The Short Stories of Ernest Hemingway: Critical Essays

The Short Stories of Ernest Hemingway: Critical Essays

Edited, with an overview and checklist, by Jackson J. Benson

Duke University Press   Durham, North Carolina   1975

Library of Congress Catalogue card no. 74-75815
I.S.B.N. 0-8223-0320-5
Third printing, 1976
Printed in the United States of America

This book is for my parents,

William Alexander Benson

Freda Sperling Benson

Contents

4. An Overview of the Stories

5. A Comprehensive Checklist of Hemingway Short Fiction Criticism, Explication, and Commentary

Acknowledgments

This volume is to a great extent a cooperative venture by many scholars, since without the generosity of the authors of the articles in this collection, it could not have been published. I am also grateful for the many kindnesses and courtesies extended to me by the editors and publishers who had custody of these essays in their original publication.

I would like to thank the compilers of all the Hemingway checklists and bibliographies which have been published over the years. The hard work of these scholars is, of course, the basis for my own checklist. In particular, I am indebted to William White for several checklists gathered in various periodicals and to Audre Hanneman for her *Ernest Hemingway: A Comprehensive Bibliography*. My gratitude is also due to my colleague, James Hinkle, for his contributions to the checklist, to the several assistants who have helped me shelf-check the items on the list, and to the librarians at the Malcolm Love Library who helped me so often to locate and obtain materials.

Introduction

We have on record one hundred nine pieces of published and unpublished short fiction written by Ernest Hemingway, and there are no doubt manuscripts in private hands that have yet to be accounted for. Of these one hundred nine items, fifty-five can be labeled "published short stories," leaving out juvenilia, the fables, the vignettes from *In Our Time*, and the story fragments posthumously published in *The Nick Adams Stories*. Of the published short stories, twenty-nine were written and published in the middle and late '20s, twenty-four in the decade of the '30s, and two in the middle '50s. The stories which have received the most attention from critics and anthologists are almost evenly divided between those written in two relatively brief periods, from 1923–1927 and from 1933–1936.

Hemingway's short stories have had an enormous popularity and influence. Depending on how one measures such a thing, the stories may well have had as much impact as the novels—a rare occurrence in an age wherein novels are thought of as major works and short stories are often considered peripheral, the by-products of apprenticeship. Of the fifty-five published stories, at least three, "The Killers," "The Snows of Kilimanjaro," and "The Short Happy Life of Francis Macomber," have become as famous as any of the Hemingway novels—as famous as anyone else's novels, for that matter. And although few modern American stories can rival the familiarity of such perennial favorites as Hawthorne's "Young Goodman Brown," Ring Lardner's "Haircut," or Stephen Crane's "The Open Boat," at least another dozen Hemingway stories come close, including "A Clean, Well-Lighted Place," "Soldier's Home," "My Old Man," "The Undefeated," and "The Gambler, the Nun and the Radio." One would be hard put to think of eight or ten stories by another modern American which have had as much influence, not only on the general reading public, but on other writers, and on the whole flow of modern literature and language.

Although anthologists choose their stories for a variety of reasons, not all of them literary, some indication of a story's popularity and influence can be gained by looking at the relative frequency of its anthology appearances. Up through 1968, Hemingway stories were included in anthologies four hundred ten times (in school, general, and exclusively Hemingway collections). By far the most popular story as measured by anthology inclusions has been "The Killers" (thirty-seven different collections in the U.S., exclusive of collections devoted solely to Hemingway's works).[1] The number for "The

---

1. Based on the *Short Story Index* and Supplements to 1968, and Landon C. Burns, "A Cross-Reference Index of Short Fiction Anthologies and Author-Title Listing," *Studies in Short Fiction*, VII (Winter 1970), 160–61.

Killers" is more than twice the number of inclusions for the next most popular story, "The Undefeated" (seventeen). Following closely are "My Old Man" (sixteen), "In Another Country" (fifteen), "The Snows of Kilimanjaro" (fourteen), "The Short Happy Life of Francis Macomber" (thirteen), "A Clean, Well-Lighted Place" (thirteen), "The Gambler, the Nun, and the Radio" (eight), "Fifty Grand" (eight), and "Indian Camp" (eight).

A great many stories which the critics have found worth discussing are not listed as having been included in any (nonexclusively Hemingway) collection, among them stories like "Fathers and Sons," "A Way You'll Never Be," and "A Canary for One." Other stories, generally considered among Hemingway's best, have received only slight attention from the anthologists, including "Soldier's Home," "Now I Lay Me," "The Battler," and "The End of Something." The Hemingway story which appears most often in school and college anthologies is "A Clean, Well-Lighted Place" (followed closely by "The Killers"). The popularity of this story, a recent phenomenon, may be due to the intense interest in existentialism in English departments of the '60s. (The story, and its concept of "nada," is prominently noted in one of the most popular general discussions of existentialism, William Barrett's *Irrational Man: A Study in Existential Philosophy*.) In the general anthology, some of the stories have had rather ironic use, considering their contents. "The Gambler, the Nun, and the Radio," for example, which deals very little with gambling and a great deal with the suffering of a gambler dying from a gun-shot wound, is included in a collection of favorite gambling stories, while "Big Two-Hearted River," a story of impending emotional breakdown, is included in *The Fireside Book of Fishing*, by R. R. Camp.

In years gone by, when people were a bit more prudish and educators a bit more cautious, editors had some difficulty in finding a Hemingway story appropriate for school use. Such squeamishness probably explains why such stories as "Fathers and Sons" (teen-age promiscuity, discussion of masturbation), "Up in Michigan" (rape, drunkenness), "A Natural History of the Dead" (gore), and "The Sea Change" (homosexuality) have been totally avoided. It also may explain why a mediocre story like "My Old Man" has been so popular and why one of Hemingway's worst, "A Day's Wait," has been used at all. In the freer climate of the last decade or so, however, more pungent stories, such as "A Clean, Well-Lighted Place" (blasphemy), "Indian Camp" (childbirth, suicide), and "Hills Like White Elephants" (abortion), have tended to replace the innocuous.

Other stories have become favorites for what some would call the wrong reasons. Certainly in earlier times, stories like "The Undefeated" were used to teach school boys a sturdy, Victorian version of life, which has only a distant relationship to the content of the story and the Hemingway code. Some stories, such as "My Old Man," can easily have a moral tacked on to them, and others provide easy opportunities for classroom discussion. How many thousands of students have worried about the meaning of that leopard on Kilimanjaro or about whether Mrs. Macomber shot her husband on purpose?

There is much evidence from textbook discussions, from criticism and from the lack of it, to support the contention that many stories have been ignored (and misused) by teachers, editors, and scholars simply because for a generation or more they were not understood. A major problem which has often blocked a full comprehension of the dimensions contained within many Hemingway stories arises from the Hemingway technique of working very subtly toward depth of meaning from a deceptively simple-appearing surface. A companion problem has been that so many Hemingway stories hardly seem to be stories at all.

"Big Two-Hearted River" is the classic example of the "pointless" Hemingway story that was misunderstood and therefore either ignored or misused. First published in 1925, the story was treated for two decades as a nature story, a fishing narrative with typical Hemingway attention to realistic detail. Its inclusion in fishing story anthologies has already been noted. Only with Malcolm Cowley's Introduction to the *Portable Hemingway* in 1945 did most critics and teachers begin to perceive the story's darker undertones, undertones that came into even sharper relief when, in 1952, Philip Young assembled the psychological history of Nick Adams. As in so many Hemingway stories (and now, of course, the modern story as a genre), the point of the story is not carried in the action, such as it is, nor presented by exposition, but is contained in the very texture of the language itself, its rhythms, imagery, irony, and tonal modulations. Although many of Hemingway's best stories were written nearly a half-century ago, it is only within the last few years that we have begun to reach out to comprehend the full breadth and depth of Hemingway's remarkable achievements within the short story form. In his Nobel Prize acceptance speech, Hemingway wrote this statement, no doubt with his own reception by the critics in his mind: "Things may not be immediately discernible in what a man writes, and in this sometimes he is fortunate; but eventually they are quite clear and by these and the degree of alchemy that he possesses he will endure or be forgotten."[2]

II

As the extensive checklist at the end of this volume certifies, a great deal of writing has been done on the short stories. Yet, after looking at the check-

2. As quoted in Carlos Baker, *Hemingway: The Writer as Artist* (Princeton: Princeton University Press, 1952), p. 339. This statement was called to my attention by Gerry Brenner in "*To Have and Have Not* as Classical Tragedy: Reconsidering Hemingway's Neglected Novel," which will be published in a collection, *Hemingway in Our Time*, edited by Richard Astro and Jackson J. Benson.

list closely, those who have read widely in Hemingway criticism are reminded that much of that which has been written is too general, too trivial, or too heavily focused on a very few of the most popular stories to be of much value to the serious student of the stories as a whole.

In large part the purpose of this book is to bring together out of this welter of material many of the best essays on the stories, while trying to maintain the widest possible range of commentary. My purpose beyond this is to present a useful book, one which will encourage a wider reading within the stories that have too often been overlooked. Here, I would hope, we have some indication of what we have and do not have, of what we know and what we do not know. As a general principle, I have favored more recent criticism, and the majority of articles have been published within the last few years. With very few exceptions, the articles have been reprinted here for the first time.

The first section of the book brings together several essays with a broad focus, emphasizing qualities, themes, and connections within the stories as considered in various groupings. The second section is totally devoted to one aspect or another of technique in the stories. I have placed special emphasis on technique for two reasons: one, it is at the center of Hemingway's greatness as a short story writer, and two, it is something frequently commented on but seldom dealt with in detail. More analysis, certainly, needs to be done on method in the short stories.

The third section is composed of essays that for the most part are focused on a single story. The primary aim in this central section is to provide as much insight as possible into the detailed texture of a number of different stories. I stress the phrase "different stories," because I think that too often we tend to speak of the "Hemingway story" as if Hemingway invented a standard formula from which he never departed. Although there is much that ties the stories together, Hemingway should be given more credit than he has been given for constant experimentation and for the achievement of extensive variety in form and technique. In addition to variety of story, I have also attempted in this third section to give as much indication as possible of the wide variety of approach used in the interpretation of the stories by critics.

I have reserved any comments I may have about particular stories, about underlying themes and techniques common to the stories as a whole, and about Hemingway's role as a writer of short stories for the "Overview" presented in Section IV. At the end of the book is the "Comprehensive Checklist," which grew from modest beginnings several years ago as a short, selected list, to a monster which has haunted and very nearly overcome its creator. Although any label such as "Comprehensive" will inevitably be taken by some as a challenge to search for omissions, the label does accurately describe the effort to make the list as useful as possible for student and professional scholar. By organizing the list for use specifically in dealing with the short stories, the scope and focus differs considerably from other more general checklists and bibliographies. I have given emphasis to providing special help to those who may be concerned with reviewing the criticism of any single story.

San Diego State University   JACKSON J. BENSON

1. Story Groupings

Hemingway and Faulkner: Two Masters of the Modern Short Story / Ray B. West, Jr.

It seems clear that the two most significant American writers of fiction in the first half of the twentieth century are Ernest Hemingway and William Faulkner. Whether their reputations are based primarily upon their novels or upon their short stories is not important. Undoubtedly their popular reputations are based upon their novels. Critics have persisted, however, in calling attention to the excellence of their short stories. In fact, it is probably in the realm of the short story that the supremacy of these two authors is least in question. Their art, interesting and important as it always is, falters occasionally in even the best of their novels—and the best (such works as *A Farewell to Arms* and *The Sound and the Fury*) come nearer to being extended short stories than they do to approaching the limits of the novel form. The best of their stories stand comparison with the finest works of all time, with the stories of Chekhov, Maupassant, Balzac, Flaubert, and Joyce in Europe; with the works of Hawthorne, Melville, Poe, and James in America.

Both authors are wholly the product of the twentieth century. Ernest Hemingway was born in Illinois in 1898, and he published his first collection of short stories in 1924. William Faulkner was born in Mississippi in 1897, and his first short stories appeared in magazines in 1930, in book form in 1931. Since the summer of 1950, when the *Collected Stories of William Faulkner* appeared, the total output of both authors has been readily available. Ernest Hemingway's *The Fifth Column and the First Forty-Nine Stories* has been in print since 1938, and it has since been reissued in a popular edition as *The Short Stories of Ernest Hemingway*.

Ernest Hemingway's first volume of short stories *In Our Time* contained such well-known stories as "Indian Camp," "The Doctor and the Doctor's Wife," "The End of Something," "Soldier's Home," "Mr. and Mrs. Elliot," "Cross-Country Snow," "My Old Man," and "Big, Two-Hearted River." His second volume *Men Without Women* appeared in 1927, and included in it were stories such as "The Undefeated," "In Another Country," "Hills Like White Elephants," "The Killers," and "Fifty Grand." *Winner Take Nothing* appeared in 1933 and included such stories as "A Clean, Well-Lighted Place," "Wine of Wyoming," and "The Gambler, The Nun, and The Radio." *The Short Stories* mentioned above added four previously unpublished stories, at least three of them among Hemingway's best: "The Short Happy Life

Ray B. West, Jr., "Hemingway and Faulkner: Two Masters of the Modern Short Story," is chapter 4 from *The Short Story in America: 1900–1950* (Chicago: Henry Regnery Company, 1952), pp. 85–106. Reprinted by permission of Henry Regnery Company.

of Francis Macomber," "The Capital of the World," and "The Snows of Kilimanjaro."

William Faulkner's first volume *These Thirteen* contained such stories as "Victory," "Ad Astra," "All the Dead Pilots," "Red Leaves," "A Rose for Emily," "A Justice," and "That Evening Sun." His second volume *Doctor Martino, and Other Stories* was published in 1934 and included "Doctor Martino," "The Hound," "Smoke," "Wash," "Elly," "Mountain Victory," and "Honor." From this point on until the publication of *Collected Stories* in 1950 it is difficult to say which of the published collections Faulkner considered to be, strictly speaking, short stories at all, since such volumes as *The Unvanquished* (1938), *Go Down, Moses, and Other Stories* (1942), and *Knight's Gambit* (1949), while they contained stories often published separately in magazines and anthologies, possess a loose kind of unity in their totality, and since selections from them were not included in the *Collected Stories*.

As a matter of fact, the problem is more complicated than this even, since Faulkner often published excerpts from his novels as short stories. Sometimes such excerpts were rewritten, sometimes not. My own belief is that the fact that Faulkner did not include a previously published short story in *Collected Stories* does not necessarily mean that he did not consider it to be a short story; rather, that since the particular ordering of stories in the collected edition was obviously designed to fill in the mythical background of his legendary Yoknapatawpha County, he included only stories from those volumes which did not contain such an ordering or stories which had not previously had book publication.

Certainly, however, it would be a great mistake not to consider such a story as "Spotted Horses," which appears as a section in *The Hamlet* (1940), as a short story simply because it appears elsewhere as an integrated part of a novel. There would be even less reason for so considering such pieces as "Ambuscade" and "Raid" from *The Unvanquished* or "Pantaloon in Black," "Delta Autumn," "Gold Is Not Always," and "The Bear" from *Go Down, Moses*. Stories included in *Collected Stories*, not previously printed in book form, include "The Tall Men," "Mule in the Yard," "A Courtship," "Lo," "My Grandmother Millard," and "Golden Land."

In any general discussion of the work of Ernest Hemingway it has become a commonplace to refer to evidence from his novels which seem to indicate a gradual shifting from a philosophy of despair in *The Sun Also Rises* and *A Farewell to Arms* to an attitude of social and moral acceptance beginning in *To Have and Have Not* and culminating in *For Whom the Bell Tolls* and *Across the River and into the Trees*. Such a development is less obvious in the short stories, and indeed the short stories have been the starting point, if not the basis, for whatever qualification has been made of such a theory. It is true that the short stories of *In Our Time* present a series of portrayals in the same somber mood as that depicted in the early novels, portray a world of lost values and lost illusions; yet, we have come to recognize that underlying such a world there existed for Hemingway an orderly if shrunken universe of recognizable value. Though the abstract ideals of justice, honor, and patriotism are lost forever, the concrete realization of what these abstractions are meant to stand for exists eternally in the natural universe. It exists in the simple sensation of fishing or hunting; in the common pleasures of eating, drinking, and sleeping; in the admirable exercise of one's physical prowess and skill in warfare, the boxing ring, or the bullfight; in all of those activities where one acquires the ability to live with a knowledge of pain and death. Such a world becomes increasingly visible in such stories as "The Undefeated" and "The Killers" from *Men Without Women*, "The Capital of the World" and "The Short Happy Life of Francis Macomber" from *The Short Stories*, and it becomes finally overstated and sentimentalized in "The Snows of Kilimanjaro" from the same book.

Parallels have been drawn between Hemingway's early work and *The Waste Land* of T. S. Eliot, and certainly there is a resemblance, if only a superficial one. While Eliot sets the sterility of modern life against a rich background of historic and religious myth, Hemingway contrasts the emptiness of ordinary living with the heightened and ritualized activity of warfare and the sports ring. Actually, however, the parallels (for whatever they are worth) seem closer in the case of Faulkner and Eliot, for William Faulkner's eclectic and disintegrating present, the world of carpetbaggers and Snopeses, stands in meaningful contrast to both the ambiguous innocence of primitive Indian life and the rich decay of Southern aristocratic society.

Since Faulkner seems most consciously intent upon weaving his total work into an elaborate mosaic to portray the history of his mythical county in Mississippi, neither the stories nor the novels alone present the complete background chronicle. Yet each separate work draws upon it for an energy and an additional level of meaning without being dependent upon a full understanding or recognition of it for its essential unity as an independent story or novel. Here it is, perhaps, that both Faulkner and Hemingway (but Faulkner in particular) appear to be widening the bounds of our modern concept of the short story, perhaps even to do violence to our understanding of the modern story as a self-contained literary work. The fact remains, however, that though the background materials add another significant level to the total body of work by each author, the best of the short stories depend very little upon it. Or, to put it another way, where they do depend upon it, such material is supplied within the story itself.

All literature makes an appeal to commonly held values, usually values which have come into existence as exigencies of community living and which are held in common by most members of society. For an author to make such an appeal is not ordinarily considered a breach of unity in his work, since the appeal is no more than that made in all art—the appeal of the object within a work of art as a symbol of the life which it is intended to represent. The world of values is truly a part of the living world of human activity which it is the artist's aim to depict in his art. Thus, Hawthorne made such an appeal when he had much of his fiction deal with a world governed by standards of New England puritan culture. Mark Twain created his most satisfying comic effects by juxtaposing a stern New England morality against the freer, more pragmatic attitudes of frontier society. Henry James, in creating a fiction in which the opposing concepts of Old World culture and the new American liberalism came into close contact, was appealing directly to our common understanding of the cultural differences represented by Europe and America.

There is a sense, however, in which the modern writer of fiction may be said to have created his own somewhat special background of myth and value. Community belief operates less effectively today than it has in the past, and Ernest Hemingway's appeal to the world of war and sport, William Faulkner's continual reference to a mythical Southern past, serve as over-all metaphors to bring about a rejuvenation of old values in terms which will strike the modern reader as immediate, fresh, and related to his own complex needs.

In these terms, we might say that a story such as Hemingway's "The Undefeated" presumes a knowledge of right conduct in the face of physical danger and possible death. Within this generality of belief, however, there exists a separate code governing the specific behavior of the bull ring. Our awareness of these concepts governs our reaction to the events of the story and the judgment we make concerning the actions of the characters. Thus, we begin by fearing the attempts of Manuel Garcia to obtain employment as a bull fighter. He is too old. He has been inactive too long. Indeed, as the story progresses, he does fail according to our understanding of the particular kind of performance which the successful matador is expected to provide. The spectators show their disapproval by showering him with cushions, one of which ironically causes him to receive the injury which (it is implied) may result in death. Yet there is an important sense—a sense which we understand because of our general knowledge of how a brave man acts in the face of danger and defeat—in which Manuel is not defeated. Despite his age and his loss of skill, he retains the courage and bravery which we recognize as the mark of a successful—an *undefeated*—man.

This level of the story does not, of course, represent the story itself. There are more concrete and more subtle events which raise the whole action to a plane where it may be thought to be an imitation of life itself, containing the complexity and richness of life, but it is upon this level that the principal meaning of the story resides. There are, likewise, other levels—level upon level of meaning, penetrating to the heart of the action, all relating to this central meaning, organizing and controlling the materials in such a way that they will contribute to the enrichment of the central theme. All are disclosed in the same manner: by referring to a common body of belief, by presenting the materials in such a manner that we may, consciously or unconsciously, recognize not only the principal intentions, but all of the minor, contributing intentions of the work as well.

It has been suggested that modern art, in particular, has grown out of a dissatisfaction with existing belief. Ernest Hemingway has been seen as a rebel against those standards of conduct which generations before World War I appeared to accept as adequate and perfectly satisfactory. There is a sense, however, in which this represents the condition of all art. To put it another way, each artist recognizes the impossibility of his age, or any age, achieving any final or absolute knowledge of truth. Nineteenth-century romanticism in England and in America, particularly during the latter half of the age, was relatively complacent; but complacency became an impossibility following the shock of war. The questions the artists seemed to be asking were: "What values of the past are illusory? Which have value for us today? In what terms do they have value? Are there new values more suitable to present, and are they also illusory or are they vitally related to our needs?"

These and similar questions seem to lie behind the artistry of both Hemingway and Faulkner. In particular, William Faulkner chooses the changing social conditions of the South following the Civil War as a setting for a body of fiction which is never far from a preoccupation with the meaning of change in terms of the static—and absolute—social structure of the past. In such a story as "A Rose for Emily," [1] this concept is mirrored, first of all, in the very description of the setting in which the action takes place. Emily's old house is seen as the impervious but dated family mansion, standing in obsolete ugliness, surrounded by garages and cotton gins, wagons and gasoline pumps. A house which must have seemed an architectural triumph in its own day has now become a symbol not only of the certainty of decay but, in its relationship to the machinery of modern life, a symbol also of the relationship of past and present. It is in these terms, too, that Miss Emily herself is portrayed, first, in her own day as a slender figure in white, silhouetted against the door with her stern and uncompromising father, then, as a pathetic and colorless figure teaching china painting to a generation of children, finally, as a frustrated mistress of a Yankee laborer, retreating into the shadowy past of her old mansion, attempting, almost by force of will alone, to halt the natural process of decay and death, to preserve a love which never existed.

This subject is more complex than the subject of Hemingway's "The Undefeated," the concept of its underlying myth less easy to draw upon. Nevertheless, it is a difference of degree only, for the significant discoveries are made through the particularities of action and scene, not in a mere recogni-

1. For a more complete analysis of this story, see Ray B. West, Jr., and Robert Wooster Stallman, *The Art of Modern Fiction*.

tion of the total, over-all view. Hemingway's most characteristic method of establishing atmosphere—of communicating his attitude toward his materials —is by the use of a style which presents the action of war, of the hunt, the prize fight, and the bull ring with an almost ritualistic intensity of detail, thus suggesting that such activities are to be taken with a seriousness almost equal to that of religious ceremony; that is, he concentrates our attention upon isolated details until we see them as symbols of ethical significance. Faulkner, on the other hand, employs a variety of stylistic devices, varying from the suggestive and rich description of an object to the weighted and complicated discourse of an "intelligence" centered in one of his characters. Faulkner's effect is often gained by the coupling or juxtaposing of unusual words, words often so unfamiliar in context that they force an exceptional concentration and examination before yielding up their meaning. Thus, when we read that Miss Emily's house was left, "lifting its *stubborn* and *coquettish* decay above the cotton wagons and the gasoline pumps," the two personifying adjectives make us aware of the horribly grotesque nature of the subject. They also prepare us for a more explicit statement concerning the subject, which is not a concern merely with old houses but with the quality of their oldness. As the unnamed narrator of Faulkner's story tells us, Miss Emily and the old Confederate soldiers confuse "time with its mathematical progression, as the old do, to whom all the past is not a diminishing road but, instead, a huge meadow which no winter ever quite touches, divided from them now by the narrow bottle-neck of the most recent decade of years." Emily's house was like an old harlot, stubbornly and coquettishly (but also grotesquely) denying the passage of time. It was like Emily, denying the death of her father and of Homer Barron, until trapped finally by the fact of her own. In addition, Emily's tragedy was by extension the tragedy of that segment of Southern society which worships its past and denies the existence of its present. By further extension, it is the tragedy of mankind, Southern and Northern, American or European, confronted by the necessity to select and honor that of the past which is applicable and helpful, to recognize and accept that of the present which is beneficial or which cannot be escaped.

The differences in method between Ernest Hemingway and William Faulkner consist primarily in Hemingway's intense concentration upon those activities which have developed formal means of dealing with life at its most active moments and in Faulkner's examination of life in the present in terms of social and religious forms which he finds existing in his Southern past. The method of each implies a complementary, if not equal, value to be found both in the forms of the past and in the actions of the present. Each is concerned with breaking down and examining the forms which they draw upon. However, neither author is satisfied merely to illustrate the simple truth or falsity of them. Each sees his subject as complex and multiform, so that the stories become an embodiment of the final theme, or idea (which is never quite the same as the underlying myth), existing only as the idea exists within it. The stories do not exist as actions, paralleling and illustrating preconceived attitudes and ideas.

Within the body of the work of each of these authors there is, however, a division into two more or less separate types of short story, practiced more or less equally by each, as each is practiced more or less equally by most contemporary writers of the short story. The first type is of the kind described above, the completed action in which the myth is introduced, examined in terms of a present action, its ambiguities disclosed, even, occasionally, resolved. Of this type we would consider Hemingway's "The Capital of the World" and, insofar as it succeeds, "The Snows of Kilimanjaro"; Faulkner's "The Tall Men," "Turnabout" (a much underrated story, and one in which Faulkner's method comes closest to Hemingway's), and many others. The second type, sometimes called "the story of initiation" or "the story of recognition," is one in which the problem is presented, usually through the consciousness of a central character, in all its distracting and confusing complexity. This kind of story usually portrays the progress of a character from innocence to knowledge. In theological terms, that knowledge is a knowledge and a recognition of evil. To adopt a more secular term we might say, however, that it represents a knowledge of the limitations of existence—the limitations of both nature (the present) and the myth (the past).

This second type has been a favorite with American authors. One reason for its appeal, I think we can assume, is that it can be stated in terms suggestive of the principal philosophical dilemma of our time. Merely by making use of the conventional phrase, "the American tradition," we can, I think, suggest the dilemma, since the very tradition to which we refer represents a rebellion against tradition, a rebellion particularly against the forms of European culture, but also a rebellion against any form which tends to become excessively restrictive or fixed—as forms inevitably tend to become. The rejection of a particular form is certainly desirable if the form has come to function primarily in its own interest—that is, as a means of preserving itself, not as an adequate method of government or as a means of achieving social justice. The dilemma of all who retain even the slightest respect for form results from the tendency of a highly formal society to perpetuate customs and manners which have little or no relationship to life in the present, as opposed to the tendency of an overliberal society to deny all formal social or political structure. These are the extremes which Henry James used in his fiction: the myth of European decadence contrasted with our concept of the vigorous but innocent utilitarianism of the New World.

The story of initiation makes direct use of the dilemma. It suggests that the ordinary means of dealing with the problems of existence are, first, to recognize that there is a problem, second, to understand that the problem is capable of only a limited solution. It assumes that a primary step in the achievement of knowledge is the recognition that though human justice is desirable, it is not immediately attainable. It assumes, further, that an important stage in the process of self-understanding has been achieved when one learns to live with knowledge. Such is the initiation which all must undergo. The exact terms in which the discovery occurs, however, is the subject matter of the story—the subject matter of such stories as Hemingway's "My Old Man," "The Killers," and "A Clean, Well-Lighted Place," or of Faulkner's "That Evening Sun."

The particular subject matter of Hemingway's short story "A Clean, Well-Lighted Place" is the discovery that traditional religious forms no longer serve to define man's place in the modern world: "It was all a nothing and a man was nothing too." The most one can do is to seek the comfort and dignity of "a clean, well-lighted place." In a savage parody of the Lord's Prayer, which defines the theological frame of reference for the story, the emptiness and futility of modern life is set off against the traditional expressions of humility and belief: "Our nada who art in nada, nada be thy name thy kingdom nada thy will be nada in nada as it is in nada. . . ." The "discovery" in this story is a reader's recognition, his discovery of the pathetic need of mankind for even the most limited kind of security and order. The characters are a barman, a waiter, and an old man, none of them possessing the dignity even of names. Some critics have maintained that the subject of this story is "nada"—nothing.[2] But it is also the story of modern man's search for dignity amidst the destruction of old values. The pathos is occasioned by our recognition of the extremely limited nature of the relief as set against an implicit lost plenitude.

The discovery in "My Old Man" and "The Killers"[3] is shared by the principal characters. The boy, Joe, of the first story, is forced to recognize the truth about his father, which is that though he was "one swell guy," he was also a crook and a cheat. Nick Adams, in "The Killers," faces the final fact of the irrationality of death, and thus of evil, in his being confronted with the facts of Ole Andreson and his relationship with the world of "the killers." At the same time, it is a realization by the reader of the means for dealing with such knowledge as is represented in the characters of Ole, who is doomed to death for a violation of the code of gangsterdom; Sam, who refuses even to acknowledge the existence of such a world; and George, who has learned to accept and live with his knowledge.

2. See particularly Mark Schorer, *The Story: A Critical Anthology.*
3. For an extended analysis of this story, see Cleanth Brooks and Robert Penn Warren, *Understanding Fiction* (New York, Appleton-Century-Crofts, 1943).

Faulkner's "That Evening Sun" is similar in that it displays the exposure of the three children of Jason Compson to the state of terror inhabited by their Negro maid, Nancy, whose wanton living midway between the worlds of whites and blacks has left her unprotected by the code of either, susceptible both to the lawful fury of Mr. Stovall and to the animal-like fury of her Negro lover. The discovery is complicated, as it is in "The Killers," by the fact that each of the principal characters makes his own adjustment to the facts. The boy Jason, in "That Evening Sun," assumes that because he is "not a nigger," he is protected from Nancy's terror. Caddy Compson, like Nick Adams of "The Killers," is intrigued by the nature of evil itself; while Quentin (who is the narrator of the story, and through whose eyes the incidents are seen) seems to have recognized that the knowledge of evil is a permanent condition of human life.

Not all stories divide themselves easily into these two types. There is another—perhaps even a higher—kind of story which appears to combine the elements of both. In such a story the initiation occurs, but it occurs primarily as a preparation for a series of actions which display the effects of such knowledge upon the human character. As such, it defines in modern terms the specific conditions (usually tragic) under which it is possible for the modern hero to live with the conflicting knowledge of man's nobility *and* his meanness. If it is a higher form of story than those already discussed, it is higher than the first because the first type of story must make its appeal primarily in terms of traditional values, or values already more or less fixed in the reader's consciousness; it is higher than the second because the second type, such as "The Killers" or "That Evening Sun," deals primarily with definition, with the conditions under which human tragedy is to be enacted, not with the tragedy itself. As examples of this type I would suggest such stories as Hemingway's "The Short Happy Life of Francis Macomber" and Faulkner's "The Bear."

Perhaps it is wrong to cite such stories as examples of a type. In structure they are similar to "The Undefeated" and "A Rose for Emily." They are similar, however, primarily in that they exhibit a completed, rather than a continuing, action. They differ only insofar as "The Short Happy Life" and "The Bear" create, at least in part, the background myth against which the events are enacted. They pick up and incorporate the ritual of initiation, which in "The Killers" and "That Evening Sun" represents the whole of the action, and they use it primarily to define the terms in which the larger, more all-encompassing action takes place. They are more completely satisfying, not only because they are more contemporary in the specification of their subject matter, but also because the mythical background is objectified and concretized by reference to events in the story, not made to depend so completely upon abstract concepts such as "honor," "pride," "decorum," etc. In short, they are both *more contemporary* and *more completely realized.*

Briefly, "The Short Happy Life"[4] deals with man's behavior when confronted, at moments of crisis, with the problems of sexual relations in modern marriage, physical terror, and death. More specifically, it deals with the result of that knowledge upon the actions of Francis Macomber, an American sportsman engaged both in discovering a basis for living with his wife and in facing up to the physical danger represented by the events of a big-game hunt. Macomber's discovery is a recognition of the sterile basis of his marriage, forced upon him by a recognition of his own cowardice and of his wife's infidelity. It is not until he has faced these facts honestly that he is capable of willfully pitting his own courage against the animal courage of the water buffalo. The discovery—or initiation—is made in terms of modern (particularly, American) marriage. It represents an examination of the terms of much modern living, reflected in the lives of Francis and Margot Macomber, as well as an examination of the traditional concepts of marital fidelity. The resolution, ironic, even ambiguous, is the resolution presented in all tragedy but provided in terms of modern man's conflict between purely utilitarian and materialistic values and the traditional values of courage, fidelity, and honor.

In such general terms, "The Short Happy Life" is little different from Faulkner's important and interesting story, "The Bear." The differences in method, however, between the two stories are both illuminating and provocative. If we are attracted by the riches enclosed and contained by the relatively simple structure of Hemingway's story—the richness of specification and implication, we may well be puzzled, as many readers have been, by the complex scaffolding employed by Faulkner to deal with similar themes.

The pitting of man against the animal has its roots deep within our mythological past. In our own time it has taken on added significance because of its particular aptness to a situation in which nature has become more and more dominant while the stature of man as something outside of nature has shrunk to an apparent insignificance. Thus, the figure of the animal contains not only its original metaphorical designation as an image for man's human limitations, but it has become also ironically symbolic of modern man's predicament as a highly cultivated, abstract, and sterile figure; that is, it has become an aptly ambiguous image, reflecting in two directions. It reveals both the degree of humanity which man has lost by his separation from nature and the degree of human isolation achieved through a purely materialistic concept of man as minute atom in the material universe.

The action of Faulkner's story centers about the hunt for a particularly

4. For an extended analysis of this story, see Ray B. West, Jr., and Robert Wooster Stallman, *The Art of Modern Fiction.*

durable and malignant bear, an animal which, through its very durability and malevolence, has earned itself a name—"old Ben." The specific details of the hunt, which are disclosed over a period of several years in the story, are viewed through the eyes of a young Southerner, Isaac McCaslin, grandson of Carrothers McCaslin, one of the original settlers of Faulkner's mythical Southern county. Isaac is introduced to the wilderness by his cousin, Cass Edmonds; Major de Spain, owner of the land where the hunt takes place; General Compson, Civil War veteran and the son of a former governor of the state; Sam Fathers, whose Indian father conceived him by raping a Negro slave; and Boon Hogganbeck, "in whom some of the same blood ran which ran in Sam Fathers, even though Boon's was a plebeian strain of it": aristocrats and landowners, on the one hand; the dispossessed and deracinated, on the other. Major de Spain is an aristocrat, however, primarily in the sense that he owns the property by law; in another and, Faulkner implies, more real sense, Sam Fathers, the son of an Indian chief and a Negro slave, shares possession of the land with old Ben. He, like the bear, is *of* the land and at the same time master of it by virtue of his skill and knowledge. So far as young Ike, Cass Edmonds, General Compson, and Major de Spain possess that skill and knowledge, they too are rightful possessors of the land. When man becomes, like Boon or like Lion (the mongrel dog which Sam Fathers and Boon train to hunt the bear), simple, malignant animal power, he does not possess, he merely rapes; he becomes a creature of greed and power.

Events of the story are divided into five sections. The first deals with young Ike's introduction to the wilderness and ends with his first sight of the bear, whom he couldn't see (though old Ben had seen him) until he had discarded watch, gun, and compass (the metal, mechanical guides, symbols of man's mastery as well as of his dependence and fear) and delivered himself up to nature itself. The second section opens with Ike's ritualistic baptism by Sam Fathers in the blood of Ike's first buck, and it concerns itself principally with the capture and training of Lion, the powerful mongrel with whose help the hunters draw the first blood from old Ben. Section three contains the successful hunt in which the bear is cornered and killed by Lion and Boon, the dog catching the bear by the throat, the man clinging to his back and stabbing him with powerful strokes, more telling than the blasts of the gun which he could never master. (It is significant to our definitions above that these sections were published separately in magazines in 1934 and 1935 as separate stories entitled "Lion" and "The Bear Hunt." The former is obviously a story of initiation when read out of its larger context.) The death of the bear means the death of old Sam Fathers too, not so much because of the exertion and exposure of the hunt, as because following the death of old Ben—the passing of the wilderness—"he just quit." Section four represents a kind of litany in which Isaac McCaslin relates his reasons for relinquishing his rights to the land bequeathed him by his fathers; for, as he explains to his cousin Cass:

I cant repudiate it. It was never mine to repudiate. It was never Father's and Uncle Buddy's to bequeath to me to repudiate because it was never Grandfather's to bequeath them to bequeath me to repudiate because it was never old Ikkemotubbe's to sell to Grandfather for bequeathment and repudiation. Because it was never Ikkemotubbe's fathers' fathers' to bequeath Ikkemotubbe to sell to Grandfather or any man because on the instant when Ikkemotubbe discovered, realized, that he could sell it for money, on that instant it ceased ever to have been his forever, father to father to father, and the man who bought it bought nothing. (Pp. 256–57)[5]

This section recounts the evil prefigured in the history of the McCaslin-Edmonds property, much of it suggested in excerpts from the commissary accounts to which Ike refers as he speaks: the buying of the land from Ikkemotubbe, the Chickasaw chief; the assembling of slaves, including Tomasina, the mother of the half-breed descendants of Ike's grandfather, Carrothers; the death of Tomy (as she was called) by self-drowning because she felt disgraced; the willing of $1,000 to the son, Tomy's Turl (Terrel), in attempted expiation; the family background and the national background, until:

The boy himself had inherited it as Noah's grandchildren had inherited the Flood although they had not been there to see the deluge: that dark corrupt and bloody time while three separate peoples had tried to adjust not only to one another but to the new land which they had created and inherited too and must live in for the reason that those who had lost it were no less free to quit it than those who had gained it were:—those upon whom freedom and equality had been dumped overnight and without warning or preparation or any training in how to employ it or even just endure it and who misused it not as children would nor yet because they had been so long in bondage and then so suddenly freed, but misused it as human beings always misuse freedom, so that he thought *Apparently there is a wisdom beyond even that learned through suffering necessary for a man to distinguish between liberty and license.* (Pp. 289–90)

These are the terms in which Isaac McCaslin has come to see not only the problems of the South but the problems of human existence as mirrored in the South. Most specifically, however, they are the problems of our time—the growth of greed and power from the pastoral-primitive Indian days through the agrarian slave society preceding the Civil War and into the mercantile rapacity not only of reconstruction but of the modern world. Section five applies these attitudes in terms of the final events of the story.

5. Page references to quotations refer to *Go Down, Moses, and Other Stories*, original edition (New York, Random House, 1942).

Isaac McCaslin returns to the wilderness as it is being destroyed on the one hand by the lumber company which has moved in and begun to cut the timber, and on the other hand by the lone survivor, Boon, or by the attitudes he represents, an attitude not too dissimilar to that of the lumbermen—Southern industry, the mongrel breed, just as Boon and Lion are mongrels. Boon is discovered by Ike in the last scene, his back against a tree in which he has cornered an unbelievable number of squirrels; he is frantically hammering at the dismembered and useless gun in his lap, furiously shouting: "Get out of here! Dont touch them! Dont touch a one of them! They're mine!"

Behind Ike, the mechanical efficiency of the industrial world; before him, the barbaric inefficiency of Boon. Both filled with the same furious greed. But greed and power are not enough. Survival demands skill and endurance, and neither the lumber company nor Boon has enough of either to outlast nature. This is perhaps as near as we can come to summarizing the complex theme which William Faulkner has bodied forth in this, one of the most noteworthy achievements of the twentieth-century short story.

However, it is not solely on the basis of individual achievement that we value the short stories of Ernest Hemingway and William Faulkner. Though we may hold it as a personal opinion that "The Short Happy Life of Francis Macomber" and "The Bear" are the two finest examples of the modern short story, we should find it difficult to prove that they were more effective as short stories than, say, Katherine Anne Porter's "Flowering Judas" or Robert Penn Warren's "Blackberry Winter." The final value of Hemingway and Faulkner exists, it is true, in terms of the excellence of their finest stories; but it exists also as an extension of that excellence, in the impressive total body of their work—a total which perhaps can be matched only by Henry James among short-story writers in America since Hawthorne. Such value exists also in the position of these men as innovators—in those qualities which mark them as not only different but superior to a generation which preceded them. The twentieth century called for revaluation, for a reexamination of the moral and aesthetic principles upon which both American life and American art had been established. Ernest Hemingway and William Faulkner, each in his own way, represent the vanguard of such revaluation in American fiction; and, different though they may seem in many ways, their similarities outweigh the differences. If it becomes increasingly difficult to see them as experimenters—as the *avant-garde*, it is above all because their values have become accepted and incorporated into the tradition. They are not so much revolutionaries as they are counter-revolutionaries. They did not so much deny existing values as they insisted upon a thorough reexamination of them, a reexamination in terms of the life of their times. In the great tradition of literature this is the mark of the genuine artist. Because in their generation and in their media they were the first to see the need and to fulfill it, they justify the title "masters" of the modern short story.

The Complex Unity of *In Our Time* / *Clinton S. Burhans, Jr.*

I

Among writers on Hemingway, few discuss *In Our Time* as more than a collection of short stories and sketches reflecting the experiences at the core of Hemingway's writing and foreshadowing many of the themes and techniques of his subsequent work. Even Philip Young and Stewart Sanderson, who see the book as at least loosely unified, discuss this unity primarily in the Nick Adams stories. But *In Our Time* incorporates these stories in a broader unity of form and theme and in a complexity of structure well worth exploring. Reading the book for these qualities yields unexpected and exciting dividends, for it reveals that *In Our Time* is indeed a consciously unified work built on a noble model and containing the careful artistry and the central vision of the world and the human condition which characterize Hemingway's writing from beginning to end. As such, *In Our Time* is not only the first of Hemingway's major works but also the best introduction to his thought and art in the rest.

II

When it was published on October 5, 1925, *In Our Time* was the culmination of a long development and a combination of previously published and new work. Several of the sixteen interstory vignettes had originated as newspaper dispatches; six had appeared in *The Little Review* for April 1, 1923; and all, as well as two of the stories which began as vignettes, were published together in Paris as *in our time* in January, 1924. Of the fourteen stories, ten had been published earlier. For the 1925 *In Our Time*, Hemingway took the vignettes of the Paris *in our time*, made two of them into the stories "A Very Short Story" and "The Revolutionist," changed the order of the rest and used them as interchapters between the stories, and added four new stories, "The End of Something," "The Three Day Blow," "The Battler," and "Cat in the Rain." And finally, for the 1930 edition of the book, he added the introductory sketch now entitled "On the Quai at Smyrna." Clearly, in all this maneuvering, Hemingway was getting at something more coherent and significant than a simple anthology of loosely related stories and sketches.

The title points in the same direction by suggesting that a common theme unifies the individual pieces which comprise the book. Several critics have

Clinton S. Burhans, Jr., "The Complex Unity of *In Our Time*," *Modern Fiction Studies*, XIV (Ernest Hemingway Special Number) (1968), 313–28. *Modern Fiction Studies*, © 1968, by Purdue Research Foundation, Lafayette, Indiana.

implied such a theme by identifying the title as an ironic echo from the Book of Common Prayer: "Give peace in our time, O Lord"; and certainly *In Our Time* defines a world and a human condition in which there is very little peace of any kind. Moreover, in the Paris edition of the vignettes in 1924, the title *in our time* is printed on a cover format composed of newspaper clippings—designed, apparently, to suggest to potential readers that the book reflects the events and qualities of contemporary life. And by keeping for the expanded *In Our Time* of 1925 this title under which the vignettes had appeared as a separate and unified work, Hemingway subtly implies that they are not subordinate introductions to the stories but the essential context in which the stories must be read and understood.

III

Writing to Edmund Wilson on October 18, 1924, Hemingway remarks that he has "finished the book of 14 stories with a chapter of *in our time* between each story—that is the way they were meant to go—to give the picture of the whole between examining it in detail. Like looking with your eyes at something, say a passing coastline, and then looking at it with 15X binoculars. Or rather, maybe, looking at it and then going in and living in it—and then coming out and looking at it again. I sent the book to Don Stewart at the Yale Club about three weeks ago. When he was here he offered to try and sell it for me. I think you would like it, it has a pretty good unity."[1] Hemingway's intention is clear: he means *In Our Time* to be more than a casually linked anthology. And a study of the book's structure, theme, and form demonstrates the high degree of his success: it has indeed "a pretty good unity."

In the vignettes (including the "Smyrna" sketch) which begin and end *In Our Time* and separate its stories, it is wasted effort to seek any one-for-one relationship between the vignettes and the individual stories. Charles Fenton is correct in saying that "there has frequently been an attempt to endow the vignettes either with a biographical sequence or with a sketch-by-sketch relationship to the short stories. . . . The effect of these distortions is to belittle Hemingway's intention and achievement in the vignettes."[2] But if they are seldom immediately related to the stories they separate, neither were they written on random themes nor placed between the stories helter-skelter. Fenton illustrates the painstaking artistry Hemingway lavished on the vignettes and suggests that they can be arranged in three groups: war, bullfighting, and journalism.[3] But this arrangement seems faulty because it is

1. *Hemingway and His Critics*, ed. Carlos Baker (New York: Hill and Wang, 1961), p. 60.
2. *The Apprenticeship of Ernest Hemingway: The Early Years* (New York: Compass Books, 1958), p. 228. Fenton's studies of the vignettes are brilliant and invaluable.
3. Fenton, p. 229.

based on two unifying principles rather than on one: two of the groups, war and bullfighting, are based on content: the third on compositional source. On the common principle of content, the groupings comprise nine on war, six on bullfighting, and two on crime.

Significantly, in placing the vignettes around and between the stories, Hemingway follows neither these groupings nor the order in which the vignettes first appeared in *in our time*—significantly, because in their resulting order, the vignettes reflect a clear pattern. The "Smyrna" sketch and the first seven are concerned with war; the next one with crime; the next six with bullfighting; the following one with crime; and the last one with war. From war to crime to bullfighting to crime to war—the pattern is definite and balanced; moreover, it suggests a unifying theme. By surrounding bullfighting with war and crime, Hemingway places violence and death on which man imposes order and meaning at the center of a world of chaotic disorder and violence, thus implying subtly that from the first—bullfighting—he can learn something about the second—the world—and about how to live in it.

The arrangement of the short stories reflects an equally unified design. The book begins and ends with stories about Nick Adams; and the stories in between concern either Nick, a central character like him in all but name, or themes introduced and developed in these stories. And reinforcing this general unity of character and theme, Hemingway arranges the stories—with one exception—in a roughly chronological order and in a pattern of alternating geographical locales.

Of the fourteen stories, seven deal directly with Nick, three ("A Very Short Story," "Soldier's Home," and "Out of Season") with central characters essentially like Nick, and four ("The Revolutionist," "Mr. and Mrs. Elliot," "Cat in the Rain," and "My Old Man") with themes closely related to the other stories. The first five stories reflect Nick's boyhood in pre-World War I America. These are followed by a vignette—the only one clearly and closely related to the stories it separates—in which Nick, now a young man, is wounded in the war. After this vignette, "A Very Short Story"—itself originally a vignette and obviously made a story for this purpose—concerns a wounded central character first in a military hospital and then back in postwar America. The next story reveals the problems of a returned veteran in postwar America, and the next—again, a former vignette made a story for both structural and thematic reasons—reveals a different kind of veteran in postwar Europe. Then a story which begins in America and ends in Europe is followed by four in Europe, and the book ends with Nick Adams back in America in his boyhood locale but now a mature man bearing a very large burden of experience.

As he did with the vignettes, then, Hemingway arranges the stories of *In Our Time* in a subtle and significant structure. From youth to maturity, from innocence to experience, from peace to war to peace again, and from America to Europe and back to America, he exposes a central consciousness, what-ever names he gives it in the different stories, to the basic realities of the world and the human condition. Like the vignettes, too, the subtle structural design of the stories reflects a unifying theme and one which develops in de-tail and from several perspectives the theme suggested by the vignettes: man, particularly contemporary American man, must face up to the world and the human condition as they really are and then cope with the problem of living as a human being in such a world.

IV

If the structure of the vignettes and of the stories and the intimate relation-ship between the two point to a central theme unifying *In Our Time* at its deepest levels, their content argues the same thematic unity even more force-fully. Here, Hemingway is saying, here are the world and the human condi-tion with the masks off, with all the fraudulent illusions stripped away. It's not a pretty world and certainly not a very safe or comfortable one for men to live in; but, taken as it really is, it's a world men can live in with meaning and value if they look in the right places for them.

"To give the picture of the whole between examining it in detail"—Hem-ingway in his letter to Wilson defines unequivocally his thematic purpose in both the vignettes and the stories. Centering on war, bullfighting, and crime, the vignettes are significantly related in substance as well as in structure. War, of course, concerns the chaos and violence of conflict between and within nations; crime is the lesser chaos and violence within social groups; and bull-fighting, in Hemingway's view a spectacle combining real rather than merely acted violence and tragedy controlled by esthetic forms and rules, symbolizes a way to face a world and a human condition characterized by war and crime. In these impressionistic sketches, then, Hemingway outlines the world and the human condition as he sees them and suggests what man must be and do in such a world; and the stories derive their unifying significance as detailed explorations of the premises posed in the vignettes.

In this context, the vignettes can be grouped not only by general content but also by common theme. Six focus on events and characters reflecting primarily the qualities which to Hemingway identify the world as it really is "in our time." The Smyrna, Adrianople, and cabinet minister sketches show helpless civilians and animals caught up in war and revolution; the Mons garden and the barricade vignettes reflect two different views of combat; and the vignette of the policemen highlights what happens to law and order in the wrong hands. Taken together, these six outline a world of disorder, cruelty, violence, brutality, suffering, and death. Significantly, these con-stitute most of the first half of the vignettes; counting "Smyrna" as the first, they are numbers 1, 3, 4, 5, 6, and 9. As such, they surround and occur between the first half of the stories—those concerning Nick Adams in his youth and those dealing specifically with World War I. These six vignettes, then, reflect in general the world which Nick, the soldier in "A Very Short Story," and Krebs in "Soldier's Home" experience in detail.

A second group of five vignettes, while continuing to reflect the nature and the qualities of the world, centers even more specifically on various ways in which men immediately threatened by such a human condition respond to it. Troops marching to the front are all drunk, officers and men alike, and one officer is so frightened that he wants the kitchen fires put out even though the front is fifty kilometers away. Wounded, Nick Adams decides to wash his hands of the whole business and make "a separate peace"; and another soldier, terribly afraid under shelling, prays and makes promises to Christ, only to shun such promises when the shelling is over. A criminal facing execution loses all control of himself, and a king caught up in a revolution thinks only of not being shot and of escaping to America. Together, these vignettes show men responding to harsh experience with fear, drunkenness, disillusion, hypocritical prayer, and dissociation. None of these responses, however understandable, is either admirable or very practical; and the sketches reflecting them—2, 7, 8, 16, and 17—occur at the beginning, in the middle, and at the end of the book as constant reminders that natural and uncontrolled responses to the world as it really is "in our time" are simply not enough.

The remaining vignettes, the six on bullfighting, complete the thematic "picture of the whole" by dramatizing the attitudes and qualities through which man can face the human condition and make it meaningful. In *Death in the Afternoon*, Hemingway defines the aspect of the bullfight which most interests him. It is, he says, a literal tragedy, not the mimetic shadow play by which most other peoples cope esthetically with tragedy. In the bullfight, there is always death; and when it is over, the corpses do not get up and go home to dinner. The fight takes place on an open stage beneath a hot sun; it contains life's basic realities—violence, suffering, inevitable death; and it imposes human meaning and order on these realities by containing them within the forms and rules of esthetic ritual and by requiring that the bullfighter stake his life against the bull's with courage and grace. Written some eight years before *Death in the Afternoon*, these vignettes reflect in outline and in subtle shading the same view of the bullfight which Hemingway details in the later work.

The first one emphasizes the very real dangers and the inflexible requirements which the bullfighter must accept. A bullfight consists of six bulls fought two each by three bullfighters, and all six bulls must be killed. Here, the first bull has wounded two bullfighters and been taken away to be killed, requiring the third bullfighter to face the task of fighting five bulls. He has no choice; and he does what he must do without complaint or evasion and with all the courage and skill at his youthful command. The next vignette cap-

sulizes the basic conditions of the bullfight and of the greater world it drama-
tizes by looking unflinchingly at its most pitiless detail: the savaging of the
picador's horse. Such conditions accentuate the preceding young bullfighter's
bravery and determination; and the following two sketches contrast two more
bullfighters. One is so incompetent that the crowd cuts off his pigtail, after
which he goes to a cafe and gets resignedly drunk; the other works the bull
and kills him with courage, skill, and grace, thereby giving dignity and meaning to a spectacle which the incompetent bullfighter had degraded into clumsy
butchery. The final two bullfight vignettes make a coda to the preceding four.
Here, one bullfighter is so frightened by what he must face in the ring that
afternoon that he tries to escape by getting drunk and dancing in a fiesta
parade, leaving another bullfighter to confront the multiplied jeopardy of
the young one in the first sketch—fighting additional bulls beyond his own.
And in the last vignette, the second bullfighter is killed, showing that not only
horses and bulls but also men die in this tragedy, as ultimately they must in
the larger tragedy outside the bullring.

As a group, these vignettes recapitulate the implications of the other two
thematic groupings. Here again, in the conditions of the bullring, are the
basic qualities of the real world and its human condition: cruelty, violence,
suffering, and death. Here, too, are the ineffective and unsatisfactory ways
men respond to experience in this world: incompetence, fear, drunkenness,
and evasion. But the bullfight vignettes go further to show the qualities men
must and can have to live as men in such a world and human condition:
courage, responsibility, determination, skill, and grace. The world, Hemingway implies, is for most men in one way or another only a bullring in disguise;
and these positive qualities enable men not to escape its inevitable realities
but to impose on them a human dignity and value. Stressing this thematic
projection of the "picture of the whole," the bullfight sketches—numbers 10,
11, 12, 13, 14, and 15—dominate the last half of the vignettes. And in this
position they occur between and provide background for stories most of
which deal not with the initiation themes of the first six or seven stories but
rather with the problems of living in the world as it really is.

For if the vignettes are masterfully organized in structure and theme to
reveal the "picture of the whole," the stories are no less impressively arranged to examine "it in detail." If they do not have the unity of central
character and event and the consistent development of a novel, they have
nevertheless a complexly interwoven thematic unity in themselves and in
their relationship to the vignettes which seems too often overlooked. For the
stories explore and develop in a variety of characters and events the two
themes working centrally in the vignettes: the problem of recognizing and
accepting the world and the human condition as they really are; and the consequent problem of trying to live with meaning and value in such a world
and human condition.

The first five stories reflect both problems; but, inevitably in view of Nick's age, they focus primarily on the first, on his initiation into actuality. In a series of crucial experiences involving the most fundamental human realities and relationships—pain and suffering, birth and death, conflict and violence, love and loss, topsy-turvy disorder—Nick is forced to recognize that the world and his place in it are neither comfortable nor orderly and that few human stories have a conventional happy ending. In "Indian Camp," he discovers that nature is not always beautiful and orderly in her processes nor concerned at all with human suffering. Disturbed by the screams of a woman in severe labor, he learns from his doctor father that babies don't always come into the world head first as they should; and he watches as his father performs a Caesarian with a jack-knife and no anesthetic. The woman's husband lies in the bunk above with an injured foot, and afterwards they find him lying dead in a pool of his own blood. Unable to "stand things," he had cut his throat with a razor.

Paradoxically, the man's love for his wife and his identification with her suffering had led to death; only the doctor's cool detachment and objective professionalism could relieve her pain and bring the baby into the world. "Her screams are not important," he tells Nick. "I don't hear them because they are not important."[4] Birth and death, Nick discovers, are alike commingled with violence and suffering; and in between, man lives on the knife-edge of paradox. Going home across the lake, with the sun rising above the hills and fish jumping in the warm water, Nick feels sure he will never die. But this feeling clearly rises from its own denial: like Hemingway in *Death in the Afternoon*, Nick knows now that "all stories, if continued far enough, end in death, and he is no true-story teller who would keep that from you."[5]

Of all the Nick Adams stories in the book, "The Doctor and the Doctor's Wife" is the only one not obviously centered on Nick and on what he learns from experience in the world of actuality. Here, his father backs down from a senseless fight with a man who wants to avoid working out a debt he owes the doctor, and Nick's mother refuses to believe that anyone could really behave so. Nick doesn't appear in the story until the last few lines, when his father finds him reading beneath a tree and tells him his mother wants to see him. Without hesitation, Nick replies that he wants to go with his father, and does.

Whether or not Nick saw his father's quarrel and retreat is uncertain, but there is at least some indication that he did. Such is the implication of the story's position amid other accounts of Nick's deepening understanding and insight; in this direction, too, point his immediate desire to go with his father and his consequent rejection of his mother's appeal. But the issue is not essential; the story serves the same thematic function in either event. Extend-

4. *In Our Time* (New York: Scribner's, 1958), p. 17.
5. *Death In The Afternoon* (New York: Scribner's, 1960), p. 122.

ing into society "Indian Camp's" focus on nature's disorder, violence, and indifference to human suffering, "The Doctor and the Doctor's Wife" contrasts three ways of looking at man and his interrelationships. At one extreme is Dick Boulton, primitive, violent, and amoral, willing to beat up the doctor to avoid paying what he owes him. At the other is the doctor's wife, romantic, sentimental, and religious, unwilling to believe that anyone could be so motivated. In between is the doctor, rational, nonviolent, and civilized, recognizing Dick for what he is but too intelligent to take a meaningless beating for some quixotic concept of bravery. This, then, is the real world which Nick must learn to live in, both in nature and in society. And whether or not he saw the quarrel, Nick's immediate choice to go with his father into the woods implies an acceptance of the doctor's position in denial of the two extremes which challenge it.

In the next two stories, Nick's education in actuality deepens. Apparently simple and artless but complexly woven and brilliantly evocative, "The End of Something" and "The Three Day Blow" are as much two episodes in a single story as are the two parts of "The Big Two-Hearted River." In "The End of Something," Nick falls out of love and learns thereby that violence, suffering, and death are inner as well as outer realities. There is no reason for his falling out of love, no explanation for it; like falling *in* love, it just happens. Nick and Marjorie like to picnic by the ruins of a lumber mill. Here an industry had thrived; but when, in the natural course of things, the trees were used up, the industry had gone. So it is with love, Nick discovers: far from being the endless enchantment of romance, love is only one among the mysterious and uncertain "somethings" which make up the natural facts of human experience. Love had come to him, and now it had gone; and the point of the story is less Nick's falling out of love than his appalled recognition that he can.

In "The Three Day Blow," Nick and his friend Bill talk and drink while an early autumn storm blows around the cottage. They discuss the peat flavor of Irish whiskey, but neither has ever seen peat (46); baseball, but conclude that " 'there's always more to it than we know about' " (47–48); and novels of impractical romance and thwarted love (49–50). Against this background of ignorance and obscurity, they talk about the equally mysterious end of Nick's love for Marjorie. " 'All of a sudden everything was over,' Nick said. 'I don't know why it was. I couldn't help it. Just like when the three day blows come now and rip all the leaves off the trees' " (58). Bill warns him that he might get involved with Marjorie again, and Nick is surprised into new joy. If falling in love is not absolute, neither is falling out of love, and perhaps he *will* love Marjorie again. "There was not anything that was irrevocable. . . . Nothing was finished. Nothing was ever lost" (59–60). In any event, Nick now looks at love in perspective: outdoors, "the Marge business was no longer so tragic. It was not even very important. The wind blew everything like that away" (60–61).

"The Battler" takes Nick away from his family and friends and involves him in a world in which everything is topsy-turvey. An apparently friendly brakeman knocks him off a freight train. In a "hobo jungle," he meets "the battler," a former champion boxer now a punch-drunk bum recently out of jail for hitting people—for which, of course, he had been idolized in the ring. His career had been destroyed when he married his manager, a woman who looked so much like his sister that the public insisted on treating her as such even though she wasn't. "The battler" is being cared for by a Negro whom he had met in jail. The Negro had been sentenced for knifing someone, but he treats "the battler" with sympathy and understanding and protects Nick from him when he suddenly becomes nasty and wants to fight with the boy. Nick leaves with more lessons learned: the world is a confused and treacherous place, but not without love and compassion.

As these stories present Nick with the actualities of the world and the human condition, the next two stories deepen this initiation theme into disillusion. Neither protagonist is named Nick Adams; but both, without any substantial or significant change, could be young Nick a few years later. "A Very Short Story" was originally a vignette in the 1924 *in our time*, but Hemingway prints it here as a story, apparently to make use of its disillusion theme. Moreover, the vignette which precedes it practically forces the reader to associate the protagonist of "A Very Short Story" with Nick Adams. In this vignette— the only one which links two stories so directly—Nick moves from his boyhood Michigan world to the greater world of his young manhood, and he finds their actualities much the same. Wounded in the general slaughter of World War I, he decides to make "a separate peace." Similarly, the protagonist of "A Very Short Story" is a wounded American soldier. He falls in love with his nurse, and they decide to marry, but she insists on their waiting until he returns home and is settled in a good job. While he is gone, she falls in love with an Italian major and dismisses her earlier affair as puppy love. Later, the disillusioned American gets gonorrhea making love in a taxi. As Nick Adams learned that love can come and go like an autumn storm and as he found that war is ultimately stupid butchery, so the protagonist of "A Very Short Story" discovers that love, no matter how deep and true, can be betrayed and lost—and even for the best reasons.

In the second of these disillusion stories, "Soldier's Home," a Marine—again, similar in background and experience to Nick Adams—returns from fighting in most of the major American battles to the Midwestern world in which he had grown up and finds himself isolated and a stranger. Krebs had been a good soldier; whatever else the war had been for him, he had found being a soldier simple and honest, and he had been proud of doing his job well. But no one cares what really happened in the war; only sensational lies will arouse their interest, and he is forced to tell lies that tarnish his memories and destroy his pride in them. Moreover, he finds the relationships of civilian life based on politics, intrigue, sentimentality, and still more lies. He had come home wanting "to live along without consequences" (93), wanting "his life to go smoothly" (101), but this the world will not permit. Ironically, Krebs is disillusioned less by the war than by the normal peacetime world which the war has made him see too clearly to accept.

For Nick Adams and others like him, then, the world "in our time" turns out to be exactly what the vignettes suggest it is—a puzzling and disillusioning place in which beauty and wonder, love and compassion, are strangely mixed with cruelty, violence, suffering, loss, alienation, and death. But the vignettes also imply that recognizing the world for what it is forms only one dimension of the human problem: equally vital is the consequent dimension of imposing a human order and meaning on such a world. And in the next two stories, Hemingway turns from the actuality of disillusion to the problem of man's idealism confronted by it.

In "The Revolutionist," the narrator describes a sensitive and idealistic young Hungarian communist whom he obviously likes and admires, not for the young man's beliefs but for the way he holds them. His idealism is neither cheap nor easy: the world has made him pay an awful price for it. He has been jailed and tortured for his ideals and knows he will be again, but he responds to cruelty, violence, and suffering not with self-pity or bitterness or detachment but with a stronger faith and a deeper joy in the beauty and kindness and love he also finds in the world. Within experienced and tested idealism, he has in full measure that courage which Hemingway defines as grace under pressure. Like Villalta and Maera in the bullfight vignettes, the young revolutionist personifies the way a man can face the violent and disillusioning actualities of the world and give his life order and meaning and value.

This realistically positive significance in "The Revolutionist" and the story's central place in the book help to explain why Hemingway changed it to a story from its original form as a vignette in the 1924 *in our time*. For the hard-earned idealism of the young revolutionist contrasts directly with the childish romanticism of "Mr. and Mrs. Elliot" in the following story. Here, a twenty-five-year-old poet and graduate student weds a forty-year-old formally fragile Southern-belle tea-shop owner. Both view life ideally and love romantically: they have kept themselves "pure" while waiting for the one great and perfect love their romanticism has led them confidently to expect. Innocent and inexperienced, they marry in an exaltation of ignorant bliss; and almost at once actuality begins to puncture their expectations. Disappointed, they become frustrated, restless, and thoroughly miserable.

Trying to escape themselves and their situation in a new romanticism of travel and foreign exoticism, the Elliots end up quarrelling and drifting apart, she into an incipient Lesbian relationship and he to drinking and bad poetry. Unlike the young revolutionist, their ideals are abstract, untested, and unearned without roots in experience and knowledge. Consequently, Mr. and Mrs. Elliot are totally unprepared for the disillusioning actualities of life and of real human relationships, and they are bitterly disappointed. Worse, they respond to this disappointment by seeking escape in further romanticism and in dissipation and perversion and are therefore unable to learn anything from their experience or on its basis to give their lives any meaning or order or value.

At the center of *In Our Time*, then, these two stories focus on idealism and romanticism in conflict with disillusioning actuality and on two contrasting responses to this conflict. "The Revolutionist" suggests that man can preserve his idealism and live meaningfully by it even amidst an actuality which would destroy it, so long as his idealism is neither a denial of that actuality nor an attempt to disguise it or hide from it. And "Mr. and Mrs. Elliot" highlights the inevitable disappointment and disillusion awaiting those who try to live in an imagined perfection divorced from actuality.

From a focus on initiation into life as it really is "in our time," on some of the characteristic disillusions of that life, and on the problems of giving it a human meaning and value, Hemingway in the next three stories explores in further detail the paradoxical and topsy-turvy nature of the human condition and the difficulties of living in it. Here, the characters are neither young innocents in their first contacts with actuality nor mature people shaken by profound disillusion nor contrasting idealists; instead, they are ordinary people in ordinary situations which have developed unaccountably contrary to what the people involved have expected or desired. "Cat in the Rain" centers on a young American wife in an Italian hotel room with her husband. As he lies on the bed reading, she looks out the window and sees a cat under a table trying to find shelter from the rain. She wants to bring it inside; and the husband, after a perfunctory offer to get the cat, allows her to go for it. Once outside, however, she finds the cat gone and returns disappointed. A few minutes later, a maid brings the animal to her: the hotel manager had gotten it for her.

These apparently trivial events reveal that for the young wife marriage has become a strange reversal of the relationship she had obviously expected. She wants to wear her hair long; her husband likes it cut short like a boy's. She wants a dining room and silver of her own and a dressing table with a mirror to brush her hair in front of and new clothes; instead, she lives in hotel rooms. In short, she is feminine and domestic and wants a family to love and be loved by, but she has only a husband who takes her for granted.

Nothing is as it should be for her: a stray cat becomes her home and family, and the attention and affection she yearns for come from a stranger, the hotel-keeper.

Even more capriciously abortive are the events in "Out of Season": here, literally everything goes inexplicably wrong for everyone. A young couple vacationing in Cortina are taken fishing by a man who has been working in the garden of their hotel and who sees in being hired as their guide a source of money and of higher status. But he is drunk and gets drunker celebrating his new position; the young couple can't understand him and are quarrelling; it's out of season for fishing; the townspeople look on with contempt; it is raining, windy, and cold; and the wife finally goes back to the hotel. When the husband and the guide reach the river, the husband has no lead for his line, and they can't fish. The guide talks him out of an advance to try again the next day, and they make an appointment; but the husband doesn't intend to show up. The world, it would seem, goes sometimes "out of season"; and everything man expects or wants or seeks collapses when he reaches for it. In these two stories, Nick Adams' world in "The Battler" becomes everyone's world "in our time."

"Cross Country Snow" reflects the same world but subordinated to a central emphasis on living in it with meaning and order. The story brings Nick Adams on stage again: he and a friend are skiing in the Swiss Alps and stop for a short while at an inn, after which they leave to finish their skiing. In this model of narrative economy, Hemingway again suggests a world in which things can unexpectedly go wrong: Nick skis too fast, hits a patch of soft snow, and falls; he can't telemark because he has a bad leg; the waitress in the inn is pregnant but unmarried; and the unplanned pregnancy of Nick's wife means that against both their wishes they must return to the States. But, turning the coin of the preceding two stories, "Cross Country Snow" centers not on the nature of the world and the human condition but on Nick's and George's response to it.

Both would like to drop everything and just ski across the world, with time out for fishing, free from all care and obligation. But neither takes such dreams seriously; and both know that they will go back to their responsibilities—George to school and Nick to his pregnant wife. They have no illusions about the world and the human condition: Nick understands the plight of the waitress and sympathizes with her; and when George wishes they could promise to meet sometime in the future to ski again, Nick says, "there isn't any good in promising" (147). Both have accepted the world for what it is and are giving it value and order by the way they live in it. As they make skiing meaningful and beautiful by knowing what to do and doing it, taking the inevitable falls when they come but getting up and going on, so they make life meaningful by doing what they know they must do. And they have learned to recognize what they must do by having faced the world as it is, by having lived in it; thus, they can impose on life an order learned from living, an order that doesn't need codification or verbalization. Like skiing, which is "too swell to talk about" (143), it is a felt, not articulated, order.

The world as it actually is "in our time" set against man's expectations and hopes; and his consequent problems and difficulties in trying to live in it with meaning and order—these, then, are the central themes which Hemingway explores "in detail" in the stories as he had made them "the picture of the whole" in the vignettes. Completing this pattern, the final two stories function as a coda, each restating and focussing sharply on one of these two unifying themes. Indeed, this function helps to explain the otherwise puzzling position of "My Old Man": on the surface, the story seems to belong both chronologically and thematically with the early Nick Adams stories. But in its young narrator's complete initiation and total disillusion, particularly as expressed in the last line, "My Old Man" makes a stark restatement of one major theme and a perfect bridge to the compelling restatement of the second in "Big Two-Hearted River."

"My Old Man" is a Sherwood Anderson tale of a young boy's initiation into an amoral universe and corrupt world ruled by fortuity. He loves and admires his jockey father and doesn't know or refuses to see that his father has worked with gamblers to purposely lose races. Possibly because of his son, possibly because he can't stand throwing any more races, the father wins a race he is supposed to lose and is forced out of racing—he still has his license, but no one will give him a mount. Finally, a friend gives him a tip on a fixed race, and he wins a large sum on it—though, again, the boy refuses to believe that the race is fixed, that anyone could want a good horse to lose. The father buys the losing horse, races it honestly, and is killed with the horse in a bad spill. Leaving the track, the boy hears some fans applauding his father's death because of his past sins, and the boy is left with nothing.

The story reflects a world of chance, amorality, corruption, injustice, and violence, in which doing right or being honest brings no salvation. The boy's father succeeds when he is corrupt and fails when he is honest; he is killed by accident in an honest race and is remembered only for his earlier corruption. Recalling the loss of all that he had loved, the boy thinks: "seems like when they get started they don't leave a guy nothing" (173).

Ending "My Old Man," this line serves equally well as the introduction to "Big Two-Hearted River." For Nick Adams, here completing the pattern begun in the first five stories, personifies the second of *In Our Time's* central themes: the fundamental problem of living in the kind of world and human condition suggested by young Joe's summary conclusion. Older, more experienced, and dubiously wiser, Nick has been profoundly damaged psychologically and emotionally, probably by the war and its aftermath. He has "left everything behind" (179) and returned to Upper Michigan where he had fished as a boy, seeking in the primal realities of nature and in the craft of fishing a meaning and order on which to rebuild his life. Leaving the burned-out town of Seney behind as he had left behind his burned-out world, he hikes up into the hills, makes camp by the river, and spends a day fishing. And in the end, he finds in these activities and in the manner in which he pursues them, at least the beginnings of the spiritual renewal he so desperately seeks.

The story functions in the tension between the threat of psychological and emotional eruption rumbling just beneath the thin crust of Nick's self-control and his almost obsessive efforts to strengthen and extend that discipline by concentrating on every detail and the sequential order of his activities. "He knew where he wanted to strike the river" (182); and even though he becomes tired and hot, he refuses to turn towards it sooner. When he gets there, he makes camp and knows that "he was there, in the good place" (186). In the morning, he forces himself to cook and eat breakfast: "he was really too hurried to eat breakfast, but he knew he must" (195). He fishes with a craftsman's devotion to detail and sequence and keeps a careful brake on his emotions: "he did not want to rush his sensations any" (204). He avoids the swamp; "in the swamp fishing was a tragic adventure," and he "did not want it" (211). Still, in imposing the human meaning and order of camping and fishing on the primal realities of nature, Nick begins to heal. Like the grasshoppers around Seney, who have adapted to their changed environment by turning black to match it (181), Nick readies himself for adaptation to his changed world: "there were plenty of days coming when he could fish the swamp" (212). The world in our time, it would appear, is not one most of us made or would have made; but we can nevertheless, if we will, live in it with meaning and order and value.

v

Many writers on Hemingway have pointed out that "My Old Man," one of his earliest stories, reflects the influence of Sherwood Anderson and that *The Torrents of Spring* (1926) is at least partly a lampooning declaration of full independence from Anderson. Between these extremes, however, *In Our Time* testifies to the deep and continuing influence of the older writer. In 1925, the year in which *In Our Time* was published, "Hemingway told Scott Fitzgerald that his first pattern had been Anderson's *Winesburg, Ohio*";[6] and in its complex unity, in Hemingway's avowed intention "to give the picture of the whole between examining it in detail," *In Our Time* turns the clear light of an ironic and contradictory actuality on the world of the first quarter of the twentieth century as *Winesburg, Ohio* had shone it on midwestern America.

Like its model, then, *In Our Time* is neither anthology nor novel but a

6. Fenton, p. 149.

new form, a literary hybrid, with something of the variety of the anthology combined with something of the unity of the novel. Moreover, in its view of the world and of man's efforts to live in it with meaning and order, in its conscious and intricate structure, in its ironic and symbolic method, and in its lean, intensified style, Hemingway's first book reflects the central intellectual and esthetic concerns which dominated his life and writing from beginning to end. Grow and develop, broaden and deepen, these concerns may, but change essentially they seldom do; and the later harvest is implicit in these, its first shoots. Better than any other single work, more than any one or few of its stories and vignettes, the unified whole of *In Our Time* introduces Hemingway's world and the art in which he creates it.

"Big World Out There": The Nick Adams Stories[1] / *Philip Young*

I proposed publishing this book almost 25 years ago; maybe I should be excused for taking a special interest in it. Bring out all of Hemingway's Nick Adams stories in one volume, I presumptuously suggested in a 1948 letter to Charles Scribner, and print them in the chronological order of Nick's advancing age. There were 15 of these stories then, several of them pretty well known, like "The Killers" and "In Another Country," and all of them in print for 15 years or many more. But Nick himself was scarcely known at all; people had practically no idea who he was or what he was like, the main reason being the jumbled ages at which one met up with him in the various collections of Hemingway's short fiction. He would surface as a soldier, say, then as a boy, then a child, a married man, and a soldier again. The coherence of his adventures was obscured, you might say, and their overall significance was just about invisible.

Mr. Scribner replied that since he did not think Mr. Hemingway would approve of the idea there was no point in pursuing it, and the matter was dropped as far as I was concerned. There it lay, as in a corner, twitching once in a while, until the fall of 1967, when I began going through the Hemingway

Philip Young, " 'Big World Out There': The Nick Adams Stories," *Novel: A Forum for Fiction*, VI (Fall 1972), 5–19. Copyright © 1972, and permission to reprint granted by Philip Young.

1. This essay was initially conceived as an introduction to the new chronological collection—including eight unpublished tales and fragments—involving Hemingway's hero, Nick Adams, called *The Nick Adams Stories* (New York: Scribner's, 1972), 268 pp., $7.95. A brief preface by Philip Young now introduces the collection.

manuscripts in an attempt to identify things. It was rather early in the game that I happened on something called "Summer People," 40 sparsely-covered sheets of pen and ink—a Nick story, and very likely the first one. Mary Hemingway had already given me a typescript of a much later and longer, though unfinished, piece of Nick fiction—the last one—which she called "The Last Good Country." And it was at just this time that Scribner's asked me to "have an idea" for a book. I don't quit easy, and soon found myself proposing to Charles Scribner, Jr., what I had prematurely recommended to his father—*The Nick Adams Stories*, with two new entries.

I didn't have that title in mind, and it was certainly not my idea that the rest of the new material that was uncovered (much of it by Carlos Baker, at Princeton) be printed here. The notion that We Must Have It All—every scrap that turned up and had Nick in it—has prevailed, which is to say that the trade publisher has out-pedanticked the academy. (The fact that Hemingway never destroyed these bits and pieces means little; he didn't throw out grocery lists, and didn't plan to print them someday either.) A lot of people are wondering how the author would have felt to know that such trivial fragments as "Crossing the Mississippi" and "Wedding Day" have been presented to the public as "stories," and that his new book opens with something called "Three Shots," which he discarded as a completely false start before beginning again from scratch to write "Indian Camp." It's a pretty safe bet that he wouldn't be happy about it.

One last disclaimer for the record: I didn't edit anything, either. Indeed there has not been much editing, except in the case of "The Last Good Country," where a good deal has been cut from what Hemingway wrote. But here the judgment is favorable: the cuts were either necessary, to piece together two long and different openings present in the manuscript, or desirable, where the text was wordy, or the pace slow, or the taste dubious. The job has been done skillfully by Scribner's.

Beyond the trivial Preface, the only other things I am indeed responsible for in this book are the selection and ordering of the "real stories"—matters that are not as simple as may first appear. Actually there isn't any completely satisfactory way to arrange them all, as readers are going to discover when they confront Nick as an adolescent veteran of the great war; and on that puzzle, one of those debates that delight some of us, and enliven (a little) the lesser critical journals, is already getting under way. But enough of the record; if we back away from it to take the large view of this book it is clear, whatever else may be said, that as we follow Nick across the span of a generation in time we have got a story worth following. As it turns out, Hemingway arranged it (consciously or otherwise) in five distinct stages—that is, the original fifteen stories occur in five segments of Nick's life, three stories to each part. "The Northern Woods," as the first section is called, deals with heredity and environment, parents and Michigan Indians. "On His Own" is all away from home, or on the road, and instead of Indians, prizefighters. "War" is exactly that, or as the author put it later on, "hit properly and for good." Then "A Soldier Home": Michigan revisited, hail and farewell. And fifth, "Company of Two": marriage, Europe revisited, and finally looking backward, a sort of coda.

Maybe it will also appear now and at long last that in Nick Hemingway gave us the most important single character in all his work—the first in a long line of fictional self-projections, the start of everything. Later protagonists from Jake Barnes and Frederic Henry to Richard Cantwell and Thomas Hudson were shaped by Nick, were all to have (if only tacitly) his history behind them. So had Hemingway. Not that everything that happens to Nick had happened to him. Indeed the author remarks right here, in the fragment called "On Writing," that "Nick in the stories was never himself. He made them up." To an extent that is of course true; the autobiography is transmuted. But it is bemusing that at the very moment when the writer is categorically disassociating himself from his persona he makes him interchangeable with himself, as the "he," the consciousness of the piece, shifts from Nick to Hemingway back to Nick again (pp. 237–40). But the real point is that this extended and disciplined self-portrait became a significant story in its own right: the story of an American born with the century, complicated in boyhood and badly hurt in a war, who came to terms with what happened and turned it to lasting fiction. And now, after all these years, it's time to have at this episodic narrative for the last time—to uncover, with the help of the biographers, its roots in the author's experience, assess the new material, remark what has not already been remarked to death about the old, and attempt a new judgment of what it all adds up to.

I

The earliest scent of Nick's trail can probably be picked up in a little story called "Sepi Gingan" which the author published when he was still at Oak Park High. A juvenile but already violent tale, apparently set in Hortons Bay, Michigan, the heart of Adams country, it is told by an Indian (who will appear in a mature Nick story) to a nameless boy who is Nick in all *but* name, about another Indian who was killed by a dog and left on the Pere Marquette railroad tracks, where a train "removed all the traces." Another Indian, drunk, who had "laid down to sleep on the Pere Marquette railway tracks and had been run over by the midnight train," figures in a new Nick "story" (it has no plot) that is here called "The Indians Moved Away," and relates how that happened. (An early piece, it was found in the manuscripts without a title; also found was an early title, "They Never Came Back," without a story; they probably should have gone together.)

Indians figure as well in all the stories Hemingway published alive about

Nick as a young boy, of which "Indian Camp" is first in several ways. It was the first Nick story to see print; it is the earliest according to his apparent age; it is the opening story of *In Our Time*, the first real book of stories. It is also perhaps the most violent, and unintentionally portentous, of all Hemingway stories, and it lays down what was to become the basic pattern of all his fiction, which is to expose a character to violence, to physical or psychological shock, or severe trial, and then to focus on the consequences. The consequence of violent birth and death in "Indian Camp" is muted—a calm discussion of suicide between Dr. Adams and his small son, the portent being that the originals for both of them were destined eventually to commit it. The story itself, with its jack-knife Caesarian, is invented. "Of course," Hemingway once remarked (again in the piece called "On Writing") "he'd never seen an Indian woman having a baby. . . . He'd seen a woman have a baby on the road to Karagatch and tried to help her. That was the way it was."

The way it started, however, in the eight longhand pages that Hemingway discarded but Scribner's prints as "Three Shots," was on a fishing trip. Uncle George (Ernest's uncle) and his brother, Dr. Henry Adams, were out fishing at night. Nick was back at their tent and frightened. But he was not so much afraid of the dark as "of dying. . . . It was the first time he had ever realized that he himself would have to die sometime." In throwing out this section of the story Hemingway was struggling, successfully, with what he once called the most difficult problem for writers: "knowing what you really felt, rather than what you were supposed to feel. . . ." Thus at the end of "Indian Camp" as we have it, Nick "felt quite sure that he would never die." What you were supposed to feel has given over to something subtler and deeper. Children don't really believe in their own demise. Death is obviously something that happens to other people.

Perhaps it was because he had been camping that Dr. Adams set off to deliver a baby with no better equipment than a knife and some gut leaders. He is an ambiguous figure generally, who does not unwrap his medical journals; and on his next appearance, in "The Doctor and the Doctor's Wife," it's his courage that's in question. Two Indians, Dick Boulton and Billy Tabeshaw (of "Sepi Gingan"), come to cut wood for him. When Boulton tries to pick a fight, only to have the doctor walk off, the problem of whether his exit was sensible or unmanly can be left to the reader. The author probably did not intend a choice; he said that the story, based on an actual incident, is about the time he discovered that his father was a coward. On the other hand Dr. Hemingway said he liked the piece, and at the end when Nick has to choose in a small way between the doctor and his wife (who is a Christian Scientist) he immediately chooses his father.

"Ten Indians" appeared two years after the story of the doctor's dilemmas and in a different book. But a little something was lost before the two stories were brought together, and tensions in the Adams family are seen against the cheerful ease with which the neighboring Garners get along. This pair of tales must also have been linked in the author's mind in another way. As the Garners return in a wagon from Petoskey with Nick aboard they pass the slumbering bodies of nine Indians, who have excessively—and inappropriately—celebrated the Fourth of July. ("Them Indians," says Mrs. Garner.) The tenth Indian is Prudence Mitchell. And now there are none: Prudie does not appear in the story, but she was Nick's girl, and when he gets home the doctor tells him he has seen her "having quite a time" in the woods with another boy. What we are not told is that in life this Indian girl, who sometimes worked for Mrs. Hemingway, was Prudence Boulton, daughter of the man who perhaps humiliated the doctor—who in turn may take satisfaction in telling Nick what he saw.

As for Nick, he is about to learn again what he really feels. "A Broken Heart" was the original title of "Ten Indians"—an ironic one, since Nick is about to learn that his own heart is quite intact. But we are not done with Prudie, later Trudy. She figures in three episodes of Nick's life, and the author often spoke of her, especially in connection with the loss of his virginity. His authorized biographer, Carlos Baker, put this down as "wishful thinking," which is probably right. But another biographer, Constance Montgomery, reports having been told that Prudence Boulton died young, perhaps in childbirth, and she passes along a rumor that the child was Ernest's. There are *no* grounds for believing this, and it would not bear repeating but for the fact that, before it was cut from "The Last Good Country," it came out that Nick indeed had got Trudy pregnant. And in his last appearance he will think back on this girl who "did first what no one has ever done better." (Them Indians.)

II

Hemingway left home in October of 1917, heading for Kansas City by train, and some years later he remembered in a very brief sketch how as Nick he first saw the Mississippi from a coach. It had been away from home, or on the road, that Nick's adolescence was spent—but on freights or on foot, not in coaches. And one would be "ill advised," as Hemingway once remarked, to think of the first of these stories, called "The Light of the World," as a "simple tale." He tried once to explain it by saying that although it is "about many things," it is really

a love letter to a whore named Alice. . . . And the point of it is that nobody . . . knows how we were then from how we are now. This is worse on women than on us . . . and that is what I was trying for in the story.

This helps in reading the piece, but leaves out *too* many things, one of which is the religious note sounded by the title. The reference to Jesus is crucial ("I am the light of the world. . . ."), for it is what points to the fact that the champion prizefighter named Ketchel has become, in the minds of the two mammoth prostitutes, a sort of fire sale Christ crucified: "I loved him like you love God," "His own father shot and killed him. Yes, by Christ, his own father," and so forth. At the end Nick (clearly, though he is not named) and Tom (in life an Indian boy named Mitchell) seem to have nowhere much to go. It is getting dark, and as they leave the railway station where they listened to the whores arguing over which of them had been loved by Ketchel it looks as if the point of the story is really that the light of the world has gone out. In *Winner Take Nothing*, moreover, Hemingway put this story right after "A Clean, Well-Lighted Place," the most pessimistic of all his stories ("Our nada who art in nada. . . ." and so on). With the breakdown of faith and "light" in both stories, it is a good bet that he thought of these as another pair, thematically related. He coupled them again when he said of "A Clean, Well-Lighted Place," "May be my best story. That and 'The Light of the World,' which no one but me ever seemed to like."

Perhaps no one but he ever seemed to understand all of it. For that we need an answer to the unresolved question of Ketchel's first name. Alice and Peroxide agree that it was Steve; a homosexual cook asks if it wasn't Stanley. It is usually assumed that there was only one Ketchel, that everyone has in mind the same fighter, and that in the argument over which woman had actually loved him it is Alice who is telling the truth. But the point this time is that both women are lying (it's worse on them than on us): neither one of them has got her lover's first name right. The facts are that the boxer who "knocked Jack Johnson down" was Stanley Ketchel, as the cook thought. He was murdered in 1910, but not by his father. In 1915 Steve Ketchel fought Ad Wolgast to a draw.

The facts are further that Ad Wolgast had won the lightweight championship of the world from Battling Nelson in the year of Stanley Ketchel's death. It was one of the bloodiest brawls of the era, and Wolgast eventually became punch-drunk. In 1917 he was declared legally incompetent; ten years later he was committed to an asylum in California where he died in 1955. From small-town Cadillac, he was known as the Michigan Wildcat, and when Nick encounters him in "The Battler" Hemingway calls him Ad Francis.

Nick is traveling alone in "The Battler," but along the same railroad (The Grand Rapids and Indiana) as before. Hiking along the rails after having been knocked off a freight, he encounters Ad and a companion in a sort of two-man hobo jungle. It turns out to be a tough experience, and for the first time—but as a striking forecast of things-to-come—we see Nick definitely shaken at the end. When in "The Killers" he meets up with some gangsters and Ole Andreson, the fighter who will no longer resist being killed, he is shaken a bit more.

Hemingway once said that Gene Tunney had asked him, "Ernest wasn't that Andre Andreson in 'The Killers'? I told him it was. . . ." (This was astute of Tunney; Andreson was so obscure that, next to this story, his best chance of being remembered was for falling clean out of the ring and knocking himself out—or so he claimed—when boxing a much smaller man in 1915.)[2] Hemingway also once explained what his story does not—"why the boys were sent to kill" him:

> the Swede was supposed to throw the fight but didn't. . . . All afternoon he had rehearsed taking a dive, but during the fight he had instinctively thrown a punch he didn't mean to.

He is also said to have told Tunney that "the town wasn't Summit, New Jersey, but Summit, Illinois. But that's all I told him because the Chicago mob that sent the killers was and, as far as I know, is still [1955] very much in business."

Exactly what at that late date he might have said that would have meant a thing to any gangster if Tunney had passed it along is very far from clear. The point seems to be that Hemingway continued to spin fictions about his fiction even after the fiction was in print. On many occasions he presented actual events as tales, and sometimes he told tales as fact. "The Last Good Country" is a good example of the latter practice. The final story of Nick on the road, and hitherto unpublished, Hemingway used to tell it (invent it, actually) about himself—about how *he* as a boy had escaped the game-wardens by taking off into the Michigan forest. It was good practice, and in 1952 he began inventing the tale for Nick.

The way it all got started is that about a week after his sixteenth birthday Ernest was working at Longfield, the family farm across the lake from Windemere, when two "beastly, insinuating, sneering" wardens came to the house "on business": "How about that young man about eighteen . . . ?" (Mrs. Hemingway is writing this to her husband, back in Chicago practicing medicine; the letter is mentioned in the story.) "They had two witnesses that he had shot a big game bird—had it in his boat, and they were after him." As soon as they went, she sent his year-older sister Marcelline "to row at top speed to the farm and warn Ernest to go to Dilworth's and stay until further notice."

> Now here's what happened. He shot a crane. . . . He wrapped it up and left it in the launch. . . . When he returned . . . he found it gone and a young boy who said he was the game warden's son came up to him and asked about the bird . . . "just drumming up business for my father. . . ." I don't know whether he had best risk it to come back to Windemere or not.

2. Oddly there was also a fighter named *Ole* Anderson whom Tunney knew, since in the third round of a bout held in Jersey City in June of 1920 he knocked him out.

At this point there is a disagreement on details, but the result was that Ernest paid a fine and the incident was ended. He identified the bird as a great blue heron, biggest he had ever seen, and explained that he had taken an impossible shot at it only to drill it right behind the eye. (Why in writing the story he changed it to a deer is hard to understand.) But the older he got the more he embroidered things, until he had the narrative of a runaway boy and his sister Littless—probably based on both Ursula Hemingway, who used to run away and "meet Ernie in Petoskey," and Madelaine (or Sunny) Hemingway, who was the family tomboy.

Familiar voices, familiar rooms. Prominent in the story, Packard's general store and post office at Hortons Bay on Lake Charlevoix appeared in "Up in Michigan" and in "Sepi Gingan." The Dilworths, to whom his mother sent Ernest, lived there, and there like Mrs. Packard in the story Mrs. Dilworth served the public fried trout or chicken dinners. Like Nick, Ernest brought her rainbows (illegal if he sold them) and split wood. The girl of "Up in Michigan" was a waitress there; so was Marjorie, with whom Nick was to have an affair later on. The hotel the Packards also run in the story must be the Echo Beach Hotel on nearby Walloon Lake, where the Hemingways used to stay before it burned down and they bought Windemere. Trudy we have met before. Mrs. Tabeshaw is probably Billy's wife. Michigan was a small world.

Although we may read "The Last Good Country" as a short story it is obviously not one. Rather long already, it is nowhere near finished when it simply stops. If the plot at its original pace were to be resolved, Hemingway was clearly headed for a full-length novel. For once, however, there is a "plot plant," so that one can guess, at least, how Nick is going to get out of the jam he is in: a warden with curious feet is going to have to call off the hunt—*and* his son, if the boy is on the trail—in exchange for continued silence on Packard's part regarding a far more serious and unpunished offense than Nick's. And though we leave off in mid-air, Hemingway has already accomplished a great deal. We get to know Nick better here than we have ever done before. And the "Hemingway heroine" is never more real than in her youngest appearance as his kid sister. Right down to the short hair, Littless is the wonderful if slightly unreal child that grew up to be Catherine Barkley and all the others. Indeed the piece immediately attracted, on publication, such damaging epithets as "mawkish" and "puerile." And it is true that here, for the only time with Nick, Hemingway treads the boundaries of sentimentality (his characteristic brinkmanship), occasionally trampling them.

But this does not automatically disqualify or cancel out the story; its real distinction lies in the fact of its genre, which is related to sentiment and unprecedented for Hemingway: sky-blue pastoral, with but one cloud in sight to keep things real and moving. Up to now, "idyllic Michigan" has been mainly an exaggeration on the part of his critics. But we leave these children on a level of peace and contentment he never occupied before—in mid-air suspended. And in this sense if in no other the story does "end." There is nowhere to go from a dream. Or from a myth: the familiar American story, most notably Huck Finn's, of a magical journey from the irritants of civilization to an unspoiled state of nature, an odyssey of a loving couple in escape of society—and of its epitome, the law. A Michigan forest was prefigured by the Mississippi River, and the kids' camp in it by a raft.

In this passage one is never alone. Van Winkle in the Catskills, Thoreau at Walden, are incomplete. To make it work there must be love. But the love must be forbidden: two males, Huck and Jim, Ishmael and Queequeg, Deerslayer and Chingachgook—or siblings, Nick and Littless. Only in Hemingway's version are sexual overtones explicit (some were cut), and only here is the partner of another sex rather than race. But as she says, Littless is not *really* a girl yet. Indeed she is something of a boy. For just as Huck dressed as a girl, in calico gown and sunbonnet, and "practiced around all day to get the hang of things," so Littless wears overalls and a boy's shirt, cuts her hair short, and moves around "practicing being a boy." But in all these stories, hints of physical love serve always to highlight the innocence of actual relationships. Without the overtones, we would never think to realize how immaculate is the conception. "The Last Good Country" is at one with its precedents in expressing a yearning for escape from ordinary life into a charmed kinship under the ennobling conditions of earth or water in the new security of a new home: raft, ship, or campfire.

And if it seems a stubborn truth that these are after all a boy and his sister in the forest, different overtones are also audible. Hansel and Gretel were not entirely happy with their mother either. They lived by a great forest, where they too picked berries and bedded down in a sort of "cathedral," as the Adams children call it, where an evil witch (or warden's son) may find them. Hemingway gets by natural means the magic that the fairy tale achieves with fourteen white-winged angels and the sound of heavenly music.

III

There is a time limit on adolescence and enchanted forests. And the title of an unpublished poem, "Killed. Piave—July 8, 1918," indirectly conveys the reversal in Nick's fortunes whereby after leaving him at Camp Number One, as happy as he will ever get, we pick him up again as a soldier, miserable and badly wounded, in Italy. The date commemorates the night on which the author was hit "for good" ("killed" is what almost, or metaphorically, happened; Piave is the river where it happened) at Fossalta, which is north of Venice. Hemingway did record the fact of Nick's wounding directly, but he slighted the event by entering it in an untitled, one-paragraph sketch (here reprinted from an inferior early text), placed between two actual stories of *In Our Time*, where readers scarcely noticed it. A more effective transition between Michigan and Italy was severed when in 1925 he abandoned at page 26 a novel called *Along with Youth*, that appears in this book as "Night Before Landing," in which Nick was crossing to France in May of 1918 on the liner *Chicago*. Hemingway had, of course, been in Italy as an ambulance driver for the Red Cross, and a week after his wounding he was shipped to a Red Cross hospital in Milan. The most badly damaged part of him was a knee; after two months he could walk to the Ospedale Maggiore for physiotherapy. Returned to the front to see his friends, he came down with jaundice and was sent back to Milan, where he had fallen in love with an American nurse he hoped to marry. Out of these events and their effects he wrote, in addition to *A Farewell to Arms*, three stories of Nick Adams.

In "Now I Lay Me" Nick is suffering from insomnia, one result of his wounds. As befits the title he thinks back to his childhood and says his prayers "over and over." The reader is meant to recall a later line of "Now I Lay Me"—"If I die before I wake"—as Nick remarks that he

> had been living for a long time with the knowledge that if I ever shut my eyes in the dark and let myself go, my soul would go out of my body. I had been that way . . . ever since I had been blown up at night and felt it go out of me and then come back.

This story, set near the front, is closely linked to "In Another Country," which is set in Milan. Both stories—which were originally two parts of a single one, as the manuscript shows—deal with the effects of Nick's wounds, psychological and physical. In the first of them his Italian orderly tells him he'd be all right if he'd only get married; in the second a bereaved Italian major tells him he must *not* marry, must find things he cannot lose.

In "A Way You'll Never Be," which falls chronologically between these two, it is clear that the psychological damage is more severe than the physical. Hemingway once explained his title saying he wanted to show a girl who was going crazy that Nick had been "much nuttier" than she was going to get. The story deals, he also said, with "things that happened to me in a trench outside Fornaci," which is near Fossalta. If so, things were really grim; Nick's mind goes utterly. And it may be that what particularly "frightened him so that he could not get rid of it . . . that long yellow house and the different width of the river," is the scene of his wounding—and Hemingway's, Lt. Henry's, and Col. Cantwell's, who also "had been hit, out on the river bank."

But the best of these, and one of the best of all Hemingway stories, is "In Another Country." "It opens," Scott Fitzgerald wrote long ago, with "one of the most beautiful prose sentences I have ever read": "In the fall the war was always there, but we did not go to it any more." It was like a sport one has lost interest in. The visiting team was the Austrians, meeting the Italians, at home; Nick, a ringer, is benched as befits his incapacity. He takes his therapy in Milan, but the focus is on that major—"in another country," as Marlowe's famous lines go—whose "wench is dead." Hemingway himself was not to make out much better with his girl, Agnes von Kurowsky, the Red Cross nurse who became Catherine Barkley. She did not follow him home to the States as he expected, and he turned his bitterness into a "sketch" which he later named "A Very Short Story." He did not call the jilted soldier Nick, however, and the piece remains more sketch than story. Thus Hemingway returned to Michigan from the war, "blown to pieces," according to a Petoskey doctor, and still alone.

IV

"It's the account of a boy on a fishing trip," to call again on Scott Fitzgerald, writing this time about "Big Two-Hearted River." "Nothing more— but I read it with the most breathless unwilling interest I have experienced since Conrad first bent my reluctant eyes upon the sea." In 1926 Hemingway was happy to settle for such published praise. But Fitzgerald might have asked himself why nothing more than a fishing trip should have galvanized his attention. If he had done so he might have discovered that he was responding perfectly to what Hemingway called in those days "my new theory that you could omit anything if you knew that you omitted . . . and make people feel something more than they understood." The things he had left out before were never really crucial, but this time an omission made all the difference. As he pointed out years later, "The story was about coming back from the war but there was no mention of the war in it."

There is no doubt, however, that the perilous state of Nick's nervous system, unmentioned in the story, accounts for the intensity of the writing, which is what arrested Fitzgerald. Here is the quintessential Hemingway style: simplicity, forged under great pressure, out of complexity. The trout, "keeping themselves steady in the current with wavering fins," reflect as in a mirror. He decides not to fish "the swamp," which would be to complicate things; besides, that's where "the river narrowed," which may remind him of the "different width" of the river at Fossalta. Acting, and not thinking, his trip proves a remarkable success. He will carry his scars, but will never be badly shaken again. Fishing is better therapy than Milan's; for Nick the war in Italy ended in Michigan.

"If he wrote it he could get rid of it," Nick will think later on. "He had gotten rid of many things by writing them." And in his next appearance so much has been purged that he seems—most disconcertingly—less the struck-down veteran of a war than a prewar adolescent. But Hemingway was still writing out of his own experience—seeing himself, at each stage of the narrative, as Nick—and the events that gave rise to the next three stories took place in the postwar summer of 1919, through half of which he was in fact still the teen-ager that Nick seems. Indeed a year later, Marcelline observed, her brother was "more like a boy of sixteen than a man approaching his twenty-first birthday." Nick at this age will bear her out, and several details in the stories date them as postwar—rum-runners, for instance, and the business about "not thinking."

"The End of Something" and "The Three-Day Blow" are as closely related as chapters in a novel. In the former Nick breaks off his affair with a girl named Marjorie. Just as Hortons Bay has run out of the logs that made it a lumbering town, leaving nothing but the foundations of the mill, which she calls "our old ruin," so their relationship has run its course and is left in ruin by Nick—one of the things, perhaps, that he got rid of by writing it. But the break-up, it turns out, was a plot in which a friend named Bill conspired, and in "The Three-Day Blow" they discuss the matter, along with the joys of bachelorhood and literature—especially Maurice Hewlett's *Forest Lovers*, which at points strikingly resembles "The Last Good Country"— as they get happily drunk on Bill's father's whiskey. "Now she can marry someone of her own sort," Bill tells him, which suggests that what Hemingway omitted this time is that in life, as already mentioned, Marjorie (Bump), though a respectable high-school girl, was a summer waitress at Mrs. Dilworth's Pinehurst Cottage. Nick is uncomfortable about the whole business, but then he realizes that just as love can run out so estrangement is not necessarily permanent, and he feels better.

"You are constantly aware of the continual snapping of ties that is going on around Nick," Fitzgerald wrote of this pair of stories—an observation so acute that it reads more like a prediction, since it is in "Summer People" that Nick really begins snapping his ties to Michigan, and there is no evidence that Fitzgerald ever saw the story. At any rate it has never been published before, or even typed.

Ernest went into a church on September 30, 1920, one of his biographers tells us, with a girl named Kate. He burned a candle, prayed for everything he wanted and was rewarded, he wrote in a letter, with a small "Adventure with a touch of Romance." If the Kate of "Summer People" was the Kate of actuality perhaps she was the reward, which is sexual. In any event, Nick has one last adventure up in Michigan, and it tells us as much about him and his maker as might a chapter of factual biography. Imperfectly paced, and itself rather boyish, it is not the best Nick story we have. Nor is it the least of them, but it is almost certainly the first: the manuscript shows repeated vacillation on the protagonist's name. Nick, Hemingway writes, and crosses it out; Allan the same; Wemedge, which becomes here as before Nick's nickname, the same; again and finally Nick, all the way through.

As an apparent first-try at a very early story, "Summer People" is remarkable for the deftness with which seemingly unlike things are brought together. Nick plunging his arm into a cold spring on a hot night at the start sharply prefigures his small adventure with Kate at the end. Along the way, the swimming, diving, conversations, thoughts, ambitions—as well as the interlude with the girl, and a prayer—are gathered in the boy's realization that he is "different," which is presumably the point. Different in all the ways of the story. Even if he does not entirely act on it, his knowledge of girls is "beyond his years"; the manner of his diving is unusual, and another prefiguration of the intercourse later on; he swims underwater, not on top of it, and so forth. All differences culminate in the crucial one, the hope and belief that he will be a great writer.

Evidence in the manuscripts shows clearly that Hemingway intended to revise and publish this story, which raises the question of why he never did. Perhaps he thought it was unprintable at the time, at least in this country. (Gertrude Stein told him that "Up in Michigan" was *inaccroachable*, and at the time she was right.) More likely, though, he "didn't want to hurt living people," the reason he once gave for why he didn't write a "wonderful novel" about Oak Park. His summer people were not just living; they had been his very closest friends. Most of all, "Summer People" would have hurt Hadley Richardson, his first wife by the time he wrote the story. It was Kate, Hadley's close friend, who had introduced her to Ernest. (He was in turn to introduce Kate to a close friend of his, the late John Dos Passos, whom she married.) Indeed in September of 1921 when Ernest married Hadley at Hortons Bay, the town of the story, near Windemere, where they spent their honeymoon, the original for every single character in "Summer People"— Nick, Kate, Bill, Odgar, and the Ghee—was in the wedding party. Kate (sometimes Butstein or Stut, just as in the story) was Katharine Smith, a bridesmaid. Bill, the same Bill as in the two previous stories, was her brother, William B. Smith, Ernest's best friend and an usher (who eventually became a speechwriter for Harry Truman). Odgar, or Carl, also an usher, was J. Charles Edgar, an older man but long-time friend who had housed Ernest when he worked in Kansas City for the *Star*. The only person involved who would not be hurt was another usher, the Ghee (significance unknown)— Jack Pentecost, who was along on the trip to the Fox River that became "Big Two-Hearted River."

Kate Smith was eight years older than Ernest, and her brother states categorically that "Ernesto did not have an affair with my sister." But Hadley was just as old. Anyway it didn't matter, Hemingway thinks for Nick later on, that the best of his writing was "made up." "None of it had ever happened. . . . That was what the family couldn't understand." (Perhaps because a lot of it had happened.) But "Summer People" was far too close to home. And by the time the family was mostly gone, and Kate decapitated in an automobile accident, her husband and brother and Hadley still lived, and

Hemingway was in far other country. He published no Nick Adams fiction after 1933; by the time Kate died his manuscripts were widely dispersed; he may even have forgotten the story. But it is a significant one—of Nick's graduation into a bigger world. Summer people are insulated; they matter but for a season, don't really belong. Nick is at the center of this transient population, but he has a secret that neither summer nor year-round people are in on: because he is different he can have what he wants, as he thinks. And that entitles him to belong elsewhere. If his final prayer comes true he is not temporary at all, but the man for all seasons he became.

At this point, however, Nick can only aspire to be a writer. He's not old enough yet, and, as he remarks, doesn't know enough. ("Wait.") As with Hemingway, the wait proved short, and it's a reasonable guess that the end of "On Writing" records the very moment when the mature career began. Irrelevant anachronisms concerning bullfighters and so forth set aside, the piece emerges as Hemingway's Farewell to Michigan. Nick is Letting Go: relinquishing the past, the Northern Woods, summers, friends, and even fishing. At the end the piece moves into action. Nick releases the trout he has caught and kept alive, simply cuts the line he had been fishing with that snagged, then relieves the rabbit of two ticks on its head that were killing it. He is freeing everything for one thing, "work." This because he has a sort of tick in his own head—very different from the one that agitated "Big Two-Hearted River," to which this material was once illogically appended. It has dawned on him that he has learned (from Cezanne, as explained) how to build in prose the land and landscape that contain "Big Two-Hearted River." Nick, in other words, is off to start the story that Hemingway had just finished. It won't be long now.

V

Meanwhile Nick has married Helen (Hadley in the manuscript of "Wedding Day"), and once again the scene shifts abruptly to Europe, where things turn out to be relatively uneventful—two episodes only, loosely connected in that both involve skiing and touch on marriage. "An Alpine Idyll," about the peasant who used to hang a lantern from the mouth of the frozen corpse of his wife, is said to be a tall tale told tourists by natives in Austria. (Nick asks his friend, "Do you think it's true?") In "Cross Country Snow" it is again the stubborn reality of a woman's body that impinges on the skiing; Helen is pregnant and Nick is taking her back to the States to have the child. (If he remembers what Bill told him, "Once a man's married, he's absolutely bitched," we do not hear about it.) And on this dying fall, taking "the run home," Nick's adventures—but for a reprise—are abruptly ended.

They needn't have been, had Hemingway chosen to pursue that marriage to Helen, for he wrote several stories in which Nick could have easily been the husband, and Helen the wife. But he tended to smuggle certain things away in his fiction; if they were compromising or shameful and he wanted to get rid of them he chose masks less transparent than Nick's. In "Soldier's Home" he had disguised his misery on returning to Oak Park from the war by giving Harold Krebs an experience of battle different from his own or Nick's, and by moving both his mother and Oak Park to Oklahoma. "Up in Michigan" was based on personal experience at Hortons Bay, and he set it there, but cast himself as Jim Gilmore, a short blacksmith with big mustaches. Similarly he skirted the breakdown of his marriage to Hadley, but did write a group of stories which are set abroad and show a marriage very like his own in a state of progressive disarray. He once called "Out of Season," where there is only a hint that things may go bad, a "literal transcript" of himself and Hadley. And although he said that the man and wife of "Cat in the Rain" were a "Harvard Couple," they sound like much the same people. In "A Canary for One," "I and my wife" are separating, and in "Homage to Switzerland" Mr. Johnson is being divorced.

That child, however, was born—a son called Schatz in "A Day's Wait," a story which could have been included in this book, except that it is really about the boy. In life John, or Jack, or Bumby Hemingway, he figures prominently in the Bimini section of *Islands in the Stream* as Schatz again, or Thomas Hudson, Jr., oldest son of the last major protagonist. He is also the son in "Fathers and Sons," in which Nick looks backward to his boyhood and rounds it off. Nick is now thirty-eight and a writer; the son is about the age of Nick when he first appeared in "Indian Camp." The action has covered a generation. The doctor who discussed suicide with his boy in the first story has now committed it, though we are told only that he is dead—another important omission. And as Nick remembers how useless his father was on the subject of sex, which he learned about from Trudy instead, so now he cannot talk to his boy about the doctor's death, though he knows that sooner or later they will have to visit "the tomb of my grandfather" (the boy has been raised abroad). A son is now father to the son, things have come full circle, and in his collected *First Forty-Nine Stories* Hemingway put this one forty-ninth.

The tale is told, but if Nick's history seems in retrospect to amount to slightly more than the sum of its chapters it may be because his progress through the first third of our century is at once representative, distinctive, and personal. Representative as a national passage from the innocence of a shaky prewar security through the disillusionment of a European ordeal-by-fire, and the rejection of much that a previous age had stood for, to "normalcy." Distinctive for memories of specific experiences the exact like of which we never had. And personal as the recreated autobiography of a culture hero of his time. But if anyone still feels more than he can account for in remembering Nick, he might ask what if anything Hemingway omitted from the story as a whole. The answer is so obvious that it might never dawn on us. The Nick Adams fiction is about leaving Oak Park, but there is no mention of Oak Park in it.

The text may be taken from Marcelline. When Ernest was flopping loose in their suburban house on his return from the war he spoke to her one day about "all the other things in life that aren't here. . . . There's a whole big world out there. . . ." What he omitted is what he escaped from. What he escaped to, for the rest of his life and all of his career, moves against a background he expunged. Oak Park was rejected for Michigan, and when that became a small world it was in turn put behind for a greater one. All that is simple to understand. But it is hard to realize today how great was the *need* for rebellion—how preposterous were things *At the Hemingways*, the name of Marcelline's affectionate book. Home was a Victorian matriarchy, and it has been said more than once that Hemingway was the only man in the world who really hated his mother. She had considerable pretentions to the arts; she sang, composed, and later painted. Her response to *The Sun Also Rises* was "I can't stand filth!" Her husband, though a busy doctor, kept house far more than she did. ("Dr. Hemingway did most of the cooking. He'd fix the kids' breakfast and then take the Mrs. her breakfast in bed.") She raised Ernest as closely as possible as a twin, a twin girl, to Marcelline. They looked alike, and were "dressed alike," his sister writes, in "gingham dresses and in little fluffy lace-tucked dresses. . . . We wore our hair exactly alike in bangs." (Harold Loeb, Robert Cohn in *The Sun Also Rises*, traces the source of Hemingway's insistence on his masculinity to this. It was as if he were forever saying "Damn it, I'm *male*.")

Few could have outdone Grace Hemingway in the intensity of her middle-class respectability, but for all his profession, and love of the outdoors, Clarence Hemingway was one who did. A lifelong teetotaller, he "abhorred" the playing of cards in any form, and would not permit anyone in his presence to say darn or gosh. Dancing school was morally repulsive—" 'leads to hell and damnation,' he kept muttering." When *in our time* was published he sent back six copies, returning even the single one his wife wanted to keep. "He would not tolerate such filth in his home, Dad declared." Later on when his son was becoming famous he is known to have answered sadly the question of how the boy was making out: "Ernest's written another dirty book."

What Hemingway called "Mr. Young's trauma theory of literature" is not retracted: the wounds in Italy are still climactic and central in the lives of Hemingway and all his personal protagonists. Nor is there any reason to withdraw the notion, which the author also objected to, that he wrote chiefly about himself; he was not lacking in imagination, but to live his life as he wished, then to write about it, was the way he basically operated. Neither is there any reason to abandon the idea that the adventures of Nick Adams were foreshadowed by *The Adventures of Huckleberry Finn.*

But a different emphasis can be put on this combination. Huck's rebellion was of course from Aunt Sally—and St. Petersburg, which Twain did not omit. Nick's rebellion is a given—omitted but as basic as the wound, and prior to it. Almost nothing Hemingway ever wrote could be set in Oak Park; it is extremely doubtful that he could have written a "wonderful novel" about the place. What he could write about happens "out there"—an exact equivalent for what, departing "sivilization" for the last time, Huck called "the territory." In the overall adventure, life becomes an escape to reality. No reward whatever is promised, and the cost in comfort and security is high. Out there can kill you, and nearly did. But it beats "home," which is a meaner death, as Ernest tried to tell Marcelline.

The Two African Stories / *Carlos Baker*

In the other two stories which grew out of his African adventure, Hemingway abandoned his experimental attempt to see whether an "absolutely true book" like the *Green Hills of Africa* could compete on terms of equality with a work of the imagination. In "The Short Happy Life of Francis Macomber" and "The Snows of Kilimanjaro" he was still determined to tell "the truth"; but now he was ready to invent the characters, and to imagine the circumstances in which they were to be entangled. The circumstances in these two stories differ markedly. At the same time they share certain inward thematic stresses. Both deal, for example, though in varying ways, with the achievement and loss of moral manhood. Both look further into the now familiar men-without-women theme. The focal point in each is the corrupting power of women and money, two of the forces aggressively mentioned in the *Green Hills of Africa* as impediments to American writing men.

Francis Macomber does not write. He is a wealthy American sportsman hunting the Tanganyika plains with his wife. But he must nevertheless wrestle with problems relating to women, money, and moral manhood. Easily the most unscrupulous of Hemingway's fictional females, Margot Macomber covets her husband's money but values even more her power over him. To Wilson, the Macombers' paid white hunter, who is drawn very reluctantly

Carlos Baker, "The Two African Stories," is from chapter 8 of *Hemingway: The Writer as Artist* (Princeton: Princeton University Press, 1972, 4th edition), pp. 186–96. Copyright 1952, 1956, 1963, 1972, and permission granted by Princeton University Press.

into the emotional mess of a wrecked marriage, Margot exemplifies most of the American wives he has met in the course of his professional life. Although his perspectives are limited to the international sporting set, the indictment is severe. These women, he reflects, are "the hardest in the world; the hardest, the cruelest, the most predatory, and the most attractive, and their men have softened or gone to pieces nervously as they have hardened."[1] With Margot in mind, this story might well have carried the title which Hemingway attached to one of his despatches from Tanganyika to *Esquire*: "Notes on Dangerous Game." The lion and the buffalo are vanquishable in a way that Margot is not.

Too much money and a woman also underlie the predicament of Harry, the dying author in "The Snows of Kilimanjaro." Having given up to a luxurious way of life by marrying wealth and then growing into complete dependence on it, he has died artistically long before his physical death. What harrows him more than the knowledge of approaching dissolution is the consciousness of all the literary riches, none of them committed to paper, which will go with him underground. Worst of all are the sharply etched memories of his former life—Liberty, Integrity, Opportunity—qualities which were all once joyously owned and now are all irrecoverably lost.

So both stories are moral tragedies tipped with irony. Macomber dies at the very moment he is commencing to live. Harry's death by gangrene symbolizes all spiritual suicides among American writers. "We destroy them in many ways," said Hemingway sardonically in the *Green Hills of Africa*. "First, economically. They make money . . . increase their standard of living and . . . are caught. They have to write to keep up their establishment, their wives, and so on, and they write slop . . . not on purpose, but because it is hurried. . . . Then, once they have betrayed themselves, they justify it and you get more slop."[2] Whether through women or the desire for money, self-betrayal is what kills a man before he has lived out his time. Women and money are nothing but instruments and agents: they exist, sometimes passively, sometimes aggressively, to help the individual writer in his moral self-destruction. If he surrenders, the fault is his own. The emphasis on the value of integrity in these short stories suggests that they may be thought of as two more chapters in the history of Hemingway's artistic obsessions.

The happy life of Francis Macomber begins on the plains of East Africa and lasts about thirty minutes. The tall young man has previously disgraced himself before his wife, his British white hunter, and his gun-bearers, by ignominious flight from a wounded and charging lion. Besides the loss of his own self-respect, such as it was, the extreme mental tortures of the experience include the barbed and vicious scorn of his wife, the lifted eyebrows and unspoken insults of the white hunter Wilson, and the visible disapproval

1. *The Fifth Column and the First Forty-Nine Stories*, p. 107.
2. *Green Hills of Africa*, p. 23.

of the native boys in his entourage. After a night of torment, during which he is obliged to watch his wife sleepily returning from the Englishman's tent, the party goes after buffalo. Since the wife knows her husband for a coward, she seems to have him where she wants him, which is under her thumb.

Suddenly, in the midst of the second day's shooting and with the white hunter as an aid, Macomber loses his fear. His wife at once senses and hates this change because it undermines her power. But Wilson silently welcomes Macomber into manhood, and together they enter the tall grass after one of the wounded buffalo, leaving the wife behind them in the open car.

Almost immediately the buffalo charges. Fearless and happy in its path stands Macomber, a coward no longer, reveling in his new-found self-trust, firing repeatedly until the buffalo is practically upon him. Then a bullet from his wife's Mannlicher plows through his skull from back to front and the short happy life is over.

The great technical virtue of this story—and it is one of Hemingway's favorites possibly for this reason—is the development of an emotional intensity to a degree seldom approached in modern literature. The ragged feelings generated by the lion-incident and verbalized in a kind of noonday nightmare during the conversations in the dining-tent, are just short of unendurable to any who have entered into the spirit of the situation. Yet the tension actually mounts when, during the next day's shooting, we watch the Macombers in their contest for the possession of a soul.

Hemingway silently points up this contest by the varying positions of the central trio in their boxlike open car. On the way to the lion, Macomber sits in front, with Margot and Wilson in the back. After that day's débâcle, Macomber slumps in the back seat beside his frozen wife, Wilson staring straight ahead in the front. When Macomber has proved himself with the three buffalo, it is Margot who retreats into the far corner of the back seat, while the two men happily converse vis-à-vis before her. And finally, as Macomber kneels in the path of the buffalo, it is his wife from her commanding position in the back seat of the car who closes the contest.

Of equal interest is the skill with which Hemingway balances off the two days of hunting against each other. Part of the balance is achieved by the repetition of first effect: the buffalo, like the lion of the preceding day, is wounded, takes cover, and charges without warning. This time, however, the charge moves into a reversed moral situation. Between times, by various devices, the reader has been fully awakened to the degree of physical courage needed in facing wounded and dangerous animals. But where the lion was an instrument for the establishment and build-up of emotional tension, the oncoming horns of the buffalo are the pronged forceps for Macomber's moral birth. Two different worlds fill the two adjacent days.

The yardstick figure, Wilson, a fine characterization, is the man free of woman and of fear. He is the standard of manhood towards which Macomber rises, the cynical referee in the nasty war of man and wife, and the judge who presides, after the murder, over the further fortunes of Margot Macomber. His dominance over the lady is apparent from the moment she sees him blast the lion from which Macomber ran. But he accepts that dominance only because it is thrust upon him. The kind of dominance he really believes in, and would gladly transfer to the suffering husband, is well summarized in a passage from Shakespeare's *Henry IV* which he quotes as a kind of tribute to Macomber's own loss of fear on the second day: "By my troth, I care not; a man can die but once; we owe God a death . . . and let it go which way it will, he that dies this year is quit for the next. . . ." [3] Having brought out, almost by accident, this attitude he has lived by, Wilson is much embarrassed. "But he had seen men come of age before and it always moved him. It was not a matter of their twenty-first birthday."

Those who object that true manhood is not necessarily proved by one's ability to face a charging beast may be doing Hemingway an injustice. Dramatically speaking, physical courage is often a convenient and economical way of symbolizing moral courage. We are glad, for example, at Hamlet's skill and bravery with the foils. In this African story Hemingway is obviously dealing with both kinds of courage, though, as the situation naturally requires, it is the physical aspect which is stressed.

It would be possible to argue that Francis and Margot Macomber are more nearly caricatures than people. The probability is that the line-drawing in their portraits is the natural consequence of an approach to material chosen for its intrinsic emotional intensity rather than to provide opportunity for depth of characterization. One rightly concludes that they are as fully developed as they need to be for the purposes of the narrative. Further development might well impede the quick march of the short, happy life.

Still it is true that Hemingway's satirical steam, never far below the surface, tends to erupt whenever he deals with leisure-class wastrels. The tendency is visible, for example, in the accounts of Cohn and Campbell in *The Sun Also Rises*. In *Death in the Afternoon*, the author scornfully watches the bored, sport-shod, ex-collegians who leave the *corrida* early. The same reaction appears in his sketches of the wealthy yachtsmen in Key West harbor in *To Have and Have Not*, part of which was written at the same time as the Francis Macomber story. It is almost as if, throughout the Depression, Hemingway had resolutely set himself to oppose F. Scott Fitzgerald's temperamental conviction that the rich are glamorous. As Hemingway's scorn rises, the satirical steam-pressure rises with it, and the result is often close to caricature.

If the story of the Macombers is judged, as it probably should be judged, in terms of an experiment in the development of emotional intensity, it is hard to match. As an instance of tragic irony, exemplified in overt action, it

3. *The Fifth Column and the First Forty-Nine Stories*, p. 131. The Speech is made by one of the country soldiers, Feeble, in *II Henry IV*, III, ii, 253–58.

has its faults. But dullness is not one of them, and formally speaking the story is very nearly perfect.[4]

"The Snows of Kilimanjaro" is a tragedy of a different order.[5] Its setting is the final afternoon and evening in the second life of a writer named Harry, dying of gangrene in a camp near the edge of the Tanganyika plains country. "Francis Macomber" proceeds through and by action; "The Snows of Kilimanjaro" is an experiment in the psychology of a dying man. Like *Across the River and Into the Trees*, it contains almost no overt physical activity, though much is implied. Judged in terms of its intention, it is a triumphant piece of writing.

Hemingway's own experiences on safari help to account for the origin of the story. The undeveloped germ of "Francis Macomber" may have been the occasion when Hemingway and M'Cola entered a bush-covered area in pursuit of a lion they heard but never saw. The general outline of "The Snows" was almost certainly suggested by Hemingway's own grave illness, the flight out of the plains country, and the distant view of the enormous, snow-capped mountain of Kilimanjaro. During the flight east, and no doubt also during the period of treatment in Nairobi—his head aching and his ears ringing from the effects of emetine[6]—Hemingway had ample time to reflect on a topic which would naturally occur to him in such a situation: the death of a writer before his work is done. As in "Francis Macomber," however, most of the other circumstances of the story were invented or overheard.

Like Hemingway, the writer Harry in the story has been "obsessed" for years with curiosity about the idea of death. Now that it is close he has lost all curiosity about it, feeling only a "great tiredness and anger" over its inexorable approach. "The hardest thing," Hemingway had written in the *Green Hills of Africa*, is for the writer "to survive and get his work done."[7] This is mainly because the time available is so short and the temptations not to work are so strong. Harry has succumbed to the temptation *not* to work at his hard trade. Now his time is over, and possessive death moves in.

The story gains further point and poignancy from another obsession of Harry's, the deep sense of his loss of artistic integrity. Despite the difference between London and Tanganyika and the lapse of time between the rule of Edward VII and that of Edward VIII, Hemingway's position is that of Henry

---

4. This story was Hemingway's choice for *This Is My Best*, ed. Whit Burnett, New York, 1942. He so wrote Mr. Burnett 5/12/42.

5. Hemingway once told Roger Linscott that he regarded "The Snows" as "about as good as any" of his work in short fiction. "On the Books," *New York Herald Tribune Book Review*, December 29, 1946. The story was finished April 7, 1936. EH to Maxwell Perkins, 4/9/36.

6. The principal alkaloid of ipecac, used as a specific in the treatment of amoebic dysentery.

7. *Green Hills of Africa*, p. 27.

James in "The Lesson of the Master." Harry's dying self-accusations are well summarized in the words of Henry St. George, the sold-out novelist in James's novelette. "Don't become in your old age what I have in mine," he tells his young admirer, "—the depressing, the deplorable illustration of the worship of false gods . . . the idols of the market; money and luxury . . . everything that drives one to the short and easy way."[8] The dying writer in Hemingway's story has followed that route, and his creeping gangrene is the mark he bears. He knows that he has traded his former integrity for "security and comfort," destroying his talent by "betrayals of himself and what he believed in." Henry or Harry, England or Africa, the lesson of the master is the same: Thou shalt not worship the graven images of false gods, or acquiesce in the "life of pleasant surrender."[9]

Although the setting of "The Snows of Kilimanjaro" is as completely un-Jamesian as one could possibly imagine, the themes which the story engages are, on the contrary, very close to those regularly employed by James. "I wonder," Hemingway once ruminated, "what Henry James would have done with the materials of our time." One answer might be that a modern James would simply have altered the costume, the idiom, and certain of the social customs which appear in his novels. The themes, which were matters of greatest interest to him, would scarcely need to be changed at all. The close reader of "The Snows of Kilimanjaro" easily recognizes and responds to its theme of confrontation. The dying writer is far different from the ghost of his former self, the young, free, unsold writer who took all Europe as his oyster and was seriously devoted to his craft. As he listens to the self-accusations with which Harry tortures himself, the reader acquainted with James may be reminded of "The Jolly Corner." In this long story, an American expatriate, returning to his old and empty house at the corner of the American city street, finds himself beleaguered by the ghost of his other self, the ravaged man he might have been had he not followed his esthetic ambitions to Europe. Although the situation is obviously quite the opposite of the one detailed by Hemingway, the strategy is exactly the same: the face-to-face confrontation of an ego by an alter ego. The corner of the tent in which Harry finally dies might well be called, in an echo of Jamesian irony, the jolly corner.

The story is technically distinguished by the operation of several natural symbols. These are nonliterary images, as always in Hemingway, and they have been very carefully selected so as to be in complete psychological conformity with the locale and the dramatic situation. How would the ideas of death and of immortality present themselves in the disordered imagination of a writer dying of gangrene as he waits for the plane which is supposed to carry him out of the wilderness to the Nairobi hospital? The death-symbols were relatively easy. Every night beasts of prey killed grazing animals and

8. James, *Works*, New York edition, Vol. 15, p. 36.
9. *The Fifth Column and the First Forty-Nine Stories*, pp. 158, 160, 162.

left the pickings to those scavengers of carrion, the vultures and the hyenas.

It is entirely natural that Harry, whose flesh is rotting and noisome—is, in fact, carrion already—should associate these creatures with the idea of dying. As he lies near death in the mimosa shade at the opening of the story, he watches the birds obscenely squatting in the glare of the plain. As night falls and the voice of the hyena is heard in the land, the death-image transfers itself from the vultures to this other foul devourer of the dead. With the arrival of his first strong premonition of death, which has no other form than "a sudden, evil-smelling emptiness," Harry finds without astonishment that the image of the hyena is slipping lightly along the edge of the emptiness. "Never believe any of that," he tells his wife, "about a scythe and a skull." His mind has been far away in the days of his former life in Paris, and now it has come back to Africa. "It can be two bicycle policemen as easily, or be a bird. Or it can have a wide snout like a hyena." Death has just come as if to rest its head on the foot of the cot, the direction from which the infection will rise up towards the vital center. Presently it moves in on him, crouching on his chest so that he cannot breathe.

Harry's dying directive, "Never believe any of that about a scythe and a skull," is an important commentary on Hemingway's own habitual approach to the development of natural symbols. He is prepared to use, where they conform to the requirements of an imaginary situation, any of the more ancient symbols—whether the threes and nines of numerology, or the weight of the Cross in Christian legend. But the scythe and the skull, though ancient enough, simply do not fit the pattern of Harry's death and are therefore rejected in favor of the foul and obscene creatures which have now come to dominate Harry's imagination.

Like the death-symbol, the image for immortality arises "naturally" out of the geography and psychology of the situation. When the weight leaves his chest, Harry finds that morning has brought the rescue plane to carry him to Nairobi. Helping him aboard, Old Compton says that they will have to refuel at Arusha. Everything happens as if it were actually happening—the take-off, the long view of the plain and its moving animals, the hills and forests to the east passing in slow majesty under the belly of the plane—until it dawns on Harry that for some reason they have by-passed Arusha. At first he does not know why. But as the plane emerges from a rain-squall, he suddenly sees ahead of them the square top of Kilimanjaro, "wide as all the world," incredibly white in the sun. "Then he knew that there was where he was going."

While he was in Africa Hemingway learned that the Masai name for the western summit of Kilimanjaro is Ngàje Ngài, which means "House of God." The association between mountainous terrain and the idea of home was, however, already an old one in his mind. He had used it symbolically in the Burguete section of *The Sun Also Rises* and also, far more extensively, in the

Abruzzi and the Montreux locale-images of *A Farewell to Arms*. "I will lift up mine eyes to the hills," runs the Psalm, "from whence cometh my help." But there is no psalm-quoting in the back-to-earth dénouement of Hemingway's story. There is only Harry's wife Helen, waking in the middle of the night down in the flat plains-country, far from Kilimanjaro, and calling to a husband who does not answer.[10]

Anyone interested in the methods by which the patterns of experience are translated to the purposes of art should find abundant materials for study in the three stories—nonfiction and fiction—which grew out of Hemingway's African expedition. The foreword to the *Green Hills of Africa* contains an implicit question. Given a country as interesting as Africa, and given the shape of a month's hunting-action there, and given the author's determination to tell only the truth, the question then becomes this: Can such a book possibly compete on equal terms with a work of the imagination? The answer is that it certainly can *compete*, provided always that the narrative is managed by a very skilled writer who takes both truth (the truth of "the way it was") and beauty (the extremely careful formal construction) as his watchwords. Yet the experiment proved also that the narrator who takes no liberties with the actual events of his experience, who tells things exactly as they were, who invents nothing and suppresses nothing important, will place himself at a real disadvantage in the competition. He gives the opposition too large a handicap. Good as the *Green Hills of Africa* is in two respects (verisimilitude and architectonics), it lacks the intensities which Hemingway was able to

---

10. Psalm 121 might do as a motto for Hemingway's collected works. In this connection one might suggest the relevance of the leopard whose enigmatic history is given in the epigraph of "The Snows." "Close to the Western summit of Kilimanjaro there is the dried and frozen carcass of a leopard. No one has explained what the leopard was seeking at that altitude." Professor C. C. Walcutt (*Explicator* 7, April 1949, item 43) sees that the conflict in Harry's life is between a "fundamental moral idealism" and an "aimless materialism." When Harry looks at Kilimanjaro, he sees it as a symbol of Truth, the "undefined ideal for which he has struggled." The leopard is then a symbol for Harry's moral nature. It is not logical that Harry "should continue to believe in man and search for meanings and values"; neither is it logical that "a purely predatory leopard" should have reached that snowy height. What drove the leopard there "is the same sort of mystery as the force that keeps idealism alive in Harry. All reason, in a predatory world, is against it, but there it is." Following this line, Professor E. W. Tedlock, Jr. finds that both leopard and mountain symbolize the preservation of integrity for Harry. "In contrast to the leopard's dried and frozen carcass," writes Tedlock, "Harry lies dying of a gangrenous leg amid heat and glare." The physical infection is the result of carelessness—"the typical analogue of a spiritual infection also resulting from carelessness." Thus we have both physical and spiritual decay, while leopard and mountain represent those things which do not decay. Professor Tedlock calls attention to how often Harry's thoughts "revert . . . to experiences in high altitudes and snow." Physically, this can be explained as the "feverish man's desire for coolness and relief"; spiritually the reversions represent a longing for "the good life" of the past (see *Explicator* 8, October 1949, item 7). For full information on the actual leopard and its discoverer, see John M. Howell, editor, *Hemingway's African Stories*, New York, 1969.

pack into "The Short Happy Life of Francis Macomber," and it cannot possibly achieve anything like the genuine pathos of "The Snows of Kilimanjaro." The experience of wrestling with the African book, followed as it was with the writing of the two short stories, undoubtedly established one esthetic principle very firmly in Hemingway's mind. The highest art must take liberties, not with the truth but with the modes by which the truth is projected. This was no new discovery for Hemingway. But for any serious writer it is a useful maxim.

No Money for the Kingbird: Hemingway's Prizefight Stories / *Charles A. Fenton*

> "You don't have to box that godamned Ward Price every morning after working all night and have him knock your ruddy block off."
> "Go to hell," said your correspondent.
> "Why do you do it?"
> "God knows. I suppose because he would think I was yellow if I stopped."
>
> Hemingway, in *Esquire*, 1935

One of the first stories Ernest Hemingway ever published, in his high school literary magazine, was about boxing.[1] It was a very slick story—slick, that is, in the sense that its plot was an O. Henry twist and its punch line an old vaudeville gag—and it included a great deal of genteel and literary language, but its principal interest today is in its juxtaposition, at one point, of the words "amateur" and "professional." Professionalism has always been very important to Hemingway. He is a man with a high sense of craft.

During Hemingway's adolescence, for example, it was completely natural that a boy who was both big for his age and interested in things that required skill should turn to boxing rather than, say, to collecting merit badges or mastering baseball. Every town in America had its gym and its stable of aspiring pugs. The Chicago sports pages gave a great deal of space to Gun-

Charles A. Fenton, "No Money for the Kingbird: Hemingway's Prizefight Stories," *American Quarterly*, IV (Winter 1952), 339–50. Copyright, 1952, Trustees of the University of Pennsylvania. Reprinted by permission of *American Quarterly*.

1. Ernest Hemingway, "A Matter of Colour," *The Tabula*, XXII (April 1916), 16–17.

boat Smith and Jack Johnson and Philadelphia Jack O'Brien. It was the era of the great Search for A White Hope. Little boys asked for and received fourteen-ounce gloves on Christmas. What would *you* do if a masher attacked *your* sister? The White House itself had recently been occupied by a zealous pugilist. An ex-middleweight champion had written a book about this chapter in fisticuffs—*The Roosevelt I Knew: Ten Years of Boxing with the President and other Memories of Famous Fighting Men.* By the time Hemingway had published "A Matter of Colour" in the Oak Park *Tabula*, boxing was also patriotic and in the national interest; a Canadian sergeant major fathered a small volume on *Boxing for Beginners* whose subtitle was "With Chapter Showing Relationship to Bayonet Fighting." Amateur boxing made considerable progress in these years, but on the whole the sport was largely professionalized. Hemingway's own initial contact with the fraternity, as Malcolm Cowley has pointed out, contained elements of both.

He persuaded his father to pay for a course of boxing lessons advertised by a Chicago gymnasium. The first lesson was an invitation to spar with Young A'Hearn, "a crack middleweight" training for his next bout. "I'll take it easy," A'Hearn promised him, but soon they were trading punches and then Hemingway was lying on the floor with a broken nose. The rest is pure Hemingwayesque of the Nick Adams vintage.

"I knew he was going to give me the works the minute I saw his eyes," he told a friend later.

"Were you scared?"

"Sure, he could hit like hell."

"Why did you go in there with him?"

"I wasn't that scared."

Hemingway was one of the few students who appeared for the second lesson. He finished the course and continued to practice boxing. Two years later his left eye was injured in a sparring match and the doctors thought for a time that the other eye might be affected.

Despite the new skill that he was acquiring, and despite the fact that he competed for—and seems to have made—virtually every extracurricular activity in the school, he wasn't very happy, and twice he ran away from home. Perhaps it was on one of these flights, as Cowley has suggested, that he met the punch-drunk welterweight of whom he wrote in "The Battler," the "former champion fighter" who now moved nomad-like around the country, psychopathic, wary, "living like a gentleman" with his Negro keeper. The fighter was excited by the boy's account of the brakeman who had knocked him off a moving freight with a trick punch. "It must have made him feel good to bust you," says Ad Francis, "seriously." His own face is terribly marked.

. . . In the firelight Nick saw that his face was misshapen. His nose was sunken, his eyes were slits, he had queer-shaped lips. Nick did not perceive all this at once, he only saw the man's face was queerly formed and mutilated. It was like putty in color. Dead looking in the firelight. . . . He had only one ear. It was thickened and tight against the side of his head. Where the other ear should have been there was a stump.

Appropriately, the first thing he had noticed about the boy was his eye and the bump over it. "Where did you get the shiner," he says, interested, gleeful, too eager even to answer Nick's "Hello!" Blows are all he'd ever understood—or, worse, enjoyed—about boxing. "I could take it," he brags to the boy. "They all bust their hands on me. They couldn't hurt me." This is his pride, his achievement, his badge. Like Young A'Hearn, who enjoyed belting hell out of green amateurs, he was a fighter but not a professional. His own aberration was only slightly more grotesque than Young A'Hearn's; where the latter liked the punching, he liked the taking. He is a prelude to the obscene veterans of *To Have and Have Not*. Young A'Hearn and Ad Francis were gross, ugly, unprofessional. This was the way you ended if you didn't respect and understand the craft. It was important to know them, but they were only the first rungs on the hierarchial ladder that led to Jack Brennan.

But before one reached Brennan there were other fighters to be studied and assessed. None of them was quite like Young A'Hearn or Ad Francis, nor, of course, were they like Jack Brennan, but they all derived in part from them. There was Ole Andreson, for example, in "The Killers." He had been a heavyweight, a big man who was too long for the beds in Mrs. Hirsch's rooming house in Summit. He had never been a champion. He had, however, been important enough to have been of service to the kind of gamblers who can afford such trigger men as Max and Al. Andreson probably had been in the main bouts. Traces of the professional ritual, of which we will see so much in Jack Brennan and "Fifty Grand," are apparent by implication in Ole Andreson. Whether or not he was once a willing tool of the mobsters we don't know; clearly, however, he ultimately balked at some final outrage against the code.

"I got in wrong," he tells Nick.

Perhaps he didn't take the dive he was paid for. Perhaps, like Bill Gorton's Vienna Negro in *The Sun Also Rises*, he was up against an opponent so inept that the bargain couldn't be consummated. "My God, Mister Gorton, I didn't do nothing for forty minutes but try and let him stay. That white boy musta ruptured himself swinging at me. I never did hit him." Whatever it was that Ole Andreson had done, all he was doing now was waiting to be shot by two hoods who had never seen him. The ritual of professionalism was over for him, as it must be over some time even for the Jack Brennans. But for Ole

Andreson it would be a vile, inappropriate climax, as illegitimate as the doublecross by which Morgan and Steinfelt had hoped to retain his crown for the unwilling Jack Brennan in "Fifty Grand."

It is in "Fifty Grand," indeed, that the entire mechanism of boxing's ritual, hinted at in these other stories, is finally exposed completely to our scrutiny. The locale itself, of course, is set entirely within the professional milieu. The action is characteristically Hemingway in its dramatic, tightly knit economy; like all of the best of his short stories, "Fifty Grand" has a compactness which is almost of the theater. Hemingway is always popular with playwriting students who are asked to transpose a short story into a one-act play.

Thus there are four scenes, two quick vignettes wedged between two longer sketches full of characterization and atmosphere. The first scene, brief, fragmentary, is in a saloon near a metropolitan gym. Years later, when he did write a full-length play, Hemingway launched *The Fifth Column* with precisely the same swift strokes. The third scene, equally brief, is in Brennan's Manhattan hotel, on the afternoon of the fight. It serves, of course, to heighten the tension that precedes the championship bout, and yet even it, as we watch Brennan, his second, and his manager play cribbage, is entirely of the boxing world. The other two scenes are also wholly of that professional climate, the first at the Jersey training camp, the second in the ring itself at the Garden. In both these scenes we can watch the hierarchy of professionalism.

A minor character of considerable importance, for example, speaks one of the story's first lines. "He can't hit you, Jack," Soldier Bartlett comfortably assures Brennan, and if we do not then comprehend his inanity, certainly it becomes clear very soon. "I wish to hell he couldn't," Brennan answers, decisively, and Jerry, the narrator—who, like Brennan, knows perfectly well that Walcott can hit the aging champion—makes a much more acute and revealing comment. "*He* looks easy to hit." Walcott, like Ad Francis and Ole Andreson, is a fighter but not a professional. "He ain't going to last like you and me, Jerry." His face is almost as marked as Ad Francis'. But these subtleties of the craft are beyond Soldier Bartlett, the kidder, the clown, the easy optimist and perennial sparring partner. There's no place for him in this kind of training camp, readying a champion who's over the hill, too old to sweat, too tired to sleep, with nothing but his courage and his skill and his pride to sustain him.

"Well," Brennan tells Bartlett, "you better go back to town, Soldier." One of the minor rewards of being as good as Brennan, as Jerry had already observed in Hanley's saloon, was that you could say what you wanted to say when you wanted to say it. Thus when Bartlett, insensitive and belligerent, wants to know why he's being fired, Brennan tells him, coldly, honestly, "You talk too much." Bartlett, of course, not a pro, sees the issue on the most personal, unprofessional level. He puts it on a sort of Toots Shor level of sportsmanship. A champion should be a good guy, a pal, a free spender.

Jerry tries to soothe him. "He's nervous and crabby. He's a good fellow, Soldier."

"The hell he is. The hell he's ever been a good fellow."

We begin to realize that Soldier is probably right, that Jack probably never was—nor could be—a good fellow in any conventional sense. Unlike Soldier, however, we also realize that being a good fellow does not equate with being a champion. This has always been a difficult truth for the American public, an audience of good fellows themselves who want to be assured that their heroes are just like them, only more so. Ring Lardner, to whom Hemingway owed so much technically in these early years—he later inscribed one of his novels "To Ring Lardner from his early imitator and always admirer"[2]— had probed a little of this himself in the closing paragraphs of "Champion." Brennan sums it up when he finally gets in the ring with the challenger. "So you're going to be one of these popular champions," he says to Walcott. "Take your goddamn hand off my shoulder." It's a little bit like Durocher— a pro—and his celebrated "nice guys finish last." Professionalism is not an automatic by-product of either membership in the guild or of championship in the craft. When "Fifty Grand" ends, the reluctant challenger is champ, but he is not a professional in the sense that Brennan is. He could never say, as Brennan had said before the fight, "I'll give them a good show."

Brennan, unlike Francis and A'Hearn and Andreson and Walcott, has given up a great deal along the way to achieve the skill. He misses his wife. "You ain't got any idea how I miss the wife. You can't have any idea what it's like. It don't make any difference where I am. You can't have any idea what it's like." His daughters are ashamed of him. If Soldier Bartlett doesn't grasp the professionalism, how can a couple of adolescent kids. " 'Who's your old man,' some of these society kids say to them. 'My old man's Jack Brennan.' That don't do them any good." To compensate for that he has to be unnaturally frugal. "Hell," Jerry assures him, "all that makes a difference is if they got the dough," and Brennan, knowing that, had long before stopped playing the horses, and he undertips the rubber, and he writes his wife instead of calling her long distance. Of course, if you're a champion you don't take anything for nothing. "That was good liquor," Hogan says, conversationally. "Put it on the bill," Brennan tells him abruptly. Not that he can drink very often, of course. Only when he can't sleep. "It's better for him than not sleeping," Hogan and Jerry realize. But usually the pleasures of liquor and all the fraternity that normally go with it are excluded. "I like liquor pretty well. If I hadn't been boxing I would have drunk quite a lot." This too you give up to attain the professionalism which will justify itself in those few seconds when Brennan, holding onto his insides, out-thinks every man in the Garden. Brennan himself is aware of it, though only the expensive,

2. Ernest Hemingway, "Defense of Dirty Words," *Esquire*, IV (September 1934), 158D.

bootleg liquor can make him discuss it. "You know," he says, "I missed a lot, boxing. You know, I miss a lot, Jerry."

Only Jerry, of all the guild members, is eligible for these confidences. Not a champion, a shadowy, mysterious figure in some ways—he's been away "a long time," so long he's never seen Walcott fight, nor does he know Morgan and Steinfelt—he nonetheless is linked with Brennan, as we have already seen, by the champion himself. He had been the same kind of fighter, and now he is a very good second indeed. "Walcott ain't going to last long. He ain't going to last like you and me, Jerry." Like all the Hemingway narrators, he is rather unconvincingly endowed by the author with virtual omniscience. He understands everything, he is delicately responsive to whatever occurs in their world. He even has a premature, Cassandra-like glimpse of what ulti- mately takes place.

"Something might happen," he warns the champion who plans to bet on the opponent he knows he cannot beat. Brennan scoffs. "You can't ever tell," Jerry says stubbornly, and, of course, he's absolutely right. Even a champion can't control those factors which are beyond the ritual, factors like a com- placent and bogus challenger, factors like Morgan and Steinfelt, the sharp- shooters, the operators, the wise boys. Only the newspaper men think you can always tell, and they too have their place in this hierarchy, a low place, lower than Soldier Bartlett and Ad Francis, lower certainly than Hogan, not quite as low as Morgan and Steinfelt.

"What the hell do they know about whether a man's right or not?" says Jerry contemptuously. They are completely outside the ritual, nonpartici- pants, risking nothing, giving up nothing, the vocational equivalents of the literary critics with whom Hemingway was beginning to feud at this time. "For every writer produced in America," Hemingway had sneered in 1924, "there are produced eleven critics." Jack Brennan, obviously, equates with writer; sportswriter equates with critic. "Critics are the eunuchs of literature," Hemingway declared,[3] and now in "Fifty Grand" Jerry speaks in the same terms. "I don't care who they are. What the hell do they know?" Only Morgan and Steinfelt are more odious.

These two are truly aliens, bringing to the training camp their own brand of corruption and insensitivity. Locked doors, whispers, Broadway wit, casual and meaningless intoxication, and, finally, the doublecross. The isolation of the professional is complete as Brennan sits in their midst, and the hierarchy of Hemingway values is never more explicit.

Jack doesn't say anything. He just sits on the bed. He ain't with the others. He's all by himself. He was wearing an old blue jersey and pants

3. Ernest Hemingway, "And to the United States," *transatlantic review*, I (May 1924), 355–57.

and had on boxing shoes. He needed a shave. Steinfelt and Morgan were dressers. John was quite a dresser too. Jack sat there looking Irish and tough.

John—John Collins, his manager—has his place too in the hierarchy. The chain which leads from the trigger men and gamblers to Soldier Bartlett, which even has a place in it for Hogan's health-farm patients, which leads on from Walcott to Ad Francis and Andreson, through Hogan and Jerry and finally to Brennan, would include Collins somewhere between Francis and Andreson. For a time he appears to fall even below the writers—after all, it's he who brings the gamblers out to the camp—and his zealousness for Brennan's welfare, apparently an exclusively material zeal, is visibly fading now in proportion to his fighter's declining future.

> "Why the hell don't you come out here when the reporters was out! You want Jerry and me to talk to them?"
> "I had Lew fighting in Philadelphia," John said.
> "What the hell's that to me? Why the hell aren't you out here when I ought to have you?"
> "Hogan was here."
> "Hogan," Jack says. "Hogan's as dumb as I am."

As the story closes, however, it is Collins, awed, who assesses what they have seen, restoring to himself a certain dignity that comes, in any craft, from merely being able to recognize professionalism when one encounters it. "You're some boy, Jack," John says. Like the referee—"go in there, you slob," the latter had told Walcott after the deliberate foul—and like perhaps half a dozen others in the jammed Garden, Collins understood what had taken place in those last minutes.

> He was holding himself and all his body together and it all showed on his face. All the time he was thinking and holding his body in where it was busted. Then he started to sock. His face looked awful all the time. He started to sock with his hands low down by his side, swinging at Walcott. Walcott covered up and Jack was swinging wild at Walcott's head. Then he swung the left and it hit Walcott in the groin and the right hit Walcott right bang where he'd hit Jack.

It was the most exciting and yet, at the same time, the most perceptive and functional climax of any of Hemingway's short stories. He has frequently been criticized for the shallowness of his symbolism—"The Snows of Kilimanjaro" is a case in point—but here the symbolism of the fouled boxer is complete and worthy. It is the kind of thing that negates the commentary which has persistently patronized Hemingway as a writer dealing exclusively with uncomplex, trivial personalities.

The most widely publicized review of this type—and it was merely a more elaborate version of scores of others which have been written at one time or another—was Lee Wilson Dodd's in the *Saturday Review of Literature*. He called it "Simple Annals of the Callous"—it was, in fact, a review of *Men Without Women*, which included "Fifty Grand"—and Dodd attacked "the narrowness of his selective range," which confined him to "people who are very much alike, bullfighters, bruisers, touts, gunmen, professional soldiers, hard drinkers, dope fiends."[4] We, on the contrary, have seen the diversity which exists within one of Dodd's smug categories—bruisers—and we recognize the range and dissimilarity of the people in "Fifty Grand." Notice that when Jack Brennan was "holding himself and his body together" he was not merely a muscular lout reacting to agony. "He was thinking. . . ." When he had solved his problem, professionally, he began to act—professionally. "He started to sock." It was not by chance that he "was swinging wild at Walcott's head." It was the professional solution to a difficult and unexpected problem. When Walcott covered up, his body would be exposed. Then Brennan "swung the left and it hit Walcott in the groin." Collins was right. "You're some boy, Jack."

Nowhere in this story, it is worth noting, does Hemingway use the word "courage," a word which has always been loosely and, frequently, derisively, linked with his work. It is apparent, however, that courage is a part of Brennan's behaviour, and yet, notice, though he is in one sense no braver than Ad Francis—"they couldn't hurt me, they bust their hands on me"—Francis would never have been capable of this. Mere guts is not enough. "Thinking" was the operative word in the paragraph we have quoted and examined. This, again, is what distinguishes the professional.

> There wasn't anybody ever boxed better than Jack. . . . Jack is always calm in close and he doesn't waste any juice. He knows everything about working in close too and he's getting away with a lot of stuff.

Remember too that all this skill and grace has its price. Part of that price we have already seen. The loneliness, the separation. There is more even than that. The skill and the grace may look automatic, effortless, but they're not. "We worked over Jack plenty, in between rounds. . . . I worked on his legs. The muscles would flutter under my hands all the time I was rubbing them. He was sick as hell." And then, finally, in the eleventh round, just before the doublecross, Brennan states—and Jerry interpolates—his creed.

> "I think I can last," Jack says. "I don't want this bohunk to stop me."
> It was going just the way he thought it would. He knew he couldn't

4. Lee Wilson Dodd, "Simple Annals of the Callous," *Saturday Review of Literature*, IV (November 19, 1927), 322–23.

beat Walcott. He wasn't strong any more. He was all right though. His money was all right and now he wanted to finish it off right to please himself. He didn't want to be knocked out.

This kind of thing exposes with finality the "dumb ox" legend—launched by Wyndham Lewis[5]—which has grown up around Hemingway's characters. Hemingway returned to this thesis many times, and if "Fifty Grand" has not clarified the relationship of courage to professionalism, as well as the hierarchy within which the relationship exists, Hemingway ten years later provided, in his account of the Baer-Louis fight, an even more explicit declaration as he recorded the obscenity of Max Baer, the nonprofessional fighter.

II

It was for *Esquire* that Hemingway reported that fight between the clownish ex-champion and the young Detroit Negro.[6] It was without question the best of the thirty-five articles which he printed at one time or another in his friend Arnold Gingrich's magazine. He called it "Million Dollar Fright," and though there is no public record that Max Baer ever read it, it was certainly not the kind of press the Hollywood Harlequin was accustomed to.

The fight ended, of course, in the fourth round, when Baer took a count of four, rose partially, to a kind of crouch, and stayed in that position for the full count. The working press was on the whole charitable, as usual, maintaining that Baer had at least "struggled to one knee." The New York *Times* reported that the bout was "the ultimate in competition," a fight that "lived up to the best traditions of the ring from every viewpoint."[7] It's possible that the reporter—James Dawson—was being ironic, but it is even more probable that like, once again, the sports editor in Lardner's "Champion," he was merely assessing the audience. "It wouldn't get us anything but abuse to print it. The people don't want to see him knocked." Certainly pictures of the fight do not indicate that Baer made any great effort to regain his feet. John Kieran, writing under the reportorial freedom of a columnist's by-line, was more in agreement with Hemingway, and his record of the action has echoes of much of what we have seen in "Fifty Grand."

> . . . Baer had no defense. He never had any from his earliest days in the ring. He scorned to learn anything about it. . . .[8]

5. Wyndham Lewis, "The Dumb Ox: A Study of Ernest Hemingway," *American Review*, III (June 1934), 289–312.
6. Ernest Hemingway, "Million Dollar Fright," *Esquire*, IV (December 1935), 35, 190B.
7. New York *Times*, LXXV (September 25, 1935), 1.
8. John Kieran, "Sports of the Times," New York *Times*, LXXV (September 26, 1935), 27.

One sees in that the inevitable parallel to Ad Francis and Walcott. Even the remark which Baer is supposed to have made to Dempsey—and which was not included in Hemingway's article—is reminiscent of Ad Francis. "I took it," he said to his sponsor.[9] But Kieran's account of the fight, and Hemingway's earlier analysis of Ad Francis, is mild in comparison to what the latter writes now of Max Baer.

> . . . The Louis-Baer fight was the most disgusting public spectacle, outside of a hanging, that your correspondent has ever witnessed. What made it disgusting was fear.

Hemingway then drew upon the hunting experience with which he was at the moment saturated—this was in late 1935, shortly after the publication of *Green Hills of Africa*—to clarify his point.

> There is no money in it for the kingbird when he chases off the eagle. The kingbird is a slate-colored, white-breasted fly-catcher, small, trim, neatly built, quarrelsome and a bully; but he likes to bully birds about eight to ten times his size. His only offensive weapon is a small not over-sharp beak to peck with and a heart to back it up. Equipped with this and a quick darting flight, he will attack, chase away, and administer punishment to crows, hawks and eagles which could all destroy him in an instant if he were afraid of them. The kingbird works in close. Your correspondent suggests that if Maxie Baer ever attempts to fight publicly, for money, again, he should first be given a forcible feeding of kingbird eggs.

He related the whole matter of fear and courage to this professional world we have been discussing.

> All human beings have fear just as all human beings perform certain natural functions. But children are trained not to perform these functions in public and fighters are trained not to be frightened while fighting. If they know their trade they have something else to think about. If they do not know their trade and are frightened while fighting, they have no business being fighters anymore than a game-cock that runs has any business being a game-cock.

Thus Hemingway makes what is for him the ultimate accusation, an accusation which accounts in part for his impatience and seeming intolerance in other areas of life, his impatience with some of his colleagues—Scott Fitzgerald, for example, and Thomas Wolfe—with the critics, and with, on occasion, himself. "Max Baer had never bothered to learn his trade."

9. New York *Times*, LXXV (September 25, 1935), 27.

Seen within this framework of professionalism, Hemingway's work and the statement it makes become much more forceful and persuasive. The public ridiculousness which has often been thrust upon him vanishes. He once went four rounds with Tom Heeney, the New Zealand heavyweight—a pretty good heavyweight—and one can be sure that he didn't do it merely for the publicity. As an act it was itself as much a part of the code we have been analyzing as anything he has written about that code. One simply doesn't write from guesswork. You must find out all you can about something and then record it as honestly and as minutely as possible.

"Watch what happens today," he once told a young writer who was cross-examining him as they rode out to fish. "If we get into a fish see exactly what it is that everyone does. If you get a kick out of it while he is jumping remember back until you see exactly what the action was that gave you the emotion. Then write it down making it clear so the reader will see it too and have the same feeling that you had." [10]

That was the impulse which caused him to enter a Spanish bullring and retire shortly with a broken rib. He is very vulnerable when he does these things. It thus became entertaining for literary New York to learn—erroneously—from Isabel Patterson's *Herald Tribune* column of "a singular encounter between Ernest Hemingway and Morley Callaghan," in which the latter was supposed to have knocked out cold the man who was both his boxing and his writing tutor. [11] It was also very amusing when one of his friends told Gertrude Stein that Ernest was very fragile. "Whenever he does anything sporting something breaks, his arm, his leg, or his head." [12] It has even made him the legitimate prey of nightclub drunks. "So you're Hemingway? Tough guy, huh?" one of them once said, and pushed him in the face. [13] Unless we understand the morality and creed that boxing, for example, represents to him, there is little chance that we will understand the rest of his writing. He is considerably more than an interpreter of pugilism, but each area of experience that he has examined was approached in terms of the same code we have seen here.

10. Ernest Hemingway, "Monologue to the Maestro," *Esquire*, IV (October 1935), 21, 174A, 174B.

11. Isabel Patterson, "Turns with a Bookworm," *New York Herald Tribune Books* (November 24, 1929), 27.

12. Gertrude Stein, *The Autobiography of Alice B. Toklas* (New York: Harcourt Brace and Company, 1933), p. 267.

13. *Time*, XXXIII (January 23, 1939), 41.

Of Wasteful Deaths: Hemingway's Stories about the Spanish War / *Martin Light*

Five short stories that arose from Ernest Hemingway's involvement in the Spanish Civil War have received little attention until now.[1] They deserve notice, however, because in them Hemingway gives expression to his major preoccupations and his perennial themes and because they exist as significant records of the Spanish experience out of which came his major novel, *For Whom the Bell Tolls*.

Perhaps these stories were ignored or dismissed because they were not readily available. They were published in *Esquire* and *Cosmopolitan* in 1938 and 1939, too late for inclusion in the comprehensive collection called *The Fifth Column and the First Forty-Nine Stories*. It is said that Hemingway did not entirely care for them and did not wish to see them reprinted. They may have received scant notice because there are of course two dozen other Hemingway short stories that absorb all critical interest. Yet such reasons seem insufficient to allow us to ignore 35,000 words by a writer of Hemingway's importance.[2] These stories complement the reportage on Spain that is available in *By-Line: Ernest Hemingway*, a recent best-seller. They deal with the nature of courage, the making of a "separate peace," the conflict between loyalty to friends and loyalty to a cause, the futility of fighting in poorly-planned battles, and the agony of waiting for purposeless death. They exhibit Hemingway's skepticism about language as he explores the difficulties of converting experience into words that tell the truth and speculates about the role of the writer in relation to people and events he has known. They show Hemingway's way of symbolizing (and offer some reflections on the process and appropriateness of symbolization) and they reveal his characteristic irony. If they do not transmit that special excitement, sympathy, and pity that emanates from Hemingway's best fiction, they have interest of an estimable

1. The situation has been changing. Four of the stories have now been reprinted in *The Fifth Column and Four Unpublished Stories of the Spanish Civil War* (New York, 1969). See also Julian Smith, "Christ Times Four: Hemingway's Unknown Spanish Civil War Stories," *Arizona Quarterly*, XXV (Spring 1969), 5–17.

2. In most studies of Hemingway the stories are either not mentioned or given one sentence. John Muste, however, devotes three pages to them in his book on writers of the war. He says, "None of the [*Esquire*] stories is successful; all suffer from wordiness, pointlessness, and a general lack of precision"; each "is disturbingly juvenile in one way or another," *Say That We Saw Spain Die* (Seattle, 1966), pp. 90–93; Warren French, however, gives sympathetic treatment to two of the five stories in *The Social Novel at the End of an Era* (Carbondale, 1966), pp. 91–94; 108–109.

order, nevertheless. They convey a dark mood, but they show faith in human resilience.

The Spanish Civil War began in July, 1936. Carlos Baker tells us that "between the two Februaries of 1937 and 1939 [Hemingway] made four extended journeys to Spain" and that "chiefly in his ancient haunts around Madrid but also often in the field, Hemingway lived and wrote during the greater part of the struggle."[3] Mussolini's Italian troops were defeated in the fighting called the Battle of Guadalajara between March 8 and 18, 1937, and Hemingway afterward walked the battlefield at Brihuega and described it in dispatches. He spent the following month in and around Madrid, sent more reports, and worked on the essential project of this first trip—the film *The Spanish Earth*, for which, after serving as guide to the director and the cameraman, he wrote the narration. Two short stories which mention filming can be thought of as taking place during that spring: "Night Before Battle" and "Under the Ridge." Hemingway also placed the action of *For Whom the Bell Tolls* in late May of the same year.

The second trip began on August 14, 1937. He wrote dispatches and *The Fifth Column* during the fall of 1937. Professor Baker says that the play "sought to present Hemingway's tough-minded apprehension of the state of things in Madrid. . . . Civilians were dying in the daily bombardments, food was becoming scarcer, hopes of lifting the siege were growing dim, and the malignant growth of treason operated deep in the city. By comparison and in retrospect, the spring of 1937 had been gay."[4] Two of the short stories we will examine take place during this dark winter of bombardment and treachery: "The Denunciation" and "The Butterfly and the Tank." Like the play, they too give Hemingway's sense of things in Madrid that fall. Hemingway returned to the United States on January 28, 1938. On March 19, he left for Spain again. He sent NANA dispatches from Barcelona, Tortosa, the Ebro Delta, Castellon, and Madrid from April 3 to May 11, and published monthly articles in *Ken* from April to September. The trip itself ended on May 31. The most important literary event of these months was the writing of the short masterpiece "The Old Man at the Bridge." It appeared in the May issue of *Ken* among Hemingway's articles, essays, and editorials, but it has the shape of a short story and is so classified in his collected work. The narrator encountered the old man on Easter, in April, 1938; the Nationalists were then marching toward the Mediterranean, forcing a Republican retreat across the Ebro River.

The fourth trip began in early September, 1938, and ended in February,

---

3. Carlos Baker, ed. *Hemingway and His Critics: An International Anthology* (New York, 1961), p. 6. For the chronology I draw upon that book and Professor Baker's indispensable study, *Ernest Hemingway: The Writer as Artist* (Princeton, 1963). See also his *Ernest Hemingway: A Life Story* (New York, 1969).

4. *Hemingway: The Writer as Artist*, p. 234.

1939. Two crucial events of the conflict occurred: Barcelona fell in January, 1939, and the Nationalists entered Madrid in late March, ending the war. For Hemingway, several significant publishing events also took place during this two-year period. *The Fifth Column and the First Forty-Nine Stories* appeared on October 14, 1938. It contained the play and all the stories that had been printed in magazines and collections up to that date, including "Old Man at the Bridge." Next, the five stories we are concerned with here appeared in two magazines: in *Esquire*, vol. 10, "The Denunciation," November, 1938; "The Butterfly and the Tank," December, 1938; and, in vol. 11, "Night Before Battle," February, 1939; and in *Cosmopolitan*, vol. 106, "Nobody Ever Dies," March, 1939; and, in vol. 107, "Under the Ridge," October, 1939. (The order of publication does not correspond to the order of action within the stories.) Finally, Hemingway began writing *For Whom the Bell Tolls* in mid-March, 1939, and published the book on October 21, 1940.

One preliminary matter is worth noting. According to the New York *Times* of August 6, 1958, Hemingway tried to stop *Esquire* from reprinting three stories in an anthology called *The Armchair Esquire*. He charged that reprinting would result in injury and damage beyond the commercial value of the stories. His lawyer's paper suggested that change in the political climate "can affect the writings of authors either favorably or unfavorably." But a day later Hemingway declared that he was dropping the suit. The *Times* of August 7 quotes him as saying that the publisher had had no permission to reprint and that two of the stories "were not as good as I wanted them and I wanted to revise them before letting them go into book form." His revisions, he said, were not political: "I only wanted to remove some of the clichés." His only concern has been to write stories that "are straight and good." He had not tried to write fiction that was pro-Loyalist or anti-Loyalist, though his attitude toward the war itself was pro-Loyalist. He then allowed "The Butterfly and the Tank" to be reprinted in the anthology without change.[5]

I

The three stories that appeared in *Esquire* are set principally in Chicote's bar in Madrid. In "The Denunciation," the narrator, who is called "Enrique" and "Mr. Emmunds," says that the incident he is writing about took place in November, 1937. The rebels were shelling Madrid; bombs were killing civilians. The mood was dark and tempers were short, though there was no despair. "The Denunciation" tells how Luis Delgado is handed over to the Security Police as a spy. Delgado has been flying with the fascists for over a

5. Arnold Gingrich and L. Rust Hills, eds. *The Armchair Esquire* (New York, 1958), pp. 135–44.

year, but the narrator remembers him from earlier times as a pleasant and honorable fellow. It is a waiter who calls the police to denounce Delgado, but the narrator supplies the telephone number and thereby implicates himself in what he knows to be a betrayal of an old acquaintanceship. The emotional interest of the story lies in Hemingway's account of the feelings of the narrator under the stress of mixed loyalties.

Chicote's was a favorite bar in the old days, says the narrator. The habitués had been "good guys," though many of them were now on Franco's side. Delgado, who had frequented the bar years before, should not be in Chicote's. Though he is a fascist, he is wearing a loyalist uniform and is talking to three young loyalists at the other side of the room. Perhaps he is there to gather information; perhaps he intends to steal a plane. He is foolish to be in Chicote's at all. But the narrator recalls that Delgado had always been very brave and very foolish. He remembers San Sebastian in 1933, when he and Delgado had been at the pigeon shoots and had bet against each other. Delgado had lost a good deal of money to the narrator, but he had conducted himself well, making it seem an honor to pay his debt.

A waiter, recognizing Delgado and knowing him to be a fascist, is troubled. First he and the narrator decide that it is none of their business that Delgado is in the bar. But the waiter remains uneasy and returns to the table to ask the narrator whether he agrees that there is a responsibility to report Delgado. The narrator tells him, "If you wish to, go to the telephone and call this number. Write it down." The waiter makes the call. To avoid being present when Delgado is hauled away, the narrator returns to the Hotel Florida. He tells himself that the waiter's decision was probably the right one, but he is upset by his own role in the denunciation. So he calls Pepe, "the strange and deadly voice" at police headquarters. Delgado, who is soon to be shot, has not yet been told that the waiter denounced him. The narrator therefore asks Pepe to say that he, the narrator, did it. And he feels much better. "All we old clients of Chicote's had a sort of feeling about the place," he thinks. He knows that that was why Delgado had gone back there. Preserving Delgado's faith in Chicote's was a small act of kindness: "I did not wish him to be disillusioned or bitter about the waiters there before he died."

In moving quickly through a summary of the story, I have necessarily slighted some important material. First, there is the evocation of Chicote's bar, the scene of three stories. It has been a nonpolitical place, where the best-looking girls in town showed up, where the drinks were wonderful, and where the waiters were always pleasant—"the best bar in Spain, certainly." In Hemingway's work, a good bar or cafe is a kind of club or secular sanctuary. Patrons share a special brotherhood. The waiters attend and serve and witness and suffer; they operate within an honored tradition and they maintain high standards of conduct. At a bad cafe the waiters may be rude and perhaps dishonest (as we shall see in "Night Before Battle"); at a good one they are wise and priestlike. Robert Weeks points out that a cafe can be the setting for that typical Hemingway drama in which people chat, play cards, or drink beer "quite unaware that sitting among them is a man whose world is coming to an end."[6] So it is in *A Farewell to Arms* when Frederic Henry, leaving the hospital where Catherine is dying, pauses at a cafe. In "A Clean, Well-Lighted Place," two waiters talk about an aged man who sits in their cafe as long as he is allowed. The young waiter is unsympathetic toward the desperation within the old client, but the middle-aged waiter "knows what it is to experience the horror of nothingness" (as Weeks phrases it) and tries to explain it to the younger. In "The Capital of the World," one waiter defends the rule that all shall remain on duty until the clients wish to leave, and another waiter defends the urgencies of politics which are drawing him to an early meeting that night. Paco, the central figure of the story, meanwhile dreams of becoming a great bull-fighter, and, in an ironic ending, dies from a knife-wound during bull-fighting practice in the kitchen. It is consistent with Hemingway's work as a whole, therefore, that Chicote's becomes the setting for dramatizations of the tensions of wartime.

In addition, there is a portrait of the companion Hemingway provides for the narrator to talk to—John, a Greek comrade "who had been buried by an airplane bomb" and had been sent to a "rest home or something of the sort." He now has buzzing in his head. There is also a substantial characterization of Delgado, who, when he lost a lot of money, had "made it seem a great privilege to pay." Of the narrator, himself, I think we might repeat what E. M. Halliday says about Frederic Henry: "he suffers a torpor brought on by too many months of living close to the war."[7] The story tries to make us understand the motives for the narrator's act of complicity in the denunciation. Delgado was wrong to be in loyalist uniform; let no one misunderstand the significance of a treacherous act. For instance, in the "Preface" to *The Fifth Column and the First Forty-Nine Stories* Hemingway discusses the necessity of shooting members of the fifth column. "They deserved to be [shot], under the rules of war, and they expected to be" (p. vi). Neither fanatics nor sentimental Americans should doubt it, or the necessity of it. In an article called "Treachery in Aragon," published in *Ken* on June 30, 1938, Hemingway recalls an incident of April in the previous year. An American writer, a good friend of his,[8] came to Madrid to locate a friend and former translator who he had heard was being held in prison. The writer would absolutely guarantee the translator's loyalty, but Hemingway already knew that

6. "Introduction" to Weeks, ed. *Hemingway: A Collection of Critical Essays* (Englewood Cliffs, N.J., 1962), p. 14.

7. "Hemingway's Ambiguity: Symbolism and Irony," *American Literature*, XXVIII (March, 1956), 16.

8. It was John Dos Passos. See Baker, *Hemingway: A Life Story*, pp. 305–306, for additional complexities surrounding this matter.

the man had been shot as a spy two weeks earlier after a long and careful trial. American liberals, he says, are too naive to believe in treachery. But, he concludes, "we who have seen this war for a long time have learned that there are all sorts of treachery just as there are all sorts of heroism in war."

In "The Denunciation," the narrator regrets the circumstance that seemed to require him to put the cause before proper regard for friendship. Caught between fellowship and politics, he, in a moment of what he calls "Pontius Pilatry," accedes to the demands of politics. What interests us further in this connection is his cynical remark about writers. For he says that as he gave the waiter the phone number of the police, he had been indulging "the always-dirty desire to see how people act under an emotional conflict, that makes writers such attractive friends." Therefore, finally, the narrator sacrifices his own reputation with Delgado in order to preserve an honorable ideal above politics—that is, to preserve Delgado's memory of the good feeling, the good food, the good companionship, and the right behavior that are associated with Chicote's bar. The narrator allows his own name to be dishonored, while preserving the reputation of a place where the code of good behavior had lived. John Muste, calling the whole story a parody of the gestures of the code hero, finds the final paragraph "appalling" in its "fake concern" for Delgado and in its "insensitivity toward the waiter's feelings."[9] But Muste is too severe. The waiter is not forced to bear the burden of guilt, for in fact the narrator pauses to speak to the waiter to reassure him that the denunciation was just and at the end reassumes the burden which he had passed to the waiter. War can provoke conflicts of loyalties—loyalty to the cause which lies behind the war as against loyalty to friends, loved ones, and oneself. It is a conflict never lightly dismissed, but the decision in Hemingway's work is always in favor of loyalty to the individual. The narrator in "The Denunciation" fears he has betrayed not only Delgado, but a revered place and his own principles. No wonder he tells this tale in a gloomy mood and leaves behind a sense of something ever painfully unresolved.

"The Butterfly and the Tank" is the next of the stories. The time is again November, 1937, the dark winter of setbacks and tensions. The city is under siege. Chicote's is crowded. The narrator enters, hungry and irritable. He sits down with a strangely-matched couple, a terrible-looking, forceful girl and a weak young man. Again he reflects bitterly that although he is a writer and is supposed to have an insatiable curiosity, he is too tired to care about these people.

The action concerns a civilian who has a flit gun and squirts a waiter. After being thrown out by some soldiers, the man re-enters and squirts the whole company. The soldiers push him to the side and shoot him. They burst from the bar, and the narrator mocks the efforts of the police, who arrive to go through the motions of an investigation even though the assassins are of

9. Muste, op. cit., pp. 92–93.

course gone. Whereas the narrator was at first simply annoyed at the whole episode, now a small measure of sympathy arises as he gazes at the dead "flit king," little and pitiful on the floor, who had no undershirt and whose shoes were worn through. The narrator tells the girl at his table that he thinks the whole thing "a pretty good story" and that he will "write it sometime." She says he should not, for it would be prejudicial to the Cause. At this stage, the narrator says he sees the episode as comic, and he will write about it because it has nothing to do with politics.

But the next day—"a fine, bright, cold early winter day"—his attitude changes significantly. For if, in his resolve to make use of the incident, he has dispensed with the girl's shallow political objections, he now has to overcome other obstacles raised by the manager of Chicote's. At Chicote's the manager and the waiters are talking about what has happened. It is a sad thing, a rare thing, says the manager; the flit-gun man had eau de cologne in the gun; it was a joke, just gaiety, not in bad taste. The narrator is reluctant to agree, since these are times of quick tempers and it was proper that the flit-king respect the tense atmosphere. He reacts bitterly to the manager's "relentless Spanish logic." Then he learns that the flit-king was a cabinet-maker called Pedro whose wife had come just a few hours before to mourn the body. Pedro had fought in the early days of the war, but had had weakness in the chest. The narrator is annoyed by the manager's interpretation of events, but he is also reacting more sympathetically toward Pedro. "I don't like this story very well," he says. The manager, attempting to explain what had taken place— attempting to find a formula which would account for the incident and the death—says of the flit-king: "His gaiety comes in contact with the serious-ness of the war like a butterfly [the narrator here interrupts sarcastically, "Oh very like a butterfly"] . . . and a tank." The narrator comments: "This pleased him enormously. He was getting into the real Spanish metaphysics." Now the narrator hears that he *must* write about it. The manager attempts to dictate the terms in which the story should be understood: "You must call it The Butterfly and the Tank. . . . The title is very elegant. . . . It is pure liter-ature." We are left, however, with the narrator's final ironic comment. He sits there on "that cheerful morning, the place smelling clean and newly aired and swept, with the manager who was an old friend and who was now very pleased with the literature we were making together and I . . . thought of the wife kneeling there and saying 'Pedro. *Pedro*, who has done this to thee, Pedro?' And I thought that the police would never be able to tell her that even if they had the name of the man who pulled the trigger." The final lines of the story seem an echo of Stephen Crane's "The Blue Hotel." Who, after all, is responsible for this death? A force larger than the behavior of any in-dividual has killed Pedro. It is Pedro himself, it is the war, it is everyone. That might be an answer to the question Pedro's wife asks, if it is any kind of an understandable answer at all.

One interesting aspect of the story is that Hemingway had used the flit-gun episode in *The Fifth Column*. Dorothy Bridges tells the protagonist, Philip Rawlings, about something she had seen at Chicote's. A man had been shot the other night, "just a poor man who was squirting everyone with a flit gun." The man hadn't meant any harm, yet someone shot him. "He lay on his back and his face was very gray and he'd been so gay just a little while before. . . . They didn't cover him up and we had to go and show our papers to a man at a table just beside where he was and it was *very* depressing, Philip. And he had such dirty hose and his shoes were completely worn through on the bottoms and he had *no* undershirt at *all*" (pp. 25–26). Dorothy Bridges' version of the incident is different from the one we see in the short story. She thinks primarily about her own discomforts, an attitude conveyed in the way the italicized words dictate that her speech be read. Philip's reaction is brief and the matter is not further explored.

Langston Hughes has also reported the incident. He had known the young English couple in the bar. Hughes says that Hemingway exaggerated their ugliness and that they were not so foolish or cowardly as he portrayed them. Hughes briefly tells about the ragged little Spaniard who had come drunkenly into the bar with the flit gun and who had been shot. Hughes says, "I was interested in observing what Hemingway did to real people in his story, some of whom he described almost photographically."[10]

What Hemingway did was more than just describe photographically and add a few details, however. "The Butterfly and the Tank" shows how Hemingway recreated experience so as to evoke significance. We watch the narrator reveal the growth of his understanding of what had taken place. At first he saw the incident as a comedy of little people acting foolishly. Then he rejected its political implications. But the next day, the manager and the waiters force it within a scheme. They see it as "misunderstood gaiety coming in contact with the deadly seriousness." They have jumped to a "metaphysical" explanation, says the narrator, and he sneers at what they are doing. They have prepared a formula of symbols: Pedro is a "butterfly"; the atmosphere of war that has taken hold of Chicote's bar is a "tank"; the butterfly thrusts itself against the tank and of course is smashed. But the manager is like a bad writer. He leaps too quickly toward an explanation that fits a scheme. The narrator saw little in Pedro that resembled a butterfly except his sprawling frame—no complexity of design, no color, no delicacy. He saw Pedro lying there in worn shoes and he thinks it truer to say that Pedro was a drab dead sparrow. The narrator wants an account without imposed meanings and artificial symbols.

Carlos Baker has said about Hemingway's attitude toward symbolization: ". . . the symbolic in Hemingway's writing must come as naturally as the

10. Langston Hughes, *I Wonder As I Wander: An Autobiographical Journey* (New York, 1956), pp. 364–365.

leaves to a tree or it had better not come at all. He seems early to have rejected the arbitrary importation of symbols."[11] It is clear that when writing of the Spanish War Hemingway found reason to reaffirm such principles. Because he had seen the tanks and because he had seen dead men, he thought of them only as they are. "Literary" literature is a disservice to truth. Yet, when he finally comes to write the story of the flit-king, Hemingway allows the manager's title to stand. And now we read it ironically, as the manager never intended. As E. M. Halliday has pointed out, at his best Hemingway puts symbol and irony to the service of the re-creation of reality.[12] "The Butterfly and the Tank" is not a story to ignore. It is not only moving in itself, but is significant as an example of Hemingway's aesthetic practice.

"Night Before Battle," takes place in April, 1937, about eight months earlier than the time of the stories discussed above. The narrator, who is called "Edwin Henry," has been making a film, just as Hemingway was doing that spring. The narrator arrives at Chicote's in a dark mood because the day's offensive has been a failure. He meets a friend, Al Wagner, a tank driver. They sit down with a Spaniard whom they call the "little man with the thick lensed glasses," and talk about Largo Caballero, the prime minister. As a socialist, Largo Caballero was attempting to hold together a united front government. The communists were not altogether pleased with him, but had nonetheless built him up as the "Spanish Lenin." He had taken the Ministry of War for himself and he had been instigating a series of strategic maneuvers. It was he who had ordered the futile frontal attacks then taking place, and the little man mocks him. After the little man leaves, Al Wagner and the narrator discuss the hopeless plans for tomorrow when the tanks will attack some thoroughly prepared positions. Suddenly, Al Wagner says (in Hemingway's masterful way of exploding an emotional bomb without warning, confirming our suspicion that surface conversation has been covering deep inner tensions), "Listen, Hank, I don't want to talk a lot of crap but I think I'm going to get killed tomorrow." He goes on, "I don't mind dying a bit. Dying is just a lot of crap. Only it's wasteful. The attack is wrong and it's wasteful. . . ." Wagner talks on at length, trying to rid himself of his anxieties. He speaks expertly about the secret use of tanks and about the inexperienced men he has to lead, men he may not be able to move forward. But as he leaves the bar, Wagner tells the waiter that there is hope; his tone changes as he voices propaganda ("you, the rear-guard, must be as firm as we will be at the front"). The narrator witnesses Wagner's belief in the political cause despite the truth his own eyes have seen. Wagner has political faith and human weakness. He tries with his words to bolster the confidence of the waiter, but he cannot convince himself. The narrator at no time in any of these stories is misled by the party line, though his humanitarian concern for

11. *Hemingway and His Critics*, p. 15.
12. Halliday, op. cit., p. 9.

individuals leads him to tell them he agrees with them while he indicates to us his own skepticism.

Wagner and the narrator go to the Hotel Florida. A group has gathered in the narrator's room, playing cards and drinking. Wagner has a bath, but he cannot remove the smudges from beneath his eyes. He gambles and loses everything. There is a brief scene at a restaurant. Unlike Chicote's, here the waiters are rude and deceitful. The food is poor and the service bad, and it is necessary to bribe the waiter to get decent drinks.

The long night continues. Back at the hotel, Al and the narrator encounter Baldy, a drunk and talkative flyer. A group of flyers in the narrator's room ask Baldy to describe the way it was when he shot down a Junker that day. Baldy's account raises the same questions that we have seen before, regarding the proper manner of recreating experience. After much persuasion, Baldy gives a "literary" account ("I was looking back and down and they [the men] were coming out of her, out through the blast furnace door, dropping out trying to get clear, and the chutes opened up and they looked like great big beautiful morning glories opening up . . ."), but one flyer says, "You ought to write for *War Aces*. Do you mind telling me in plain language what happened?" So Baldy recounts the experience: "We dove onto them with all four guns until you could have touched them before we rolled out of it. . . ." Probably Baldy's account serves also as a foreshadowing of what Al Wagner's death may be like in a flaming tank.

Wagner borrows money and loses it gambling again. Obviously he now has no luck. But after a nap he says he is OK; he has gotten things into perspective: "All you need is a perspective." He gives the narrator an envelope containing "pictures and stuff" to send back to his brother. The narrator and Al say they'll meet tomorrow night at Chicote's. "What time?" asks the narrator. "Listen, that's enough," Al responds. "Tomorrow night at Chicote's. We don't have to go into the time." The final paragraph reads:

> If you hadn't known him pretty well and if you hadn't seen the terrain where he was going to attack tomorrow, you would have thought he was very angry about something. I guess somewhere inside of him he was angry, very angry. You get angry about a lot of things and you, yourself, dying uselessly is one of them. But then I guess angry is about the best way that you can be when you attack.

The narrator sees advantages in anger, but Robert Jordan thinks something rather different near the beginning of *For Whom the Bell Tolls*. He reflects upon the right mood for a soldier: "All the best ones, when you thought it over, were gay. . . . There were not many of them left though. No, there were not many of the gay ones left" (p. 17). Al Wagner is a good one, but he has lost his gaiety. "Night Before Battle" has an atmosphere of inevitable death. But neither abiding earth nor love supply relief, as they do in *For Whom the*

Bell Tolls. Though the story is long and loosely constructed, it reflects the mood of the night. It records much talk—talk loose and "wet"—the only relief for the weary and worried mind. In the "Introduction" to *Men at War*, Hemingway wrote: "Worrying does no good. . . . A good soldier does not worry. He knows that nothing happens until it actually happens and you live your life up until then" (p. xvii). Yet in his fiction, Hemingway shows worry spinning anyway. Al Wagner is a sympathetic portrait of a good soldier inescapably worrying. Robert Jordan will command himself, "Turn off the thinking now, old timer." Jordan knows that he would rather not be a hero, but decides he will do what he is asked. Wagner says the same: the attack is no good, but "my duty is to do what I'm ordered to do."

The first of the two stories which appeared in *Cosmopolitan*, called "Nobody Ever Dies," is, I think, the weak one of the five. Although the setting is Cuba, the protagonist, Enrique, has just returned from fifteen months of fighting in Spain, an experience which he describes at length. There is political terror in Cuba, too, and thus in the story two struggles against fascism cross each other. Trapped in a house with his friend Maria, while an informer and the Havana police threaten them outside, Enrique justifies war by lapsing into propaganda: "We must proceed so that we will never again fall into revolutionary adventurism." He tells Maria that her brother is dead in Spain, as are "the flower of our party." When she laments the death of her brother, Enrique reminds her that "we are all brothers" and that the cause is worth it. Maria, denouncing the death of good men "in failures in a foreign country," tells Enrique that he talks like a book, not like a human being. Again we see Hemingway's skepticism of literary and political language. Yet the direction of this story underlines slogans and mottoes rather than refutes them. Enrique shows Maria the wound in his back, and her sudden pity leads to an embrace that is described tritely ("her lips an island in the sudden white sea of pain"). As the house is raided, Enrique and Maria run out in different directions. Enrique is shot down. The story ends with a new sense of dedication within Maria. She is compared to Joan of Arc, and her courage under capture frightens the Negro who had betrayed her to the police. In general, idealism soars aloft in the story; it is not brought to earth in Hemingway's customary manner, except when Enrique describes the fighting and the dead he has seen. The ending rises cheaply upward. Seeing Maria's dedication, the Negro fingers his voodoo beads, "but they could not help his fear because he was up against an older magic now." "Nobody Ever Dies"—the title itself is a slogan. The story is the only one of this group that falls below respectable standards.[13]

The other *Cosmopolitan story*, "Under the Ridge,"returns to the Spanish setting, though to the battlefield, not to Chicote's. It is a fascinating story, one of the best among the five. It explores several subjects: the hostility of

13. But it was reprinted apropos of Castro's revolution; see *Cosmopolitan*, CXLVI (April, 1959), 78–83.

the Spanish soldiers toward foreigners, even toward those who form the International Brigades; the making of a "separate peace"; the treatment of those who inflict wounds upon themselves to remove themselves from battle; and the cruel meaning of totalitarianism of any kind, for here the villains are not fascists but communists on the loyalist side. Warren French finds it "difficult to imagine how a story could more directly indict the Communists as the destroyers of what the author thought most valuable in the world—inexperienced, willing youth and self-possessed maturity." [14]

It is spring, 1937, again, as it was in "Night Before Battle," when Hemingway was visiting the lines to film *The Spanish Earth*. On a bright April day the narrator comes down out of battle to a ridge where the Spanish troops wait in reserve. He thinks of the failure of the attack, and he watches the work of the ambulances. He talks with a soldier from Extremadura who hates foreigners and who asserts (and reasserts, to the point of annoyance) that he has no fear. Suddenly, a mysterious figure crosses the scene. It is a Frenchman, who looks like a man walking in his sleep, "walking alone down out of the war." Two Russians in leather coats follow him out of sight up the hill where they shoot him. The narrator explains his sympathy for the Frenchman's separate peace: "I understood how a man might suddenly, seeing clearly the stupidity of dying in an unsuccessful attack, . . . seeing its hopelessness, seeing its idiocy, seeing how it really was, simply get back and walk away from it as the Frenchman had done . . . not from cowardice. . . . I understood him as a man." Nonetheless, the narrator tries to justify the action of the Russians. It is the discipline necessary in wartime, he says. However, the Extremaduran soldier replies, "And to live under that sort of discipline we should die?" He asks the American to listen to a tale.

He tells the story of Paco, a boy from Extremadura, who became frightened during the bombardment and shot himself in the hand. "Such people have their wounds dressed and are returned at once to the line," he explains. "It is just." But Paco's case was special. His hand had to be amputated and he remained in the hospital, where he was well-liked and made himself useful. Yesterday (the Extremaduran soldier goes on) the two Russians and an officer from the Brigade brought Paco here. He was warmly greeted by the soldiers, who were willing to tolerate his fears. But "when such people with the leather coats and the pistols come it is always a bad omen." The Russians took him to the place where he had wounded himself and shot him without warning. "It is for this that I now hate Russians as well as all other foreigners." The narrator understands. He and the soldier shake hands. The narrator, departing for Madrid, concludes, "The nearest any man was to victory that day was probably the Frenchman who came, with his head held high, walking out of the battle. . . ." "Under the Ridge" looks back to Frederic Henry's separate peace in *A Farewell to Arms* and forward not only to the Spanish partisans'

14. French, op. cit., p. 93.

distrust of foreigners in *For Whom the Bell Tolls*, but also to Pilar's recognition of cruelty on the loyalist side in her account of the massacre of village officials and priests. Though the story does not compromise either Hemingway's admiration for courage or his dislike of cowardice, it does affirm his concern for each individual case.

II

Hemingway conceded that the Spanish Civil War brought its surprises, even to one like himself who had seen a good deal of fighting over a period of about twenty years. One of the NANA dispatches almost has the form of another short story. It is about Jay Raven, whom Hemingway visits in a hospital outside Madrid. Raven, who had been a social worker, has lost most of his face and has been injured in the legs and feet. While telling about the action in which he was wounded, Raven puts his hand in Hemingway's. There were no callouses and the fingers were smooth, Hemingway notes. "Holding his hand and hearing him tell it, I did not believe a word of it. . . . The story did not sound right. It was sort of the way everyone would like to have been wounded." But as he returns from the hospital, Hemingway meets Raven's commanding officer, Jock Cunningham, who confirms that Raven's account is accurate. "We talked for a while and he told me many things," Hemingway writes. "They were all important, but nothing was as important as that [15] what Jay Raven, the social worker from Pittsburgh with no military training, had told me was true. This is a strange new kind of war where you learn just as much as you are able to believe." [16]

Some of the ideas treated in these stories had appeared earlier in Hemingway's work. Some were to appear in *For Whom the Bell Tolls*. Malcolm Cowley has pointed out that Hemingway had the habit of returning to the same themes, "each time making them a little clearer—to himself, I think, as well as to others." [17] Through the voice of Frederic Henry in *A Farewell to Arms*, Hemingway had announced his verbal skepticism: "I was always embarrassed by the words sacred, glorious, and sacrifice. . . . I had seen nothing sacred, and the things that were glorious had no glory and the sacrifices were like the stockyards at Chicago. . . ." [18] Stories like "The Butterfly and the Tank" and "Night Before Battle" are sarcastic about the "literary" view of experience. In *For Whom the Bell Tolls* Robert Jordan doubts that big words

15. In *By-Line: Ernest Hemingway* (p. 267) this key word was accidentally left out, depriving the sentence (and the narrative) of its special meaning—that human nature does not submit to stereotype.

16. William White, ed. *By Line: Ernest Hemingway. Selected Articles and Dispatches of Four Decades* (New York, 1967), pp. 262–267.

17. "Introduction" to Cowley, ed. *The Viking Portable Library Hemingway* (New York, 1944), p. ix.

18. *A Farewell to Arms* (New York, 1929), p. 196.

make killing defensible or palatable (p. 165). Hemingway mocks false metaphors in a scene between Pilar and Primitivo above the bridge. Primitivo worries whether fragments from the blown bridge will come as far as he is. Pilar says not to worry. Primitivo replies, "But I remember with the blowing of the train the lamp of the engine blew by over my head and pieces of steel flew by like swallows." "Thou hast poetic memories," Pilar says. "Like swallows. *Joder!* They were like wash boilers" (pp. 443–44). The stories we have examined can be seen as part of Hemingway's search for a true way to recreate the Spanish experience.

The best of the stories of the Spanish Civil War, "Old Man at the Bridge," ends as the old man sits at the river bank, worrying about his cat and the other animals he had to leave behind. Refugees rush past him. The narrator says, "There was nothing to do about him. It was Easter Sunday and the Fascists were advancing toward the Ebro. It was a gray overcast day with a low ceiling so their planes were not up. That and the fact that cats know how to look after themselves was all the good luck that old man would ever have." The five stories studied here suggest that there was little enough luck also for Delgado, John the Greek soldier, Pedro, Al Wagner, the Frenchman, Paco, and many other victims of that fateful war.

2. Story Technique

The Revision of "Chapter III" from *In Our Time* / *Charles A. Fenton*

The first version of "chapter 3" of *in our time* was cabled to Toronto from Adrianople on October 20, 1922.[1] A revision was published as the third of the *Little Review* series in April, 1923. The final draft which Hemingway gave to Bill Bird for *in our time* was completely declarative.

> Minarets stuck up in the rain out of Adrianople across the mud flats. The carts were jammed for thirty miles along the Karagatch road. Water buffalo and cattle were hauling carts through the mud. No end and no beginning. Just carts loaded with everything they owned. The old men and women, soaked through, walked along keeping the cattle moving. The Maritza was running yellow almost up to the bridge. Carts were jammed solid on the bridge with camels bobbing along through them. Greek cavalry herded along the procession. Women and kids were in the carts crouched with mattresses, mirrors, sewing machines, bundles. There was a woman having a kid with a young girl holding a blanket over her and crying. Scared sick looking at it. It rained all through the evacuation.

The 1922 cable, although it had many points of likeness with the finished vignette, differed from it in several important respects. Its last two paragraphs were general ones, describing the relief agencies that were operating in Thrace. These paragraphs had no validity for the redrafting of the dispatch into the vignette; none of the material appears in the second, *Little Review* draft, or in the final, *in our time* version. The cable's first three paragraphs, however, do constitute that first draft.

> In a never-ending, staggering march the Christian population of Eastern Thrace is jamming the roads towards Macedonia. The main column crossing the Maritza River at Adrianople is twenty miles long. Twenty miles of carts drawn by cows, bullocks and muddy-flanked water buffalo, with exhausted, staggering men, women and children, blankets over their heads, walking blindly in the rain beside their worldly goods.
> This main stream is being swelled from all the back country. They

Charles A. Fenton, "The Revision of 'Chapter III' from *In Our Time*," from chapter 11 of *The Apprenticeship of Ernest Hemingway: The Early Years* (New York: The Viking Press, 1958), pp. 229–36. Copyright, 1954, by Charles A. Fenton. Reprinted by permission of Farrar, Straus & Giroux, Inc.

1. Toronto *Daily Star*, October 20, 1922, 1 (second edition).

don't know where they are going. They left their farms, villages and ripe, brown fields and joined the main stream of refugees when they heard the Turk was coming. Now they can only keep their places in the ghastly procession while mud-splashed Greek cavalry herd them along like cow-punchers driving steers.

It is a silent procession. Nobody even grunts. It is all they can do to keep moving. Their brilliant peasant costumes are soaked and draggled. Chickens dangle by their feet from the carts. Calves nuzzle at the draught cattle wherever a jam halts the stream. An old man marches bent under a young pig, a scythe and a gun, with a chicken tied to his scythe. A husband spreads a blanket over a woman in labor in one of the carts to keep off the driving rain. She is the only person making a sound. Her little daughter looks at her in horror and begins to cry. And the procession keeps moving.

The three paragraphs for the *Daily Star* were more than competent journalism. They were well-written by any standards. This was the cable which so impressed Lincoln Steffens, when Hemingway showed it to him at Lausanne in December, 1922. When Steffens wrote about the incident almost ten years later, in his autobiography, he even used some of Hemingway's own words. Steffens remembered the story as "a short but vivid, detailed picture of what [Hemingway] had seen in that miserable stream of hungry, frightened, uprooted people."[2] Steffens inevitably recalled the story in terms of adjectives; Hemingway had used a variety of modifiers in the cable. The process of redrafting began here.

Save for such virtually corporate words as "thirty," "mud," and "Greek," the *in our time* vignette contained only ten legitimate adjectives: *no*, used twice, *loaded, old, yellow, soaked, solid, young, scared*, and *sick*. Three were participles, and the twice-employed "no" was not a conventional descriptive adjective. Hemingway relied in the final draft on four basic modifiers, *old, yellow, young*, and *sick*. This was in sharp contrast to the cabled first draft, where, sharp and clear as he made it, he nevertheless used almost thirty adjectives. He relied there on compound modifiers such as "never-ending," "muddy-flanked," and "mud-splashed." He used such adjectival sequences as "exhausted, staggering," and "ripe, brown." He used such familiar modifiers as "worldly goods," and pejorative adjectives like "ghastly." This was one of the devices Hemingway had in mind when he spoke later of the limitations of journalism. "In writing for a newspaper," he declared in 1932, "you told what happened and, with one trick and another, you communicated the emotion aided by the element of timeliness which gives a certain emotion to any account of something that has happened on that day."[3]

2. Lincoln Steffens, *Autobiography of Lincoln Steffens* (Harcourt, Brace, 1931), p. 834.
3. *Death in the Afternoon* (Scribner's, 1932), p. 2.

There were other tricks which the necessities of deadlines and hasty readers compelled a reporter to rely on. Hemingway's best journalism, of which the Adrianople cable was an example, used the tricks sparingly, but they could not be concealed. "If a writer of prose knows enough about what he is writing about," Hemingway said in 1932, "he may omit things that he knows and the reader, if the writer is writing truly enough, will have a feeling of those things as strongly as though the writer had stated them. The dignity of movement of an ice-berg is due to only one-eighth of it being above water."[4] In newspaper writing, however, most of the effects had to be well above the surface; none of them could be totally submerged.

The 1922 cable for example, was directed for the reader by a series of comments from the author. "They don't know where they are going," Hemingway had written of the refugees. He was deliberately shaping the reader's response as a supplement to the overt impact of the scene he was describing. He continued the prodding when he told his Toronto audience that "now they can only keep their places." "It is all they can do to keep moving," he added later. Even the most obtuse reader would sense the tragedy, but the dimension which Hemingway later termed the architectural element of writing was necessarily lost by this reportorial steering. There was additional, less direct commentary to guide the newspaper reader. When Hemingway wrote of the "brilliant peasant costumes," now become "soaked and draggled," he was also pushing his audience toward a reaction. Phrases such as "to keep off the driving rain" and "in horror" were equally pejorative, designed to get through quickly to readers who ran while they read.

All of this relatively heavy shaping was cleansed from the vignettes. The ultimate effect became proportionately more forceful by virtue of the new understatement and compression. In the *in our time* draft the reader's horror was far greater because he seemed to be reaching his own conclusions. The sketch was also made more evocative, at a subtler level, by the new image Hemingway introduced. The metaphor of the cable was both strong and familiar. Hemingway had enforced it by the most direct exposition. "Now they can only keep their places in the ghastly procession," he cabled, "while mud-splashed Greek cavalry herd them along like cow-punchers driving steers." The grim likeness between the procession and a cattle drive is retained in the vignette, but it has ceased to be the central image. In a direct way it survives only in the verb of the ninth sentence. In the second draft, in fact, for the *Little Review*, Hemingway eliminated "herded" altogether. His substitution of "rode hard on" did not satisfy him. It was too explicit.

That momentary choice, however, did contain an element of the new image—driftwood, or, even more precise, the log floats Hemingway had seen all through his boyhood in northern Michigan. He re-emphasized the

4. Ibid., p. 192.

verb "jammed," used only once in the cable. The reference to the camels is an entirely new one, particularly important because it permitted the introduction of the gerund "bobbing." Gerunds, indeed, had a new importance in the vignette. The form, with all its utility for the communication of movement and flow, occurs ten times in the sketch. Approximately one out of every thirteen words was now a gerund. Not content with this emphasis, nor with the exhaustive revision as a whole, Hemingway inserted an additional, eleventh gerund when the vignette was republished in 1925 in *In Our Time*; in the sixth sentence he changed "walked" to "walking." [5]

The effect of the driftwood image was to vivify the paragraph. The equation with a log jam is fresher and more denotative than the cattle metaphor. The procession is still moving forward, as in the cable, but its progress is even more sluggish; it is resisted, as a log jam is resisted, by its own pressure. The frame within which the scene is held has been altered to fit the new image. An artist in the best of his journalism, Hemingway had bound the cable by the procession metaphor. "In a never-ending, staggering march," he had cabled in the first line, "the Christian population of Eastern Thrace is jamming the roads towards Macedonia." The last sentence of the first draft had knotted the image. "And the procession," he concluded in 1922, "keeps moving."

For the second, *Little Review* draft, the frame was completely remade. The first line of the vignette not only states the image and introduces the frame, as had been done in the cable, but also initiates the affirmation of the image. "Minarets," the sketch begins, "stuck up in the rain out of Adrianople across the mud flats." As the reader moves into the paragraph, the minarets become the long poles which are scattered upright along the path of a log run. Throughout the body of the sketch there is a constant emphasis and restatement of the saturated, almost submerged quality of the scene. The waterlogged immobility is in every line. "It rained," the vignette ends, "all through the evacuation."

This was not the last step in the process of revision. The compositional structure of the cable had been primarily one of paragraphs and cumulative effect. The second and third drafts became exercises in directional composition, more subtle than the adjectival steering of the cable. It was a prelude of the pictorial device that would be tested in an occasional Ruhr dispatch in April and May of 1923. "Chapter 3" of *in our time* is dominated by two figures who had been merely part of the crowded scene in the *Daily Star* cable. The woman in labor, and her weeping daughter, are no longer details in the panoramic sweep of cavalry, an old man, cows, water buffalo, carts, a husband, men, women, children, calves, a young pig. Hemingway has drawn the wom-

5. The gerund was retained in the Scribner 1927 edition of *In Our Time*. The 1930 edition reverted to the *in our time* form, as have subsequent editions.

an and her child out of the procession and made them the central object.
Were the vignette an etching, they would be in a lower corner, the procession
behind and around them, illuminated by the story which is told in the faces
and positions of these two victims. This was the Goya-like quality Hemingway deliberately sought to inject into the vignettes of *in our time*; a large,
incomprehensible human tragedy was vivified by the episode within it. The
husband did not survive the rewriting. Now the weight of our response falls
upon the young girl, and the horror of her situation is thereby magnified.
There is not even a father to shield her.

Such a deletion was a functional pruning of the same kind which persuaded
Hemingway to rearrange in each draft the pitiful list of possessions the refugees clutched. In the cable he used the phrase "worldly goods," stale and un-
evocative, supplemented by the entire third paragraph's precise catalogue.
For the *Little Review* all this excessive clutter was reduced to a single sentence. "Women and kids were in the carts crouched with mattresses, mirrors,
sewing machines, bundles, sacks of things." In the final draft for *in our time*,
still anxious to eliminate the unspecific, Hemingway erased "sacks of things."
The possessions were the more poignant by their specific meagerness.[6]

The transformation of experience into final draft had been a complicated
process, extending over a period of several months and marked by absorption
so scrupulous that as late as 1930, when Scribner's republished *In Our Time*,
Hemingway continued to make revisions in the vignette. At that time he
repressed the surviving cablese by inserting "There was" in the fourth sentence. He added a comma in the tenth line after "carts," and, still preoccupied with pictorial composition, he described the woman in labor as having
a "baby" rather than a "kid."

This concern with precision was much more than a characteristic of youthful intensity or expatriate craftsmanship. It has continued all through Hemingway's mature work, a persistent reflex dictated by his own artistic demands. A Hemingway manuscript is a facsimile of the three drafts of "chapter
3" of *in our time*, adjectives crossed out, more precise modifiers inserted
above the erasures, punctuation meticulously altered to give weight to key
words, good verbs replaced by better ones. The vignettes of *in our time*, made
possible by both the demands and the inadequacies of newspaper work, are
the solid base of Hemingway's work.

6. This particular revision actually went through four drafts rather than three. On
October 23, 1922, three days after sending the cable from Adrianople, Hemingway
mailed from Sofia a long dispatch about the refugee procession. In it he began the
condensation of detail. "I walked five miles with the refugees [sic] procession along the
road, dodging camels, that swayed and grunted along, past flat wheeled ox carts piled
high with bedding, mirrors, furniture, pigs tied flat, mothers huddled under blankets
with their babies, old men and women. . . ." Toronto *Daily Star*, November 14, 1922, 7.

A Clean Well-Lighted Place / *Frank O'Connor*

Ernest Hemingway must have been one of the first of Joyce's disciples. Certainly, so far as I can ascertain, he was the only writer of his time to study what Joyce was attempting to do in the prose of *Dubliners* and *A Portrait of the Artist as a Young Man* and work out a method of applying it. It took me years to identify Joyce's technique and describe it with any care, and by that time I realized that it was useless for any purpose of my own. So far as I know, no critic had anticipated me, but Hemingway had not only anticipated me; he had already gone into business with it on his own account, and a handsome little business he made of it.

In dealing with *Dubliners* I have already described the peculiarities of Joyce's prose in his first book, but Joyce reserved some of its principal developments for his autobiographical novel. The passage I quoted from it in *A Mirror in the Roadway* to illustrate the technique is as good as any other for my purpose.

> The soft beauty of the Latin word *touched* with an enchanting *touch* the *dark* of the evening, with a *touch* fainter and more persuading than the *touch* of music or of a *woman's* hand. The strife of their minds was quelled. The figure of *woman* as she appears in the liturgy of the church *passed* silently through the *darkness*: a white-robed figure, small and slender as a boy, and with a falling girdle. Her *voice*, frail and high as a boy's, was heard intoning from a distant choir the first words of a *woman* which pierce the gloom and clamour of the first chanting of the passion.
>
> Et tu cum Jesu Galilaeo eras—
>
> And all hearts were *touched* and turned to her *voice*, shining like a young star, shining clearer as the *voice* intoned the proparoxyton, and more faintly as the cadence·died.

This, as I have said, seems to me a development of Flaubert's "proper word," a word proper to the object, not to the reader; and as well as imposing on the reader the exact appearance of the object in the manner of an illustrator, seeks also to impose on him the author's precise mood. By the repetition of key words and key phrases like "touch," "dark," "woman," and "pass," it slows down the whole conversational movement of prose, the

Frank O'Connor, *The Lonely Voice: A Study of the Short Story* (Cleveland: World, 1963), pp. 156–69. Reprinted by permission of the World Publishing Company. Copyright © 1962, 1963 by Frank O'Connor.

casual, sinuous, evocative quality that distinguishes it from poetry and is intended to link author and reader in a common perception of the object, and replaces it by a series of verbal rituals which are intended to evoke the object as it may be supposed to be. At an extreme point it attempts to substitute the image for the reality. It is a rhetorician's dream.

But when you really know *A Portrait of the Artist as a Young Man* you recognize exactly where the beautiful opening of Hemingway's "In Another Country" came from.

> In the *fall* the war was always there, but we did not go to it any more. It was *cold* in the *fall* in Milan, and the dark came very early. Then the electric lights came on, and it was pleasant along the streets looking in the windows. There was much game hanging outside the shops, and the snow powdered in the fur of the foxes and the *wind blew* their tails. The deer hung stiff and heavy and empty, and small birds *blew* in the *wind*, and the *wind* turned their feathers. It was a *cold fall* and the *wind* came down from the mountains.

There! You have realized how cold and windy it was that fall in Milan, haven't you? And it didn't really hurt, did it? Even if you were not very interested to begin with, you have learned one or two very important things that you might otherwise have ignored. Quite seriously, this is something you don't recall from other famous passages of literature, written by predecessors of Joyce and Hemingway, because in neither of these passages is there what you could call a human voice speaking, nobody resembling yourself who is trying to persuade you to share in an experience of his own, and whom you can imagine yourself questioning about its nature—nothing but an old magician sitting over his crystal ball, or a hypnotist waving his hands gently before your eyes and muttering, "You are falling asleep; you are falling asleep; slowly, slowly your eyes are beginning to close; your eyelids are growing heavy; you are—falling—asleep."

Though Joyce was the most important single influence on Hemingway, and one can trace him even in little pedantries like placing the adverb immediately after the verb when usage requires it either to precede the verb or to follow the object, as in "he poured smoothly the buckwheat batter," he was not the only influence. Gertrude Stein and her experiments with language were also of some importance. Her experiments—usually rather absurd ones —were intended to produce a simplification of prose technique like the simplification of forms that we find in the work of certain modern painters. Her mistake—a blatant vulgarization of Joyce's fundamental mistake—was to ignore the fact that prose is a very impure art. Any art which formally is practically indistinguishable from a memorandum issued by a government office is necessarily impure. "Prosaic" is a term of abuse, though in fact it should have a connotation as noble as "poetic."

As practiced by Hemingway, this literary method, compounded of simplification and repetition, is the opposite of that we learned in our schooldays. We were taught to consider it a fault to repeat a noun and shown how to avoid it by the use of pronouns and synonyms. This led to another fault that Fowler christened "elegant variation." The fault of Hemingway's method might be called "elegant repetition." His most elaborate use of it is in "Big Two-Hearted River."

> There was no underbrush in the island of *pine trees*. The *trunks* of the *trees* went straight up or slanted toward each other. The *trunks* were straight and *brown* without *branches*. The *branches* were *high above*. Some interlocked to make a solid *shadow* on the *brown forest floor*. Around the grove of *trees* was a bare space. It was *brown* and soft underfoot as Nick walked on it. This was the over-lapping of the *pine*-needle *floor*, extending out beyond the width of the *high branches*. The *trees* had grown tall and the *branches* moved *high*, leaving in the sun this bare space they had once covered with *shadow*. Sharp at the edge of this extension of the *forest floor* commenced the sweet fern.
>
> Nick slipped off his pack and lay down in the *shade*. He lay on his *back* and looked up into the *pine trees*. His neck and *back* and the small of his *back* rested as he stretched. The earth felt good against his *back*. He looked up at the sky, through the *branches*, and then shut his eyes. He opened them and looked up again. There was a wind *high* up in the *branches*. He shut his eyes again and went to sleep.

This is part of an extraordinarily complex and simple-minded literary experiment in which Hemingway sets out to duplicate in prose a fishing trip in wooded country, and it is constructed with a minute vocabulary of a few dozen words, like "water," "current," "stream," "trees," "branches," and "shadow." It is an elaboration of the device I have pointed out in *A Portrait of the Artist as a Young Man*. In some ways it anticipates Joyce's "Anna Livia Plurabelle" though in general it resembles more an experiment in Basic English. The curious thing is that I have worked with scores of young Americans—people who knew their Hemingway far better than I did—and they had never noticed the device. Perhaps this is what Hemingway and Joyce intended; perhaps I read them in the wrong way, but I do not know of any other way to read prose. And I feel quite sure that even Joyce would have thought "Big Two-Hearted River" a vulgarization of his rhetorician's dream.

However, Hemingway went one better than his master when he realized that precisely the same technique could be applied to dramatic interludes, and that the repetition of key words and phrases in these could produce a similar simplification with a similar hypnotic effect. Where Joyce writes "the other hand careered in the treble after each group of notes. The notes of the air sounded deep and full" Hemingway will write:

> "You oughtn't to ever do anything too long."
> "No, we were up there too long."
> "Too damn long," John said. "It's no good doing a thing too long."

This is a new thing in storytelling, and it is worth considering at some length. There is a fairly straight-forward example in "Hills Like White Elephants," a story in which a man tries to persuade his mistress to have an abortion. There are certain key words in the dialogue like "simple" and key phrases like "I don't want you to do it if you don't want to."

> "Well," the man said, "*if you don't want to* you don't have to. I wouldn't have you *do it if you didn't want to.* But I know it's *perfectly simple.*"
> "And *you really want to?*"
> "I think it's the best thing to do. But *I don't want you to do it if you don't really want to.*"
> "And *if I do it* you'll be happy and things will be like they were and *you'll love me?*"
> "*I love you now.* You know *I love you.*"
> "I know. But *if I do it*, then it will be nice again if I say things are like white elephants, and you'll like it."
> "*I'll love it. I love it now* but I just can't think about it. You know how I get *when I worry.*"
> "*If I do it you won't ever worry?*"
> "*I won't worry about that* because it's *perfectly simple.*"
> "Then *I'll do it.* Because *I don't care about me.*"
> "What do you mean?"
> "*I don't care about me.*"
> "*Well, I care about you.*"
> "Oh, yes. But *I don't care about me.* And *I'll do it* and then everything will be fine."
> "*I don't want you to do it* if you feel that way."

The advantages and disadvantages of a style like this are about evenly divided. The principal advantage is clear. Nobody is ever likely to get the impression that he is accidentally reading a government memorandum or a shorthand report of a trial. If Goethe is right in saying that art is art because it is not nature, this is art. Even in very good stylists of the older school of storytelling there is often a marked struggle at the beginning of the story before the author can detach himself from what is not storytelling and the story becomes airborne, a paragraph or more of fumbling prose like the tuning up of an orchestra; but in Hemingway the element of stylization cuts off the very first sentence from whatever is not storytelling, so that it rings out loud and clear like music cutting across silence. Turgenev's "Living Relic" begins with the words "A French proverb runs: 'A dry fisherman and a wet hunter present a sorry sight.' Never having had any predilection for fishing . . ."—a leisurely enough opening in the manner of his period. Chekhov's "Sleepy" begins with the single word "Night," which is more urgent through perhaps a little trite. The first sentence of "In Another Country" is a perfect opening phrase, mannered enough to jolt the reader awake without making him go to see if the front door is locked: "In the fall the war was always there, but we did not go to it any more." In the same way, when Hemingway ends a story it stays ended, without giving us the feeling that perhaps we have bought a defective copy.

The obvious disadvantage is that it tends to blur the sharp contrast that should ideally exist between narrative and drama, the two forms of which storytelling is compounded. Ideally, the former should be subjective and persuasive, the latter objective and compulsive. In one the storyteller suggests to the reader what he believes happened, in the other he proves to him that this in fact is how it did happen. In a good story the two aspects are nearly always kept in balance. In a Hemingway story drama, because it is stylized in the same way as the narrative, tends to lose its full impact. Dialogue, the autonomous element of drama, begins to blur, and the conversation becomes more like the conversation of alcoholics, drug addicts, or experts in Basic English. In Joyce's "Grace," the author's irony gives the conversation of the men in the sick room the same dull, claustrophobic quality, but there one can excuse it on the ground that his aim is comic. There is no such excuse for the conversation in Hemingway's story.

Of course you may say if you please that the drama there is implicit rather than explicit, and that it is made sufficiently clear that the man does not love the girl—after all he indicates it by saying "I love you now" and "I love it now" too close together—and that she knows it and is offering up her unborn child for the sake of a man she feels sure will leave her, but the dialogue by which two people communicate or try to communicate with one another is missing. And here, I think, we may be touching on a weakness in both Joyce and Hemingway. To the rhetorician dialogue must so often seem unnecessary since he knows so many ingenious ways of evading it.

Not that Hemingway often took his rhetoric to the fair as Joyce did. In fact, if we exclude "Big Two-Hearted River," which is only a caricature of a literary method, there never was much of the real experimenter in him. He was a practical writer, not a research worker, and he took from the research workers like Joyce and Gertrude Stein only what he felt he needed, in the spirit of an American efficiency expert studying the tests of a group of scientists to discover how he can knock a second or two off the time it takes to move a lever. When you compare the passage I have quoted from *A Portrait of the Artist as a Young Man* with the passage from "In Another Country," you can see that Joyce is already letting his own theory run away with him, while Hemingway uses precisely as much of it as he needs to create the effect that he himself has in mind.

In fact, from a purely technical point of view, no other writer of the twentieth century was so splendidly equipped. He could take an incident—any incident, no matter how thin or trivial—and by his skill as a writer turn it into something one read thirty years ago and can still read today with admiration and pleasure.

One can see his skill better when the material *is* skimpy and he has to rely on his ability as a writer. There is nothing in "Che Ti Dice La Patria" that could not have been observed just as well by any journalist reporting on a hasty trip through Fascist Italy—someone is rude, a young man in a shady restaurant says that the two Americans are "worth nothing," an insolent policeman holds them up for fifty lire, that is all—but no journalist could have given us the same feeling of the sinister quality of life in Italy at the time. And when Hemingway ends his description of it in a final poker-faced sentence it stays ended—"Naturally, in such a short trip we had no opportunity to see how things were with the country or the people." "Fifty Grand" is just about as dull a subject as a writer's heart could desire but the story itself can still be reread.

But the real trouble with Hemingway is that he so often has to depend upon his splendid technical equipment to cover up material that is trivial or sensational. For much of the time his stories illustrate a technique in search of a subject. In the general sense of the word Hemingway has no subject. Faulkner shows a passion for technical experiment not unlike Hemingway's, and, like Hemingway's picked up in Paris cafés over a copy of *transition*, but at once he tries to transplant it to Yoknapatawpha County. Sometimes, let us admit, it looks as inappropriate there as a Paris hat on one of the Snopes women, but at least, if we don't like the hat we can get something out of the woman it disguises. Hemingway, on the other hand, is always a displaced person; he has no place to bring his treasures to.

There are times when one feels that Hemingway, like the character in his own "A Clean Well-Lighted Place," is afraid of staying at home with a subject. In his stories one is forever coming upon that characteristic setting of the café, the station restaurant, the waiting room, or the railway carriage—clean, well-lighted, utterly anonymous places. The characters, equally anonymous, emerge suddenly from the shadows where they have been lurking, perform their little scene, and depart again into shadows. Of course, one has to realize that there is a very good technical reason for this. The short story, which is always trying to differentiate itself from the novel and avoid being bogged down in the slow, chronological sequence of events where the novel is supreme, is also seeking a point outside time from which past and future can be viewed simultaneously, and so the *wagon lit* setting of "A Canary for One" represents a point at which wife and husband are still traveling together though already apart—"we were returning to Paris to set up separate residences"—and the railway station setting of "Hills Like White Elephants" the point where the abortion that must change everything for the lovers has already been decided on though it has not yet taken place. The story looks backward and forward, backward to the days when the girl said that the hills were like white elephants and the man was pleased, and forward to a dreary future in which she will never be able to say a thing like that again.

But though this is perfectly true, it forces us to ask whether the technique is not limiting the short-story form so as to reduce it to an essentially minor art. Any realistic art is necessarily a marriage between the importance of the material and the importance of the artistic treatment, but how much of the importance of the material can possibly seep through such rigid artistic control? What has happened to the familiar element in it? If this girl, Jig, is not American, what is she? Does she have parents in England or Ireland or Australia, brothers or sisters, a job, a home to go back to, if against all the indications she decides to have this baby? And the man? Is there any compelling human reason why he should feel that an abortion is necessary or is he merely destructive by nature?

Once more, I know the formal answer to all these questions: that Hemingway's aim is to suppress mere information such as I require so as to concentrate my attention on the one important thing which is the abortion. I know that Hemingway has been influenced by the German Expressionists as well as by Joyce and Gertrude Stein, and that he is reducing (or enlarging) these two people into the parts they would play in a German Expressionist tragedy—*Der Mann* and *Die Frau*—and their problem into the tragedy itself—*Das Fehlgebären*. But I must respectfully submit that I am not German, and that I have no experience of Man, Woman, or Abortion in capital letters.

I submit that there are drawbacks to this method. It is all too abstract. Nobody in Hemingway ever seems to have a job or a home unless the job or the home fits into the German scheme of capital letters. Everybody seems to be permanently on holiday or getting a divorce, or as *Die Frau* in "Hills Like White Elephants" puts it, "That's all we do, isn't it—look at things and try new drinks?" Even in the Wisconsin stories it comes as a relief when Nick's father keeps himself out of harm's way for an hour or two by attending to his profession as doctor.

Even the submerged population that Hemingway writes of is one that is associated with recreation rather than with labor—waiters, barmen, boxers, jockeys, bullfighters, and the like. Paco in "The Capital of the World" is a waiter with a soul above waitering, and he dies by accident in an imitation bullfight that I find comic rather than pathetic. In the later stories the neurotic restlessness has developed out of the earlier fishing and shooting into horse racing, prize fighting, bull fighting, and big-game hunting. Even war is treated as recreation, an amusement for the leisured classes. In these stories practically no single virtue is discussed with the exception of physical courage, which from the point of view of people without an independent income is usually merely a theoretical virtue. Except in war it has little practical application, and even in war the working classes tend to regard it with a certain cynicism: the hero of the regiment is rarely a hero to the regiment.

In Hemingway the obsession with physical courage is clearly a personal problem, like Turgenev's obsession with his own futility, and it must be recognized and discounted as such if one is not to emerge from one's reading with a ludicrously distorted impression of human life. In "The Short Happy Life of Francis Macomber" Francis runs away from a lion, which is what most sensible men would do if faced by a lion, and his wife promptly cuckolds him with the English manager of their big-game hunting expedition. As we all know, good wives admire nothing in a husband except his capacity to deal with lions, so we can sympathize with the poor woman in her trouble. But next day Macomber, faced with a buffalo, suddenly becomes a man of superb courage, and his wife, recognizing that Cressida's occupation's gone and that for the future she must be a virtuous wife, blows his head off. Yet the title leaves us with the comforting assurance that the triumph is still Macomber's, for, in spite of his sticky end, he had at last learned the only way of keeping his wife out of other men's beds.

To say that the psychology of this story is childish would be to waste good words. As farce it ranks with "Ten Nights in a Bar-Room" or any other Victorian morality you can think of. Clearly, it is the working out of a personal problem that for the vast majority of men and women has no validity whatever.

It may be too early to draw any conclusions about Hemingway's work: certainly it is too early for one like myself who belongs to the generation that he influenced most deeply. In a charitable mood, I sometimes find myself thinking of the clean well-lighted place as the sort of stage on which Racine's heroes and heroines appear, free of contact with common things, and carrying on their lofty discussions of what to Racine seemed most important. The rest of the time I merely ask myself if this wonderful technique of Hemingway's is really a technique in search of a subject or a technique that is carefully avoiding a subject, and searching anxiously all the time for a clean well-lighted place where all the difficulties of human life can be comfortably ignored.

Point of View in the Nick Adams Stories / *Carl Ficken*

Despite the succession of heroes from Jake Barnes to Thomas Hudson, one of Ernest Hemingway's most interesting characters remains his first creation, Nick Adams. The later heroes may seem tougher, more like the image Hemingway was building for himself; but Nick Adams has special qualities which make him stand out as one of Hemingway's most fully-revealed characters. Through a dozen short stories mentioning his name, Nick Adams grows as a person of rare sensitivity and self-perception: He is a loyal son, a wandering youth, a soldier briefly, a hospital patient, a sportsman, a father; he is capable of great friendships and he is something of a loner; he is one who has made many discoveries about life and has finally suffered a shocking wound; he is a thinker—not a sophisticated intellectual, but a man who tries to understand what has happened to him. Naturally, Hemingway must do many things well to achieve his success with Nick Adams; one of his major accomplishments is that he employs a narrative perspective which keeps the focus constantly on the hero and allows the hero to tell his own tale.

I

Early critics of Hemingway did not pay too much attention either to the Nick Adams stories as a whole or to Hemingway's handling of point of view; yet, when he published a first-person novel, he was readily identified with his protagonist. It may be that the use of the third person in the earlier stories was a sufficient fake to keep critics off the autobiographical trail: One result was that Hemingway's image began to develop more in relationship to Jake Barnes than to Nick Adams. The Baker biography and Philip Young's studies of Nick Adams have successfully demonstrated that the Nick stories grew out of Hemingway's childhood memories, his boyhood adventures and his war experiences. Baker is able to show, with almost every story, a parallel between Hemingway's life and Nick's. In some cases, it is just that Hemingway's father was a doctor and that they lived near an Indian camp in the summers; in others, it is that Hemingway's father did commit suicide, and that Hemingway himself did experience a serious wound which he either felt to be, or made to be, traumatic.[1]

None of this is to say that Nick Adams is Ernest Hemingway or that these stories are a "Portrait of the Artist." Hemingway did bring to the stories a

Carl Ficken, "Point of View in the Nick Adams Stories," *Fitzgerald/Hemingway Annual, 1971*, Matthew J. Bruccoli and C. E. Frazer Clark, Jr., eds. (Washington, D.C.: N.C.R. Microcard Editions, 1971), 212–35. Copyright © 1971 by The National Cash Register Company. Reprinted by permission of Microcard Editions.

fertile imagination: he created Nick Adams, not *ex nihilo*, but out of both his life and his strong, imaginative powers. Nonetheless, the author's hand is deeply involved in this character: All through the stories the relationship between author-narrator-character is especially close. It was important for Hemingway to "write out" of himself the Nick stories, just as it was important for Nick to camp and fish and cook out his problems. As Professor Young has noted, Nick is, for Hemingway, a "special kind of mask." [2] Clearly, Hemingway always stands right behind his narrator no matter who that narrator might be, but in the Nick stories a side of the writer's own personality shows through, a side which he apparently at other times attempted to cover over with his inevitable bravado.[3]

At the beginning of his writing career in the 1920s, Hemingway was working at, among other things, the problem of point of view. In his first publication, *Three Stories and Ten Poems*, 1923, he told two of the stories through an omniscient third-person narrator and the other in the first person; "My Old Man," in fact, remains one of the classic examples of the unreliable, first-person narrator. Of the *in our time* sketches, one half are in the first person and one half in third person; of the *In Our Time* interchapters, six are first person and ten are in some form of third person; three of the *In Our Time* stories are in the first person, the rest in a variety of third-person forms. And, of course, the first two novels are told by their main character, although Hemingway did attempt to rewrite *The Sun Also Rises* in the third person.[4] What is most significant about all this is that, throughout the period in which most of the Nick Adams stories were written, Hemingway was working from a variety of narrative perspectives and had already begun to establish his primary point-of-view techniques.[5]

In the Nick Adams stories, written over a span of ten years, Hemingway worked out a means of relating point of view to the development of character—that is his essential achievement in the handling of narrative perspective in these stories. Besides that, of course, he demonstrates great versatility. His treatment is by no means simple or clear-cut; no two stories are exactly alike in point of view. A study of Hemingway's technique in the Nick Adams stories, limited to those stories in which Nick's name is specifically mentioned, reveals a definite correlation between Nick's own state of mind and the degree to which the narrator probes into that mind. As a general rule, subjectivity intensifies in the stories around Nick's traumatic wound. In the earlier stories, when Nick is younger and less capable of understanding what is happening to him, the point of view is more objective, so that the reader knows less of what Nick is thinking; in the stories around the wound, the narrative perspective is most complex and Hemingway departs most decisively from an easily identified point of view; then, as Nick grows past the wound, a measure of objectivity returns. It isn't quite that simple, of course, because "The Killers," in which the narrator is almost absent—the most objective story, in other words—takes place when Nick is in his teens; and, the earliest story, "Indian Camp," offers a brief, but crucial, insight into Nick's thoughts. Yet, if the stories were listed on a scale of increasing subjectivity in point of view, the wound-recovery stories would be at the subjective end of the scale. Or, the stories might be placed on a scale which moves toward and then away from subjectivity, toward and then away from the wound. On such a scale only at two places are the stories out of line chronologically, even though they were neither written nor did they appear in this order.[6] None of this is to suggest, of course, that Hemingway consciously plotted such a development or that he was aware in every story of this relationship between point of view and character development. Yet examination of the stories reveals that Hemingway matched his narrative perspective with his hero's mental state—no small accomplishment for a writer in his late twenties, consciously done or not.

In part, it is the fact that Hemingway is working at point of view with such special skill that makes a study of the problem worth while. He is experimenting with point of view; he is working at getting into the mind of his character, just as were his contemporaries. Many of Hemingway's stories, with the distinctive point of view, were written in the years between the celebrated examples of point of view innovation: Joyce's *A Portrait of the Artist as a Young Man* and *Ulysses* in 1916 and 1919, Virginia Woolf's *To the Lighthouse* in 1927, and Faulkner's *The Sound and the Fury* in 1929. Yet, Hemingway's point-of-view technique has received little notice: In the more than forty years since the first Nick stories and the first-person novels, one general study[7] and one analysis of point of view in *The Sun Also Rises*[8] have appeared; a few stories raise occasional comment,[9] but for the most part Hemingway's treatment of point of view is neglected by the critics. Perhaps Hemingway's work with narrative perspective is not the most brilliant achievement of the century—one must not claim *too* much, after all—but careful study of these stories indicates that he was extremely diligent in striving for precise points of view and that he came up with something, if not new, at least significantly different from the usual literary patterns. The problem in talking about it is to say just *how* it is different.

II

One of the difficulties in discussing point of view is that of finding the precise defining terminology. It seems as though every scholar who dares to talk about the subject employs a different set of terms.[10] Clearly, the most traditional terms (first person, third person, omniscient author) do not begin to make sufficiently sharp distinctions for a great deal of modern literature; it is understandable that critics should seek new labels to capture the subtle variations of narrative perspective, but the result is additional confusion in terminology. Indeed, when one tries to apply the terms from any one general discussion of the subject to a specific author, he finds that the categories don't fit, that they don't cover the individual effects achieved by that author. Hemingway, for example, has at least three different kinds of third-person narration in the Nick Adams stories; traditional labels do not work neatly with those stories.

Still, discussion is impossible without identifying terms. Rather than invent a new set, I have chosen those terms which apply most directly to Hemingway's techniques and which can serve as fairly easy handles for this study. These stories, again, do not fit perfectly into any categories; it is more accurate to see them on a subjective-objective scale. Nonetheless, the shades of difference between the narrators need to be clarified, insofar as that is possible. Four general categories of narrator seem to work in these stories (in each category a brief quotation from one of the stories will serve as a temporary identification of the type of narration). The "Effaced Narrator" is one who merely observes the action but cannot see into the minds of the characters; this is the objective end of the scale and is represented in the Nick Adams stories only by "The Killers" ("From the other end of the counter Nick Adams watched them."[11]). The "Author-Observer" is an omniscient author in that he may know what is in the mind of more than one character at any given time, but he is a mere observer in that he reports only what is immediately before him ("Marjorie . . . loved to fish with Nick . . . . He was afraid to look at her"[13]). The "Center of Consciousness" is a narrator who reflects the mind of one central intelligence (here, Nick himself), albeit with varying intensity ("Nick's hand was shaky. He reeled in slowly . . . . He'd bet the trout was angry . . . . That was a trout . . . . By God, he was the biggest one I ever heard of"). The "Narrator-Agent" is, of course, the first-person narrator telling his own story ("That night we lay on the floor in the room and I listened to the silk-worms eating,"[14]). Of these four forms, the Effaced Narrator is farthest from the central character's mind and the Narrator-Agent is, naturally, closest.

Such variation in point of view is a way of adding dimension to the character of Nick Adams. If the reader sees Nick both from an objective narrator's position and as Nick sees himself, then the reader has a deeper, more rounded insight into the character. Such a perspective is not usually possible since one of the rules of the writing game is that point of view must be consistent; because Hemingway is writing short stories, however, and because he is willing to play with the "Center of Consciousness" narration, he gains additional development of his hero.

At the same time, through all the movement in point of view, Hemingway manages to maintain Nick's place as the central character of the stories. However far the reader or narrator stands from Nick, however little he knows of Nick's thoughts, Nick remains the key figure. Hemingway accomplishes this, not only thematically by making the meaning of the story rest with Nick, but also by keeping a spot focus on Nick, mentioning his name, identifying other characters through their relationship to him, giving brief, almost imperceptible, insights into Nick's actions. This identification of Nick as the central character, in other words, increases as the narrator comes nearer Nick's mind; but even when the narrator is barely there, when he is most effaced, the reader is still made conscious of Nick's presence. To discuss Hemingway's narrators in the order of their distance from the protagonist is to watch a camera gradually move in, closer and closer to Nick Adams. The following study will progress from the objective toward the subjective: It will begin with the Effaced Narrator of "The Killers" and then discuss the Author-Observer, the Center of Consciousness and the Narrator-Agent.

III

Effaced Narrator

"The Killers" often serves as the primary illustration of a point-of-view technique common to Hemingway and other twentieth century writers.[15] It is an especially fine example of the Effaced Narrator, since it has narration reduced to a minimum, few descriptive sentences, little stage direction, nothing added to the simple "he said," and considerable dialogue. If the story were to be made into a play, no "narrator" off-stage would be necessary to tie the action together, nor would there be any authorial direction to tell actors how to say their lines; in fact, there is less "authorial intrusion" in this story than there is in most drama (even Becket cannot resist an occasional "violently," or "indifferently"). The narrator is practically effaced.[16]

All this is true. And yet, in "The Killers," the narrator is only *practically* effaced. Hemingway allows the narrator enough power to put an occasional spotlight on Nick Adams. The story is a good example of the Effaced Narrator, but the author has made some exceptions in the technique, not so as to mar the story's effectiveness, but so as to place Nick Adams unambiguously at the center. The exceptions to the rule, then, are worth noting. The story opens with a closeup of Henry's lunchroom; clearly an observer of that first scene description is necessary and that observer—or Effaced Narrator, as he should be called to avoid confusion with the next category—stands inside the lunchroom. "The door of Henry's lunch-room opened and two men *came in*. They sat down at the counter" (italics mine).[11] After an initial, conventional exchange between the waiter, George, and his customers, the Effaced Narrator again provides description, again from the inside: "Outside it was getting dark. The street-light came on outside the window." Then the focus shifts to Nick: "From the other end of the counter Nick Adams watched them. He had been talking to George when they came in." That sentence

provides a focus on Nick, a still-shot showing what Nick is and has been doing, and the focus is accentuated by the use of his full name. Yet, obviously,
the vantage point for the observations rests outside Nick: The Effaced Narrator stands so that he is able to see both ends of the counter. The following
conversation is reported objectively, with only brief comment by the Effaced
Narrator about the actions or external appearance of the characters. Even in
straight dialogue lines, attention falls on Nick when the killers ask for his
name, a question they do not direct to George. Even when Nick is off-stage
and the external action rests with George, what is happening to Nick, tied up
in the kitchen, is more important and represents a more shaking experience
than what happens to George: Nick, after all, "had never had a towel in his
mouth before." [17]

Through it all, the Effaced Narrator stays with the central action of the
story and never reveals anything of what could be in anyone's mind, except
through dialogue. The only line suggesting Nick's feeling is the one in which
the narrator said: "It sounded silly when he said it." [18] That can, of course,
be taken objectively too: The Effaced Narrator is not saying that it sounded
silly to Nick so much as that it sounded silly to him, or to any observer.
Finally, the Effaced Narrator reveals what Nick saw, and by implication
what he felt, as he left Ole: The fully dressed fighter was "lying on the bed
looking at the wall." [19] Nothing in these examples breaks the rules of this
kind of narration; but, within this approach, Hemingway is also able to place
Nick sufficiently forward in the account so that the meaning of the story has
to do with Nick's discovery of what life is like through those killers and Ole
Andreson's reaction to them. This narrator is not so "effaced" then as to be
nonexistent: the author's hand is clearly there directing steady, if gentle, attention to Nick Adams.

Author-Observer

The next step in the narrowing focus is to allow the narrator to look into
the minds of the characters. Such a narrator, identified as an Author-
Observer, handles "The Doctor and the Doctor's Wife," "The End of Something," and "Indian Camp." The former story is the only one wherein the
observer has no access at all to Nick's thoughts, but does have some ability
to see into the minds of the characters. The Author-Observer of this story
also follows the central action from its beginning when Dick Boulton and
two Indian boys come into the Adams's yard to "cut up logs for Nick's
father." [20] The story continues objectively until the Author-Observer provides a small inside view of Dick Boulton: "He knew how big a man he was.
He liked to get into fights. He was happy." [21] The Author-Observer stays with
Dick and the boys until they leave the grounds; then he picks up the doctor
inside the cottage. The Author-Observer is able to know that the doctor is

"irritated"[21] about a pile of unopened medical journals, that he was "very fond"[22] of his gun, but no more than that can the reader discover apart from the objective report of action. Finally, in the last sentence of the story the doctor comes upon Nick in the woods reading and that's the first time Nick has been in the story. About Nick nothing can be known except that he prefers to go hunting with his father rather than to obey his mother's call, and that he knows how to find some black squirrels.

The difficulty with this story is that Nick is so far out of the action: He is in no sense the central character of the story; no evidence in the story suggests that Nick witnessed either one of his father's encounters that day. Some critics seem to assume that Nick did hear all this and that he was consequently initiated further into the nature of his father and mother, that he made discoveries about his parents[23]; but the text says quite plainly that the doctor went out the gate—through which Dick Boulton had entered the grounds at the beginning of the story—and followed a path into the hemlock woods where he found Nick. The boy could have witnessed both scenes, of course, and hurried back to the woods so that no one would know, but nothing in the story supports such an hypothesis. Hemingway does keep the focus on Nick by identifying the doctor at the outset as Nick's father; in fact, until Dick Boulton calls him "Doc" a full page into the story, the reader only knows of "Nick's father." It would seem then that the story is about Nick's father, and about his mother; Nick did not have to see what happened that day: The story presents for the reader the conditions under which Nick grows up. His discovery about his father and mother is no sudden thing, sprung upon him by observing these two incidents; it is a gradual awareness of what those two people are like and what they are doing to one another and that knowledge shapes him as surely as any of the initiations through which he must go. The narrative perspective of the story, through a fairly objective Author-Observer, keeps Nick in the reader's mind, simply by the use of his name and, at the same time, allows for a brief focus on Nick's parents and the role they have played in the boy's development.

Nick is the central character in "The End of Something," but the Author-Observer reveals just a little of what is in the minds of both Nick and Marjorie. He tells us that Marjorie "was intent on the rod all the time they trolled."[12] that she "loved to fish with Nick"[12]; further, Marjorie responded "happily" to Nick's rather matter-of-fact announcement that there would be a moon. Nick's attitude throughout the early moments of the story contrasts sharply, of course, with Marjorie's, but the reader knows about that mainly through Nick's actions and the flats and sharps of his conversation. Only by slight touches does the Author-Observer let us know what Nick knows: That the moon would soon rise, that he "was afraid to look at Marjorie,"[13] that he heard and "felt" Bill's approach. Since the story is about the break-up of Nick and Marjorie and about Nick's reaction to that break-up, it is important that the reader be able to see into the minds of both parties, even if only in such slight glimpses. It is important to know that Marjorie was happy in the relationship, that Nick was the one who took action; and the Author-Observer can do that most economically and with less strain on the dialogue, by allowing some insight into Marjorie's mind. The focus stays, finally, on Nick, inasmuch as he is the one whom the Author-Observer chooses to watch after the separation; but, the double focus at the beginning helps to enforce the sense of separation once Nick is left in the spotlight.

"Indian Camp" really belongs to this category, too, although its final sentence represents a deeper penetration into Nick's thoughts than exists in any of these first three Nick stories. It is, of course, the first story chronologically, but it belongs in this position on the objective-subjective scale because of that final look into Nick's mind. The final words of the story indicate that Nick "felt quite sure that he would never die"[24]; such a reflection by the Author-Observer parallels the language of the Center of Consciousness. While the last words qualify this story for the Center category, the rest of the story belongs to an Author-Observer; for that reason the story falls at the end of this category.

Up to that last sentence, the Author-Observer tells only what any person watching the action could assume: the facts that Nick "heard" the oarlocks,[25] that his "curiosity" about the childbirth ran out,[26] that he "felt" the warmth of the lake water,[24] that the doctor was "satisfied" with the cleanliness of his hands, that he felt and then lost "post-operative exhilaration"[27]—all these facts could be reasonable guesses by any observer. The last sentence, however, is more than a guess; it represents Nick's own thoughts, his reaction to what he had seen: "In the early morning on the lake sitting in the stern of the boat with his father rowing, he felt quite sure that he would never die."[24] That one sentence, by an Author-Observer who is able to read Nick's mind, not only attaches this story to Nick Adams, but also has thematic significance for the whole series of stories. It is the first instance of Nick Adams as a Center of Consciousness, a hint of the way Nick's thoughts were later to capture his stories. The focus of the story is kept on Nick—despite the fact that the Author-Observer allows fleeting gazes into the doctor's thoughts too—by having his name begin the third sentence of the story and by identifying the other two main characters through their relationship to Nick: "Uncle George" and "Nick's father." In fact, Nick's father is identified as the "doctor" only four times, after the birth and while Nick is at some distance from the action.

Center of Consciousness

With "Three-Day Blow" the narrative technique of the Nick Adams stories turns sharply and with increasing depth into the personality of the protagonist. Providing almost the same effect as first-person narration, these stories offer, in varying degrees, an inside view of Nick's mind and are presented by a narrator who may best be identified as a Center of Consciousness: a narrator who sometimes stands apart from Nick and reports his actions, but who also sometimes stands within Nick and expresses Nick's mental process as though it were unmediated. It is this latter effect which muddies the point-of-view waters. Traditionally, the term "Center of Consciousness" applies to a work in which the narrator speaks of the main character in the third person, yet knows as much as that character knows. What is most significant about Hemingway's development of this narrative perspective is that he brings into the narration first- and second-person accounts in order—and this is the heart of the matter—in order to gain further penetration into the mind of the character.

"The Three-Day Blow" is a good example of a story in which the narrative focus rests clearly with Nick, moving from time to time inside his mind, behind his eyes, yet without the intense introspection of the later stories. Even though the story is mainly dialogue, Hemingway works at establishing the sensory perceptions of Nick, so that the reader is kept aware of what Nick sees, hears, feels, as well as what he thinks. When Bill leaves the room, Nick is the Center who notes: "He went out to the kitchen and came back"[28]; another observer could say that "They sat in front of the fire,"[28] but then so could Nick say, "We sat in front of the fire." Such a positioning of characters does not depend upon a neutral observer or an Effaced Narrator, as does the placement of Nick at "the other end of the counter" in "The Killers." Further, when Bill leaves the room a second time, Nick hears him walking overhead[28]; and when Nick leaves the room, we follow him and are aware of his every action.[29, 30] The reader sees, as Nick sees, Bill pouring a drink: "Bill reached down the whisky bottle. His big hand went all the way around it. He poured the whisky into the glass Nick held out."[31] That is distinctly Nick's view of the scene, a view from the Center.

The total effect of the story is increased by the fact that Hemingway never really goes to Bill: The reader never knows what Bill thinks, except as Nick might guess it, as when he thinks of Bill, "He was also being consciously practical."[29] The directions for Bill's part of the conversation are consistently limited to "he said," whereas Nick "confesses" or asks "respectfully" or says "sadly."[29] This narrative perspective is strengthened in the middle of the story when Nick has had quite a bit to drink: the liquor tells on Nick, the Center, when he comes through the kitchen with a log and knocks a pan from the table. In the description of picking up his mess and then a moment later in the account of his passing the mirror, there is a sense of slowed reaction; the narrative is told not by a sober observer, but by a slightly tipsy Nick:

He laid the log down and picked up the pan. It had contained dried apricots, soaking in water. He carefully picked up all the apricots off the floor, some of them had gone under the stove, and put them back in the pan. He dipped some more water onto them from the pail by the table. He felt quite proud of himself. He had been thoroughly practical.[29, 30]

Then later, Nick

went out into the kitchen again. He filled the pitcher with the dipper dipping cold spring water from the pail. On his way back to the living room he passed a mirror in the dining room and looked in it. His face looked strange. He smiled at the face in the mirror and it grinned back at him. He winked at it and went on. It was not his face but it didn't make any difference.[30]

Hemingway, therefore, establishes Nick as the Center of Consciousness both by revealing his thoughts and by providing an impression of his sensory responses.

"Ten Indians" follows a pattern which becomes familiar in the stories: an opening setting Nick up as the central character, a body largely in dialogue, and a conclusion focusing sharply on Nick's thoughts. Again "Nick" is the subject of the first sentence and we learn immediately that he "remembered" how many Indians he had seen on his way home with the Garners after a Fourth of July ball game. In the dialogue and the brief descriptive paragraphs, Nick *sees* the lights of Petoskey[32] (a neutral observer can reveal what a character looks at but not what he sees); he feels "hollow and happy inside" when he is teased about Prudie[32]; he hears his father moving in another room.[33] Further, the action is always with Nick: His father "brought in" the food, later "went out" of the kitchen, then "came back" and the reader knows of Nick's father's movements only what Nick himself can observe. The final paragraphs of the story show Nick's reaction to the news he has received about Prudie's "infidelity"; his thought about the matter is fairly objective and subdued, but the reader is told that Nick heard and felt the cool night wind and that he finally "forgot to think about Prudence."[33] Only Nick himself could say, "he was awake a long time before he remembered that his heart was broken."[33] Even though this story was published outside the *In Our Time* sequences, its narrative technique places it properly on the objective-subjective scale for this time in Nick's life.

In "The Battler" the narrative perspective undergoes a subtle shift: The Center of Consciousness is more thoroughly revealed, is more apparent to the reader, through the use of what I shall call an indirect first person. The core of this technique, so essential to Hemingway's development of point of view, lies in sentences which stand apart from a "he thought" introduction, sentences which stand alone as thoughts of the Center, framed the way his mind would formulate them. The third paragraph of the story, for example, illustrates this variation in the usual third-person pattern:

That lousy crut of a brakeman. He would get him some day. He would know him again. That was a fine way to act.[34]

In that paragraph, the second and third sentences are proper for a third-person narrator, the "He" referring to Nick; but the first and last sentences are Nick talking to himself, they represent what he said, even though they are not quoted and not introduced by "he said." Further, the report of what the brakeman had said to him can come only as Nick tells it. Whenever, in fact, Nick begins to talk about another man, the pronoun "he" may refer to himself or to the other man:

"Come here, kid," he said. "I got something for you."
He had fallen for it. What a lousy kid thing to have done.[34]

That first line comes directly from Nick and is much clearer and simpler than had an observer had to say something like, "He remembered that the brakeman had said, 'Come here, kid.' " The second "he" obviously refers to Nick and the sentence could just as easily read, "I had fallen for it. What a lousy kid thing to have done." Inasmuch as the latter sentence remains the same in either case, it represents, again, an indirect first person.

The next few descriptive paragraphs are almost objective reporting about Nick's hike along the railroad track to the fireside of Ad Francis, but Nick's sensations are constantly there (he was hungry and his eye ached[35]) and the lines could easily be done in the first person. The body of the story is, of course, largely made up of dialogue between Nick, Ad Francis and Bugs; passages of dialogue rival those in "The Killers" in objectivity, but with the difference that the reader here rarely knows anything of how Ad and Bugs say things or what they are thinking while he always knows how Nick is feeling or thinking. Almost every page keeps Nick's consciousness foremost through reminders that Nick is "embarrassed," feels "a little sick,"[36] tastes good food,[37] and finally hears and sees the fireside scene from a distance.[38] When we are told that Ad said something "seriously,"[36] or "happily,"[39] or that Bugs "soothed" Ad,[38] it is clear that these are the Center's impressions; those stage directions need not reflect insight into the characters' minds by an overseeing author: They simply represent Nick's idea of the way the voices sounded to him. In "The Battler" Nick is the Center of Consciousness, the narrator of his own story.

With "Cross-Country Snow," we interrupt the chronological order of the stories and move beyond the wound; Nick, here, is some years past the war, married, about to become a father. The story is rather objective, made up mostly of dialogue and brief descriptive paragraphs, with very little of Nick's own thoughts aside from dialogue. Only one pair of sentences really enters his mental process and there Hemingway uses the first person, without quotation marks and followed by "he thought."

> The girl came in and Nick noticed that her apron covered swellingly her pregnancy. I wonder why I didn't see that when she first came in, he thought.[40]

That unquoted first person again brings the reader a little further within Nick's mind, even though the rest of the story is so very objective. This is a more secure Nick Adams than the man of the wound stories; so it is appropriate that the narrative perspective should be as objective as it had been before the wound; still this Nick has now a store of experiences behind him, his mind is full of images and any window to them can show a great deal.

What Nick thinks, even though we know so little of it, is important for the theme of the story. A little later we are to learn that Nick's wife's pregnancy is a cause of his separation from George; our one glimpse into Nick's mind, therefore, fits the theme and causes Nick's thoughts to stand out. Nick's mental confusion, first unawareness and then marked notice, with regard to pregnancy at this point leaves range for the reader's imagination to play with Nick's thoughts, and it avoids what might become sentimental in direct connection with his own wife. The only other comment in the story about the thoughts of Nick comes in these sentences: "George and Nick were happy. They were fond of each other. They knew they had the run back home ahead of them."[41] That, to be sure, sounds like an omniscient narrator; but, according to the pattern already established in the stories, it is just the sort of thing Nick could say or think: he is confident in his relationship with George; he knows George's mind well enough to guess that George feels as he does at this moment.

Despite some ambiguity about the narrative perspective in this story, despite its objectivity and its heavily dramatic qualities, the focus is no less on Nick, but it is kept there sensually rather than mentally. In the second paragraph we are told that George had "dipped out of sight"[42]; naturally he could not have dipped out of the sight of an Author-Observer, but he could dip out of Nick's sight. Then as Nick skis, "a steep undulation in the mountain side plucked Nick's mind out and left him only the wonderful flying, dropping sensation in his body."[42] When he falls in the snow, we are told that he was "feeling like a shot rabbit" and that his nose and ears were "jammed full of snow."[42] A little later, as George and Nick climb back toward the lodge, Nick hears "George breathing and kicking in his heels just behind him."[40] And at the end of the story, Nick feels the cold when they go outside and sees George on the road ahead of him. This accumulation of sensory perceptions, then, keeps Nick as the central agent of the story so that what the reader sees and feels come through that Center. Further, that part of the story which does belong to the Effaced Narrator technique establishes a terse dialogue entirely appropriate to the awkwardness and affected indifference of this separation.

"Fathers and Sons" is also on the other side of Nick's war-time wound; it is the final story in the Nick sequence and shows an older, more mature Nick, reflecting on a great deal of what has gone before and especially, since he is driving with his own son, reflecting on his relationship to his father. These flashbacks offer a deep penetration into Nick's mind and so represent an additional movement toward subjectivity. Many of the flashbacks are similar to the early childhood stories, but now the action is frequently described in the perfect or past-perfect tense rather than in the simple past. As Nick's mind returns, however, to those childhood days, the older days get closer, so that at one point Nick's reminiscences begin to take the shape of a story, now in the past tense, about Nick and his Indian friends, Trudy and Billy.[43] And this little story, of three pages, is told from the same narrative perspective as the earlier stories, such as "Ten Indians"; that is, the story is largely dialogue, with a brief glimpse at Nick's thoughts and feelings. The effect is that of a story within a story, a narrator within a narrator; the smaller story is less subjective than the larger one; it is Nick talking about Nick talking about Nick; it is the Center becoming briefly an Author-Observer. The differences we have been noting in Hemingway's narrative perspectives are especially obvious here since two different forms appear side by side.

Most of "Fathers and Sons" is a report of Nick Adams's day-dreams as he drives along a highway in the United States: some of the thought is close to the surface, sparked by what he sees; some of the thought moves by association to his own past, even to the depth of that interior story about Trudy; a large portion of the thought is expressed in the more informal and more controlled second person ("In shooting quail you must not get between them and their habitual cover"[44]). The use of the second person is a still further step toward subjectivity; Hemingway treats the second person much the same way he treats the indirect first person, that is, in what amounts to the character talking to himself. If the work were being rewritten as a first-person narrative, all the second-person sentences could stand without change because they appear in the text just as a person might speak them. The second person as Hemingway uses it here, in other words, is a more informal, more conversational form; therefore, it moves the reader closer to the Center. Hemingway brings the second person into an easy mixture with the third, keeping the focus objectively on Nick but also adding a sense of closeness to him as the teller of the action.

> His father was as sound on those two things [fishing and shooting] as he was unsound on sex, for instance, and Nick was glad that it had been that way; for some one has to give you your first gun or the opportunity to get it and use it, and you have to live where there is game or fish if you are to learn about them, and now, at thirty-eight, he loved to fish and to shoot exactly as much as when he first had gone with his father.[45]

This story, then, has as its protagonist and as its Center of Consciousness an older Nick Adams, one who has been through a great deal, who still is troubled by his relationship to his father and by his father's suicide, yet one who is a little more in control of his life and his thought than he had been for a while after the war. It is the narrative perspective which helps to establish this kind of Center.

"Big Two-Hearted River" has only one character and so represents Nick totally as a Center of Consciousness and is perhaps the best example of the Hemingway third-person Center. This is Nick's story entirely: No other characters enter the picture except as Nick makes characters of a grasshopper or a trout, except as he remembers an old friend named Harry Hopkins. The third-person narration has those same qualities, apparent in other stories, of objective reporting and subjective identification with the protagonist. This story is too completely packed with illustrations of the technique already mentioned in connection with other stories for us to recount every one of them. Generally, however, the same principles are operating, intensified. At no point in the story does the focus come from any observer other than Nick; at every point first person would work. At the outset, Nick watches the train move "out of sight" and the reader is immediately placed so that he sees through Nick's eyes. In fact, one of the amazing things about this story is the way the author constantly surrounds the character with sensory images so that the reader feels he has stepped into Nick's skin. Many of the verbs are *look*, *watch*, *see* verbs, with the effect that the reader is always seeing what Nick sees. Furthermore, the reader feels, with Nick, a heavy pack, aching muscles, hunger and even happiness and that "old feeling" which Nick occasionally gets. It isn't just the power of clear descriptive language that causes the reader to experience all this with Nick; it is also that the perceptions come to the reader through Nick. There is nothing else to feel and see except what Nick feels and sees. And, of course, at every step of the way, the reader knows what Nick is thinking: It is as though every impression of Nick's mind makes up the continuation that is this story.

The narrative perspective of "Big Two-Hearted River" becomes most complex as the story draws to a close, as Nick comes closer to the swamp. In the story, Hemingway also uses the second person on several occasions: When Nick thinks about the proper way to handle trout, for example, the narration slowly moves into Nick's mind from the beginning of the paragraph with its objective report, "He had wet his hand before he touched the trout," to: "Nick did not like to fish with other men on the river. Unless they were of your party, they spoiled it."[46] The next to the last sentence shows Nick's mental attitude; the last sentence is Nick's own unspoken formulation of that attitude. Nick talks to himself again in the second person later on when he thinks about the difficult fishing near the bank:

The very biggest ones would lie up close to the bank. You could always pick them up there on the Black . . . . It was almost impossible to fish then, the surface of the water was blinding as a mirror in the sun. Of course, you could fish upstream, but in a stream like the Black, or this, you had to wallow against the current and in a deep place, the water piled up on you. It was no fun to fish upstream with this much current.[47]

Clearly this is a crucial moment for Nick; he is thinking everything out carefully: The narration shows all that when the Center actually talks to himself.

In this story, Hemingway takes an additional step into the mind of his hero by once slipping into a direct use of the first person. The occasion is the climactic moment after Nick loses the big trout. Here the reader is aware, within a single paragraph, of movement into Nick's mind, from an objective report of the action to Nick's thoughts to the indirect first person to first person. In quoting the paragraph here, I shall divide it and number it in order to illustrate the steps of this movement.

1) The leader had broken where the hook was tied to it. Nick took it in his hand. [An objective report]
2) He thought of the trout somewhere on the bottom, holding himself steady over the gravel, far down below the light, under the logs, with the hook in his jaw. Nick knew the trout's teeth would cut through the snell of the hook. [Third-person Center, within Nick's mind]
3) The hook would imbed itself in his jaw. [Now, third person refers to the trout; the sentence could be spoken by a narrator-Nick]
4) He'd bet the trout was angry. [Third person is back to Nick, but note easily it could be changed to "I'd bet"]
5) Anything that size would be angry. That was a trout. He had been solidy hooked. Solid as a rock. He felt like a rock, too, before he started off. By God, he was a big one. [All indirect first person; could easily be placed in quotation marks]
6) By God, he was the biggest one I ever heard of.[48]

This beautiful and important story, then, makes a significant contribution to Hemingway's narrative technique because it is in this story that Hemingway achieves his deepest penetration so far into the mind, now a terribly troubled mind, of Nick Adams. Hemingway achieves this depth by complicating the Center of Consciousness role with the addition of first- and second-person sentences. Furthermore, the style of the story is fitting as a play-by-play picture of the narrator's own mind. This is the carefully controlled mind of a man meticulously searching for restoration from incoherence. The precise details, the concentration of each simple action, the tedious, logical thought of this story is exactly what Nick Adams must do for himself; since he is the Center of Consciousness, the one through whom the story is told, that very precision represents the steps he must take to regain control.[49]

The mind of Nick Adams is in a more troubled state in "A Way You'll Never Be" than it is in "Big Two-Hearted River," because that former story is closer in time to the wound Nick received. What has been true of the other Center of Consciousness stories is true of this one: The story is again told in the third person, but clearly from Nick's own point of view; it could as easily be told in the first person; much of the story still contains some of the familiar objective dialogue; sometimes, the story uses direct and indirect first person. The central episode of this story, for point of view, is that in which Nick's mind is at its most disintegrated state; when Nick tries to rest on a bunk, his mind wanders in and out of past experiences. These two pages of loosely connected thoughts come to the reader through Nick's consciousness, of course, and the movement into the first person and what we have called the indirect first person also enforces the mental disintegration. The long section begins with reference to Nick, "He was very disappointed," and moves by word and image association to:

> I'd shoot one but it's too late now. They'd all be worse. Break his nose. They've put it back to five-twenty. We've only got four minutes more . . . . Bail them out as you go. What a bloody balls. All right. That's right.[50]

The whole passage changes person as rapidly as it does subject and both changes work together to portray Nick's mental state: it is through his confused consciousness that the reader gets all this. The account is far different from the controlled day-dreaming of "Fathers and Sons"; a comparison of the two stories, both of which show Nick's mind moving into the past, demonstrates the greater degree of subjectivity in "A Way You'll Never Be."

Narrator-Agent

"Now I Lay Me" is the only first-person narration in the Nick Adams stories; obviously the Center of the other stories is not the Narrator-Agent. Hemingway is telling this one in the first person as, in fact, he might have told a number of the others in the first person by shifting only the pronouns. The Narrator-Agent of "Now I Lay Me" is identified concretely in one reminiscence when his father addresses him as "Nick." The basic pattern of the story is familiar since it begins and ends with that focus on the narrator and has an extended and more objective dialogue in the middle. But there are differences, even within that pattern. For one thing, the dialogue section in this first-person narrative is almost entirely dramatic:[51] the Narrator-Agent intrudes for only two short lines ("We smoked skilfully in the dark" and "We were both quiet and I listened to the silkworms"[52]) and less than a fourth of the lines are introduced by the "I said" or "he said." Hemingway, in other words, lets the dialogue work for him and keeps his Narrator-Agent honest by not having him comment further on the conversation.

The second difference in the pattern of this story is that the opening section is longer: The Narrator-Agent gets to say more in this story than did the Center in his. And that fits too. If the author decides that he is going to write in the first person, it must have something to do with a desire to get more deeply into the mind of his narrator: it is appropriate, therefore, that the Narrator-Agent should have more time to make his case. And, in this story, Nick does probe more deeply into his own thoughts, he is more analytical, there is a greater sense of awareness in the introspection. At times, he is simply reflecting—"I would think of a trout stream I had fished along when I was a boy"[53]—but at other times, he is more than a reflector—"On those nights I tried to remember everything that had ever happened to me, starting with just before I went to the war and remembering back from one thing to another."[54] It is that very backward movement which characterizes this story in theme and in narrative technique, for Nick is trying to dig into his own mind enough to understand some things about his parents—some things which he has not heretofore been able to understand, which have been an unabsorbed part of his "education" (see "The Doctor and the Doctor's Wife"), which have contributed to his present condition.

The use of the second person in Nick's reflections in this story serves as a connection with the same practice in the other stories. In the sentence, "You can hear silk-worms eating very clearly in the night and I lay with my eyes open and listened to them,"[55] the second person does not seem at all out of place, because it is the way Nick thinks: The second person is a kind of general comment which goes well with the first person, as a personal and conversational form. In "Now I Lay Me," then, Hemingway's narrative perspective reaches its most subjective level, goes most deeply into the mind of Nick Adams; it is his use of first person which makes it so. One of the beauties of the story is that the starkly objective dialogue section keeps the story from becoming sentimental or overladen with self-pity in the same way that Nick's conversation with the soldier pulls him out of his introspection.

IV

The Nick Adams stories, taken together, provide an overview of Ernest Hemingway's narrative technique in one segment of his literary career. Some general conclusions can now be drawn in summary of the preceding analysis.

1. The basic schema on which this paper operates—the objective-subjective scale—cannot be forced too far. Variations in the pattern clearly exist:

They must, since Hemingway was not working from the pattern in the first place; they must, since too precise a pattern would call attention to itself and away from the work. The scale is useful only insofar as it serves as a tool for getting at the stylistic qualities and thematic concerns.

2. Quite obviously, then, Hemingway is working carefully and skillfully with point of view in these stories. If anything can put the lie to the charge that Hemingway's early work is mere reporting or that his writing lacked maturity, it is a realization of the precision with which he works at point of view. Even though he probably did all this subconsciously, his control of the perspective, his experimentation with the form, his ability to relate point of view to theme, all mark him (needless to say?) as a great writer.

3. Study of points of view in these stories reenforces the importance of the Nick Adams sequence for a total picture of Hemingway and his work. Nick's sensitive personality deserves a high place among Hemingway's heroes because it adds another dimension to the writing and because it reminds us of another side of Ernest Hemingway (in the sense that Nick is a special mask). The trout streams of upper Michigan are as important as (I am tempted to claim "more important than") the cafe tables of Paris.

4. Because of the relationship between the author and his mask, Hemingway needs to work these stories out mainly in the third person. He is able to avoid—at least until scholars begin snooping—that easy identification in the public mind between the author and his first-person narrator.

5. A corollary of that is that Hemingway gains objectivity by presenting most of these stories in the third person. Such an observation is a commonplace of point-of-view criticism, of course; but it is appropriate here. Just because he was so close to the experiences of Nick Adams, Hemingway needed to establish some distance between himself and his hero; he needed to steer clear of any intimation of self-pity; he had to make Nick a believable narrator and character. The third person helps to do all that.

6. At the same time, Hemingway apparently wanted to get as far into the mind of Nick as he could. To put it another way, he wanted to write what he felt to be true and that meant burrowing deep into himself. He wanted to talk about initiations and traumatic wounds, and in order to do that effectively and honestly he had to show, in as many ways possible, how his hero reacted to experiences.

7. Hemingway was, therefore, unable to follow exactly the established pattern of point of view. In order to achieve the proper combination of objectivity and subjectivity, he had to work out variations of an omniscient author or a Center of Consciousness pattern. One way to do that was by allowing the Center occasional second- and first-person language.

8. Finally, most significantly, Hemingway was able to build a relationship between his point-of-view technique and his overall characterization. As Nick matures and goes through his initiations, the point of view becomes increasingly subjective. The stories immediately following the wound show a disordered state of mind and are presented through a complicated narrative perspective. In no small degree, point of view provides the means by which Hemingway develops, with such penetration, the character of Nick Adams.

1. Carlos Baker, *Ernest Hemingway: A Life Story* (New York: Charles Scribner's Sons, 1969).

2. Philip Young, *Ernest Hemingway: A Reconsideration* (University Park: Pennsylvania State Press, 1966), p. 62.

3. See Young's chapter, "The Man and the Legend," and especially his discussion of the Nick Adams side of Hemingway: ibid., p. 157.

4. Baker p. 163.

5. The third-person narrators of the *In Our Time* interchapters are five times nearly absent, three times representative of a single center of consciousness, once given limited insight into the minds of the characters, and once a narrator who sets himself apart by his use of the second person. The *In Our Time* stories have three first-person narrators, two of whom function as storytellers ("you ought to have seen"), and five non-Nick third-person narrators. Of the latter five, two narrators have limited insight into the minds of the characters, while three focus on a central consciousness.

The two first-person novels are not exactly alike in narrative technique: Jake Barnes is an objective narrator, rarely revealing his own thoughts and feelings, using the more informal and personal second person in only ten passages; Frederic Henry, on the other hand, frequently probes his own consciousness, frequently uses the second person. Hemingway is doing nothing very unusual in these first-person narratives, but he does establish, partially through point-of-view technique, a distinction between the narrators.

6. A study of the composition dates as given in Baker shows no apparent relationship between the time of writing and the type of narrative perspective.

7. E. M. Halliday, "Hemingway's Narrative Perspective," *Sewanee Review*, LX (April–June 1952), pp. 202–218.

8. John S. Rouch, "Jake Barnes as Narrator," *Modern Fiction Studies*, XI (Winter 1965–1966), pp. 361–370.

9. For specific studies, see Cleanth Brooks and Robert Penn Warren, *Understanding Fiction* (New York: Appleton-Century-Crofts, 1943), pp. 303–312, on "The Killers"; Warren Beck, "The Shorter Happy Life of Mrs. Macomber," *Modern Fiction Studies*, I (November 1955), 28–37; Austin McGiffert Wright, *The American Short Story in the Twenties* (Chicago: University of Chicago Press, 1961), pp. 391–393, on "Cross-Country Snow" and "An Alpine Idyll."

10. The most helpful general discussions of point of view are: Wayne Booth, *The Rhetoric of Fiction* (Chicago: University of Chicago Press, 1961), a major and essential volume; Brooks and Warren, "Focus of Narration: Point of View" in *Understanding Fiction*, pp. 659–664; Norman Friedman, "Point of View in Fiction: The Development of a Critical Concept," *PMLA*, LXX (December 1955), 1160–1184; Caroline Gordon, *How to Read a Novel* (New York: Viking Press, 1957), pp. 72–144; Wright, "The Narrator," in *The American Short Story in the Twenties*, pp. 280–288.

11. Ernest Hemingway, *The Fifth Column and the First Forty-Nine Stories* (New York: Charles Scribner's Sons, 1938), p. 377.

12. Ibid., p. 206.   13. Ibid., p. 208.

14. Ibid., p. 461.

15. Brooks and Warren, pp. 303–312; Booth, p. 151.

16. It is interesting that of *The First Forty-Nine Stories* only three can be said to have an Effaced Narrator: "The Killers," "Hills Like White Elephants," and "Today is

Friday" which is in play form; the Effaced Narrator would seem, therefore, to be an atypical Hemingway technique rather than an earmark of his style.

17. Hemingway, op. cit., p. 384.

18. Ibid., p. 385.   19. Ibid., p. 386.
20. Ibid., p. 197.   21. Ibid., p. 199.
22. Ibid., p. 200.

23. See Young, pp. 32–33 and Joseph DeFalco, *The Hero in Hemingway's Short Stories* (Pittsburgh: University of Pittsburgh Press, 1963), pp. 33–39.

24. Hemingway, op. cit., p. 193.

25. Ibid., p. 189.   26. Ibid., p. 191.
27. Ibid., p. 192.   28. Ibid., p. 214.
29. Ibid., p. 218.   30. Ibid., p. 219.
31. Ibid., p. 215.   32. Ibid., p. 430.
33. Ibid., p. 434.   34. Ibid., p. 227.
35. Ibid., p. 228.   36. Ibid., p. 229.
37. Ibid., p. 232.   38. Ibid., p. 236.
39. Ibid., p. 231.   40. Ibid., p. 283.
41. Ibid., p. 284.   42. Ibid., p. 281.
43. Ibid., pp. 591–593.   44. Ibid., p. 586.
45. Ibid., p. 588.   46. Ibid., p. 323.
47. Ibid., p. 327.   48. Ibid., pp. 324–325.

49. I have treated this story as a unit, not considering its two parts as separate stories. The objectivity of Part I, taken by itself, would cause it to be placed on the scale about where "Three-Day Blow" is. Yet, taken with Part II, as it must be, the story belongs here. I would even argue—and the paragraph above is a part of the argument—that the objectivity of Part I is an aspect of the Center's effort to retain control of a disturbed mind. The very objectivity is the careful mind's work, so it is not the same treatment, does not have the same depth, of the earlier Center stories.

50. Hemingway, op. cit., p. 506.

51. An objective story by a first-person narrator is not unusual for Hemingway, of course. Sixteen of *The First Forty-Nine Stories* are in the first person and they show as much variety within that narrow form as do the third-person narratives. In some stories, the Narrator-Agent gives no hint as to his own thoughts ("Che Ti Dice La Patria" and "Canary for One" are examples of extremely objective narratives); in some the Narrator-Agent gives only brief insight to his own thoughts ("Day's Wait," "Wine of Wyoming"); in others he is consciously a storyteller ("The Mother of a Queen"); in others he is very subjective ("After the Storm," "Alpine Idyll").

52. Hemingway, op. cit., p. 466.   53. Ibid., p. 461.
54. Ibid., p. 463.   55. Ibid., p. 465.

The Reliable and Unreliable Narrator in Hemingway's Stories / *Sheldon Norman Grebstein*

In regard to Hemingway's craft, the salient question about those stories which employ the I-witness or I-protagonist mode is how the narrative voice in a particular work shapes its characterizations and communicates its meanings. We must once more be warned against approaching Hemingway's I-narratives with the comfortable supposition that the first-person narrator invariably functions as a reliable spokesman for the writer's ethic or as his thinly disguised persona. Even in those cases where the I-narrator's attitude or values (or, to use the classic Hemingway word, *code*) can be equated with the writer's, we notice certain ambiguities. A few representative stories will illustrate the varying distances at which Hemingway stands from his first-person speakers.

Two examples of I-narrator accounts in which the writer impersonates a character very unlike himself are "Fifty Grand" and "Mother of a Queen." In the first the speaker is Jerry Doyle, a trainer for the story's prizefighter-protagonist, Jack Brennan. In "Mother of a Queen," the narrator is one Roger, ex-business manager and former friend of a Mexican matador named Paco. In both stories the narrator's proximity to the protagonist and his familiarity with the milieu, prize ring and bullring, produce the appropriate idiom and atmosphere of authenticity. This alone lures the reader into accepting the narrative at face value. However, since in both cases the speaker's version of action and character is the only account we have, his reliability becomes a crucial consideration. It is precisely this question of reliability which lends complexity to all I-narratives, yet, surprisingly, the question has not been sufficiently stressed in readings of "Fifty Grand," among Hemingway's most popular stories, and has been totally ignored in "Mother of a Queen." These stories require a closer look.

On the surface, a surface so convincing no critic has ever peeked behind it, "Mother of a Queen" professes to be the portrait of an utterly contemptible matador who betrays virtually every commandment in the Hemingway code. Not only is the man immediately identified by the speaker as a "queen"— and Hemingway's scorn for homosexuals resounds throughout his work—he is accused of other serious breaches of conduct: miserliness, dishonesty, treachery to friends, incompetence, disregard of obligations to filial duty and

From *Hemingway's Craft*, by Sheldon Norman Grebstein (Carbondale: Southern Illinois University Press, 1973), pp. 56–67. Copyright © 1973 and reprinted by permission of Southern Illinois University Press.

family honor, total absence of pride as a man and as a Spaniard. All this we learn from a witness who was once the matador's intimate associate but has broken with so repulsive a creature and now publicly vilifies him. Just there lies the problem. Not only should the narrator's vehement hostility and contempt (as well as his readiness to tell the story to any who will listen) arouse our suspicions about his reliability, Hemingway also provides us with an important clue to the narrator's bias. Toward the end of his monologue he says: "I got the car out to go to town. It was his car but he knew I drove it better than he did. Everything he did I could do better. He knew it. He couldn't even read and write." [1]

Once we remark this element of competition and jealousy, "Everything he did I could do better," we must discount at least some of the speaker's testimony and perhaps most of it. Several intriguing possibilities emerge. For one thing, the shape of the story changes. It is no longer a simple I-witness account, with the matador as protagonist, but as much about the narrator himself. Indeed, a rereading of the story with that in mind reveals that in almost every episode the narrator himself is the hero: he is punctual and efficient where the matador is negligent; he fulfills his duties where the matador evades his; he upholds the standards of honor which Paco disgraces, and so on. Too, all the charges laid by Roger against Paco become suspect. If the matador is truly a homosexual, why does he consort with women or want to impress them? If it is Paco's custom to have a liaison with his manager, why has he not made a pass at Roger? If the narrator keeps possession of the cashbox, why not help himself to what he claims is owed him? Why does he call the matador a "bitch"?—a strange epithet for a man to use, even to a homosexual. It seems more typically what one homosexual would call another. Furthermore, despite his boast, the narrator omits one important field of competition from his claim of superiority: he offers no evidence that he himself has ever faced the horns of a bull. If all these conjectures do not amount to overwhelming proof that Roger is a thoroughly unreliable narrator, I do suggest that once we take Hemingway's cue and query the speaker's honesty, the story becomes much more interesting and substantial than anyone had thought.

"Fifty Grand" has been studied recently by such able critics as Earl Rovit and Sheridan Baker, among others. Baker notes with amusement the narrator's peculiar and narrow sophistication in the tough world of his métier, while Rovit stresses the absurdity of the story's central situation wherein the protagonist can only win by losing.[2] However, neither Baker nor Rovit (who

1. *The Short Stories of Ernest Hemingway*, Modern Standard Authors Edition (New York: Charles Scribner's Sons, n.d.), p. 418. All subsequent page references will be included in the text.

2. Earl H. Rovit, *Ernest Hemingway* (New York: Twayne, 1963), p. 61; Sheridan Baker, *Ernest Hemingway: An Introduction and Interpretation* (New York: Holt, Rinehart, and Winston 1967), pp. 61–62.

characterizes the narrator as uncommitted and somewhat naïve) treats the story in enough detail to fully explain the narrator's role or settle the issue of his reliability.

The technique itself supports the speaker's credibility. Unlike "Mother of a Queen," which is entirely a monologue, "Fifty Grand" is much more objective. That is, although the only speaking voice we hear is necessarily that of the narrator, this narrator does not constantly interpose himself between reader and protagonist. Roger reports only *his* encounters with Paco; Jerry Doyle reports a series of encounters between Brennan and a variety of characters. Furthermore, the quality of the narrator's perception, wary of making judgments and usually limited to what was actually done and said, commends his truthfulness to the reader. Nor do I wish to impugn it. Doyle is reliable, insofar as he sees. But what and how does he see?

One significant aspect of his vision has been little emphasized: his affection and loyalty to the protagonist, the reverse of the prevailing situation in "Mother of a Queen." This need not contradict the narrator's testimony nor invalidate it, but it does impinge on the story's rendition of character and add overtones to Doyle's seemingly flat and laconic voice. Hemingway sets down a number of cues which document the speaker's bias in favor of the protagonist: "He liked me and we got along fine together." Doyle tells us early in the story; "He's a good fellow," Doyle assures another character who attacks Brennan; "Well, he's always been fine to me," Doyle says to another critical acquaintance; "You're the only friend I got," Brennan confesses to Doyle in an unguarded moment. Also, we notice Doyle's immunity to Brennan's edged tongue, his truthful responses to Brennan's worried queries about his shape for the fight, his attempt to placate the protagonist's fears with commonsense advice, and especially his solicitous attempt to keep Brennan from getting sick-drunk. What this brings to the story, despite the narrator's attempt to efface himself, is a more complex view of the protagonist's character. Because Doyle observes Brennan through eyes that seem wholly clear yet are slightly misted over with loyal affection, we, too, remark those human traits in the hero, the admixture of good and evil, which dignify "Fifty Grand" as more than a mere sports story and constitute its superiority to the hundreds of hard-boiled imitations. Only to such a narrator as Doyle could Brennan uncover his loneliness for his family, an emotion Doyle can recognize and record but, as a bachelor, not really share.

What the narrator, a horseplayer, does fully understand and covertly communicate is the gaming principle and the gamester's desperation, a vital part of Brennan's motivation in the crucial moment. Too, by advancing subtle hints Doyle's narration prepares us for Brennan's ability to keep his feet after a smash to his groin, when almost anyone else would fall. Throughout the story this ability—not so much courage, as readers usually interpret it, but sheer instinct to survive—is foreshadowed; at the very start Brennan says to

the narrator, "He ain't going to last like you and me, Jerry."[3] Brennan's survival instinct goes beyond the money-lust so evident in the story's literal dimension. Money is symptom, not cause. In short, the I-witness of "Fifty
Grand" can be named an "almost-reliable" narrator, dependable enough for
the reader to accept his account as substantially true, thus assuring the story
of its basically "realistic" and "objective" quality, yet biased to the extent
that we must read between the lines. In this Hemingway achieves an imitation
of life: we can agree on what happens; we cannot agree on the precise meaning of what happens.

Two other worthy stories, "Wine of Wyoming" and "The Denunciation,"
again almost without annotation in Hemingway criticism except for fleeting
references to their biographical sources, embody first-person narrators who
function significantly in the action and who convey an ethical norm which
reflects the writer's own values.[4] Although the stories seem different in almost
every way—locale, mood, situation—similarities can be descried. In both,
the narrator-protagonist's social relationships have a moral context; in both
he is thrust into the role of arbiter and adviser, which he carries out by giving
verbal advice; yet in both the narrator falls short of his own standards of conduct and cannot fully redeem himself. In these stories the ironic effect and
complexity arise not only from the disparity between the reader's clear view
and the narrator's clouded sight but also from the narrator's own recognition
of the discrepancy between his ideals and his actions.

"The Denunciation," first published in *Esquire* in 1938 and lately collected with a body of Hemingway's other work about the Spanish Civil War,
revolves around a figure who has nearly the same relationship to the writer
as Robert Jordan in *For Whom the Bell Tolls*; he is an American committed
to the Loyalist cause yet involved in acts repugnant to his personal creed.
That is, both Jordan and this protagonist are projections of Hemingway's
own experience in Spain and his somewhat ambivalent identification with
the Loyalists. In this case the narrator must decide whether or not to betray
an old acquaintance, Luis Delgado, now on the Fascist side, whom he sees
masquerading in Loyalist uniform in the Madrid café they both patronized
before the war. The café is not just a place; it is a way of life, a tradition. At
first the narrator attempts to serve both creeds by allowing a waiter, who has
also recognized the daring Fascist, to report him to counterespionage. Thus

3. Cleanth Brooks, for example, in *The Hidden God* (New Haven: Yale University
Press, 1963), pp. 13–14, praises Brennan as heroic and courageous.
4. Carlos Baker, *Hemingway: A Life Story* (New York: Charles Scribner's Sons,
1969), pp. 210, 597, identifies the prototypes for the Fontans as the Moncini family of
Sheridan, Wyoming, and says, "It follows almost exactly the events of late August and
early September, 1928, while EH and Pauline were in and around Sheridan." Of "The
Denunciation" Baker writes that it was "based . . . on an actual incident from the fall
of 1937" (p. 337). The one critical discussion I have found of "The Denunciation" is
Julian Smith, "Christ Times Four: Hemingway's Unknown Spanish Civil War Stories,"
Arizona Quarterly 25 (1969): 5–17. Smith's approach has little in common with mine.

he keeps faith with the cause which demands destruction of its enemies, yet he evades the direct responsibility of betrayal. Then, at the conclusion, in a paradoxical reversal provoked by his personal ethic, the narrator asks that the arrested Fascist be told that he, not the waiter, had reported him; thus Delgado can go to his death still believing in the splendid tradition of the café's eternal loyalty to its patrons.

By creating a narrator who demonstrates at each stage of his behavior a high degree of moral consciousness, Hemingway appears to sacrifice one of the prime advantages of the I-narrator mode, the reader's superior perception of the consequences of the narrator's actions. If the speaker sees as much as the reader, what remains for the reader to do except to listen? However, closer inspection divulges two deeper layers of meaning, one moral, one aesthetic. The narrator's vision, acute as it is, turns out to be only the eyepiece of the telescope.

First, despite the narrator's keen sensibility, he does not fully comprehend that his own tortuous moral decision is not unique to him but collects and intensifies the decisions made by all the other major characters. The precipitating decision had been Delgado's, to risk recognition in a public place behind enemy lines. From the narrator's standpoint this proves him an "utter bloody fool," but also characteristically sporting, "cheerful" and "brave." Moreover, we can infer that although the Fascist carries out a useful mission, Delgado's real motivation is his gambling impulse and his belief, announced to the narrator in the good old days when the stakes were only money, that one made the game interesting by betting more than one could afford to lose. In turn, the waiter's decision balances between his own set of personal and political ideals, whether to betray a Fascist and so uphold the cause to which he has given his sons, or to preserve the cherished name of the café and the honor of his profession as a waiter. By supplying the waiter with the number of the secret police, the narrator helps the waiter resolve his dilemma, for this can be construed as an indirect order from a preferred customer. However, by this act the narrator complicates his own problem. The waiter's dilemma would be almost comic, were not a man's life at stake.

The story's aesthetic level also attains something of the irony of the split perspective in that a number of actions unfold and are related or recalled by the narrator, but they are actions whose purport he only partially apprehends. What the narrator does not quite realize is the similarity between this episode in the café, which costs Delgado his life because his luck runs bad, and the other, years before, when the narrator had won all Delgado's money. In both episodes the narrator, a lesser but luckier man, prevails—yet without full awareness that Delgado has engaged him in a second contest. This recognition whets the reader's appreciation of the story's conclusion, for we discern that the narrator's underlying motivation is not to save the waiter's and café's good name but to repeat his earlier triumph over Delgado and ensure that the loser know the identity of the winner. In this sense the story completes the central metaphor of life as a game of chance.

The ironies of theme and character are further enhanced by our perception of certain elements ostensibly part of the story's objective scene and so routinely reported by the narrator, but without his overt recognition of their appropriateness. The narrator's conversation with the Greek comrade, which seems to be a digression, really serves a double function: as comic relief for the narrator's strained dialogue with the waiter and as corollary for the major action. The Greek's jocular accounts of his burial by a bomb and his encounter with huge octopi in deep water are paradigms for the story's motifs of the narrow margin of luck between life and death, and the wisdom of keeping away from dangerous places. Similarly, we perceive that the narrator's package of freshly butchered meat which he brings into the café and is reminded to take with him when he leaves—just after Delgado has been betrayed—objectifies his conscious self-characterization as Pontius Pilate.

So far we have observed three different uses of the first-person narrator: an unreliable I-witness in "Mother of a Queen," a relatively reliable I-witness in "Fifty Grand," and an I-protagonist in "The Denunciation." The last example of the I-narrator to be considered in the short stories might be described as an I-witness protagonist, the narrator of "Wine of Wyoming." Although these samples hardly exhaust the range of possibilities of Hemingway's first-person narrators in the short fiction, they serve quite well as models or types. For example, "God Rest You Merry, Gentlemen," "The Revolutionist," and "Old Man at the Bridge," could be grouped with "Fifty Grand"; such others as "On the Quai at Smyrna" and "My Old Man" resemble "Mother of a Queen"; and "In Another Country" and "Now I Lay Me" use an I-narrator like that in "The Denunciation." I have chosen to deal with "Wine of Wyoming" both because of its interesting technique and because it offers an opportunity for critical analysis not previously exploited by others.

I have called the narrator of "Wine of Wyoming" an I-witness-protagonist because he begins as one and becomes the other, thus combining the functions of both. As witness he speaks, or seems to speak, directly for the writer, effacing himself for much of the story and concentrating primarily on the words and actions of other characters. For three-fourths of the story's length, marked off exactly in the text by formal divisions, our attention focuses on the Fontan family, an elderly French couple and their teen-aged son. We learn only enough about the narrator to justify his presence on the scene and delineate the relationship with the Fontans which comprises the story's situation. Then, in the story's concluding section the narrator's role changes because one of his actions—his failure to keep an engagement with the Fontans to taste their newly vinted wine—precipitates the story's crisis and provides the means by which character is illuminated and values conveyed. In other words, for most of the story the narrator is needed only to tell it; in the end he is needed to make it happen. The story's irony, apprehended simultaneously by the narrator and the reader, is that a seemingly trivial decision (breaking a promise in a small social occasion) can cause irreparable damage to a fragile relationship and produce strong moral consequences.

The narrator is aligned with the Fontans in two ways. By the very nature of the story's narrative mode, his sight and hearing become the reader's. Accordingly, the narrator's affection for these people, communicated not by direct assertion but by his report of the cleanliness and order of their household, the excellence of their food and drink, and the delightfully candid and unaffected quality of their speech, converts the reader to the same attitude. Nor is our participation in the narrator's viewpoint impaired by any discrepancy or hint of unreliability in the speaker's account. His report is also authenticated in that he speaks their native language and converses with them in a mixture of French, English, and a hilarious "Franglaise" patois.

Secondly, before the story has proceeded very far, we recognize that although the narrator is American, youngish, and a writer, and the Fontans French, elderly, and barely educated, he shares their values—including their distaste for boorish Americans and the corruptions of American life. He "speaks their language" in this sense, as well. Indeed, by means of the narrator's (and the reader's) identification with the Fontans and against the "others," Hemingway poses a much more effective indictment against his homeland than those delivered as broadsides in *Green Hills of Africa*. The narrator and the Fontans represent European values: the appreciation of good food and drink, friendship based on a shared ethos; individual freedom and responsibility; self-respect as evidenced by cleanliness, order, and pride in one's work; an awareness of the greater worth of things because of their scarcity. Against these values are contrasted American behavior and standards: hypocritical and restrictive laws (Prohibition) which deny individual freedom and responsibility, and stimulate rather than suppress misconduct; people who drink to get drunk and then vomit on the table; wives who feed their husbands canned beans because they are too lazy to cook; over-abundance; prejudice; a popular culture built on the aggrandizement of sex and violence.

The story's crisis pivots on this very contrast, for in the end the narrator and the Fontans also behave like "Americans"; that is, each betrays the relationship and its common values. By not keeping his appointment with the Fontans because it was inconvenient, the narrator proves himself no better than the other customers who use the Fontans merely as a source of food and alcoholic drink. And Fontan, by drinking all the new wine he had promised to share with the narrator, demonstrates that he is prey to the same animal appetites he despises in those American *"cochons"* whom he bars from his table. Together, the narrator and Fontan suggest to us the story's theme that even the kindest and best-intentioned men are victims to their weaknesses and impulses. They, themselves, voice this recognition in their last conversation:

> "Good-by," I said. "Don't think about the wine. Drink some for us when we're gone." Fontan shook his head. He did not smile. He knew when he was ruined.
> "That son of a bitch," Fontan said to himself.
> "Last night he had three bottles," Madame Fontan said to comfort him. He shook his head.
> "Good-by," he said.
> Madame Fontan had tears in her eyes.
> "Good-by," she said. She felt badly for Fontan.
> "Good-by," we said. We all felt very badly. They stood in the door-way and we got in, and I started the motor. We waved. They stood to-gether sadly on the porch. Fontan looked very old, and Madame Fontan looked sad. She waved to us and Fontan went in the house. We turned up the road.
> "They felt so badly. Fontan felt terribly."
> "We ought to have gone last night."
> "Yes, we ought to have." (*The Short Stories*, p. 466)

As in "The Denunciation" the narrator's awareness of the nuances of the human relationship and the consequences of his behavior is underscored by objective factors in the story's action and setting, some of them within the speaker's range of perception, others not. He does perceive, as the title implies, that wine amounts to more than a drink; it is an essence. The whole contrast between Europe and America (also suggested by the title's incongruous juxtaposition), and the basis for the affection between Fontan and the narrator, depends upon their mutual response to wine, which they regard not as an alcoholic beverage but as a distillation of the good things in life—taste, in the fullest meaning. Likewise, the narrator associates the Fontans with the Wyoming they inhabit, still relatively open and free but already falling into ruin. What the narrator's perception misses, but we see, is that his very description of the story's setting, the opening view of sun-baked country, parched and dusty against distant, cool, snow-capped mountains, embodies the story's conflict and foreshadows its melancholy conclusion. The Fontans' house, with its shade tree and drink, is an oasis in this desert, but not for all. The ill-behaved are turned away. When, at the end the narrator passes through the desert, with the mountains still distant, and despite his remark about the transience of good people and good land, he does not totally admit his own part in the deterioration. The oasis has been despoiled both by those who kept it and those who came to it. The sadness of the concluding episode, and the emphasis of the story's framing scenes upon the distance between the desolate here and now and the remote ideal, also quell the often exuberant humor of the work's earlier sections. Our final impression of "Wine of Wyoming" is serious rather than comic.

A Lesson from Hemingway ("The Undefeated") / *Francis Christensen*

Several years ago, in "A Note on the Writer's Craft" (*Twentieth Century English*, New York, 1946), John Erskine discussed a "principle" which he said is known to every writer but which he had never seen discussed in print. It illustrates, he says incidentally, "the startling gulf between the grammar which is taught and learned and the grammar which is used." The principle is this:

When you write, you make a point, not by subtracting as though you sharpened a pencil, but by adding. When you put one word after another, your statement should be more precise the more you add. If the result is otherwise, you have added the wrong thing, or you have added more than was needed.

. . . the grammarian leaves with the unwary the impression that the substantive, since it can stand alone, is more important than the adjective, that the verb is more important than the adverb, that the main clause is more important than the subordinate.

In the use of language, however, the truth is precisely the reverse. What you wish to say is found not in the noun but in what you add to qualify the noun. The noun is only a grappling iron to hitch your mind to the reader's. The noun by itself adds nothing to the reader's information; it is the name of something he knows already, and if he does not know it, you cannot do business with him. The noun, the verb, and the main clause serve merely as a base on which the meaning will rise.

The modifier is the essential part of any sentence.

Erskine did not develop this principle to any extent. I have attempted to do so for descriptive and narrative, or descriptive-narrative, writing, putting

Francis Christensen, "A Lesson from Hemingway," in *Notes Toward a New Rhetoric* (New York: Harper and Row, 1967), pp. 24–37, reprinted from *College English*, XXV (October 1963), 12–18. Copyright © 1967 by Francis Christensen; reprinted by permission of Harper & Row Publishers, Inc.

the problem this way: what does a writer add to the noun and the verb and the main clause to make a point—that is, to give to the image the degree and kind of particularity his purpose requires and his sensibility and experience permit?

My purpose in this has been practical rather than theoretical. The style is the man and style cannot be taught, the clichés run. But style is not a seamless robe, and one might by analysis, I thought, determine some of the elements of a concrete style—elements common to all individual styles in the way the elements of syntax are common—and apply such an analysis in teaching composition. Mr. Kempton has said (*The Short Story,* Cambridge, Mass., 1948) that it is "the attempt of fiction to refrain from full explanation but maintain intelligibility and interest by a thin but ceaseless stream of concrete details. . . . Something like a continuum of existence is what the storyteller is after." The ability to summon and manage that thin stream or continuum may be a gift which cannot be communicated, though that is what courses in fiction writing must occupy themselves with. But the means of making the details concrete, or graphic and telling, can be studied as a separate element of style. The thin stream carries the nouns and verbs and main clauses, so to speak, and what may be added to sharpen the image can be made the subject of study and practice.

And not only that. "Nothing is clear until we have put it into words," Bergson says, "for words are the only means of translating impressions to the intellect. Hence the immense help expression gives to vision, in clarifying it. The growth of the power of language is not merely a technical development, it implies a growth of vision." If this is true, then learning to sharpen an image is learning to see an image sharply. It is not so much that we only see what we are looking for as that we are not likely to see what we cannot see how to use. In short, growth in the kind of vision that counts in writing requires a focus and a medium.

Erskine's statement of his principle is put in grammatical terms, but the analysis can also be made in what I will call rhetorical terms; and since the rhetorical terms, illustrated from description rather than from narration, afford the simplest starting point, we can begin with any simple descriptive passage which exemplifies the various possibilities, such as this from Peattie's *An Almanac for Moderns* on learning to distinguish deciduous trees in winter:

Only gradually one finds he too is learning the subtlest differences where at first all seems alike: the BRANCHES OF IRONWOOD, *like the muscles of a straining wrestler,* the SHAPES OF ELMS *like a falling fountain,* the *mottled* BARK OF SYCAMORES, the ALDERS *with their little cones,* the

HICKORIES *with their buds almost like flowers*—out of the silvery winter ranks individuals step forth, are marked, remembered.—January 25th.

The first statement, down to the colon, motivates the addition of description. The nouns in small capitals name the items the author has chosen to present; they are the *headwords* to which description is added. The italicized parts are what has been added to sharpen the image—to distinguish individuals where at first all was alike.

The simplest way to individualize a thing is to point to some *quality* or *attribute*, as "mottled" does. The second way is to point to some *part* of the object, what I will call a *detail*. Here the alders are marked by their cones, the hickories by their buds. Pointing to a quality effects in the reader's mind an over-all modification of the image suggested by the headword; it is like turning the focusing knob and seeing the blurred image spring into sharpness on the ground glass. Pointing to a detail, on the other hand, is like moving in for a close-up of some part of the tree. The third way is to go beyond the object itself and to sharpen the image by suggesting its *likeness* to something else, as is done here with the branches of ironwood and the shapes of elms. Considerable experience has convinced me that there are only these three *methods of description*, as I will call them—by qualities or attributes, by details, and by comparison. Adjectives such as *exhilarating* suggest a fourth, by *effect,* but this soon shades off into explanation. It should be noted that the nouns in what is added may in turn become headwords and have description of their own— *straining, falling, little, almost like flowers.* Any of the three methods may be used for such further-level description, and there is no limit to the number of levels. The description here is all drawn from the sense of sight, but it may be drawn from any of the senses.

From the point of view of grammar the matter is a little more complicated. A quality or attribute is always designated by an adjective, but an adjective does not always designate a quality. It may designate a detail, *thin-barked,* or a comparison, *flower-like* or *flower-soft*; and an abstract adjective, such as *beautiful*, does not picture at all but summarizes, and should be regarded as expository. The detail usually calls for a phrase—a prepositional phrase (most commonly *with, without,* or *in*) or a participial or absolute phrase. The comparison usually calls for a *like*-phrase. Any of the three may be given the weight of a predicate—"The bark of the sycamore is mottled"; "Hickories have buds, and the buds are almost like flowers." But a separate predication interrupts the narrative movement and tends toward exposition.

This, then, is what a writer may add to a noun to sharpen the picture of an *object*. He does exactly the same thing when the headword is a verb and he wants to sharpen the picture of an *action*. He uses the same three methods of description. (A separate term, *methods of narration*, seems hardly necessary). He points to some quality or detail of the action or he suggests a comparison. (We are concerned here only with adverbs of manner or attendant circumstances; adverbs of time, place, etc., take care of themselves.) Even the grammatical character of the additions is identical, except that adverbs usually take the place of adjectives.

For the rest of this paper I have chosen to narrow the discussion from what *may* be added to what one author actually *did* add, hoping thus to give some notion of the frequency of the various kinds of modifiers. I have narrowed it still further to what has been added to the *verb*, in other words, to narration. The piece chosen, Hemingway's *The Undefeated*, has the advantage of a relatively simple narrative style and of being close to pure narrative, with almost no intermixture of description or explanation. It will pass too, I suppose, for expert narration; Edward J. O'Brien, who includes it in his *Short Story Case Book*, says, "Ernest Hemingway's duel with words is as close and skilful a struggle as Manuel's with the bull."

In applying Erskine's principle to this story, I have confined my counting to the scenes at the bullring, though I have taken examples from the opening and closing scenes at the office, cafe, and infirmary. Dialog and interior monolog are excluded as belonging to the characters rather than to the author. My count shows that in the bullring scenes Hemingway used 668 predicate verbs, plus 17 sentences without predicate verbs, to sustain the stream of narrative action. Of these, 532 stand alone without modifiers of the kind we are concerned with, and 153, or one in every four or five, have modifiers. The total number of modifiers added is 236, some of which, of course, are second-level modifiers. A frequency such as this, especially when the modifiers are mainly of the relatively long types, results in a style that may be said to have a relatively dense *texture*. By comparison, the opening and closing scenes, with fewer and lighter modifiers, have a lighter texture. This concept of texture as determined by the frequency and the rhetorical and grammatical character of the modifiers and whether they are used for description or narration is useful for understanding and comparing individual styles.

In the bullring scenes Hemingway uses comparison 7 times, description by quality 35 times, and details 194 times. The proportions are 1:5:28. In almost any prose, I believe, the three methods will stand in this order, but the proportions will vary enormously.

His sparing use of comparison is what one might expect in writing where there is no play of fancy over the surface of the material. The few comparisons he does use, though, are models for a style that chooses for its immediate effect a camera-like precision in following the action. They are all simple, familiar, and appropriate to the action. The bullfighter's cape "swung out like a ballet dancer's skirt" and he "wound the bull around himself like a belt"; he pricked the cape with the tip of his sword and with the sword "spread the red flannel like the jib of a boat"; knocked to the ground and lying on his back, he fended off the bull by "kicking like a man keeping a ball in the air"; "At the end of the pass the bull turned like a cat coming around a corner and faced Manuel."

Hemingway is not given much, either, to describing an action by its quality or attributes, that is, by the use of adverbs; there are only 17 of them, or 1 to 48 verbs. This is to be expected in a writer who cares for exact rather than general effects, because the adverb of manner is no tool for a precise workman. Most of such adverbs are abstract, and the common concrete ones are mostly general rather than specific. When a writer experiments with the abverb, as Robert Penn Warren and Truman Capote have done, the adverb usually calls attention to itself: "He heard the ice settle *clinkingly* in the full glass" (Warren); "A firefly pulsing *goldenly*" (Capote). In *The Undefeated* the adverbs concerned with the horses and bulls are faintly concrete; the best one suggests rather well the quality of the horses provided by Retana: "The picadors galloped *jerkily* around the ring." But the abstract adverbs defining the attitude of Hernandez and Fuentes are an indulgent shortcut: said *cheerfully* or *happily*, walking *arrogantly* or *insultingly*.

In this story more adjectives than adverbs (18 as against 17) are added to the verb, and they are more interesting. Seven of them are complements rather than modifiers—that is, predicate adjectives used after verbs of action rather than after "empty" copulas. These "quasi-predicatives," as Jespersen calls them, make it possible to combine description with narration, so that the reader can picture the agent in the course or at the end of the action: as the sword was withdrawn, "the scabbard fell *limp*"; the gypsy was "watching *lazy-eyed*"; the sword "shot up in the air . . . to fall *red-hilted* on the sand." Others differ from these in standing outside the clause, in the appositive position. The examples in this story are not remarkable: "The bull stood, *heavy* and *dull* again after the action"; "There was the bull standing, *heavy*, firmly planted"; " 'You ever seen these fellows?' Zurito asked, *big* and *looming* beside Manuel in the dark." Although Hemingway has not used them freely, such appositive adjectives are a characteristic feature of the loosely cumulative sentences of modern descriptive-narrative style. Finally, an adjective sometimes turns up in a series of adverbial modifiers, so that description and narration are interwoven: "There he came, eyes open, *ugly*, watching the cape"; "Fuentes stood watching, his cape held against his body, *tall*, in repose, watching lazy-eyed."

The most important, by far, of the methods of describing action is by details; in this story there are 5 for every adjective and adverb and 28 for every comparison. And they are important not only in numbers but in what a writer can do with them.

I have defined a detail as a part of any given whole. In narration the "whole" is the unit of action, the segment of the continuum, named by the headword. Take, for example, this sentence from the cafe scene: "In the far corner the man was still ASLEEP, *snoring slightly on the intaking breath, his head back against the wall.*" The "whole" is the situation blocked out by the predicate of the main clause, WAS ASLEEP; the italicized phrases are the "parts," the details of the action of sleeping. A few more examples will make clear this principle: "He READ the newspaper laboriously, *forming the words with his lips as he read*"; "He felt the sword buckle[1] . . . and then it SHOT high in the air, *end-over-ending into the crowd.*" In each sentence, the italicized phrase sharpens the image by designating an action, or sometimes an attitude or posture ("his head back against the wall"), that is a subordinate part of that proposed by the headword. Though the term *detail* is convenient and will be used here, *attendant circumstances* would sometimes be more accurate: "He sat heavily in his chair, *his black cordoba hat tipped forward.*"

Descriptive details can be compressed to an adjective and are occasionally expanded to a relative clause; but narrative details are practically restricted to phrases as their vehicle. The phrases are again of three kinds—prepositional, participial, absolute.

The prepositional phrase, with the same prepositions (*with, without,* and *in*), is far less common in narration than in description. In narration the preposition is a device for converting nouns to an adverbial function, and the use of the phrase is limited by the vocabulary available. Most of the nouns could be used directly as verbs, but there is a difference in emphasis between "The bull *rushed* out" and "The bull came out *in a rush.*" Moreover, the modifiers to be used sometimes determine the choice of noun or verb. In sentences such as these—". . . with prissy little sidling steps, she started forward" and "He advanced along the shore with a creeping bow-legged hobble" (Capote)—*step* and *hobble* could not be used as verbs because their modifiers could not be converted to adverbs.

Of the 13 prepositional phrases in *The Undefeated,* 9 are based on *in* and only 4 on *with,* an unusual proportion. The *in*-phrases are all simple: "Then the bull came out *in a rush,* skidding on his four legs as he came out under the lights, then charging *in a gallop,* moving softly *in a fast gallop*"; "The bull charged *in a scramble*"; "The gypsy moved *in a zigzag.*" None of Hemingway's are typical *with*-phrases like the two from Capote quoted above. They should, strictly, be classed as absolute phrases. In a sentence such as this— "The bull, *with his tongue out, his barrel heaving,* was watching the gypsy" —the two phrases are identical except for *with,* and *with* here is simply a "marker" of the absolute.

Participial and absolute phrases are more useful vehicles for narrative details because they use a form of the verb instead of a noun. The two differ in that the subject of the participle is not contained in the phrase itself but must be inferred from other parts of the sentence, whereas the absolute has its own subject. The absolute is the ideal vehicle for details, descriptive as

1. *Buckle* here is an infinitive, not a noun.

well as narrative, because any part of the agent or the situation can be singled out for separate notice. This can be seen in a sentence where both kinds of phrases are used in a series: "Manuel SWUNG with the charge, *sweeping the muleta ahead of the bull, his feet firm, the sword following the curve,* a point of light under the arcs." *Manuel*, the subject of *swung*, is also the subject in a secondary way of *sweeping*; but Hemingway wants us to see, as parts of the same action, the feet held firm, the sword, in the other hand, following the curve of the muleta. If it were not for the absolute construction he would have to say something like "sweeping the muleta ahead of the bull, holding his feet firm, following the curve with his sword," which would not only be clumsy and wordy but put the three subordinate actions on the same plane. Finally, as a detail within a detail, he wants us to see the sword as not a sword but a point of light. The construction is a noun cluster or phrase.

The participle, the lighter of these two constructions, appears more frequently; there are two for each absolute phrase. The 121 include 11 passive participles and 11 "fused" participles, that is, participles that are not separated by punctuation from the verb they modify: "The little man sat looking at him" as contrasted with "Retana sat, saying nothing and looking at Manuel." There are 60 absolute phrases, not counting the 17 punctuated as sentences.

How Hemingway has handled details can be shown best by examples where he seems most intent on shaping the sentence to the action, trying to get the complexity of the action without losing the narrative continuity. This will show, too, all three methods working together and all the grammatical forms they express themselves through. Some of the best sentences are those describing the work of the gypsy, Fuentes:

> Alone in the center of the ring the bull STOOD, *still fixed.* FUENTES, *tall, flatbacked,* WALKING toward him *arrogantly, his arms spread out, the two slim, red sticks, one in each hand, held by the fingers, points straight forward.*

The second sentence has no predicate verb; grammatically it is an absolute phrase. *Tall* and *flat-backed* go with the subject, *Fuentes*, describing appearance rather than behavior, the first by quality, the second by detail. As a headword, *walking* takes the adverb *arrogantly* and the two absolute phrases describing the position of his arms and the way he holds the banderillos. The phrases *one in each hand* and *points straight forward*, both absolutes, modify *the two slim, red sticks held by the fingers*; these details within a detail represent a third level.

The next, relatively simple, sentence illustrates all three methods of description.

> The gypsy was walking out toward the bull again, WALKING *heel-and-toe, insultingly, like a ball-room dancer, the red shafts of the banderillos twitching with his walk.*

The second *walking* I take as in apposition to the first; it is a common practice to add an appositive noun or verb in order, as here, to separate the modifiers of manner from those of time and place, or to clear the narrative movement by keeping the subject and the verb free of modifiers. *Walking* is modified by quality in the adverb *insultingly*, by comparison in the *like* phrase, and by detail in the concluding absolute phrase; *heel-and-toe* is an adverbial noun describing by detail.

The next sentence is of a type, frequent especially in Hemingway's narratives of hunting, where the action involves two or more agents and the sentence focuses, by means of absolute phrases, first on one and then on another, with any number of third- or fourth- or fifth-level modifiers added to the absolute phrases. In this sentence, after winding the bull around himself like a belt, Manuel stepped clear,

> leaving the bull facing Zurito on the white horse, come up and planted firm, THE HORSE FACING THE BULL, its ears forward, its lips nervous, ZURITO, his hat over his eyes, LEANING FORWARD, the long pole sticking out before and behind in a sharp angle under his right arm, held halfway down, the triangular iron point facing the bull.

The absolutes in small capitals are subordinate to "Zurito on the white horse, come up and planted firm." The fear of the horse is described by two details in absolutes showing his alert ears and nervous lips, and the attitude of Zurito leaning forward by two more, showing the position of his hat and his pic. The last two phrases, a participle and an absolute, are fifth-level details picturing further the way he holds the pic. The five levels of structure in the part of the sentence I have quoted can be shown graphically as follows:

1 Zurito on the white horse,
  2 come up and planted firm,
    3 the horse facing the bull,
      4 its ears forward,
      4 its lips nervous,
    3 Zurito, / , leaning forward,
      4 / his hat over his eyes
      4 the long pole sticking out . . . under his right arm,
        5 held halfway down,
        5 the triangular iron point facing the bull.

This, to conclude, is what I have found in working out Erskine's principle. The striking thing about this analysis is its simplicity. There are two steps in picturing an object or an action in words—naming it and describing it. (Naming has been taken for granted in this paper.) For describing either an object or an action there are three methods; and each method makes use of a limited set of grammatical constructions. These grammatical constructions are an invaluable clue to the sentence patterns of current descriptive-narrative writing.

A Statistical Analysis of the Prose Style of Ernest Hemingway: "Big Two-Hearted River" / *Elizabeth J. Wells*

In order to supply the statistics necessary for this analysis of Hemingway's prose style, I was forced to look long and hard at the printed page with an attention to detail that is normally granted only poetry. Certainly a computer analysis could include more pages of type in the sampling, but the advantages of having visually and verbally gone over and over the same passages would be lost. Hemingway's prose more than repaid my attention to structural detail.

The statistics have been taken from Hemingway's "Big Two-Hearted River: Part I." "Big Two-Hearted River" is early Hemingway. It is important to note here, however, that Hemingway was not a monolithic writer. In fact, his style changed over the years from the excessively clipped expression of *In Our Time* to the more mellow expression of *For Whom the Bell Tolls*. Moreover, within this gradual change, Hemingway experimented with rambling Faulknerian sentences in *Green Hills of Africa*. In brief, the progression from the style of *In Our Time* to the style of *For Whom the Bell Tolls* was a progression toward more complexity and variety in all matters except diction. The sentences became longer and grammatically more complex. More words were included inside dependent clauses. Sentence openers became more varied. Hemingway's diction, however, remained essentially of the same monosyllabic, Anglo-Saxon cast.

Having granted a difference in earlier and later Hemingway, I have chosen to describe in detail the most extreme example of the Hemingway style to be found in his earlier stories. For it was the earlier Hemingway that created a style that has since been copied and displayed as a model for a modern, no-nonsense, prose style. By describing the extreme, this study will be des-

This paper is a revised version of part of "A Comparative Statistical Analysis of the Prose Styles of F. Scott Fitzgerald and Ernest Hemingway," *Fitzgerald / Hemingway Annual 1969.* Copyright © 1969 by the National Cash Register Company. Revision printed here by permission of Microcard Editions.

cribing, therefore, those elements of his style that are most often identified with him and which earned him a reputation as one of the most conscientious stylists of American writers.

It may be argued that subject matter and point of view affect the reliability of statistics. It would be a mistake, indeed, not to consider these matters of subject when the statistics are interpreted. A description of an author's style is, by implication, a description of his subject matter. Hemingway's fondness for simple diction is tied inextricably to the character of his male protagonists. Whenever necessary, therefore, forays will be made into the world of Nick Adams in order to interpret or qualify the statistics.

One very important limitation of this study, however, is the elimination of dialogue because the tools of statistical analysis do not readily lend themselves to work on dialogue. Also, dialogue, by definition, consists of words spoken by a character and, ideally, reflects more upon that character's manner of speech than upon the author's prose style. Not much will be lost by ignoring the dialogue of this story as there are only three short statements by Nick. These three statements do, however, affect statistics on paragraph length.

The length of a paragraph, the largest unit of written discourse, is determined by many considerations. Paragraphs written as lead-ins for dialogue will be shorter than most. But equally important is the subject matter of the paragraph, that is, whether the paragraph argues a point, provides descriptive background for future action, or describes action taking place over a time span of many years or a few minutes. The average paragraph length of "Big Two-Hearted River" is 105 words. Significantly, three out of the six paragraphs that fall under 35 words surround dialogue.

The brevity of paragraph number five, the first short paragraph in this story, is definitely used to highlight and intensify the action of that paragraph. After giving us four long paragraphs of strictly objective scene-setting in which Nick observes the ruins of Seney, Hemingway shifts to a very succinct statement of Nick's emotional reaction to the trout:

Nick's heart tightened as the trout moved. He felt all the old feeling.

This paragraph is important. It is the first indication that Nick has returned to a world that means much to him, the first indication that this is not just another excursion. And the shift in cadence from the long descriptive paragraphs to this brief statement of emotion alerts the reader to its importance. Immediately following this first short paragraph is another short one that pictures Nick following the convolutions of the stream. Once again, this particular stream is very important; it is, in fact, the occasion for the title of the story.

In the longest paragraph, 312 words, Nick is remembering something from his past. He is remembering Hopkins. The paragraph wanders as

Nick's mind wanders. But Nick does not want to think; he wants to leave the past behind him for a while. And the long paragraph which describes Nick's lapse into the past is broken off only when he acts and drinks the coffee.

Because Hemingway seldom provides any biographical background in his short stories, especially in the Nick Adams stories which are small vignettes recounting an isolated event, he does not shift from longer paragraphs of orderly narrative exposition of events that cover long time spans to shorter paragraphs of fragmented description of immediate action that cover a single event. Instead, he varies paragraph length for specific effect.

The next largest unit of written discourse, the sentence, can be studied in terms of length, structure, and patterning. Hemingway's sentences average 12 words. This statistic is even more striking in conjuction with the additional facts that only 12 percent of Hemingway's sentences are more than ten words over the average of twelve and 43 percent are five words or more below the average. This extreme brevity can be accounted for by degree of sentence complexity. Hemingway's sentences are short because 73 percent of them are simple sentences.

The immediate effect of such a style is obvious. It produces a choppy, Dick-and-Jane type of prose. The reasons for such writing are generally thought to be also very obvious. It is the paratactic syntax most often found among children who have not yet learned to subordinate their ideas and who, consequently, present ideas one after another without any relationships between them. It is most often considered to be the language of those incapable of cause-and-effect reasoning and unable to perform the more sophisticated mental activity of abstracting generalities out of specifics. But in Hemingway's case it is not a matter of being incapable of cause-and-effect reasoning and abstraction but of being unwilling to present either in this story. Although "Big Two-Hearted River" is told in the third person, we are never allowed to see more than Nick sees, and Nick, to repeat an earlier point, does not want to think. He wants to act. He is, in fact, consciously putting himself through a ritual that will keep him from thinking. Any complication, therefore, whether mental or linguistic, is, like the swamp, to be avoided. Possibilities abound for subordination in this story, but Hemingway refuses to take advantage of them. He writes, for example:

> His muscles ached and the day was hot, but Nick felt happy. He felt he had left everything behind, the need for thinking, the need to write, other needs.

Hemingway could have written instead:

> Although his muscles ached and the day was hot, Nick felt happy because he felt he had left everything behind, the need for thinking, the need to write, other needs.

Only once does Nick allow himself to search for causes and that is when he examines the sooty grasshoppers. But there is little danger in pondering the reason for grasshoppers turning black. It is, however, important to note that the paragraph that describes Nick's puzzling over the grasshoppers contains more subordinate clauses than any other paragraph in the story.

The logic of sentence structure demands that subordination establish a clear scale of values by subordinating less worthy ideas into dependent clauses. In this story little attempt is made to distinguish between the relative value of each of Nick's ritual actions. Only 15 percent of the story is told inside dependent clauses.

Of equal significance is the type of dependent clause Hemingway employs. Sixty-three percent are adverbial and only six of those adverbial clauses are introduced by the subordinate conjunctions "since," "because," or "if," all of which establish causal relationship. Instead, Hemingway is fond of the subordinate conjunctions "as" and "while," which describe concurrent action. His longest sentence, in fact, contains three such clauses:

> *As the shadow of the kingfisher moved up the stream*, a big trout shot upstream in a long angle, only his shadow marking the angle, then lost his shadow *as he came through the surface of the water*, caught the sun, and then, *as he went back into the stream under the surface*, his shadow seemed to float down the stream with the current, unresisting, to his post under the bridge where he tightened facing up into the current.

When Hemingway wishes to express step-by-step action, he most often places one action after the other without any temporal connector. To provide the subordinate conjunctions "until" and "before" (he uses only five altogether) would be to needlessly complicate the sequential nature of the events.

When faced with a problem of description, Hemingway chooses repetition rather than subordination. Notice the repetition of the words "trees," "trunks," and "branches" in the following sentences:

> There was no underbrush in the island of pine *trees*. The *trunks* of the *trees* went straight up or slanted toward each other. The *trunks* were straight and brown without *branches*. The *branches* were high above.

Any two of these sentences could be combined by using adjectival subordinate clauses. For example, one could say, "The trunks, *which were straight and brown without branches*, went straight up or slanted toward each other." This revision is certainly not an improvement and could only be justified on the basis of avoiding repetition and introducing sentence variety. But besides being one of the salient characteristics of the Hemingway style, repetition is essential to the ritual of this story.

Hemingway seldom fails to set up obvious patterns. Patterns may be created by repetition of the same key words, similar grammatical types of words, clauses that begin with the same conjunction, similar sentence structures, or similar or identical sentence openers.

Repetition of a key word can be used not only to avoid subordination, as has been illustrated, but to emphasize the importance of that word. In the following passage, Hemingway uses the word or a form of the word "smoothed" three times:

> He *smoothed* out the sandy soil with his hand and pulled all the sweet fern bushes by their roots. His hands smelled good from the sweet fern. He *smoothed* the uprooted earth. He did not want anything making lumps under the blankets. When he had the ground *smooth*, he spread his three blankets.

This is not the work of a writer of limited vocabulary. Nick Adams is not only smoothing out the ground underneath him, but also smoothing out the unnecessary complications of his past, smoothing over his bruised consciousness. He wants no problems, no "lumps." Note how Hemingway further emphasizes Nick's smoothing actions by repetition on the "s" sound, especially in the verbs.

When Hemingway wished to depict more energetic activity, he often chose the dynamic present participle. In his first description of the trout, he gives life to the stream and the fish in it by using several participial phrases to describe the scene. The trout are described as "keeping themselves steady," "holding themselves with their noses into the current," "looking to hold themselves," "facing up the current." The surface of the stream is described as "pushing and swelling." Not only are specific words repeated in these three paragraphs but the grammatical cast of those phrases used to describe the scene is identical.

It has already been established that Hemingway used dependent clauses sparingly. But when he did use them, he often repeated exactly the same type of clause, with the same subordinate conjunction introducing it. In the paragraph describing Nick's cogitation about the grasshoppers, five of the nine dependent clauses are introduced with "as" and three are introduced with "that." His tendency toward repeating similar dependent clauses reduces the inherent complexity of such clauses and increases the rhythmic, ritualistic effect of his prose.

Hemingway also often repeated the structure of the larger unit of the sentence itself. In one paragraph he includes three sentences of almost identical structure:

> *He adjusted* the pack harness around the bundle, *pulling* straps tight.
> . . . *He walked* along the road that paralleled the railway track, *leaving*
> the burned town behind in the heat. . . . *He walked* along the road *feeling*
> the ache from the pull of the heavy pack.

Most striking of all, however, is his repetition of the simple subject followed
immediately by the simple verb as a sentence opener. Notice the grammatical
plainness of the following passage which illustrates this type of repetition:

> *Nick sat* down beside the fire and lifted the frying pan off. *He poured*
> about half the contents out into the tin plate. *It spread* slowly on the
> plate. *Nick knew* it was too hot. *He poured* on some tomato catchup.
> *He knew* the beans and spaghetti were still too hot. *He looked* at the
> fire, . . .

Occasionally, Hemingway repeats both identical words and identical grammatical structures and, in addition, puts them in a pattern. In the following
passage all of the sentences begin with the simple subject, simple verb
combination, and the subject is alternated:

> *Nick stretched* under the blanket comfortably. *A mosquito hummed*
> close to his ear. *Nick sat up* and lit a match. *The mosquito was* on the
> canvas, over his head. *Nick moved* the match quickly up to it. *The
> mosquito made* a satisfactory hiss in the flame.

However trivial the contest, Hemingway is pitting Nick against the mosquito,
just as he will later, in a more complicated sport, pit Nick against the trout.
Such repetition is designed for effect. And just how effective it can become
can be best illustrated in the following passage which uses all the possibilities
of repetition. Nick has just set up camp, and Hemingway gives us this most
unusual description of Nick's emotional state:

> Now things were done. There had been this to do. Now it was done.
> It had been a hard trip. He was very tired. That was done. He had made
> his camp. He was settled. Nothing could touch him. It was a good place
> to camp. He was there, in the good place. He was in his home where
> he had made it. Now he was hungry.

Repetition of the word "done" expresses the finality of Nick's accomplishment. Repetition of the word "now," especially at the beginning of the sentences, gives the impression of shelving the past and looking with hope
toward the future. All of the cobwebs have been cleared away, and he is in
a "good place." All of the sentences, except one, are simple and most of the
verbs express state of being rather than action. At this moment Nick has
sufficiently simplified his world, provided for all his needs, and is in a static

state of simply existing. He is "settled." He is "there." Note the consistent impersonality of all of the subjects except "he": there are "things," "this," "it," "that," "nothing." In this new world that Nick has created for himself, the "things" other than himself are without personality, without threat, unable to "touch" him. He has sufficiently neutralized his world to the point where he can satisfy his needs by repeating rituals of motion, rituals so well learned that they require no thought. The stasis of the above passage is broken only when Nick acts to satisfy his hunger.

Such manipulation of words into patterns in order to produce an effect not inherent in the lexical definition of the words themselves constitutes an attempt to escape the bounds of denotative meaning by using the rich possibilities of sentence logic to carry us beyond the words. Although other techniques, such as the effective use of figurative language, may add more dimensions of meaning to a Hemingway story, the strict objectivity of numerical analysis does not allow for their consideration in this study. To count, however, is to begin to capture much of what is distinctly Hemingway. The perfect blend of form and content in "Big Two-Hearted River" was achieved by an artist who knew how to make his language do his bidding.

Hemingway and the Thing Left Out / *Julian Smith*

Having long suspected Ernest Hemingway of omitting essential details from his stories and novels, I was not surprised by his account in *A Moveable Feast* of how he deleted "the real end [of "Out of Season"] which was that the old man hanged himself. This was omitted on my new theory that you could omit anything if you knew that you omitted and the omitted part would strengthen the story and make people feel something more than they understood."[1] I can see why Hemingway left out the old man Peduzzi's suicide—his death would have distracted our attention too far from the young American couple who seem at the story's center; moreover, it wasn't necessary to actually tell us Peduzzi killed himself. That is, Hemingway had the advantage of having written under the tension of knowing what would happen—it was the tension Hemingway valued, not the Thing that caused the tension, so he left the Thing out.

Julian Smith, "Hemingway and the Thing Left Out," *Journal of Modern Literature*, I (1970–71), 169–72. Reprinted by permission of the *Journal of Modern Literature*.

1. (New York: Scribner's, 1964), p. 75.

"Out of Season," the first story Hemingway wrote after the theft of his early manuscripts, marks his true professional beginning (the only stories to survive the manuscript catastrophe, "My Old Man" and "Up in Michigan," are not of the true style). It should follow that Hemingway, having so begun, continued to experiment with the technique of leaving things out. Indeed, Carlos Baker states that Hemingway excised from "Indian Camp" "an entire preliminary episode covering eight long-hand pages. This was the story of Nick Adams, a small boy afraid of the dark, firing off a rifle to bring his father and his uncle back from jacklight fishing in the lake."[2] Hemingway seems to have reversed the technique he employed in "Out of Season": instead of building toward a moment of tension, he *started* with the tension of Nick alone and afraid on the lake, a tension later balanced by the boy's final calmness, in spite of the night's terrors, in his father's company. Having established Nick's personality, gotten him moving down an emotional track, Hemingway simply cut off the motive power, fear.

But the excision of the early scene from "Indian Camp" is the kind of editorial cut many authors make without greatly altering the effect or meaning of a story. What I mean by The Thing Left Out is illustrated in "Big Two-Hearted River," which Hemingway called a story "about coming back from the war but there was no mention of the war in it."[3] Again, the motive power, the tension, seemingly remained outside the story, but within the author's mind as he wrote. The omission is more crucial because what has been left out affects our reading. To read "Big Two-Hearted River" without reading anything else Hemingway wrote causes confusion: what is wrong with Nick? Why does he take pleasure in those simple obsessions? Not knowing the answers should not bother one greatly, for many things are unknowable, yet the reader who has read the other Nick Adams stories and knows of Nick's wounds should be much more impressed by what has been left out, impressed by the craftsmanship of a writer who has managed as a third-person narrator to avoid telling us what his hero has avoided thinking about. The effect is hard, stoic, controlled, and the reader who understands what has been left unsaid finds himself initiated into a cult.

I

Though these three stories (written in less than two years) are the only ones we positively know employ the technique of omission, it seems unlikely that other examples do not exist. I will therefore suggest that three often misunderstood stories are also built around something never clearly expressed: "In Another Country," "Now I Lay Me," and "God Rest You Merry, Gentlemen."

2. Carlos Baker, *Ernest Hemingway: A Life Story* (Scribner's, 1969), p. 125.
3. *A Moveable Feast*, p. 76.

But first, let me cite a case in which Hemingway either passed up the chance to leave something out or put it back in at the last minute. In October, 1926, two months after his first marriage ended, he submitted "A Canary for One" to *Scribner's Magazine*.[4] In this story, a young American couple, obviously not talking to one another, share a train compartment with a middle-aged American tourist who insists on talking about marriage in general and how she broke up her daughter's engagement. The story seems at first to be about this American lady, but the young couple become increasingly important until the last sentence when the husband, who narrates, tells us "We were returning to Paris to set up separate residences." I don't think Hemingway worked up here to the kind of WOW ending he disclaimed in *Death in the Afternoon*. Rather, writing under the effect of his own recent separation, writing from personal experience and perhaps even for himself, he felt no need to say what was wrong, or was incapable of revealing the problem as he wrote. But when he submitted the story for publication, he did not, I speculate, have sufficient faith in the terrible finality of the true end: "We followed the porter with the truck down the long cement platform beside the train. At the end was a gate and a man took the tickets." So he put back the thing left out by adding that O. Henry last sentence.

He was far bolder with "In Another Country," sumitted the following month and printed beside "A Canary for One" in *Scribner's Magazine*. So much has been omitted that the young American narrator, who as in "Canary" is the secret center of the story, has frequently been ignored or relegated to a minor position ("the central figure was an Italian major"; "It is the major's pain that the story is about"; "the story centers around [the major]") [5] or falsely identified as Nick Adams (Philip Young and others). He is not Nick Adams, but like the narrator of the companion story, anonymous. Nick Adams is Hemingway's adolescent alter ego; Hemingway, unsettled by the end of his first marriage, I suggest, developed two new avatars, both young, both American, both in Europe, and both bereft of love. At the end of "A Canary for One" we are informed directly of this loss of love if we have not understood it in the story; "In Another Country" *seems* to be about a middle-aged Italian major whose wife has died of pneumonia, but is actually about the young American who witnessed the major's loss without realizing he was about to suffer a similar loss.

What has been left out of "In Another Country" is the dead wench alluded to in the story's title taken from Marlowe's *The Jew of Malta* by way of T. S. Eliot's "Portrait of a Lady":

4. For dates and details of composition and submission, I am indebted throughout this paper to Professor Baker's biography.

5. See Carlos Baker, p. 177; Philip Young, *Ernest Hemingway: A Reconsideration* (Pennsylvania State University Press, 1966), pp. 58–59; Leo Gurko, *Ernest Hemingway and the Pursuit of Heroism* (New York: Crowell, 1968), p. 181.

> Thou hast committed—
> Fornication: but that was in another country,
> And besides, the wench is dead.[6]

If we read Hemingway's story as it has generally been read, the "wench" is the major's wife. Such an identification is doubly inappropriate because it puts the emphasis right back on the major in spite of the fact that the narrator has been carefully characterized long before we meet the major and because "committed fornication" connotes an illicit act, whereas the very proper major was married. It is our nameless young narrator, looking back to "a long time ago" when *he* was in another country, who has committed fornication with a "wench" now dead.

That my reading may make "In Another Country" seem an early version of *A Farewell to Arms* should be obvious: the narrator anticipates Frederic Henry and the offstage "wench" his mistress, Catherine Barkley. Carlos Baker dates the start of *A Farewell to Arms* as early March, 1928, and states Hemingway wanted to use the "in another country" quotation for an epigraph.[7] I wonder if Hemingway had a hand in choosing the direct translation of Marlowe's words for the title of the German edition of the novel, *In Einem Andern Land.*

Although there are only these two peripheral connections between the story of 1926 and the novel begun less than two years later, the direct connections are far more numerous. The narrators, young Americans attached to the Italian army, are both equally interested in medals, both wounded in the leg and afflicted by a knee that won't bend. Both walk across Milan from their hospital quarters to another hospital for mechanical therapy—and both stop to drink at the same place before returning to their hospital. The first words of the story summarize perfectly the mood of the last half of the novel following Henry's farewell to arms: "In the fall the war was always there, but we did not go to it any more." Hemingway achieves the same kind of removal from warfare through the novel's first sentence by ignoring the war entirely: "In the late summer of that year we lived in a house in a village that looked across the river and the plain to the mountains."

It would be an easy matter to insert "In Another Country" either after the marriage conversation at the end of Chapter XVIII or between Chapter XXI, in which Catherine announces her pregnancy, and Chapter XXII, in which Henry loses his chance to go on leave with Catherine and is sent back to the front. The story fits so well into the novel that it seems The Thing Left Out. But though the novel does not need the story, the story needs the novel if it is to be read with any understanding of the narrator's reason for telling it. It

6. For Hemingway's debt to Eliot and Marlowe, see Phyllis Bartlett, "Other Countries, Other Wenches," *Modern Fiction Studies*, III (Winter 1957–58), 345–349.
7. Baker, p. 190.

is of course impossible to know how much of the story line for the novel Hemingway had in mind when he wrote "In Another Country"—quite likely he was not even thinking of a full novel but of a hero very much like himself and in love, like his younger self, with a nurse.

He also knew that something would have to happen to the love affair. But what?

In 1924, in what has been called the starting point for *A Farewell to Arms*, Hemingway tried to fictionalize his unsuccessful courting of Agnes von Kurowsky, the American nurse he met in Milan. In the bitter result, "A Very Short Story," a nurse writes her suitor that she has decided to marry a mature Italian officer instead, for "theirs had been only a boy and girl affair." But such a commonplacely unromantic end to the affair is not appropriate to the autumnal mood of "In Another Country"—nor would it have been appropriate, I believe, to the mood of Hemingway right after his separation when, as he hinted at the end of *A Moveable Feast*, he felt morose and guilty for having ruined his first and most idyllic marriage.

At this point it would be well to quote the marriage conversation in "In Another Country";

> "Are you married?" [asks the major]
> "No, but I hope to be."
> "The more of a fool you are," he said. He seemed very angry. "A man must not marry."
> "Why, Signor Maggiore?"
> "Don't call me 'Signor Maggiore.' "
> "Why must not a man marry?"
> "He cannot marry. He cannot marry," he said angrily. "If he is to lose everything; he should not place himself in a position to lose that. He should not place himself in a position to lose. He should find things he cannot lose."

For some reason the narrator's odd answer to the first question, that he "hopes" to be married, has gone unnoticed. Young American males do not hope for marriage in general or as a future condition; if anything, they may hope for the opposite. In addition, the way the narrator patiently asks why a man should not marry, the way he later asks "But why should he necessarily lose it," suggests that the narrator, who has trouble speaking Italian with the intensely precise major, is making more than polite small talk, that his interest is highly personal. The major breaks off the conversation, goes into another room, makes a telephone call, and returns with the news that his young wife has died.

Had Hemingway incorporated "In Another Country" in the middle, say, of Chapter XIX of *A Farewell to Arms*, it would have ominously foreshadowed Catherine's death. Let us try such an interpolation. After the major's wife dies, Henry returns to Catherine, where, following his return in the novel itself from therapy, we find this dialog:

> "I'm afraid [says Catherine] of the rain because sometimes I see me dead in it."
> "No."
> "And sometimes I see you dead in it."
> "That's more likely."

Perhaps Hemingway was remembering "In Another Country" as he wrote these lines; what has been left out is that they form a terrible coincidence after the conversation with the major. Or take this fragment from Chapter XXI:

> "They won't get us," I said. "Because you're too brave. Nothing ever happens to the brave."
> "They die of course" [says Catherine.]

None of this, however, is proof that the story's narrator has lost his wife, fiancée, or mistress to death. Proof I cannot give; I can only assert that "In Another Country" becomes an even more impressive story if you will read it as I do. For instance, the major is obviously a "tutor" figure similar to the many tutors encountered by Frederic Henry—as such, he teaches *not* that one should not marry, but how one should accept the loss of one's wife: one returns to what one has been doing, even if it is something as ridiculous and futile as mechanotherapy for a ruined hand. Such a message would be intolerably commonplace if purely abstract, but Hemingway-Henry-nameless narrator is pulling it out of his memory at a time when it is a useable truth following the loss of his own "wife." At the same time, by dwelling on the major's loss rather than his own, the narrator shows he has learned well the major's stoic philosophy.

II

Though it is the second story in *Men Without Women*, "In Another Country" is actually the first to state the men-without-women theme. The nominal lead story, "The Undefeated," about bullfighting, was probably placed first to capitalize on the recent popular success of *The Sun Also Rises*. Further evidence that "In Another Country" is the real beginning of *Men Without Women* is to be found in the fact that it is counterpointed by the last story, "Now I Lay Me," also narrated by a young American in the Italian army who has also been wounded and who also has a conversation about marriage. But whereas in the first story the narrator wants to marry and is warned not to, in the second the narrator, who seems unwilling to marry, is advised to do so by his orderly, John.

"Now I Lay Me" ends with the narrator's confession that the orderly came "to see me several months after and was very disappointed that I had not yet married, and I know he would feel very badly if he knew that, so far, I have never married. He was going back to America and he was very certain about marriage and knew it would fix up everything." Richard B. Hovey lumps this with three other Hemingway stories about "a bachelor hero so reluctant to marry that he cannot even contemplate the possibility except with doubt and apprehension" and asserts that the narrator's "efforts to cope with his trauma require a fuller inquiry, but for the moment it is enough to note the story's obvious moral: that marriage is no help for a man who has come too close to death."[8] I have taken Professor Hovey's comment because it comes from one of the fullest and most recent readings of the story and because it so well represents the tendency of much Hemingway criticism to reduce a story to an "obvious moral."

Very little in this or any other Hemingway story is as obvious as it seems. Earl Rovit calls the orderly "a wounded fellow soldier" when it is not at all evident he is wounded and when it is absolutely certain that he is not a "fellow" soldier but a subordinate; Rovit also calls the story "a direct recounting of [Hemingway's] convalescence in Milan after the Fossalta wound"[9] despite the first words of the story ("That night we lay on the floor in the room and I listened to the silkworms eating"—odd place to convalesce, on the floor of a silk worm house) and the later information that the setting is only "seven kilometres behind the lines" (Milan was far from the front). Rather, it should be clear that the narrator, who has "been wounded a couple of times," is back at the front between woundings.

Criticism of "Now I Lay Me" is abundant and becoming increasingly synoptic. Its popularity with critics probably results from its openness to psychological interpretation: the narrator, who can't sleep partly for fear of dying before he wakes, first occupies his mind by fishing the big two-hearted rivers of imagination, then begins to remember the running warfare between his parents and his own childish involvement in that warfare. Joseph DeFalco, taking the psychological reading to its outer limits, pontificates thusly: "As he lies in bed at night unable to sleep, a willful precipitation of regressive infantile reveries marks him as suffering from some acute mental disorder."[10] The first thing wrong here is that the narrator is not in bed; he's on a blanket spread over straw on the floor. Secondly, things other than "acute mental disorder" keep one awake—dripping faucets, fear of the police, debt, mos-

8. *Hemingway: The Inward Terrain* (University of Washington Press, 1968), p. 8.
9. *Ernest Hemingway* (New York, 1963), p. 79.
10. *The Hero in Hemingway's Short Stories* (University of Pittsburgh Press, 1963), p. 105.

quitoes, straw bedding. And why must childhood memories be labeled "willful precipitation of regressive infantile reveries"? That kind of talk gives us all a bad name.

Not enough attention, on the other hand, has been given to the nagging little questions raised by the story. What exactly does the first sentence mean? "That night we lay on the floor in the room and I listened to the silkworms eating." The first two words alone offer enough problems to distract us from psychological readings. What night? Why is he *listening* to rather than merely *hearing* the silk-worms? Why does he mention "we" and not tell us who "we" are until the second half of the story? My point is that the story has still not been read carefully at the first level of meaning, the literal.

A prime example of this neglect is that no one, to my knowledge, has explained the narrator's double insistence that "I had not yet married" and "so far, I have never married." The narrator, called Nick by his hen-pecked doctor father, seems almost certainly Nick Adams, but we know from "Cross Country Snow," published in January, 1925, over two years before "Now I Lay Me," that Nick Adams is already married. There are several unsatisfactory ways around this problem. We could say that although the story was published after "Cross Country Snow" and although the narrator seems to be speaking of his present condition, that he is actually speaking prior to the time we meet him in the later story. We could say the Nick of this story is not Nick Adams, or that though generally consistent in his treatment of Nick, Hemingway cannot be held to consistency at the expense of effect. Or perhaps "Cross Country Snow" itself was a false direction in the history of Nick Adams and Hemingway changed his mind later and unmarried him ("Fathers and Sons," 1933, is the only other story in which we see Nick has ever been married). Or the narrator may be lying, or Hemingway may be ironically purging himself of his first marriage (apparently composed at about the time of his second marriage in May, 1927, the story may reflect his temporary unmarried state).

The trouble with all these suggestions is that they are too far from the story itself. Ideally, the reason for Hemingway's decision to arbitrarily change facts in the biography of Nick Adams and to end with "he was very certain about marriage and knew it would fix up everything" should be found within the story, but since it cannot be found, clearly something has been left out. If we read "Now I Lay Me" as an extension of "In Another Country" and as an early effort by Hemingway to fictionalize and romanticise his unsuccessful courtship of an American nurse in Italy, we might get this kind of plot line: the narrator of the first story disregards the major's advice, seeks to marry, but like Frederic Henry loses his fiancée-mistress; following his loss, not having deserted the Italian army at this stage in Hemingway's thinking, he returns to the front where we see him sleepless in the

summer, half a year or more after the time of the first story, and in no mood
to think of marriage, for marriage will no more cure his inner wounds than
will the therapy machines cure the major's.[11]

Unfortunately, such a reading does not explain the presence of the narrator's highly specific memories of his father's psychological emasculation:
how "after my grandfather died we moved away from that house and to a
new house designed and built by my mother" (the mother, on the death of
the patriarch, usurped the male role of architect and builder); how his mother
burned his father's collection of phallic snakes and equally phallic Indian
artifacts—arrow heads, stone axes, skinning knives, and tools. Professors
DeFalco and Hovey see the narrator as psychically emasculated, Hovey calling Nick's memories of Mom-the-destroyer "the prototype of Nick Adam's
first 'wound'—the child's fear of emasculation. This long-established and
buried trauma has been revived with terrible power through the physical
battle wound. That somehow this is the earliest memory, dredged up through
so much pain, indicates that in Nick Adams the fear of castration is stronger
than in most men."[12] Why does the narrator dwell on memories that suggest
fear of castration, and what has this preoccupation to do with the fact John
"was very certain about marriage and knew that it would fix up everything"?
I suggest the story concerns something that literally cannot be "fixed up" by
marriage, that the narrator has been sexually wounded, and that his memory
of his father's symbolic castration is selective, not random, highly personal,
not removed. In short, I am suggesting he is closer to Jake Barnes, the sexually wounded narrator of *The Sun Also Rises* (1926), than to Nick Adams.

The many similarities between the narrator of "Now I Lay Me" and Jake
Barnes might be explained away as further evidence that Hemingway himself is the common denominator among his heroes and that they do not
resemble each other as much as they resemble Hemingway. Hemingway,
Jake, and Nick of "Now I Lay Me" are all young Americans from the Mid-
west who served in the Italian army; all three are wounded and hospitalized
in Milan's Ospedale Maggiore; all love fishing; Hemingway and Jake are
reporters, Nick says he wants to be a reporter. More specifically, Nick and
Jake are afflicted by a common insomnia during which Nick remembers his
childhood and Jake remembers being hospitalized in Milan; neither can
keep his mind from "jumping" around. Jake is a Catholic and Nick says
Catholic prayers; Nick attempts to pray for his family, Jake prays for his
friends and himself. In short, *The Sun Also Rises* shows Jake Barnes seven

11. Further evidence of a relationship between these two stories is found in the fact
that a "near-final draft of what became 'Now I Lay Me'" was originally titled "In
Another Country—Two. A Story." See Philip Young and Charles W. Mann, ed., *The
Hemingway Manuscripts: An Inventory* (Pennsylvania State University Press, 1969),
p. 44.
12. *The Inward Terrain*, p. 52; see also DeFalco, p. 113.

or eight years after his wound; "Now I Lay Me" shows someone with a similar but much newer wound who has not yet made adjustments.

Though "Now I Lay Me" was published a year after the novel, it may be a fragment excised from an early version or a scene Hemingway meant to write, a scene showing young "Jake" adjusting to the new knowledge that he cannot have an ordinary marriage, all the while inflicted with the gratuitous advice that marriage "would fix up everything," a spurious message echoed in Brett Ashley's famous last words to Jake: "we could have had such a damned good time together." But, granted my suspicions are correct, why has Hemingway taken a scene from Jake Barnes' life and given it to Nick Adams? Simply because Jake is Nick, sharing the same wounds, the same experiences, even the same friends. Bill, Nick's friend and advisor in "The End of Something" and "The Three-Day Blow" (1925) shows up a year later in the novel as Bill Gorton, Jake's old friend. Nick's Bill and Jake's Bill are both based on Hemingway's friend (and best man at his first wedding) William Smith.[13] If Nick's friend Bill appears in *The Sun Also Rises*, can Nick be far behind?

In an article on the real-life sources for *The Sun Also Rises*, Bertram D. Sarason summarizes the "biographical" interpretation of Jake's wound as representing "imaginatively the blockade to a love affair with Lady Duff Twysden (the Lady Brett Ashley of the novel) which had to be foregone because of Hemingway's loyalty to his wife."[14] I think, however, that Jake's wound is just as much a part of Hemingway's romantization of his "affair" with the nurse who declined to marry him, thus inflicting a psychic wound as debilitating as the physical one. Jake's first conversation with Robert Cohn about Brett Ashley may show our author's old love wound festering and that Hemingway may have combined Duff Twysden and the nurse:

> "Have you known her a long time?" [asks Cohn]
> "Yes," I said. "She was a V. A. D. in a hospital I was in during the war."
> "She must have been just a kid then."
> "She's thirty-four now."

Hemingway's real nurse, born in 1892 like Duff Twysden and Brett Ashley, was also thirty-four in 1926, the year the novel appeared. Note too the similarities between Brett Ashley and Catherine Barkley: both are British and older than the narrators, both once cared for the narrators as V. A. D.'s, both lost lovers to the war before they met the narrators. Hemingway's romantization of his adolescent affair in these two stories and two novels

---

13. See Donald St. John, "Interview with Hemingway's 'Bill Gorton,'" *Connecticut Review*, I, ii (1968), 5–12, for an identification of Smith and Gorton.

14. "Lady Brett Ashley and Lady Duff Twysden," *Connecticut Review*, II (April 1969), 6.

had day-dream alternatives: on the one hand the hero cannot marry because the girl dies; on the other the hero cannot have a normal marriage because of a sexual wound.

If Jake Barnes's experiences are reflected in one story published after the novel, it should not be surprising to find them in another. Such, I think, is the case with "God Rest You Merry, Gentlemen" (1933). The narrator, a former cub reporter from journalist Jake Barnes' hometown, Kansas City, tells about an extremely religious youth who demanded to be castrated in order to escape sexual desire. Turned down, and not knowing what castration entailed, he cut off his penis. I think what has been left out of the story is that the identically mutilated Jake Barnes, and not an anonymous narrator, is remembering an incident that meant nothing to him at the time it occurred but later came to have a terrible relevance. Like "Now I Lay Me," "God Rest You Merry, Gentlemen" may also have been excised from an earlier mental version of *The Sun Also Rises;* if nothing else, both stories share titles calling upon divine aid in gaining the peace so sought after by Jake Barnes:

Now I lay me down to sleep,	God rest you merry, gentlemen,
I pray the Lord my soul to keep;	Let nothing you dismay . . .
And if I die before I wake,	Oh, tidings of comfort and
I pray the Lord my soul to take.	joy. . . .

Though "God Rest You Merry, Gentlemen" has been mostly ignored, there seems a hierarchy of misreadings: at the highest level of misunderstanding, critics discussing the boy who mutilates himself fail to notice the two doctors who tell the narrator about the boy. Since the boy is not even a character in the story, this reading is patently misguided. Closer to the truth comes the larger group of critics who find significant the conflict between the competent Doc Fischer and the incompetent Doctor Wilcox. Neither reading, however, explains the presence of the narrator, for the story could be told by one of the doctors or in the third person. Instead, Hemingway devotes the first hundred and fifty words to memories of the narrator, memories seemingly irrelevant to the story, and later goes to great trouble to characterize him.

The first mistake made by those who do notice the narrator is to call him Horace, the nickname used by the ironic Doc Fischer ("you don't mind me calling you Horace, do you?"). The Roman Horace was everything young Hemingway aspired to be: poet, satirist, and stoic. It is a fine name for a young Jake Barnes, a gift from the sophisticated Doc Fischer to a young aspirant who takes pleasure in false sophistication, as when he tries to interpret "*Dans Argent*," the motto on a racing car: "this I believed to mean the silver dance or the silver dancer, and, slightly puzzled which it meant but happy in the sight of the car and pleased by my knowledge of a foreign language, I went along the street in the snow." The second mistake is to underrate the narrator, as does Peter L. Hays who says "Horace is a perfect Hemingway persona, an accurate but impartial observer," but condemns him as "none too intelligent"[15] partly on the basis of his weak French. The point should be clear: the narrator has over the years acquired sufficient true sophistication, so much so he can now speak objectively of his youthful naïveté, just as Jake Barnes can tell us straightforwardly and with great dignity of his adult humiliations and cruelties.

Indeed, I can think of no Hemingway character better qualified than Jake to speak the first sentence of "God Rest You Merry, Gentlemen": "In those days the distances were all very different, the dirt blew off the hills that have now been cut down, and Kansas City was very like Constantinople." Here are the poles of Jake's existence, K. C. and Constantinople—when he was young Kansas City was the center of the world, civilization amid wilderness, a metropolis where one found *"Dans Argent"* on the hood of a car. "In those days the distances were all very different" because he had a different spatial, temporal, and intellectual scale of reference.

To see the story as about anyone but the narrator is to negate all the narrator tells us about himself, to make him superfluous. Yet on the evidence within the story, he seems totally unnecessary, and the story seems lacking in focus. Once again I am thrown back to the conclusion that Hemingway has left out the narrator's identity and his reason for telling the story. At the same time, I admire the story for its incompleteness, for it is tense, beautiful, and passing strange as written. Still, I want to know why things are as they are in the story; why, for instance, the ending dribbles away in a pointless argument between the two doctors in which the incompetent Wilcox can do no more than ineffectually and irrelevantly attempt to turn Doc Fischer's Jewishness against him.[16] I conclude that the narrator has managed to distract us from himself so we will not bother to ask too many pointed questions about him; I also conclude that the ending is dramatically realistic—at the time it happened the boy's self-mutilation was little more than an agent for increasing the tension and conflict between the two doctors and the narrator remembered the incident in that context. Jake Barnes tells us the story from a personal context, but has left out that context.

If I have gone too far with some of my readings, I repent. But I think it

15. "Hemingway and the Fisher King," *University of Kansas City Review*, XXXII (March 1966), 226.
16. *The Sun Also Rises* and "God Rest You Merry, Gentlemen" are the only works in which Hemingway has important Jewish characters—perhaps he is making up for his antisemitic portrait of Robert Cohn by the extremely sympathetic portrayal of the tutor-figure Doc Fischer. Hemingway goes out of his way to avoid stock characterization by making Fischer thin and blond and the Christian Wilcox short and dark.

better to err in the direction of seeing Hemingway as too coherent than to accuse him, as some readers of all the stories discussed have, of lacking focus, of introducing irrelevant characters and incidents, of, in short, not knowing his business. Instead, I here assert that through omission Hemingway has succeeded in the goal he stated in *A Moveable Feast:* to "make people feel something more than they understood."

3. Story Interpretations

Hemingway's Two-Hearted River / *Sheridan Baker*

Seney is a wide place in Highway M-28, as it drives straight from east to west, just about dead center of Michigan's Upper Peninsula. The railroad runs straight beside the highway on the south side. On the north, after a broad shoulder of shrub and weed, strips of still water, like canals, reflect the straight edge of the thorny stand of second-growth pine, interrupted by stretches of hummocky swamp and brushland. All along at night in the swale between road and trees you can catch the wide anxious ears of does, with eyes like coals and a white flare of tail flying, just outside the wedge of the headlights, with occasionally a dead one beside the road, hit by a car.

Seney has a few houses and cabins and gas stations and a new chartreuse motel with a natural redwood edge to its flat roof. Seney was once the center of a great white-pine forest, the wildest of logging towns. The new forest is scrubby and undernourished. Seney now trades with vacationists, many simply stopping to turn north for wilder parts. It is the home of a company that builds ready-made houses. It is also the starting point for Ernest Hemingway's only story exclusively about trout fishing—his central story, as I hope to show, in the group about Nick Adams—"The Big Two-Hearted River."

But the river Nick Adams looks into from the bridge, after he gets off the train at Seney and walks down the track, is not called the Two-Hearted River at all. It is the Fox, coming from the northwest to run under two new concrete bridges and a railroad trestle—swift and deep and clear-brown, like tea, just as Hemingway describes it, except that its color comes from swampy vegetation, not, as Hemingway says, from pebbles on the bottom. Since Hemingway does not mention the river's name in the story, his title seems simply an epithet, pointing to some vague two-faced, black-hearted, big-hearted significance that runs under the swift brown prose. It seems so, that is, until you learn that there really is a Two-Hearted River—with forks usually called "Big" and "Little"—some thirty or forty rugged crowflight miles to the northeast of Seney. The only critic to pay Hemingway's title any attention at all has taken it literally, with no overtones, and hiked Nick all the way over to the Two-Hearted in less than a day in spite of his long afternoon nap and his glimpses of the river off to the left as he walks north, working upstream. No, Hemingway's river is the Fox, all right. He has simply found a symbolic title ready-made, reaching over the swamps and pines to borrow a name closer to his meaning than the simple Fox could provide.

Sheridan Baker, "Hemingway's Two-Hearted River," *Michigan Alumnus Quarterly Review*, LXV (Winter 1959), 142–49. Copyright, 1959, and permission granted by *Michigan Quarterly Review*.

There can be no doubt that "The Big Two-Hearted River" is meaning-ful. After Malcolm Cowley first pointed this out, others have elaborated briefly. It is about the closely autobiographical Nick Adams, who recurs in a total of fourteen of Hemingway's stories. It forms a conclusion to Hem-ingway's first collection, *In Our Time* (1925), which contains among its fifteen stories seven about Nick, not counting the two halves of "The Big Two-Hearted River," conspicuously given separate numbers in the table of contents and also labeled "Part I" and "Part II." It is Hemingway's only story so formally partitioned. The doubleness of the title seems to be under-lined, and the final position in the book seems summative and emphatic. It is the only story in which Nick is absolutely alone, the only character.

The story opens with Nick standing alone on the track as the train goes out of sight behind a burnt hill. Seney is utterly burned out and deserted: "There was no town, nothing but the rails and the burned-over country." He sees the cracked foundation of the "Mansion House hotel." He walks along to the railroad bridge. The first sign of life comes from the trout "keep-ing themselves steady in the current with wavering fins." This, as Philip Young says, is exactly Nick's own breathless, shell-shocked tension. He has not seen the river for a long time. He keeps reminding himself that he is happy. He is afraid to think. "His mind was starting to work. He knew he could choke it because he was tired enough." He is meticulously neat in stretching his tent, keeping himself tensely occupied with the immediate pres-ent, shutting out the past and all distance possibilities. As he lies down for the night a mosquito drills into the silence close to his ear. He lights a match and finds the mosquito on the tent directly over his head, burns it with a "satisfactory hiss," shuts his eyes, curls up, and goes to sleep.

His first day has been reassuring. The town is gone, but the river is still there. He has leaned his forehead into his tumpline even though he realizes his load is too heavy. He has walked uphill, his muscles aching, but he has been happy. He has left the burned town, knowing the country "could not all be burned." He has found grasshoppers, sooty black, that have survived the fire of the year before, assimilating themselves to their blackened en-vironment, as lively as ever—"not the big grasshoppers with yellow and black or red and black wings whirring out from their black wing sheathing . . . just ordinary hoppers." Nick has rested his pack on one charcoal stump, sitting against it with legs stretched out in front of him, and the grasshopper he examines flies to refuge in another. Nick, too, can survive his devastation —we do not learn here what it is—he, too, can survive in a charred land. He wonders how long the grasshoppers will stay that way. He walks downhill. The char stops, and sweet fern grows in the sandy soil between islands of pine. By the river he finds meadows, and "medium sized brown" grasshop-pers, for bait. Across the river is a dark swamp, from which mist and mos-quitoes rise toward evening, but it is quiet and he has his tent, stretched as tightly as his own state of mind, equally protective in its static tension.

Nick's second day is given entirely to fishing. The recurring references to Nick's head—tumpline, the mosquito, thoughts about not thinking—combine with our almost inevitable notion that consciousness is a stream, is something fluid and moving. Nick's venture into the powerful deep river suggests a venture into his own consciousness, into his own past, into other attempts to find and catch things there, an adventure both inviting and fearful. He steps into the shocking cold of the stream. You cannot fish against a stream like this. You must follow it down. This river is just like the Black.

The Black River is the only one Hemingway names in his text. It too is an actual Michigan river, one of two, in fact, either the Black River over toward the western line of the Upper Peninsula, near Wisconsin, or the one thirty miles to the east of the Hemingway summer home at Petoskey. Again the name lends ominous emphasis to the swift river and the mental process. A happy fishing trip along the Black, with friends now gone, is the only memory of the past in the story, the only one Nick allows himself. The dip into the stream of the past is pleasant but uncomfortable. Immediately Nick reassures himself that, since he is tired, he can shut off his mind whenever he pleases. The reminiscence is about making coffee, and the coffee turns out bitter (and presumably black). Nick laughs, "It made a good ending to the story." And Nick shuts off his mind. "That was a long time ago on the Black River." Happiness, at the edge of the Black River. The poetic implications in the unobtrusive name—the black countryside, the black grasshoppers—come to us again when, later, Nick reminds himself that you can't fish against a swift deep stream like the Black River and the one he is fishing.

One of Nick's grasshoppers drops into the stream, swirls, swims, then disappears as a trout takes it. Nick hooks a big trout where the water goes smooth and dark under some logs. It gets away. Nick's hand is shaky; he feels a little sick; he thinks he had better sit down. "He did not want to rush his sensations any." It is as if he had almost caught a disconcerting idea.

After sitting on some logs in a meadow for a while, Nick returns to the stream, catches two good trout—one, strangely, from inside a hollow log, the living from the dead, a kind of birth, delivered kicking from the dark enclosure—and the river has carried him almost to where it narrows, smooth and deep, into the swamp and its low tangle of cedars. "It would not be possible to walk through a swamp like that." He does not want to go in. "He felt a reaction against deep wading with the water deepening up under his armpits, to hook big trout in places impossible to land them." In the dark, half-light, Nick feels that swamp fishing would be "a tragic adventure." He doesn't want any more fishing that day. But as he leaves he looks back. "There were plenty of days coming when he could fish the swamp." He feels, and we feel with him, that he will manage all of his own murky entanglement, that he can survive the tragic depths.

Every sentence of this story seems to sound a harmonic of larger and parallel meaning, as if it were in code. And the key is the river, the stream of consciousness, of time, of life. Fishing, as later in *The Old Man and the Sea*, becomes something ritualistic, something symbolic of larger endeavor. Hemingway himself hinted to friends that he was trying for more than mere surface in the story, as Carlos Baker notes. As Baker has said, the story progresses from a sinister town to a sinister swamp, and, even though the trip is actually a hairpin and not the straight line Baker traces, the dramatic passage from dark to dark is straight enough, and reaches as far as from birth to death.

In front of each half of "The Big Two-Hearted River" is one of the brief italicized vignettes—mostly about violent birth and death—which heads each of the "chapters" in the book. The book opens with a sketch about births and deaths and agony among Greek refugees at Smyrna—a sketch added in 1930, almost, one would suppose, to emphasize the theme, since the vignette which follows it, the vignette of Chapter I, is one of the few not about such violence. And Hemingway's opening story, "Indian Camp," is probably the most appalling birth-death story ever written. Although these apparently unrelated vignettes were printed separately as chapters in Hemingway's booklet *in our time* (1924), it is clear that he interleaved them between the stories of the *In Our Time* of the following year to counterpoint their specific journalistic violence against the numb aftermaths of most of the stories, giving his title from Evening Prayer its full and double irony: We get not peace in our time, O Lord, but either violence or numbness. The vignette of Chapter VI, for instance, the only one about Nick, has him wounded in the spine on a very hot day, propped up against the wall of a church with both legs sticking out awkwardly in exactly the position he is to take against the charcoal stump at the end of the book. The story which follows is about an unnamed major, on a very hot evening, and a transient affair with his nurse in a hospital (a preliminary sketch for *A Farewell to Arms*).

Before Part I of "The Big Two-Hearted River" a bull-fighter finds himself being gored to death in the sand, and the final sentence, *"Then he was dead,"* flows almost like a dream into the opening sentence of the story: "The train went on up the track out of sight, around one of the hills of burnt timber." Before Part II—between the two halves of the story, that is—a man too terrified to stand is hanged, while a priest, who doesn't have to do the dying, urges Hemingway's most central message on him: *"Be a man, my son"*—exactly what Nick is attempting to be on his lonely trip in the aftermath of war. Again the vignette ends in death, as the trap falls, and the story opens with a new awakening of consciousness as Nick crawls from his tent into the morning sun. "There was the meadow, the river and the swamp." When the story ends with Nick's thoughts about fishing the dark swamp—the last word, in fact, is "swamp"—after he has executed the two trout by breaking their necks, laid them out, noticed how alive they look when held in the stream, we can have no doubt that the swamp represents the darkness of death, of unknowing and the unknown, the biggest mystery of life, and that to be a man Nick must face it. The river has two hearts, the active stream and the dark swamp it leads to, the good and the evil. Experience with the blackness is good, the ultimate test of worth. The implications are big. The Big Two-Hearted River is life-and-death itself. The peace for which Nick is searching, in our time, is not unlike—in a tough, earthbound sort of way—that which passes all understanding.

Four other stories, in particular, clarify Nick's fishing trip. The details are slightly contradictory, though not necessarily so, but the psychological issue is deeply consistent: Nick has been wounded and shocked by shellfire. His will is paralyzed. He cannot leave the masculine world of guns and fly rods, weather, violence, and transient companionship, the world he has grown into, even though it has exploded under him, crippling his emotions and cutting him adrift. He is, as Hemingway usually sees him, incapable of satisfactory marriage—powerless and alone between male and female elements.

In "Cross Country Snow" (two stories ahead of Nick's fishing trip) Nick is skiing with a friend in the Alps. We learn that he "can't telemark with my leg," that the two know they will really never ski or fish together again, that Nick is married to a girl named Helen, also in Europe, that their baby is expected late "next summer," that Nick didn't want the baby at first but is now glad, that he and Helen will probably go back to the States though neither wants to, that he and Helen probably won't do any skiing—but Nick and George still have the final run for home ahead of them at the end of the story. "In Another Country" (*Men Without Women*, 1927), though presenting a man much more dismally alienated, seems related to "Cross Country Snow" —the young officer goes daily for physical therapy to a Milan hospital, his knee will not bend, his leg no longer has a calf, he hopes, vaguely, to be married.

But these two portraits are not quite consistent with the Nick of "A Way You'll Never Be," in *Winner Take Nothing* (1930), the third book of stories, the Nick also of "Now I Lay Me" in *Men Without Women* (1927), the second. This Nick is clearly the one we find fishing the two-hearted Fox River. In "A Way You'll Never Be" he is recovering from a fractured skull and wounds "in various places"; he can't sleep without a light; he has formerly been "certified as nutty"; his legs stiffen whenever they are out straight too long; he has attacks of jumbled memories and comically wild talk, but he can control them somewhat. Just as when Nick gets off the train at Seney, here in northern Italy he comes alone into an absolutely deserted town. It is not burned out, but shelled out. As at Seney, it is very hot. As at Seney, there is a river beyond the town. Here, too, he finds no change in the river. Nick lies down and tries to rest, trying to do here what he later accomplishes under the pines outside Seney. As his thoughts begin to jumble he remembers "the nights the river ran so much wider and stiller than it should." He remembers a house and willows by a canal, "but the banks weren't like this river." He remembers men wading, rifles overhead, and falling into the water. "Now he was back here at the river, he had gone through that same town, and there was no house. Nor was the river that way. Then where did he go each night and what was the peril. . . ." We remember Nick going through Seney, with no house there, and the cracked foundation of what was "the Mansion House hotel." Nick gives a long irrational and mock-serious lecture on grasshoppers to some Italians in the dugout:

> We always preferred one that we called the medium-brown. They last the best in the water and fish prefer them. The larger ones that fly making a noise somewhat similar to that produced by a rattlesnake rattling his rattlers, a very dry sound, have vivid colored wings, some are bright red, others yellow barred with black, but their wings go to pieces in the water and they make a very blowsy bait, while the medium-brown is a plump, compact, succulent hopper. . . .

He shuts his eyes to rest again; he sees the bearded man squeezing the rifle, "the white flash and clublike impact," and "a long, yellow house with a low stable and the river much wider than it was and stiller."

We learn even more about Nick and rivers in "Now I Lay Me." It is also, like "The Big Two-Hearted River," the concluding story of its volume. Again it is summer. Nick has been "blown up at night" in the early spring. He has, in fact, been "wounded a couple of times" and was eventually hospitalized to Milan, he says as he recalls the incident, after the October offensive. He can sleep if there is a light on, but when he can't have a light, seven kilometres behind the lines, he keeps himself awake to keep his soul from leaving his body. He is fairly sure it won't happen, but is still "unwilling to make the experiment." He says the Lord's Prayer, but can get no farther than "On earth as it is in heaven."

Outside the window silkworms are chewing and dropping on the mulberry leaves, as steadily as Nick's own thoughts. His favorite method of keeping awake and keeping his soul in his body is to fish carefully in his mind along "a trout stream I had fished along when I was a boy," fishing all the holes and under all the logs, having himself catch trout sometimes and sometimes lose them. He would have himself stop for lunch, "sometimes on a log over the stream," eat very slowly and watch the water. Anything to fill out the memory and keep out the anxiety. Often he would have himself run out of bait and have to take time to dig more, "but one time in the swamp I could find no bait at all and had to cut up one of the trout I had caught and use him for bait." Sometimes when his imagined stream ran through a meadow he would have himself catch grasshoppers for bait, and sometimes have himself "toss them into the stream and watch them float along swimming on the stream and circling on the surface as the current took them and then disappear as a trout rose." Sometimes he would have himself fish four or five streams a night.

> Some nights too I made up streams, and some of them were very exciting, and it was like being awake and dreaming. Some of those streams I still remember and think that I have fished in them, and they are confused with streams I really know. I gave them all names and went to them on the train and sometimes walked for miles to get to them.

Lieutenant Nick also goes back down the stream of time, as it were, to remember people and events as far back as he can. He remembers vividly a time when his mother burns his father's boyhood relics and his father rakes chipped arrowheads from the blackened ruins. Nick's orderly thinks he ought to get married to settle his mind. So Nick tries to remember girls at night, but their faces blur, and he goes back to fishing. As he tells the story of that summer, some time later, he thinks his orderly would be disappointed to learn that "so far, I have never married."

It is almost as if the Nick of this story, not Ernest Hemingway, had written "The Big Two-Hearted River" from one of his nocturnal imaginings—the train trip, the hike, the grasshoppers caught, the one tossed on the stream, the logs, the deep places, lunch on a log, catches and losses, the meadow, the swamp, with Seney a burnt relic of boyhood, now vaguely connected with the war, as Nick alone in the dark fishes along a river in his head to keep his sanity, raking the blackened remnants for something dear and valuable of the past. Nick outside of Seney is doing in actuality what war-wounded Nick has imagined, and both for the same purpose: to cover the mental chasm opened by the terror of violent pain and the fear of violent death.

When you stand on the track at Seney today, it is clear that something of imaginary streams, the traumatic wounding that caused them, and the searching-back along the flow of memories, has attached itself to the Fox River, with its new imaginary, though borrowed, name. Something of the symbolic town-house-river which hangs elusively in Nick's mind is here. The "sunken road" of "A Way You'll Never Be" seems to have given Seney—which, excepting some low mounds, lies almost as flat as a motel top—a road with "a high, fire-scarred hill on either side," like the hill the train has curved around to disappear, though the actual track stretches ahead as straight as a flat ladder to infinity.

The cracked remnants of what may be the foundation of the old White House Hotel—Hemingway's "Mansion House"—are still visible among the weeds, but it is highly doubtful that Nick, standing on the tracks in 1919, would have found Seney completely burned out and deserted. Fire records are inadequate and memories worse, but Hemingway's mention of thirteen saloons on the main street suggests that he is reaching back into Seney's colorful history for his symbolism. In its heyday in the eighties and nineties, Seney had, by most accounts, twenty-two saloons. It was completely burned out by a forest fire in 1891. It was rebuilt and burned again to some extent three or four years later, just about when the town was virtually abandoned as the logging companies moved on, leaving behind not much more than scorched sod and stumps cut tall in the winter snow. Even today you get a vague sense of the ghostliness.

But Seney was never completely abandoned. Frank P. Bohn, the only doctor in the old roaring camp, writes in the *Michigan History Magazine* (Winter, 1937) that Phil Grondin's general store is "one of the few remaining landmarks of Seney." Hemingway has apparently moved up his burning a quarter of a century and increased his devastation, just as he has borrowed the river's name and blackened his grasshoppers (a highly unlikely phenomenon, orthopterists tell me) to give his story its figurative meaning. Hemingway has also put the flat site of Seney on a hillside, letting Nick's spiritual climb tilt the very land itself, making the road northward climb up a ridge of hills, as Nick drives his forehead into his load and climbs up and away from desolation and disappointment.

When you walk along the track to the bridge, you see only brown sand on the river-bottom, no pebbles at all. There are no boulders and bluffs as you look downstream, no "big water-smooth rocks." I am told by two piscatorial professors, Earl Hilton (who first told me about the Fox) and Darwin Shrell, that the real Two Hearted River *is* bouldered and pebbled. It seems that the stones have moved over to the sandy Fox along with the name.

But, conversely, it seems clear that, in the main, the therapeutic river Nick fishes, first in mind, then in fact, is none other than the Fox itself. He gets to his imaginary rivers—even, he seems to say, to *all* of them—by train, just as surely as he later comes to Seney by train from St. Ignace (after having crossed the Mackinac Straits by ferry). Not many trout streams are so conveniently situated. Hemingway, indeed, consistently shows a kind of wilfulness in reporting fact with journalistic accuracy and then insisting that it is all fiction, that "there are no real people in this volume." On August 15, 1924, Hemingway writes to Gertrude Stein about what must be, as Charles Fenton indicates, "The Big Two-Hearted River":

. . . the long one I worked on before I went to Spain where I'm trying to do the country like Cézanne and having a hell of a time and some-

times getting it a little bit. It is about 100 pages long and nothing happens and the country is swell, I made it all up, so I see it all and part of
it comes out the way it ought to, it is swell about the fish, but isn't writing a hard job though?

I made it all up. Well. We can see the artistic distortions at work as Hemingway, in Paris, sends his mind back to the trip he made, or wished he had
made, five years earlier when he stayed, with his war wounds, at the old
summer home on the Lower Peninsula. After the war Nick still remembers
streams "I made up" and "they are confused with streams I really know."
But what Hemingway himself counts as fiction seems to contain a very high
saturation of actuality.

The imaginary remembrance of the Fox River is remarkably accurate.
You can almost convince yourself in an afternoon's hike that you have found
the very spot Hemingway had in mind. Beyond the town and Hemingway's
imaginary ridge, the land is, as he says, undulating and alive. You can see
faintly ahead through the heat waves "the far blue hills that marked the Lake
Superior height of land." You pass small humps of piny ground that indeed
look like islands. The ground is sandy and covered with fern. Once in a
while, under the fronds, you can find (unfortunately not charred) what may
be a stump from the original pine forest. There are meadows near the river.
You find no grasshoppers, but mosquitoes almost as big rise from the shoul-
der-high grass.

Logs bridge the river where the current has toppled an elm or maple.
There are several swamps that would almost do, though not cedar-tangled
and not directly in the river's path. The fast stream passes them by. The most
likely one is not across from where you like to think Nick camped, but on the
same side. "There were birch trees in the green of the swamp on the other
side of the river." And so there are. One dead birch at the swamp's far edge,
very tall and thin, right at the center of the encircling trees, is whitely chalked
against the two-tone green of hardwood and pine, forking gently up and up
like smoke from a campfire.

Looking down at the river again from the bridge at Seney, you notice almost at your knee, unbelievably, a big black grasshopper, almost two inches
long, sleek in charcoal-grey casings. Contrary to Nick's advice, you take your
hat and flail at him. He flutters and sails into the grass and shrubs on black
silk wings, edged in bright yellow. He was the wrong kind anyway. A small
black log lies halfway into the stream, and the brown water goes over like
fur, with a flare of white. The day is hot and very peaceful. The water runs
on and on. The brown sandy bottom is fluted and ridged like minature sand
dunes, layer after layer, like the dark flesh of some strange fish, or like very
old parchment, wrinkled. There are no trout at all, no pebbles. But the sun
on the ripples throws a bright yellow net, steady yet changing, like flame,

over the strange sombre bottom. Tiny flecks and dots of bark, black as ink, roll and bounce downstream with the current, between flat streamers of weed at the margins. One almost hears words and hears a young man somewhere in another country hopefully picking at a typewriter. And the quick brown Fox runs lazily and eternally over the log.

Initiation ("Indian Camp" and "The Doctor and the Doctor's Wife") / *Joseph DeFalco*

One can only guess the extent of Hemingway's knowledge and interest in analytical psychology as a discipline, but a study of his treatment of a young boy as the central character in a number of his short stories illustrates that underlying his artistry there is a perceptive understanding of the development of the human mind. Taking a character at an early age, he depicts the first insights into a world of experience. Many times these insights are not pleasant for the character, and many times he refuses to accept as real what he has viewed. At other times the character will make some minor adjustment to the experience which may not seem apparent on the literal level. At any event, throughout the sequence of short stories treating the young hero, Hemingway constellates the primal conflicts which all men through all ages have experienced. As such, these stories illustrate Hemingway's concern with and exploration of the elemental inquiry concerning man's relationship to the cosmos.

When Hemingway gave the hero of so many of his early stories the name of "Nick Adams," he was doing more than designating a simple appellation to stand for a character. Rather, he intentionally used a symbolic name as a conscious device to illustrate what the character himself would reveal throughout every story in which he appeared. Yet the employment of such a device is not as simple and surface as it may seem at first glance, for Hemingway is too much of the artist to resort to the use of an unsophisticated allegoric device in its most obvious form. Once viewed in relation to the thematic content of the stories, the naming of the hero may be seen as full-blown charactery taken to its furthest implication.

The surname is particularly appropriate inasmuch as Nick Adams is in a very real sense a second Adam. He is not in any literal sense the progenitor of a whole race, but he does typify a whole race of contemporary men who

Joseph DeFalco, *The Hero in Hemingway's Short Stories* (Pittsburgh: University of Pittsburgh Press, 1963), pp. 25–39. Copyright © 1963 by the University of Pittsburgh Press. Reprinted by permission of the University of Pittsburgh Press.

have encountered irrational elements in their environment and have been forced to deal with them. In the stories in which Nick is depicted as a young boy, he is the innocent, akin to the first Adam before the Fall. But as in the biblical story, the state of innocence is short-lived, and the serpent here too enters the "garden." In this case, however, the entry is not a blatant caricature of the forces of evil; it is the subtle growing of awareness of the incalculable events that disturb the natural order of things, of the caprice in that disturbance, and, what is more important, it is a growing of awareness of the irrational forces that operate within the self.

Hemingway directly reinforces the implications of the name "Adam" as incorporating the forces of evil and the chthonic by giving his hero a first name that might easily be associated with "Old Nick" or Satan, the archetype of evil. Having thus named his character, Hemingway in one stroke characterizes the inherited tendencies of all men. The tension created by the implications of the association of these names is in itself archetypal in its suggestion of the eternal struggle between the forces of good and evil. But the hero in the Hemingway stories encounters evil in many guises, and it goes by many names, be it a wound—literal or psychological—terror in the night, death, or anything else. Always, however, evil is inescapable and unpredictable. In many ways what the Hemingway hero must learn throughout the stories is the nature of evil, and the tension created by the struggle of opposing forces within himself provides the underlying dynamics for the learning process.

Experience itself may be one of the guises of contingent evil. Just as surely as eating the fruit of the tree of knowledge precipitated Adam's fall, so for the innocent the initial encounter with elements foreign to the womb-like existence of home and mother is the first stage of a long and dangerous journey. To the individual involved, retreat from the implications of this first encounter might seem possible, but once exposed, his own nature automatically commits him to the entire journey. If he denies the validity of the commitment, he merely postpones the inevitable or damns himself eternally to the regions of infantile fantasy.

In the short story "Indian Camp," the first of the "Nick" stories of *In Our Time,* Hemingway illustrates the compelling tendency to revert to the state of naïve innocence once the first contact with forces outside the protected environment has been made. Nick as a young boy accompanies his father, a doctor, to an Indian village where an Indian woman is to have a baby. Traveling with Nick and his father is Uncle George, who becomes a register against which the attitudes of Nick's father may be tested. The story evolves out of the central incident in which the baby is delivered by Caesarean section. Certain revelations concerning the doctor's character emerge because of the method of delivery, for he has failed to bring along the proper equipment. The operation must be performed with a jack-knife and without benefit of an anesthetic. As a result of the woman's screams during the operation, her husband, who has been lying all the while in the overhead bunk with a severe ax wound, commits suicide by cutting his own throat.

/Although the surface plot is of some consequence in itself, the major focus of the story is Nick's reaction to these events./This emphasis clarifies in light of the initiatory motif around which the story is constructed, and a seemingly slight interlude with a bizarre ending is revealed as having more than situational import. In this story Hemingway establishes a controlling symbol, the Indian camp itself. As in other stories, the camp is suggestive of the primitive and dark side of life. It is a manifestation of the intrusive and irrational elements that impose upon the secure and rational faculties where order and light prevail. For Nick, whose own home is across the lake, the night journey to the camp has all the possibilities of a learning experience. But he must be prepared to accept the knowledge it can give him. As it turns out, Nick is incapable of accepting the events he has witnessed, and the initial preview of the realities of the world is abortive.

Hemingway prepares the reader for Nick's encounter with the dark forces by employing details of setting suggestive of the mysterious and other-worldly: "The two boats started off in the dark. Nick heard the oarlocks of the other boat quite a way ahead of them in the mist. The Indians rowed with quick choppy strokes. Nick lay back with his father's arm around him. It was cold on the water" (91). The classical parallel is too obvious to overlook, for the two Indians function in a Charon-like fashion in transporting Nick, his father, and his uncle from their own sophisticated and civilized world of the white man into the dark and primitive world of the camp. Hemingway also invokes a conscious contrast in his use of another classical device, the guide figure. Here, the father takes Nick along to the camp, and he protectively has his arm around Nick. In the passage that follows, it is to his father that Nick directs the meaningful question, another traditional device of the journey artifice: "Where are we going, Dad?" The answer his father gives is indicative of the protective parental mantle that refuses to allow the child to face directly certain adult terrors. Rather than tell Nick outright, the father-guide here attempts to diminish the import of the coming event: "Over to the Indian camp. There is an Indian lady very sick" (91).

The father as guide figure for the son is to this point of the story a portrait of a nautral and harmonious relationship. Yet Hemingway has imposed the figures of the two Indians and Uncle George almost in thumbnail sketch, and their function is important in the symbolic equation that is the basic form of the story. In crossing the lake to the dark side, the Indians control the movement, and Uncle George rides in the lead boat. He smokes a cigar and gives cigars to the two Indians, reminiscent of the smoking ritual and symbolizing unity and harmony with the forces represented by the Indians. Later, Uncle George becomes emotional over the events of the delivery, signaling his further involvement. Finally, it is Uncle George's telling comment which points out the ineptitude of the father as a man of science and representative of a rational and civilized world in his dealings with dark forces that lie outside his province. This commentary occurs after the operation when, as the narrator relates, the doctor "was feeling exalted and talkative as football players are in the dressing room after a game." He then addresses Uncle George: " 'That's one for the medical journal, George,' he said. 'Doing a Caesarean with a jack-knife and sewing it up with nine-foot, tapered gut leaders.' " With telling irony Uncle George reveals all the inadequacies of the doctor in his naïve attempt to impose order in a world of disorder. He tells the doctor, " 'Oh, you're a great man, all right' " (94).

That the father as a man has not himself come to terms with the irrational and uncontrollable forces at work is made obvious by his reaction to the suicide of the Indian husband. When the delivery of the child apparently is going well, the father—in the guise of doctor-scientist—gives Nick a step-by-step account of its progress. At one point he even tells Nick that the screams of the woman are not important. But the statement is ironic, for the husband commits suicide because of the screams. When the doctor discovers the death of the Indian, his control of the situation is lost. He is left with "all his post-operative exhilaration gone." He tells Nick, " 'it was an awful mess to put you through' " (94). In this way the studied control of the father as doctor and rational man disintegrates, and all that is left is father as fallible man. In effect, the father has been stripped of his own protective mask, the doctor-scientist *persona,* and he is forced to deal with the situation as a man with an unmasked ego.

Hemingway has further imposed a significant aspect of the theme of individuation. That is, the hero is constantly forced to adjust in some manner to the prime manifestations of the irrational: pain and death in the world. The two father figures here, the doctor and the "wounded" Indian, are in apposition to each other, but each reacts in a different way. Both are equally ineffectual, however, and this fact illustrates their denial of that role. The Indian as a primitive has no effective method of dealing with the terror created by the screaming wife. On the other hand, as long as Nick's father is in the role of doctor and performs the rituals assigned to the healer, he assumes he can cope with and control the forces of life and death. When the Indian by his suicide denies his role and function as father and husband, the doctor's role as healer is at the same time put in a ridiculous light. Thus Hemingway illustrates the absurdity of man, in any guise, in his attempt to control forces which are not in his power.

The figure of Uncle George as a foil to the doctor is further exhibited in relation to the guise of the father as healer and man of science. During the delivery, when the doctor apparently has the situation under complete control, Uncle George is bitten by the woman while trying to hold her down.

His response, "Damn squaw bitch," an emotional and uncontrolled one, signifies his ability to respond naturally to pain. The doctor, in that role, affects an air of detachment in direct opposition to the responses of the uncle. With the suicide the obvious point of the unreality of such a pose is made.

When his father fails to sustain the expected role, Nick reverts to infantile dependence. At the end of the story the pair row back to the other side of the lake, and Nick questions his father about the implications of the events of the night. Nick's denial of the learning experience begins when he addresses his father as "Daddy" instead of "Dad," as he had at the beginning. But the most telling revelation of the abortive nature of the learning situation comes when he asks, " 'Is dying hard, Daddy?' " Having witnessed the bizarre events at the camp, the question reflects his inability to grasp the significance of his exposure to pain and death. Further, by slipping back into the role of the inexperienced one Nick thus effects a reconstruction of the father. Both the denial of the experience—or admission of his insensitivity to it—and the attempt to recreate the father as man into the infantile father-*imago* likeness are sublimated at this point.

Nick's refusal to accept the terrors of pain and death and the father's inability to cope with them are revealed in an ironic light in the conclusion: "In the early morning on the lake sitting in the stern of the boat with his father rowing, he [Nick] felt quite sure that he would never die" (95). But Nick has been exposed to some of the primal terrors of human experience, and his "feeling" is depicted as illusory and child-like because it is a romantic reaction to the experience he has undergone. The irony enters in the portrait of the young Nick "sitting in the stern," implying that he is in control of the boat—events; yet it is the father who rows, and he has already proven ineffectual for such a role. The details of setting further point up the irony, for "the sun was coming up over the hills." In contrast with the events of the night the sun may seem to dispel darkness, but at the same time it foreshadows the coming of night again.

In "The Doctor and the Doctor's Wife," the second of the "Nick" stories of *In Our Time*, the controlling symbol is once again the Indian camp. Here, however, instead of a journey to the camp, with all of the attendant psychological implications of such a journey, representatives of the camp are summoned across the lake to participate in the sophisticated and civilized world of Nick and his father. The locale is northern Michigan, and the fact that it is the edge of a wilderness gives the setting a significance beyond a mere backdrop. This is a border zone area, symbolically a meeting place of two opposing forces, and here Nick as the young inexperienced one will undergo the initiatory rites which eventually project him into the role of young manhood. This site is the ground of home and parental protection, and the eventual severance from this influence must be won. These functions are not separate and distinct, for on the journey toward individuation the encounter with the dark powers can come only after a complete detachment from all of the infantile regressive tendencies has been accomplished.

Nick as yet is unequipped to undertake the complete journey, but the repeated experience with stark reality and the cumulative effects of such experience eventually project him into the greater effort. In "The Doctor and the Doctor's Wife," as the title reveals, the surface conflict involves two important personages in Nick's life and posits the two diverging axes of the archetypal nursery drama. The central conflict that emerges reveals a further step in the learning process that Nick undergoes in the story sequence of which this is a part.

The plot concerns a short altercation that takes place between Nick's father and Dick Boulton, a half-breed from the Indian camp, over whether or not some beech logs washed ashore from a log boom are to be regarded as stolen, as Boulton contends, or as driftwood, as Nick's father assumes. A moral question is posed, although no one knows whether the steamer crew will return to claim the logs. After Boulton, his son, and another Indian leave without cutting the logs for the doctor, the original purpose for which they had come, the doctor with some restraint tells his wife of the argument and then leaves to go hunting with Nick.

As a half-breed, Dick Boulton incorporates the features and powers of both the white man and the Indian, symbolically the light and the dark, the known and unknown. He is a border zone figure and has available knowledge that is denied those who are committed to one or the other of the opposing regions. Through him Hemingway creates a tension of the opposites. Boulton is the exemplar who stands in rebellion against the authority of Nick's father. The encounter between the two undermines Nick's trust in his father, making the need to search for other authority figures the more urgent. Nick is by no means capable of beginning an active quest at this stage of his development, nor does Hemingway intend an obvious rebellion on Nick's part. Boulton is the revelator, and the accumulation of such encounters will later convince Nick that authority at any level is spurious.

The ringing irony of Boulton's appearance in the story is that the doctor himself summons this figure from out of the dark land of the Indian camp. In this way the doctor contributes to his own downfall in the eyes of his son. Hemingway intensifies the irony of the situation by interposing the moral question of whether or not the logs are stolen. As a representative of the society of which Nick will become a part, and as a supporter of the ethical code to which that society adheres, the doctor is defeated on a question of moral import by a representative of a supposed lower and more primitive level of culture. Thus, not only is the father figure denigrated in Nick's eyes, but also the moral framework of Nick's entire society is undermined.

The argument scene with Boulton is not the central focus of the story, but it does serve as the catalyst for the ensuing albeit inapparent nursery drama. This drama as such implies the triadic conflict of the child versus both parents in his desire to free himself from parental domination and achieve autonomy. Hemingway depicts the effects of this conflict in the second and in the final scenes of the story.

In the second scene Hemingway emphasizes the conflict and points up the breech between the two parents by injecting an additional irony. The father as doctor, scientist, or representative of the rational order of things is juxtaposed to the mother, a Christian Scientist. The irony in the utter divergence of thought between the two is brought into sharp focus when the doctor returns to the house and tersely tells his wife that he has had a row with Boulton.

> "Oh," said his wife, "I hope you didn't lose your temper, Henry."
> "No," said the doctor.
> "Remember, that he who ruleth his spirit is greater than he that taketh a city," said his wife. She was a Christian Scientist. Her Bible, her copy of *Science and Health* and her *Quarterly* were on a table beside her bed in the darkened room.
> Her husband did not answer. He was sitting on his bed now, cleaning a shotgun. He pushed the magazine full of the heavy yellow shells and pumped them out again. They were scattered on the bed. (101-02)

Other than the obvious irony of a physician's wife belonging to a religious sect which denies the necessity of his professional function, there are several other levels of consideration here. The reason for the mother's lying in a darkened room in broad daylight is not given, but the implication is that she is ill, a fact which further heightens the surface irony. Whether or not this is so, however, the detail serves to illustrate that she is ineffectual in her role as wife and mother and even as a social entity. As mother-preserver and protectress of the innocent, she is portrayed here symbolically as languishing in the womb-like province of her darkened room. As such, she is at once the fatal or terrible mother figure who would lure her son back to the womb to be smothered by her protective nature. Thus she would destroy any possibility of the son ever reaching the goal of self-realization. In classical literature this feature of the mother archetype is often depicted by the sirens who lure sailors from their natural course. The results there are identical with the psychological implications of this situation: for those who succumb to the call, death or regression is the inevitable result. The mother, like Circe who would turn men into swine, represents a romantic refusal to accept the realities of life. When the doctor tells her he believes Boulton started the argument to avoid paying a bill, she responds unrealistically: " 'Dear, I don't think, I really don't think anyone would really do a thing like that' " (102).

The lure of this wooing mother figure provides one axis—the romance of escape to the womb—of the underlying conflict inherent in the nursery drama.

Hemingway distinctly delineates the abode of the mother and the region of the father by drawing attention to the psychological schism with particular, literal details and by symbolic allusion. After the conversation between the mother and father in which it becomes obvious that they are at odds, the narrator relates: "The doctor went out on the porch. The screen door slammed behind him. He heard his wife catch her breath when the door slammed. 'Sorry,' he said, outside her window with the blinds drawn. 'It's all right dear,' she said" (102–03). The flat, inexpressive quality implied by the tone of the dialogue suggests in itself that all is not "all right" between the doctor and his wife. The fact that the doctor is "outside her window with the blinds drawn" illustrates symbolically the alienation of the father from the womb, and consequently reflects the mother-son-father triadic conflict. Thus the divergency of the two positions demonstrates dramatically the attractions which test Nick's ability to select his own course of life. Since the role of the father is to provide the impetus for the son's projection beyond the protective presence of the womb, Nick's selection must be that which will somehow come to terms with the father.

Nick's direct involvement in this interlude is first apparent when the mother tells the doctor, " 'If you see Nick, dear, will you tell him his mother wants to see him?' " (102). The fact that Hemingway has her refer to herself in the third person immediately suggests a peculiarity in her personality and perhaps a more serious psychological aberration. In effect, referring to herself as a separate entity from the "I" which is speaking accomplishes a depersonalization of her ego, a further illustration of her complete separation from the world of reality.

Nick's task is to escape from this temptress who threatens his development into maturity, and he does. At the end of the story with his denial of her, she becomes the image of frustration and unrelatedness, wasting away in isolation and solitude. Hemingway thus correlates her role as temptress-mother with her religious affiliation, neither of which is depicted as valid for the hero in his epic struggle.

For Nick, standing on the threshold of adolescence and as yet unable to make any significant break from parental domination, the possibilities of reconciling what he has witnessed seem small. Yet in the final scene he does come to terms with the situation. Finding Nick sitting under a tree, reading —an escape—the father tells him: " 'Your mother wants you to come and see her.' " But Nick rejects, " 'I want to go with you,' " and takes the first step by denying escape through mother and reconstructing the father image. There is a tinge of irony, though, for in the exchange that follows Nick is at once deferential ("Daddy") and at the same time commanding: " 'I know where there's black squirrels, Daddy,' Nick said. 'All right,' said his father. 'Let's go there' " (103). By this means Hemingway illustrates the effect of the total experience upon Nick. In a sense Nick has usurped the function of the father in his attempt to reconstruct him. Now it is Nick who is to be the guide, and significantly it is to the woods that they are to go. Symbolically, the journey is toward experience, not retreat to the womb of mother. This is in effect a completion of the symbolic equation posited at the beginning of the story where Boulton precipitated the adventure for Nick. The woods are illustrative of the dark qualities represented by the Indian, and it is into the woods that Nick is to lead the fallible father figure in order to restore him.

Of Human Dignity: "In Another Country" / *Earl Rovit*

The tutor takes a surprisingly large variety of forms in Hemingway's fiction, but, in each of his manifestations, he is always "the professional." With two significant exceptions, his activities are confined to areas where he can perform within the predictabilities of his training—fighting bulls, bootlegging whiskey and Chinamen, facing lion charges, and landing large fish. The exceptional stories recount, in part, the adventures of tutors who encounter challenges beyond the jurisdiction of their professional preparations; these are in "Fifty Grand" and "In Another Country. . . ."

"In Another Country," which is surely one of Hemingway's masterpieces in the short story form, also takes a professional into a challenge situation for which he has not been prepared, but with very different results from the satiric "Fifty Grand." The Major of the story is Hemingway's most attractive tutor figure, and he is also the most intelligent and sensitive. A professional soldier, and before the war a champion fencer, he is undergoing mechanical therapy for a wound which has left his fencing hand shrunken to baby size. Disabling wounds and death are foreseeable eventualities for professional soldiers, and the Major accepts his lot with equanimity. Out of a sense of duty he reports to the hospital every afternoon to be treated by the therapeutic machines (designed to rehabilitate industrial accidents), even though he does not believe in their efficacy. When he engages the tyro (the first-person narrator) in conversation, he insists with characteristic professional-

Earl Rovit, "Of Human Dignity: 'In Another Country,' " *Ernest Hemingway* (New York: Twayne Publishers, 1963), pp. 60, 61–65. Copyright, 1963, and permission granted by Twayne Publishers, Inc.

ism that the boy speak Italian grammatically. As Hemingway presents him, the Major is a figure of considerable dignity and somewhat stuffy rectitude who "did not believe in bravery," presumably because, like Santiago, he chooses precision and exactness over the uncontrollable results of impulse action.

But one afternoon he comes to the hospital in a very irritable mood and provokes the tyro into a rude argument over marriage in which he declaims angrily that a man must not marry. "If he is to lose everything, he should not place himself in a position to lose that. He should not place himself in a position to lose. He should find things he cannot lose." He makes a telephone call and returns to the room where the tyro is sitting.

> He was wearing his cape and had his cap on, and he came directly toward my machine and put his arm on my shoulder.
> "I am so sorry," he said, and patted me on the shoulder with his good hand. "I would not be rude. My wife has just died. You must forgive me."
> "Oh—" I said, feeling sick for him. "I am *so* sorry."
> He stood there biting his lower lip. "It is very difficult," he said. "I cannot resign myself."
> He looked straight past me and out through the window. Then he began to cry. "I am utterly unable to resign myself," he said and choked. And then crying, his head up looking at nothing, carrying himself straight and soldierly, with tears on both his cheeks and biting his lips, he walked past the machines and out the door.

One final paragraph concludes the story, in which we are told that the Major returns for his regular treatments three days later with mourning crepe on his uniform sleeve. The doctors had placed photographs of wounds before and after treatment in front of his machine. "The photographs did not make much difference to the major because he only looked out of the window."

This is the one certain case in Hemingway's work where the tutor rises far beyond the artificial boundaries that restrict his need to make decisions. As we have seen, the code of professionalism with its severe conditioning in special pragmatic skills and attitudes is designed to minimize the multiplicity of possibilities existing in any challenge situation. Or, to express it more simply, the professional attitude creates an arbitrary chart of the future—like a contour map of preselected terrain—in which only a few items are considered significant and the rest are ignored. The rationale for the adoption of such a code is suggested in the Major's passionate cry: "[Man] should not place himself in a position to lose. He should find things he cannot lose." He will eventually lose everything when he loses himself, but along the way he will be able to control his losses and also the sequence of "holding attacks" through which he wages his battles.

If such a life code were adhered to strictly, a man would have to be either "the dumb ox" (the "simpler man") of so much Hemingway criticism or an unbelievable monster of machined egotism living, as it were, in an almost impregnable pillbox with no exits or entrances. The Major of this story is neither; his adoption of a code of life does not preclude his exposure to the risks of the incalculable in spite of his angry cry of outrage. Because he is human, he has loved; and, to continue the military metaphor, he has wittingly exposed his flanks to undefendable attack. His commitment to love and his shock at his wife's death have placed him "in another country" than the one he has prepared to defend. That other country is nothing less than the human condition itself, for the human will is always vulnerable to ruthless destruction. And Hemingway's ultimate test of human performance is the degree of stripped courage and dignity which man can discover in himself in his moments of absolute despair. It would have been quite simple for the Major to have died well; his challenge is far greater than his own death (a challenge which Hemingway has typically considered a relatively easy one to face). The Major, in losing his wife, suffers a death of himself accompanied by the absurdity of his own continued life. It is meaninglessness—*nada*—that confronts the Major in full assault.

And like Jesus in "Today is Friday," the Major is "good in there." He is badly broken, but not destroyed. He refuses to resign himself to the chaos of un-meaning, but he refuses also to deny the actuality of his fearsome defeat. He holds tight to the superficial conventions of his training—the empty forms of innate courtesy and soldierly duty—and sits within them to begin the laborious process of making the broken places within himself strong again. His response can be characterized as neither acceptance nor denial; he is neither victim nor rebel. The least and the best that can be said of him is that he survives with dignity, and it is possible that he may be considered Hemingway's most eloquent portrait of ideal heroism—unquixotic, unathletic, profoundly humanistic.

The characteristic of *dignity*, so important to Hemingway as to have furnished him with one of the major themes in his fiction, is relevant to our discussion at this point. The peculiar problems of twentieth-century life have made the depictions of human dignity almost anomalous in modern literature. Our characteristic heroes have been "anti-heroes" or non-heroes, aggressive doomed men in revolt or essentially pathetic dupes at the mercy of non-malicious and implacable victimization. Dignity in either situation is difficult to ascribe to such heroes who tend by choice to divest themselves of the traditional values of rational intelligence and moral integrity on which dignity has always rested. The great majority of modern heroes in literature are purposely grotesque—picaresque saints, rebels, victims, and underground men of all shapes and colors. Their individual value as artistic achievements and embodiments of viable life attitudes is undeniable, but *dignity* is a quality largely beyond their grasp.[1] Hemingway's attempt to retain the ideal of dignity without falsifying the ignobility of the modern human condition (that impulse in his work which leads many commentators to associate his beliefs with those of classical Stoicism) is one of his signal triumphs as a modern writer. And it is generally through his characterizations of the tutor figure that this quality of dignity is manifested.

Besides the Major we can find it in Manuel ("The Undefeated"), in Anselmo of *For Whom the Bell Tolls*, in the old men of "A Clean, Well-Lighted Place" and of "Old Man at the Bridge," and finally in Santiago. It is probably significant that all of these examples are old, or at least older men. Dignity certainly does not come automatically with age in Hemingway's fiction, but is is usually denied to youth with its passions and penchant for illusions.[2]

A minimal degree of native intelligence is a basic requirement; basic also are the qualities of real humility and self-abnegation. Thus characters like Harry Morgan, Cayetano Ruiz, Wilson, or El Sordo—all in some fashion tutor figures and models of a kind of excellence—are on the lower levels of Hemingway's portraits of heroism. This point should be remembered since too many evaluations of Hemingway's life code are based on the mistaken assumption that Hemingway's code heroes can be lumped together in an indiscriminate stereotype of brute primitivism and animal virtues.

1. Two excellent discussions of this phase of modern fiction are Ihab Hassan, *Radical Innocence* (Princeton, 1961) and R. W. B. Lewis, *The Picaresque Saint* (New York, 1959).
2. A possible exception to the rule is Schatz in "A Day's Wait."

Hemingway's Concept of Sport and "Soldier's Home" / *Robert W. Lewis, Jr.*

In recent years mathematical biologists like Anatol Rapoport,[1] ethologists like Robert Ardrey and Konrad Lorenz,[2] philosophers like Paul Weiss,[3] psychiatrists like Eric Berne,[4] and even journalists like George Plimpton[5] have

Robert W. Lewis, Jr., "Hemingway's Concept of Sport and 'Soldier's Home,' " *Rendezvous*, V (Winter 1970), 19–27. Reprinted by permission of *Rendezvous*.

1. *Fights, Games, and Debates* (Ann Arbor, 1960); *Strategy and Conscience* (New York, 1964); *Prisoner's Dilemma* (Ann Arbor, 1965).
2. Ardrey, *The Territorial Imperative* (New York, 1966); Lorenz, *On Aggression* (New York, 1966).
3. *Sport: A Philosophic Inquiry* (Carbondale, 1969).
4. *Games People Play* (New York, 1964).
5. *Paper Lion* (New York, 1966).

directed our attention to games people play, and they have discovered our pastimes to be not so innocent as we had, perhaps, believed. One of our recreations, sport, of course, we had always thought of as "building character," and battlefield victories were really won on the playing fields of Eton. Such notions justified and explained sport from the time of the Greek gymnasiums. Sport was educational, and it still survives most vigorously in our school systems. But now scholars in various disciplines are suggesting that individual fights or hostilities and global confrontations (as between Russia and America) belong as much to a comprehensive theory of games as does a more narrowly defined investigation.

Many exciting applications have been suggested, but no more sensitive and penetrating comment on the modern cultural relevance of sport can be found than in much of the writing of Ernest Hemingway. In fact, one might fairly say that he anticipated modern speculation on the subject by a generation, as creative artists often do anticipate subsequent philosophical or psychological development. Hemingway did not, obviously, consciously analyze sport and then thematically embody his ideas about it in his works, but he did turn naturally and effectively to sport as subject and then found in it both metaphor and ritual for a life and a world that had lost the old rituals of religion and state.

Perhaps this is an overstatement that ignores similar thematic uses of the subject of sport in literature that preceded Hemingway's uses. But once one gets beyond Hemingway's sports journalism, one finds in his serious work several recurrent ideas expressed best through sport and expressed better by no modern writer.

Of course, on the realistic level, his descriptions and analyses of bullfighting, boxing, fishing, and hunting are often superb, but this very excellence has misled some readers into assuming this realism as an end in itself. Spanish aficionados still respect his *Death in the Afternoon;* a fish has been named after him; he was on a first-name basis with world champions in numerous sports; his milieu was the fishing port, the ski lodge, the hunting camp, the ball park, or the bull ring where we saw him in endless photos that made his image and made some highbrows denigrate him because of his associations with sport and sportsmen. In his work as in his life, these associations were a sign of "arrested development" even to some sympathetic critics; Hemingway was prevented by his own eternal adolescence from becoming anything more than a biological kind of "sport" in the literary world, an isolated instance of the primitive, untutored artist who accidentally or spontaneously hits upon a formula, a style that is original and vigorous but of limited range because of the author's limited mind. Critics who are not sportsmen might say so, and critics who enjoy sports might be afraid not to say so.

Only rarely have critics taken his seeming preoccupation with sport beyond the literal, but Edmund Wilson very early saw that Hemingway's prin-

ciples of courage, pity, and honor were those "of sportsmanship, in its largest human sense," and his only protest of the cruelties and defeats of life
was that of the sportsman who loses a game.[6] Others have noted the ascetic
or self-disciplinary side of Hemingway's interest in sport, especially dangerous sport like bullfighting and big-game hunting. He sought physical danger and seemed to think that man needs it to test and purify himself, whether
or not he plays to win. Man, including the artist, was not made for safe
havens.[7] Sport could also be heightened or intensified experience, leading in
some rare moments to a kind of ecstacy or religious feeling.[8] And sport
could be meaningful play that gave a sense of freedom, a kinetic joy, a unique
experience unrelated to practical activity.[9] It could also be metaphor for the
process of art, which Hemingway described in terms of baseball and boxing
in a way that convinced at least one fellow writer.[10]

These recognitions of the function of sport are related to the earlier mentioned idea of sport as substitute ritual, but sport as rite is distinguished from
them and is, I think, Hemingway's chief contribution to a theory of games.
It is the very meaninglessness or irrelevancy of sport to "real" life which
many of Hemingway's heroes cherish. Sport provides the "certain cleanness
and order" for which a clean, well-lighted place is also a substitute.[11] The
Big Two-Hearted River must be fished in a certain careful way, the bull must
be pic-ed properly to correct his tendency to hook, the gestures of the aficionados are holy and reserved for the initiated, and outsiders like Brett and Cohn
(in *The Sun Also Rises*) profane the rites and corrupt the novitiate Pedro.
Such instances of the sacrality of sport abound in Hemingway's work, but
they are apt to seem adolescent if viewed merely as realistic detail or as journalistic "material."[12] Merely noticing that there are at least two kinds of
sportsmen in Hemingway's work, however, suggests a complexity of ideas.
Several critics have commented on the differences between the "code" hero
(or tutor) and the Hemingway or Nick Adams type of hero (the tyro), and
the contrast also applies when the subject of sport is used as reference.[13] Nick

6. "The Sportsman's Tragedy," *The Shores of Light* (New York, 1952), pp. 341,
344. First published in 1927. For an interesting but different approach to the idea of
game in Hemingway, see Jackson J. Benson, *Hemingway: The Art of Self-Defense*
(Minneapolis, 1969), Chapter 4.
7. See especially "The Short Happy Life of Francis Macomber" and "The Undefeated."
8. See "The Big Two-Hearted River." For a brief critical comment on the point see
Ted R. Spivey, "Ecstasy and Suffering in Hemingway," *Religious Themes in Two
Modern Novelists* (Atlanta, 1965), pp. 5–6.
9. See especially descriptions of skiing as at the beginning of "Cross-Country Snow."
10. Ralph Ellison, *Writers at Work*, 2d Series (New York, 1965), p. 321.
11. "A Clean, Well-Lighted Place," *The Short Stories of Ernest Hemingway* (New
York, 1953), p. 383.
12. See the clichés and jargon of the "substitute bull-fight critic" in "The Undefeated" as an illustration of the profane view of sport.
13. See especially Philip Young, *Ernest Hemingway* (New York, 1952); Earl Rovit,

Adams and Francis Macomber are sensitive and aware in ways that Wilson (of the "Macomber" story), Manuel Garcia (of "The Undefeated"), and Jack Brennan (of "Fifty Grand") are not. The latter type of hero does not see beyond sports as an end in itself. It does not provide the rite for any faith; it is all their lives, and beyond it there is nothing. The Nick Adams or Macomber type of hero comes to sport as rite or refuge when he is blown up (literally or psychically) in the "real," non-sporting world. Macomber has to learn the virtues of sport (chiefly courage and self-discipline), but he is "born" into a happy, if short, life as a result of his initiation, of his becoming an aficionado or insider. These sensitive heroes are more admirable than the Wilsons or Brennans whose courage is mindless and merely physical. Even the mightily courageous Manuel Garcia is pathetic and is contrasted with the observant Zurito whose skill and dedication to bullfighting are not only professional but also informed in relation to the world outside the plaza de toros.

The Nick Adams aficionado knows that "outside" there is chaos: a world of "Killers," men at war who play at God and sloganeer and end up killing each other or trapping themselves. The domestic world is not better: the deaths of love, of marriage, of idealism are as painful as those of a world at war and merely protracted, the tortures subtler. The soldier playing games may have kept his illusions intact in an age of codified chivalry, but in our time even the professional like Colonel Cantwell (of *Across the River and into the Trees*) faces irreconcilable differences between war as game and war as she really is.[14] Love as game (as in the early encounters of Frederic Henry and Catherine Barkley in *A Farewell to Arms*) is equally impossible to the man who is honest with himself.

If the "games" of love and war, the chief occupations of Hemingway's heroes, are incredibly mad and yet unavoidable and foredoomed to loss, one alternate exists for the sensitive player of life's cruel sports: he may find refuge in true sport that, by definition, pretends to no relevancy and is based on purely arbitrary rules. Yet this sport can provide the only "cleanness and order" that man will ever have. He will go to desperate and absurd lengths to maintain the integrity of his particular game, just as surely as a religious fanatic will or would have.[15] (Where are the zealots in a cynic age?) Some have become obsessed with learning how to break par rather than learning how many angels can dance on the head of a pin. They are more concerned with the virtues of lowering the pitcher's mound than the seven deadly vir-

---

Ernest Hemingway (New York, 1963); and Delbert E. Wylder, *Hemingway's Heroes* (Albuquerque, 1969).

14. See Chapters III and IV of *In Our Time* and the early parts of *A Farewell to Arms* for illustrations of the hero who approaches war as casually as a spirited athletic contest.

15. The word *fan* derives, of course, from *fanatic*, originally a god-maddened man.

tues that only lead to lost causes and lost love in a fallen world. The rule
book replaces the Golden Rule and is considerably more workable. The bat
may be weighed, the base paths measured. The fly fisherman's object is not
simply to catch trout but to catch them in a certain way using certain equipment. Dynamite would be more efficacious, but it is without the arbitrary
order that is of the essence. In "The Short Happy Life of Francis Macomber,"
Margot instinctively knows where the dedicated sportsman Wilson is most
vulnerable, and that is on the point of rule or order. She calls him on the
illegality of chasing game in a motorcar, and he becomes very defensive. Regardless of the fact that Wilson thinks it was "sporting enough," such viola-
tions of the technical rule are corruptions of the very value that the game
provides.[16] Some people will do anything to win, but they can never have
the grace of those who, though losers like Santiago of *The Old Man and the
Sea,* retain the purity of form, honesty of execution, craftsmanship or stewardship and thus remain always undefeated. Their "victories" are senseless and
"moral"; like the losing team, they have built "character"; they come home
with no trophy but their own greater hearts and the admiration of a very few
aficionados (like Santiago's Manolin, Cantwell's Renata, and Manuel Garcia's Zurito) who know and value the integrity of form rescued from a form-
less world.

   The order and form of sports, then, could be a paradigm of what the
other, "real" world should be like, but the gap between controlled, clean
game and chaotic, dirty life is unspannable. Thus, one alternative is to use
sport as therapy, to turn to it as haven when the chaos of life is unbearable,
when the ship sinks or the bank fails. Nick Adams performs this self-therapy
in his reminiscences of fishing in "Now I Lay Me" and "A Way You'll Never
Be" as well as in the actual fishing trip of "The Big Two-Hearted River."[17] The typical Hemingway hero cannot himself ever escape to the uncomplicated life of a Wilson or Jack Brennan, and Santiago stands alone as
the enlightened, sensitive man who survives as sportsman and tutor of a
code that is viable, productive, and not parasitic (like Wilson's White hunting) or narrowly ethnic (like bullfighting) or crooked (like Brennan's prize-
fighting or "My Old Man's" horseracing).

   Sport is therapeutic because it can provide escape and at the same time
the appearance of meaningful pattern. A story that is relatively unsporting,
"Soldier's Home," provides an excellent illustration, perhaps the best, of
what I see as Hemingway's idea of sport, in part because it links the "real"
arenas of both war and social conflict with both images of sport and other
such meaningless or irrelevant patterns. It is an excellent story written in
a wonderfully ironic, carefully modulated style in which Hemingway is in
full control of verbal repetitions and variations on his theme.

In this story of a returned Marine veteran of World War I, sport as such seems incidental to what first appears as a casually ironic recounting of the trials of a veteran's readjustment to civilian life. But each detail is loaded, and the few references to sport—to pool, motoring, reading the sporting page of the newspaper, and girls' "indoor baseball," i.e., softball—form an important pattern of their own in this story about patterns. Patently the story tells us of the hypocrisies, shams, and self-delusions of middle-class America. More subtly it tells us of the cost of a life of lies and illusions; it leads to existential nausea and the awareness of a lack of freedom. Krebs desires that "certain cleanness and order" too, and it is not paradoxical that a certain restraint gives freedom. It is the restraint of conventional patterns that *pretend* to meaning that is sickening. Pious but hollow faith and subscription to the Protestant work-ethic are merely chaos disguised. Trust in God and work may once have had meaning, but it is now enslaving, robbing man of his existential awareness of self as it deludes him into thinking he knows and understands.

The beginning of the story is beautifully contrived in every detail. Even Kreb's former school, a *Methodist* college, connotes the order or pattern that pretends to meaning and relevance, but later when his mother tells him "There can be no idle hands in His Kingdom," Krebs answers, "I'm not in His Kingdom."[18] His pious mother tells him she prays for him all day long as he looks "at the bacon fat hardening on his plate"—wonderful objective correlative! The war has wrenched him free from methodism of all kinds.

The two pictures described at the beginning of the story depict the contrast. The young Krebs had been photographed "among his fraternity brothers, all of them wearing exactly the same height and style collar" (145). He had been already in uniform, that of the self-restricting social group. He was "collared," like the good-looking young girls whom he now likes to watch in their uniforms of similar hair style and clothes with "round Dutch collars" that "they all wore . . . It was a pattern," but it was part of a game too, that of courtship, and the girls "were too complicated"; they meant "intrigue and politics . . . He did not want to tell any more lies" (147). And so he does not court them or play their meaningless game. "Christ! What are patterns for?"[19]

In the other picture in which we see Krebs he is in a literal uniform, photographed "on the Rhine with two German girls and another corporal. Krebs and the corporal look too big for their uniforms. The German girls are not beautiful. The Rhine does not show in the picture" (145). Ironically, the real uniform is not so uni-formed, and the foursome implicitly destroys a pattern related to that of the courtship of young middle-class Americans. To

18. *The Short Stories*, op. cit., p. 151. Subsequent page references to this story will appear in the text.
19. Amy Lowell, "Patterns," *The Complete Poetical Works* (Boston, 1955), p. 76.

show "the way it was" was Hemingway's avowed aim, and so doing meant destroying such romantic illusions as that of the dashing American warrior conquering the Teuton and winning the legendary Rhine maidens. The way it was in war was not the way it was supposed to be, not in the après-guerre nor in the fighting, which Krebs is also led to lie about. The pattern demanded atrocity stories and Krebs' pretension to great fear in battle, and when he lies about his experiences in order to fit the pattern, to satisfy expectations, he not only acquires "the nausea in regard to experience that is the result of untruth or exaggeration," but he also loses "everything" (146). That is, in fabricating an autobiography in order to conform to a pattern, he eradicates the very soul of the truth of his life; he kills himself, and the existential nausea accompanies the crime.

The sardonic use of clichés with a somewhat archaic tone also emphasizes the absurdity of human patterns that are arbitrary but are thought to have meaning: "By the time Krebs returned . . . the greeting of heroes was over. He came back much too late. . . . years after the war was over" (145). (In fact, he came back less than a year after the Armistice.) The very patterns of language in a phrase like "the greeting of heroes was over" can have a numbing or enslaving effect upon the mind that accepts them as representing something real.

Krebs' reaction to his newly discovered old life seems passive, but in fact he takes several positions. At first, in respect to the socially accepted pattern of war, he succumbs to denying his own experience by lying about it. Then having been sickened, he refuses to lie about the needlessly "complicated" world of courtship, and thus he merely looks on, bemused but healthy, not suckered by the girls' patterns or the lie that every real man had to have a girl all the time. He retreats into himself and studies his present milieu dispassionately just as he also reads histories of the war to better understand his experience in it. This concerned passivity gives way finally under the assault of his parents' virtue that is offended by his "meaningless" inactivity. In the encounter with his mother, he initially holds his ground and refuses to lie and succumb to their games, but his tearful, saccharine mother is too dense, too culturally absorbed: "He couldn't tell her; he couldn't make her see it" (152). That is, she cannot understand his resistance to her god and "settling down." Again, "Krebs felt sick and vaguely nauseated" (152), but this time he will not give them the chance to kill him by making him lie again. He will leave home and try to protect his integrity.

The symbolism of sports parallels this structure of lying (for the sake of patterns), withdrawal (for the contemplation of patterns, both social and military), lying again, and then final withdrawal. Pool, motoring, and girls' "indoor baseball" (a wonderful sport) provide the references to an uncomplicated world without hypocrisy and without pretense to meaning. Truly, pool, motoring (as pastime), and girls' softball are mindless activities that are patterned (carefully patterned in the case of pool and softball), just as courtship and "getting ahead" are, but the restrictions or rules of sport are purely arbitrary and gratuitous and without pretense to meaning or significance outside themselves. (Reasons such as sport for exercise or sport for the release of hostilities or the libido are incidental since sports or games are not the only means to effect such ends, and, indeed, more rational or productive means such as calisthenics or gardening are readily imaginable and available.) Thus, the sportsman can become like the existential hero achieving freedom through the *acte gratuite*, and sports, perhaps, is more socially acceptable in establishing one's freedom than purposelessly pushing a stranger to his death, as Andre Gide's Lafcadio does.

In his initial home-coming when he tells lies and acquires "the nausea," Krebs finds refuge from "the hottest hours of the day in the cool dark of the pool room. He loved to play pool." And, perhaps not so curiously, he learns that "Even his lies were not sensational at the pool room" (146). (Is every area, even the neighborhood pool hall, a testing ground, a place where man can be found out? Where he faces "the moment of truth"?) Pool is completely irrelevant to his life, but though it is "meaningless" or absurd, it is rite.

The next sport is a somewhat tangential one, motoring, but in "Soldier's Home" it provides the subtlest illustration of the theme. The first paragraph to mention the Krebs' family automobile at first reading might seem curiously out of place or a red herring, or fractured by the absence of transitions between what immediately precedes and follows it. In itself, however, it is a neatly, ironically structured paragraph in which Hemingway repeats the word *car* four times, uses *never* once and *always* twice, begins with a "before . . . the war" phrase, and ends with an "after the war" phrase. There is also the comic notion of the father always wanting "the car to be at his command" (146–147). That is, for his "non-committal," remote-control businessman father, the car is a functional, meaningful tool, not a means to recreational motoring. But we should note that this paragraph-length discussion of the car never even alludes to motoring as sport or pastime. Two pages later, however, his mother does bring up the subject of Krebs' taking "the car out in the evenings," and he is apparently very interested in getting the use of the car (149). In this scene, then, the subject is dropped, but it comes up again when Krebs rejoins his mother at breakfast and she quizzes him on his "aim in life" (151). Krebs takes his last stand, denying his mother's god and his father's mammon. Mother Krebs plays what she thinks is trumps, the offer of the use of the car, but the sentences before and after the offer reveal that the parents' view is different from Krebs': " 'Your father does not want to hamper your freedom. He thinks you should be allowed to drive the car. If you want to take some of the nice girls out riding with you, we are only too pleased.' "

Freedom *is* the issue, and the car could be a means to it, but not with "nice" girls along. His mother instinctively and correctly makes the connection be-tween Krebs' desire for the car and his desire for freedom. But she does not see that the car must be used uselessly in order for Krebs to have that ex-treme of freedom that she cannot even imagine. He had already decided not to play the courtship game with the "nice" girls, but his mother wrongly as-sumes that he must want the car for that reason. Everything must have a reason, including life and motorcars. Since his mother has corrupted the concept of freedom and sport by linking it with fatuous parents' conventions and blindness, Krebs turns off and drops out, even though yielding one last time to his mother's tears.

Another thematic use of sport is brief but clever. When Krebs goes to eat breakfast he opens the morning paper "to the sporting page" (149), the one section of value to him because presumably, it is disinterested and cool, as the archetypal sportsman should be. But even this innocent activity en-croaches upon a socially absurd pattern, his father's irrational but no doubt common need for a certain cleanness and order in the family newspaper:

> "Harold," his mother stood in the kitchen doorway, "Harold, please don't muss up the paper. Your father can't read his *Star* if it's been mussed."
> "I won't muss it," Krebs said. (149)

And finally the mother is so upset by Krebs' nonchalance that she asks him to put the paper away (150).

The last use of sport in the story revolves around Krebs' kid sister's indoor baseball game. There is strong affection between Krebs and his tomboy sis-ter who says she " 'can pitch better than lots of the boys. I tell them all you taught me' " (150). Perhaps Krebs sees her as the only other sport in the family, and certainly she has not yet succumbed to the patterns that wait for a middle-class mid-American girl. Still, Krebs won't promise Helen that he will come to watch her game, but after the nauseating exchange with his mother (nauseating for Krebs, comic for us), he vows to leave home to escape the dishrag smothering of his mother and the lies and "complications" that his parents lead him into: "He would go to Kansas City . . . He would not go down to his father's office. He would miss that one. . . . He would go over to the schoolyard and watch Helen play indoor baseball."[20]

That is the end of the story. Once more in a moment of crisis Krebs es-capes from social patterns and finds haven among the patterns of sport, and here there might seem to be some hope that it is a prelude to a more thorough and general escape, an escape to freedom outside the context of games. Given Krebs' own inarticulateness and lack of sophistication, however, we might wonder if he has much hope, this side of the backstop, of avoiding nausea,

20. There is no inconsistency here; "indoor baseball" was what is now called softball, and it was so-called whether played indoors or out.

lies, and the ensnaring patterns of family, courtship, marriage, and gainful employment. The last mentioned sport itself, girls' indoor baseball, also challenges any small hope because even among absurd activities like sport it is extreme, a version of a stereotyped game played by incompetent girls. Yet even then Krebs goes to see it rather than visit his father or stay at home with his mother. The reference to girls' indoor baseball suggests Hemingway's awareness of the futility of a passion for sports as substitute ritual. It is self-mocking. It is not "real" baseball, it is not "real" sport. And we remember that elsewhere in Hemingway's work he was often concerned with the fact that even sport, the last refuge of a fanatic, can be corrupted and destroyed just as faith, love, and even language had been. (See, for instance, the justly famous lines from *A Farewell to Arms* in which Lieutenant Henry is disillusioned of words like *sacred, glorious, sacrifice,* and *in vain.*[21])

The fixed horse race in Chapter XX of *A Farewell to Arms*, "The Battler," "The Undefeated," "Fifty Grand," and "My Old Man" are good illustrations of the corruption that reaches even sport. Hemingway was particularly concerned with the purity of bullfighting, and *Death in the Afternoon* and "The Dangerous Summer" are in part jeremiads on the decline of the classic bullfight.

Some final questions are worth asking. Since "Soldier's Home" is conceded to be a closely autobiographical story depicting the spirit if not the letter of Hemingway's own problems with his family upon his return from service in World War I, what was *his* resolution of the conflict between empty values and his longing for freedom and meaning? And corollary to that question, why does *Death in the Afternoon*, ostensibly about bullfighting, contain so many comments about the art of writing? And, if you see where I'm going, why are there so few writers or artists in Hemingway's fiction? Or, when they do appear, why are they failures, phonies, or corrupt like Robert Cohn in *The Sun Also Rises*, Richard Gordon in *To Have and Have Not*, Harry in "The Snows of Kilimanjaro," and Hubert Elliott in "Mr. and Mrs. Elliott"? Is it significant that Harry in "The Snows of Kilimanjaro" is trying to begin a comeback, to "work the fat off his soul" by going on a hunting safari? (60). That he is conscious that his lies had got him his success and "there was no truth to tell"? (59). That he too is rebelling against patterns, that the Macombers are trapped by them and then liberated from them on a stylized hunting trip? Even the one nonwriting artist (an architect) among Hemingway's protagonists, Frederic Henry of *A Farewell to Arms*, is something of a bastard, when all is said, and his own story is something of a confessional. (And why did Hemingway choose, albeit without emphasis, to make Henry an architect?)

21. (New York, 1929; 1953), p. 191. Like Krebs, Lieutenant Henry plays billiards (Chapter XXXV), and in the hospital he says, "The baseball news was all I could read. . ." (p. 142).

Hemingway himself escaped the patterns of his middle-class family by becoming a writer (and Krebs was not), and the only other exit besides sport is art. For the sensitive man in the midst of and aware of chaos, art is the structure that does not mean but is. *Death in the Afternoon* makes the connection implicitly in the seeming digressions from bullfighting to art. The subjects are cut from the same cloth.

Hemingway's "Now I Lay Me": A Psychological Interpretation[1] / *Richard B. Hovey*

Once when he was asked the name of his psychoanalyst, Ernest Hemingway is said to have replied with a laugh, "Portable Corona No. 3."[2] The laughter is ribald in *Death in the Afternoon*, where he is contemptuous of Waldo Frank's Freudian view of bull-fighting.[3] Hemingway also seems to have taken a dim view of Philip Young's book about him: at least he found little in what he called Young's "trauma theory of literature."[4] Until Carlos Baker's authorized biography comes out and we know more about Hemingway, we can neither prove nor disprove that he read or tried to read any of the modern depth psychologists.[5] On the other hand, during his Paris years in the 1920's Hemingway could scarcely have avoided hearing talk about Freud and Jung. This likelihood becomes stronger of course when we recall his friendship with and admiration for James Joyce.

Whether Hemingway was ever consciously influenced by Freudianism or

Richard B. Hovey, " 'Now I Lay Me': A Psychological Interpretation," *Literature and Psychology*, XV (Spring 1965), pp. 70–78. Reprinted by permission of *Literature and Psychology*.

1. This article is one of the products of a generous grant awarded me by the General Research Board of the University of Maryland.

2. See Philip Young, *Ernest Hemingway*. New York, 1952, p. 136.

3. See pp. 53–54, op. cit. Frank's *Virgin Spain* is, according to Hemingway, a work of "bedside mysticism," a sample of "erectile writing," a muddle-headed result of sexual frustration. He tells us how the writing of such a book might have been prevented: "But to those inner-searching Viennese eyes peering out from under the shaggy brows of old Dr. Hemingstein, that masterful deducer, it seems as though, had the brain been cleared sufficiently, by a few good pieces, there might have been no book at all."

4. This phrase is evidently Hemingway's own. It is quoted by George Plimpton in "An Interview with Hemingway," included in *Hemingway and his Critics*, ed., Carlos Baker (in American Century Series), New York, 1961, p. 24. Originally this interview appeared in *The Paris Review*, 18 (Spring 1958).

5. Dr. Baker in his *Hemingway: The Writer as Artist*, Princeton, 1952, (3rd ed., 1963), assures us that Hemingway is "never guilty of Freudian fiddle-faddle," pp. 150–152.

whether he merely stumbled on it despite his distaste, the curious fact is that one of his most revealing stories bears striking analogies to what occurs in psychoanalytic treatment. I refer to "Now I Lay Me," which focuses on the psychic shock Nick Adams suffers as a result of his having been wounded on the Italian front.[6] Its autobiographical purport is hard to doubt; and it is plainly one of the things Hemingway wrote to "get rid of it."[7]

The setting is night, somewhere behind the Italian lines in what seems to be a makeshift hospital. The first half of the narrative is taken up with Nick's insomniac ruminations. He tries many ways to stop thinking back on the horror which has shattered his nerves. Sharing his sleeping-quarters is the lieutenant-narrator's Italian-born orderly; and the second half of the story is chiefly dialogue between these two. John, a married man and a father, talks sympathetically with the lieutenant about his worries and sleeplessness. His prescription for all such ills is marriage: "You'll never regret it. Every man ought to be married." On this point John is insistent. Though Nick then tries for a while to think of all the girls he knows and of the kinds of wives they might make, other memories blot out such thoughts. The story ends with the wounded man's statement: "He [the orderly] was going back to America and he was certain about marriage and knew it would fix up everything" (p. 371). The point is that if a man has been so close to death as Nick Adams has, love is not strong enough to win him back into more of life. Wedlock is no panacea. And this is one of four of the stories in which a bachelor protagonist is so reluctant to marry that he cannot even contemplate that possibility except with apprehensiveness.

It is interesting that here—as in "Soldier's Home" and "In Another Country"—wounding is linked with rejection of marriage. The wound is also linked with much else in the emotional life of the hero. In fact, Hemingway has never writen a more obviously psychological story—in the sense that we have here a quite explicit and rather elaborate exploration into the depths of a tormented psyche. No doubt, psychoanalytically oriented criticism has its limitations; yet no other critical tool can take us so close to the beauties and meanings of this story. If we aim to get at the larger implications of "Now I Lay Me" and of its connection with other fictions of Hemingway, if we hope to win from it a few insights into the mind and heart of its creator, some knowledge of Freud's therapeutic methods is indispenable. For the ramblings of the traumatized Nick Adams are set down—yes, with art—but also in the pattern of free-association.

6. This story first appeared in *Men Without Women*, 1927. All quotations from and references to "Now I Lay Me" are from *The Short Stories of Ernest Hemingway*, New York, 1954. Page numbers from this edition will be cited within the text.

7. In the story "Fathers and Sons," Nick Adams (evidently speaking for his creator) tells us: "If he wrote it he could get rid of it. He had gotten rid of many things by writing them" (p. 491).

As often with Hemingway, the title gives the first clue. We are being taken back to the nursery, to the child's night prayer:

> Now I lay me down to sleep;
> I pray the Lord my soul to keep.
> *If I should die before I wake*
> I pray the Lord my soul to take.

To be sure, the child does not italicize the third line, which suggests to the adult mind the fear of death, that death might come during sleep, traditionally death's second self. The title also implies a longing to return to the imagined security of early childhood—suggests regression, if you will. The connotations of the title expand when we know that Hemingway himself suffered from insomnia and when he tells us here exactly what it seemed like when the trench-mortar shell hit Nick—in language close to that used in the account Malcolm Cowley says Hemingway gave of his own wounding at Fossalta: [8]

> I myself did not want to sleep because I had been living for a long time with the knowledge that if I ever shut my eyes in the dark and *let myself go*, my soul would go out of my body. I had been that way for a long time, ever since I had been blown up at night and felt it go out of me and go off and then come back. I tried never to think about it, but it had started to go since, in the nights, just at the moment of going off to sleep, and I could only stop it by a very great effort.   (p. 363)

In other words, the threat of death is linked with sleep, Nick's fear of dying linked with his fear of losing consciousness. And the only defense—so the hero or patient believes—is not to let himself go, to keep a rigid hold on his consciousness. (The italics of course are not Hemingway's.)

But to return to Nick's ruminations—or to his free-associations. These are set down in what seems to be chaos until we recognize how the psychoanalyst's patient is supposed to behave as he lies on the couch. That is, the patient—and it usually takes him months before he begins to learn how—

8. See Cowley's "A Portrait of Mister Papa," which originally appeared in *Life Magazine*, January 10, 1949. This one has been reprinted, "Slightly revised by the author," in the collection of essays, edited by John D. M. McCaffery, *Ernest Hemingway: The Man and His Work*, Cleveland and New York, 1950. In the paperback edition of McCaffery, Avon Books, New York, p. 39, we find this: "A big Austrian trenchmortar bomb, of the type that used to be called ash cans, exploded in the darkness. 'I died then,' Hemingway told his friend Guy Hickock. 'I felt my soul or something coming right out of my body, like you'd pull a silk handkerchief out of a pocket by one corner. It flew around and then came back and went in again and I wasn't dead any more.' . . . For a long time he was afraid to sleep except by daylight, because he had been blown up at night. He thought that if he ever again closed his eyes in the darkness the soul would go out of his body and not come back." Compare also the parallel passage in Chapter IX of *A Farewell to Arms*.

is required to tell the doctor, without any self-criticism, or editing, or effort to clarify, or attempt to make sense or a good impression—exactly everything that passes through his mind. So, as his words come out, the linking of thought with thought and image with image and memory with memory and all their related emotions, appears to be totally without order. Yet, as the trained psychoanalyst listens, in time all this outpouring begins to afford him clues; these clues eventually merge into patterns; and the patterns point to deeper feelings and half-forgotten recollections of what is bothering his patient and what these surface ramblings disguise but do not totally conceal. So it is with Hemingway's insomniac, his traumatized Nick Adams.

A patient in analysis might begin his session with an observation of some external fact—say, a window blind. Similarly, Nick first notices a sound; it is the sound which the silkworms make as all night long they gnaw on the nearby mulberry leaves. Of course, Hemingway is an artist, telling us a story; so he shapes his material in ways the psychoanalyst cannot. Poetically, window blinds are not as interesting as silkworms, whose sound at night may seem sinister and relentless. They might suggest to the nervous narrator his awareness of his own mortality; and if he is literary, he might think of Poe's horrific fascination with what worms do to a corpse. The simpler and more obvious link, though—and the one employed by Hemingway—is that these silkworms cause Nick to think back on the time when he himself used worms for bait when he went fishing as a boy.

Now, the free-associations shift to recollections and fantasies about fishing. Actually, these occupy nearly a page and a half of the story. They are precise, detailed, elaborate. Such fantasies here have two functions for Nick. Practically, they while away the hours of sleeplessness. Psychologically, they help to blot out, to screen away from awareness, what might be painful contents in Nick's psyche: "I would think of a trout stream I had fished along when I was a boy and fish its whole length very carefully in my mind . . ." (p. 363). The tenacity with which Nick clings to and expatiates upon these fantasies indicates something compulsive, sickly:

> Sometimes I would fish four or five different streams in the night; starting as near as I could get to their sources and fishing them down stream. When I had fished too quickly and the time did not go, I would fish the stream over again, starting where it emptied into the lake and fishing back up stream, trying for all the trout I had missed coming down. Some nights too I made up streams, and some of them were very exciting, and it was like being awake and dreaming. Some of those streams I still remember and think that I have really fished in them, and they are confused with streams I really know.   (p. 364)

A passage like this helps us to understand "Big Two-Hearted River." In our first reading of that story, Nick Adams' extremely painstaking report of seemingly every detail and ritual in a solitary fishing trip strikes us as realism. It appears to be almost documentary realism—until we heed the anxiety it stirs and begin to surmise that all these external facts are somehow too carefully set down and too brilliantly lighted, as if the narrator were clinging to outward realities: forcing his consciousness to hold to them because, for some nameless dread, he dare not look elsewhere, and least of all look within. Read "Big Two-Hearted River" with the perspective supplied by "Now I Lay Me," and you realize that the first story is a nightmare in broad daylight. So we gain some hint of the import which fishing has in Hemingway's fiction—and in his own life. It is of course therapy and escape, but not of the simple sort enjoyed by the Izaak Waltons of this world.[9]

Why do fantasies of fishing help Nick to endure his torment? Why does the shock of a wound bring insomnia, and why do these fantasies so regularly accompany that insomnia? What emotions are bound to these images of fishing? Nick's continuing introspection leads us further and deeper. He remembers the worms and the other bait he would use and the bait he did not like to use, crickets and a tiny salamander—apparently because on the hook they writhed too much.

"But some nights I could not fish, and on those nights I was cold-awake." This impeding of Nick's fishing fantasies is unmistakably analogous to "resistance" in the psychoanalyst's patient. When the analysand stops talking, the flow of words, ideas, and recollections is blocked by some competing or conflicting currents of feeling. Such resistance alerts the psychoanalyst because it usually indicates that some still unrevealed part of the psyche may be pushing toward consciousness and meeting resistance, some feelings and memories which lie deeper and are harder to dig up. So with Nick's halting free-association:

> But some nights I could not fish, and on those nights I was cold-awake
> and said my prayers over and over and tried to pray for all the people
> I had ever known. That took up a great amount of time, for if you try
> to remember all the people you have ever known . . . (pp. 364–365)

The praying of course does not help Nick, as it would not directly help the patient in analysis. Perhaps, though, it does help. It affords Nick a small link to stir earlier memories and deeper-lying feelings. So the free-association begins to flow again. So far, the recollections and images have moved from silkworms to the battlefield wounding to fishing to bait to fishing again to praying and to remembering "all the people you have ever known." Now

---

9. This paragraph is indebted to Malcolm Cowley's introduction to *The Portable Hemingway*, New York, 1945. Titled "Nightmare and Ritual in Hemingway," this piece is included in one of a paperback series (Twentieth Century Views) *Hemingway: A Collection of Critical Essays*, ed., Robert P. Weeks (Englewood Cliffs, New Jersey, 1962).

Nick tells us he is "going back to the earliest thing you remember." With him it was:

> . . . the attic of the house where I was born and my mother and father's wedding-cake in a tin box hanging from one of the rafters, and, in the attic, jars of snakes and other specimens that my father had collected as a boy and preserved in alcohol, the alcohol sunken in the jars so that the backs of some of the snakes and specimens were exposed and had turned white—if you thought back that far, you remembered a great many people.   (p. 365)

Of all the possible "earliest" things a boy might remember, these attic souvenirs are rather remarkable. That ugliness or some painful emotion may be connected with this memory is indicated when again Nick's free-associations are interrupted with references to praying. Obviously, these memories center in the father and the mother. To the Freudian, the images are unmistakable: the tin box symbolizes the female genitals—emphatically so when it contains the wedding cake; the snakes symbolize the male organ—emphatically so, for a Caucasian, when their whiteness is recollected.

When Nick resumes, try as he will, he can remember no farther back than "to that attic in my grandfather's house. Then I would start from there and remember this way again, until I reached the war" (p. 365). In other words, Nick's earliest memory is linked to the war, specifically the war wound. And it was evidently this trauma which drove Nick into a self-analysis that took him so far back into his early childhood. As Nick pushes further his *recherche du temps perdu* we learn more about her who owned the tin box and about him who owned the whited snakes:

> I remember, after my grandfather died we moved away from that house and to a new house designed and built by my mother. Many things that were not to be moved were burned in the back-yard and I remember those jars from the attic being thrown in the fire, and how they popped in the heat and the fire flamed up from the alcohol. I remember the snakes burning in the fire in the back-yard. But there were no people in that, only things. I could not remember who burned the things, even, and I would go on until I came to people and then stop and pray for them. (p. 365)

There is fearsome fascination in this image of phallic snakes being destroyed by fire. Since there are "no people" in this memory, we do not know who burned up the contents of the jars. But we do know that the destruction occurred in connection with moving to a new house. In that move the dominating figure was the mother: it was she, not the father, who designed and built the new house. Nick cannot recall who did the burning—because that would be too painful to recall. In his next recollection, however, he tells us that he does remember who did the burning—at least enough for our purposes. It was his mother:

> About the new house I remember how my mother was always clean-ing things out and making a good clearance. One time when my father was away on a hunting trip she made a good thorough cleaning out in the basement and burned everything that should not have been there. (pp. 365–366)

When Nick's father returned that day and saw the fire still burning, he was upset. His wife greeted him with a complacent smile: "I've been cleaning out the basement, dear." Doctor Adams said nothing, kicked at the fire, leaned over it, picked something out of the ashes, and told Nick to get him a rake. Then "very carefully" he raked out his prized specimens, Indian relics: ". . . stone axes and stone skinning knives and tools for making arrow-heads and pieces of pottery and many arrow-heads" (p. 366). His only comment was, "The best arrow-heads went all to pieces." Some of these relics the Freudian would consider phallic symbols; all of them except the pottery are at least representative of masculine authority and prowess.

The immediate significance of Nick's recollections is plain. The mother is remembered as the destroyer. She destroyed possessions on which the father's heart was set. More specifically, when she burned the white snakes, she symbolically destroyed the male organ. Here, of course, is the very image, the prototype, of Nick Adam's first "wound"—the child's feared wound of emasculation. This long-established and buried fear has been revived with terrible power through the trauma incurred by the physical wound in battle. That somehow this is the earliest memory which is dredged up, back through so much pain, indicates that in Nick Adams the fear of castration is stronger than in most men. It is the mother who intensifies this fear.

If my interpretation is so far valid, we have gained here an insight into at least a few of the puzzles of Hemingway and his writings. As to "Now I Lay Me," we begin to see that its artistic unity derives from an organic unity. It is not merely a two-part story whose first half records the pointless ramblings of an insomniac casualty and whose second half informs us that Nick Adams takes no hopeful view about getting married. For in a very real psychological sense, the same "wound" operates in both halves of the story: a wound that cripples the ability to love.

To be sure, we are not informed where this Nick Adams has been hit. But his kinship to Jake Barnes and Lieutenant Henry is undeniable. When it comes to their creator, to Hemingway and his own actual wound at Fossalta on the Piave, we know that it was in the leg and close enough to the genitals for any mortal man to think of it as a threat. It might have happened, had his luck been a few inches worse.

Much of course has been made of the wounded protagonists in Hemingway's fiction. The Freudian view of "Now I Lay Me" gives us at least a glimpse as to why Hemingway was so deeply and so long affected by his own wounding and perhaps why wounding is almost an obsessive theme in his writings. After all, plenty of other men have been wounded more severely and yet have not been preoccupied with it for almost four decades. With Hemingway, the wound seems to have become part of his personality as man and as artist. That is evidently because the emotional connections between his actual battle wound and his childhood fear of castration were more direct and stronger than with most men. This may be why the wound in Hemingway's fiction is sometimes eroticized: Jake Barnes of course suffers the supreme erotic wound; Catherine Barkley makes love to the hospitalized Lieutenant Henry; Harry Morgan caresses his wife with the stump of his arm; and Renata makes a tender fuss over Colonel Cantwell's maimed hand.

"Now I Lay Me" contains other hints too. It is by fire that the mother destroys symbolically, the male organ. And of course it is by fire that Hemingway protagonists are wounded. Then, too, as we read through the short stories, it is again and again the mother figure who is the destroyer or the threatener and the mother who must be fought against—as the father did not enough fight against her to protect and save his manhood. So also, the fear of the threatening mother which is obvious in "Now I Lay Me" explains in part why, in all of Hemingway's fiction, father figures and old men are treated with more warmth and tenderness than the mothers ever are. For if the mother could so unman the father as she does here, so might a woman in a love affair emasculate her man. So, if a man cannot keep away from women, he does well at least to keep them in their place. After all, in the Hemingway world, no matter how full of danger that world is, a man is usually safer with other men.

"The Killers" / *Cleanth Brooks and Robert Penn Warren*

There are certain fairly obvious points to be made about the technique of this story. It breaks up into one long scene and three short scenes. Indeed, the method is so thoroughly scenic that not over three or four sentences are required to make the transitions. The focus of narration is objective through-

From *Understanding Fiction* by Cleanth Brooks and Robert Penn Warren (New York: Appleton-Century-Crofts, 1959), pp. 303–12. Copyright © 1959. Reprinted by permission of Appleton-Century-Crofts, Educational Division, Meredith Corporation.

out, practically all information being conveyed in simple realistic dialogue. In the first scene the revelation of the mission of the gangsters is accomplished through a few significant details—the fact that the gangsters eat with gloves (to avoid leaving fingerprints), the fact that they keep their eyes on the mirror behind the bar, the fact that, after Nick and the cook have been tied up, the gangster who has the shotgun at the service window stations his friend and George out front "like a photographer arranging for a group picture"—all of this before the specific nature of their mission is made clear.

Other observations concerning the technique of the story could be made— the cleverness of composition, the subtlety with which the suspense is maintained in the first scene by the banter of the gangsters, and then is transferred to another level in the second scene. But such observations, though they are worth making, do not answer the first question which, to the reader, usually presents itself, or should be allowed to present itself. That question is: what is the story about?

The importance of giving an early answer to this question is indicated by the fact that a certain kind of reader, upon first acquaintance with the story, is inclined to feel that the story is exhausted in the first scene, and in fact that the first scene itself does not come to focus—does not have a "point." Another kind of reader sees that the first scene, with its lack of resolution, is really being used to "charge" the second scene. He finds his point in Ole Andreson's decision not to try to escape the gangsters—to stop "all that running around." This reader feels that the story should end here. He sees no relevance in the last several pages of the story, and wonders why the author has flattened out his effect. The first reader we may say, feels that "The Killers" is the gangsters' story—a story of action which does not come off. The second and more sophisticated reader interprets it as Andreson's story, though perhaps with some wonder that Andreson's story has been approached so indirectly and is allowed to trail off so irrelevantly. In other words, the reader is inclined to transpose the question, What is the story? into the question, Whose story is it? When he states the question in this way, he confronts the fact that Hemingway has left the story focused not on the gangsters, nor on Andreson, but on the boys at the lunchroom. Consider the last sentences of the story:

"I'm going to get out of this town," Nick said.
"Yes," said George. "That's a good thing to do."
"I can't stand to think about him waiting in the room and knowing he's going to get it. It's too damned awful."
"Well," said George, "you better not think about it."

So, of the two boys, it is obviously Nick on whom the impression has been made. George has managed to come to terms with the situation. By this line of reasoning, it is Nick's story. And the story is about the discovery of evil. The theme, in a sense, is the Hamlet theme, or the theme of Sherwood Anderson's "I Want to Know Why" (p. 317).

This definition of the theme of the story, even if it appears acceptable, must, of course, be tested against the detailed structure. In evaluating the story, as well as in understanding it, the skill with which the theme has been assimilated must be taken into account. For instance, to put a concrete question: does the last paragraph of the story illuminate for the reader certain details which had, at their first appearance, seemed to be merely casual, realistic items? If we take the theme to be the boy's discovery of evil, several such details do find their fulfillment and meaning. Nick had been bound and gagged by the gangsters, and has been released by George. To quote: "Nick stood up. He had never had a towel in his mouth before. 'Say,' he said. 'What the hell?' He was trying to swagger it off." Being gagged was something you read about in a thriller and not something which happened to you; and the first effect is one of excitement, almost pleasurable, certainly an excuse for a manly pose. (It may be worth noting in this connection that Hemingway uses the specific word *towel* and not the general word *gag*. It is true that the word *towel* has a certain sensory advantage over the word *gag*—because it suggests the coarseness of the fabric and the unpleasant drying effect on the membranes of the mouth. But this advantage in immediacy is probably overshadowed by another: the towel is sanctified in the thriller as the gag, and here that cliché of the thriller has come true.) The way the whole incident is given—"He had *never* had a towel in his mouth *before*"—charges the apparently realistic detail as a pointer to the final discovery.

Another pointer appears in the gangster's wisecrack about the movies: "You ought to go to the movies more. The movies are fine for a bright boy like you." In one sense, of course, the iterated remarks about the movies, coming just after the gangsters have made their arrangements in the lunchroom, serve as a kind of indirect exposition: the reader knows the standard reason and procedure for gang killings. But at another level, these remarks emphasize the discovery that the unreal clichés of horror have a reality.

The boy to whom the gangster speaks understands the allusion to the movies, for he immediately asks: "What are you going to kill Ole Andreson for? What did he ever do to you?"

"He never had a chance to do anything to us. He never even seen us," the gangster replies. The gangster accepts, and even glories a little in, the terms by which he lives—terms which transcend the small-town world. He lives, as it were, by a code, which lifts him above questions of personal likes or personal animosities. This unreal code—unreal because it denies the ordinary personal elements of life—has, like the gag, suddenly been discovered as real. This unreal and theatrical quality is reflected in the description of the gangsters as, after leaving the lunchroom, they go out under the arc light and cross the street: "In their tight overcoats and derby hats they looked like a vaudeville team." It even permeates their dialogue. The dialogue itself has the sleazy quality of mechanized gag and wiscrack, a kind of inflexible and stereotyped banter that is always *a priori* to the situation and overrides the situation. On this level the comparison to the vaudeville team is a kind of explicit summary of details which have been presented more indirectly and dramatically. On another level, the weary and artificial quality of their wit has a grimmer implication. It is an index to the professional casualness with which they accept a situation which to the boys is shocking. They are contemptuous and even bored, with the contempt and boredom of the initiated when confronted by callow lay observers. This code, which has suddenly been transferred from the artificial world of the thriller and movie into reality, is shocking enough, but even more shocking to Nick is the fact that Ole Andreson, the hunted man, accepts the code too. Confronted by the news which Nick brings, he rejects all the responses which the boy would have considered normal: he will not call the police; he will not regard the thing as a mere bluff; he will not leave town. "Couldn't you fix it up some way?" the boy asks. "No I got in wrong."

As we observed earlier, for a certain type of reader this is the high point of the story, and the story should end here. If one is to convince such a reader that the author is right in proceeding, one is obligated to answer his question: What is the significance of the rather tame, and apparently irrelevant, little incident which follows, the conversation with Mrs. Bell? It is sometimes said that Mrs. Bell serves to give a bit of delayed exposition or even to point the story by gaining sympathy for Andreson, who is, to her, "an awfully nice man," not at all like her idea of a pugilist. But this is not enough to satisfy the keen reader, and he is right in refusing to be satisfied with this. Mrs. Bell is, really, the Porter at Hell Gate in *Macbeth*. She is the world of normality, which is shocking now from the very fact that it continues to flow on in its usual course. To her, Ole Andreson is just a nice man, despite the fact that he has been in the ring; he ought to go out and take his walk on such a nice day. She points to his ordinary individuality, which is in contrast to the de- mands of the mechanical code. Even if the unreal horror of the movie thriller has become real, even if the hunted man lies upstairs on his bed trying to make up his mind to go out, Mrs. Bell is still Mrs. Bell. She is not Mrs. Hirsch. Mrs. Hirsch owns the place, she just looks after it for Mrs. Hirsch. She is Mrs. Bell.

At the door of the rooming house Nick has met Mrs. Bell—normality un- conscious of the ironical contrast it presents. Back at the lunchroom, Nick returns to the normal scene, but the normal scene conscious of the impinge- ment of horror. It is the same old lunchroom, with George and the cook going about their business. But they, unlike Mrs. Bell, know what has hap- pened. Yet even they are scarcely deflected from their ordinary routine.

George and the cook represent two different levels of response to the situation. The cook, from the first, has wanted no part of it. When he hears Nick's voice, on his return, he says, "I don't even listen to it." And he shuts the door. But George had originally suggested that Nick go see Andreson, telling him, however, "Don't go if you don't want to." After Nick has told his story, George can comment, "It's a hell of a thing," but George, in one sense at least, has accepted the code, too. When Nick says: "I wonder what he did?" George replies, with an echo of the killers' own casualness: "Double-crossed somebody. That's what they kill them for." In other words, the situation is shocking to the cook only in so far as it involves his own safety. George is aware of other implications but can dismiss them. For neither of them, does the situation mean the discovery of evil. But for Nick, it is the discovery, for he has not yet learned to take George's adult advice: "Well, you better not think about it."

To this point the discussion of "The Killers" has been concerned with the structure of the story with regard to the relations among incidents and with regard to the attitudes of the characters. But there remain as important questions such items as the following: What is Hemingway's attitude toward his material? How does this attitude find its expression?

Perhaps the simplest approach to these questions may be through a consideration of the situations and characters which interest Hemingway. These situations are usually violent ones: the hard-drinking and sexually promiscuous world of *The Sun Also Rises*; the chaotic and brutal world of war as in *A Farewell to Arms, For Whom the Bell Tolls*, or "A Way You'll Never Be"; the dangerous and exciting world of the bull ring or the prize ring as in *The Sun Also Rises, Death in the Afternoon*, "The Undefeated," "Fifty Grand"; the world of crime, as in "The Killers," *To Have and to Have Not*, or "The Gambler, the Nun, and the Radio." Hemingway's typical characters are usually tough men, experienced in the hard worlds they inhabit, and apparently insensitive: Lieutenant Henry in *A Farewell to Arms*, the big-game hunter in "The Snows of Kilimanjaro," Robert Jordan in *For Whom the Bell Tolls*, or even Ole Andreson. They are, also, usually defeated men. Out of their practical defeat, however, they have managed to salvage something. And here we come upon Hemingway's basic interest in such situations and such characters. They are not defeated except upon their own terms; some of them have even courted defeat; certainly, they have maintained, even in the practical defeat, an ideal of themselves, formulated or unformulated, by which they have lived. Hemingway's attitude is, in a sense, like that of Robert Louis Stevenson, as Stevenson states it in one of his essays, "Pulvis et Umbra":

Poor soul, here for so little, cast among so many hardships, filled with desires so incommensurate and so inconsistent, savagely surrounded, savagely descended, irremediably condemned to prey upon his fellow lives: who should have blamed him had he been of a piece with his destiny and a being merely barbarous? And we look and behold him instead filled with imperfect virtues: . . . an ideal of decency, to which he would rise if it were possible; a limit of shame, below which, if it be possible, he will not stoop. . . . Man is indeed marked for failure in his efforts to do right. But where the best consistently miscarry, how tenfold more remarkable that all should continue to strive; and surely we should find it both touching and inspiring, that in a field from which success is banished, our race should not cease to labor. . . . It matters not where we look, under what climate we observe him, in what stage of society, in what depth of ignorance, burthened with what erroneous morality; by campfires in Assiniboia, the snow powdering his shoulders, the wind plucking his blanket, as he sits, passing the ceremonial calumet and uttering his grave opinions like a Roman senator; in ships at sea, a man inured to hardship and vile pleasures, his brightest hope a fiddle in a tavern and a bedizened trull who sells herself to rob him, and he for all that, simple, innocent, cheerful, kindly like a child, constant to toil, brave to drown, for others; . . . in the brothel, the discard of society, living mainly on strong drink, fed with affronts, a fool, a thief, the comrade of thieves, and even here keeping the point of honor and the touch of pity, often repaying the world's scorn with service, often standing firm upon a scruple, and at a certain cost, rejecting riches;—everywhere some virtue cherished or affected, everywhere some decency of thought and carriage, everywhere the ensign of man's ineffectual goodness! . . . under every circumstance of failure, without hope, without health, without thanks, still obscurely fighting the lost fight of virtue, still clinging, in the brothel or on the scaffold, to some rag of honor, the poor jewel of their souls! They may seek to escape, and yet they cannot; it is not alone their privilege and glory, but their doom, they are condemned to some nobility . . .

For Stevenson, the world in which this drama is played out is, objectively considered, a violent and meaningless world—"our rotary island loaded with predatory life and more drenched with blood . . . than ever mutinied ship, scuds through space." This is Hemingway's world, too. But its characters, at least those whose story Hemingway cares to tell, make one gallant effort to redeem the incoherence and meaninglessness of this world: they attempt to impose some form upon the disorder of their lives, the technique of the bullfighter or sportsman, the discipline of the soldier, the code of the gangster, which, even though brutal and dehumanizing, has its own ethic. (Ole Andreson is willing to take his medicine without whining. Or the dying Mexican in "The Gambler, the Nun, and the Radio" refuses to squeal, despite the detective's arguments: "One can, with honor, denounce one's assailant.")

The form is never quite adequate to subdue the world, but the fidelity to it is part of the gallantry of defeat.

It has been said above that the typical Hemingway character is tough and, apparently, insensitive. But only apparently, for the fidelity to a code, to a discipline, may be an index to a sensitivity which allows the characters to see, at moments, their true plight. At times, and usually at times of stress, it is the tough man, for Hemingway, the disciplined man, who actually is aware of pathos or tragedy. The individual toughness (which may be taken to be the private discipline demanded by the world), may find itself in conflict with some more natural and spontaneous human emotion; in contrast with this the discipline may, even, seem to be inhuman; but the Hemingway hero, though he is aware of the claims of this spontaneous human emotion, is afraid to yield to those claims because he has learned that the only way to hold on to "honor," to individuality, to, even, the human order as against the brute chaos of the world, is to live by his code. This is the irony of the situation in which the hero finds himself. Hemingway's heroes are aristocrats in the sense that they are the initiate, and practice a lonely virtue.

Hemingway's heroes utter themselves, not in rant and bombast, but in terms of ironic understatement. This understatement, stemming from the contrast between the toughness and the sensitivity, the violence and the sensitivity, is a constant aspect of Hemingway's method, an aspect which was happily caught in a cartoon in the *New Yorker* some years ago. The cartoonist showed a brawny, hairy forearm and a muscled hand clutching a little rose. The cartoon was entitled "The Soul of Ernest Hemingway." Just as there is a margin of victory in the defeat of the Hemingway characters, so there is a little margin of sensibility in their brutal and violent world. The revelation arises from the most unpromising circumstances and from the most unpromising people—the little streak of poetry or pathos in "The Pursuit Race," "The Undefeated," "My Old Man," and, let us say, "The Killers."

It has already been pointed out that Ole Andreson fits into this pattern. Andreson won't whimper. He takes his medicine quietly. But Ole Andreson's story is buried in the larger story, which is focused on Nick. How does Nick Adams fit into the pattern? Hemingway, as a matter of fact, is accustomed to treat his basic situation at one or the other of two levels. There is the story of the person who is already initiated, who already has adopted his appropriate code, or discipline, in the world which otherwise he cannot cope with. (One finds examples in Jake and Brett in *The Sun Also Rises*, Jordan and Pilar in *For Whom the Bell Tolls*, the bullfighter in "The Undefeated," and many other stories.) There is also the story of the process of the initiation, the discovery of evil and disorder, and the first step toward the mastery of the discipline. This is Nick's story. (But the same basic situation occurs in many other stories by Hemingway, for example, "Up In Michigan," "Indian Camp," and "The Three-Day Blow.")

It has been observed that the typical Hemingway character is tough and apparently insensitive. Usually, too, that character is simple. The impulse which has led Hemingway to the simple character is akin to that which led a Romantic poet like Wordsworth to the same choice. Wordsworth felt that his unsophisticated peasants or children, who are the characters of so many of his poems, were more honest in their responses than the cultivated man, and therefore more poetic. Instead of Wordsworth's typical peasant we find in Hemingway's work the bullfighter, the soldier, the revolutionist, the sportsman, and the gangster; instead of Wordsworth's children, we find the young men like Nick. There are, of course, differences between the approach of Wordsworth and that of Hemingway, but there is little difference on the point of marginal sensibility.

The main difference between the two writers depends on the difference in their two worlds. Hemingway's world is a more disordered world, and more violent, than the simple and innocent world of Wordsworth. Therefore, the sensibility of Hemingway's characters is in sharper contrast to the nature of his world. This creates an irony which is not found in the work of Wordsworth. Hemingway plays down the sensibility as such, and sheathes it in the code of toughness. Gertrude Stein says of Hemingway: "Hemingway is the shyest and proudest and sweetest-smelling storyteller of my reading." When she refers to his "shyness" she is, apparently, thinking of his use of irony and understatement. The typical character is sensitive, but his sensitivity is never insisted upon; he may be worthy of pity, but he never demands it. The underlying attitude in Hemingway's work may be stated like this: pity is only valid when it is wrung from a man who has been seasoned by experience, and is only earned by a man who never demands it, a man who takes his chances. Therefore, a premium is placed upon the fact of violent experience.

A further question suggests itself. How is Hemingway's *style* related to his basic fictional concerns. In "The Killers," as in many of his other stories, the style is simple even to the point of monotony. The characteristic sentence is simple, or compound; and if compound, there is no implied subtlety in the co-ordination of the clauses. The paragraph structure is, characteristically, based on simple sequence. * First, we can observe that there is an obvious relation between this style and the characters and situations with which the author is concerned: unsophisticated characters and simple, fundamental situations are rendered in an uncomplicated style. But there is another, and

* In some of Hemingway's work, especially in the novels, there are examples of a more fluent, lyrical style than is found in "The Killers." But even in such examples, one can observe that the fluency and the lyrical effect is based on the conjunction *and*—that there is no process of subordination but rather a process of sequence in terms of direct perceptions. The lyrical quality of such examples is to be taken as a manifestation of the "marginal sensibility," as can be demonstrated by an analysis of the situations in which the lyrical passages occur.

more interesting, aspect of the question which involves, not the sensibility of the characters, but the sensibility of the author himself. The short simple rhythms, the succession of co-ordinate clauses, and the general lack of subordination—all suggest a dislocated and ununified world. Hemingway is apparently trying to suggest in his style the direct experience—things as seen and felt, one after another, and not as the mind arranges and analyzes them. A style which involves subordination and complicated shadings of emphasis —a style which tends toward complex sentences with many qualifying clauses and phrases—implies an exercise of critical discrimination—the sifting of experience through the intellect. But Hemingway, apparently, is primarily concerned with giving the immediate impact of experience rather than with analyzing and evaluating it in detail. (We can notice, in this connection, that in his work he rarely indulges in any psychological analysis, and is rarely concerned with the detailed development of a character.) His very style, then, seems to imply that the use of the intellect, with its careful discriminations, may blur the rendering of experience and may falsify it; and this style, in connection with his basic concern for the character of marginal sensibility, may be taken as implying a distrust of the intellect in solving man's basic problems. It is as though he should say: despite the application of the human intellect to the problems of the world, the world is still a disorderly and brutal mess, in which it is hard to find any sure scale of values; therefore, it is well for one to remember the demands of fundamental situations—those involving sex, love, danger, and death, in which the instinctive life is foremost—which are frequently glossed over or falsified by social conventions or sterile intellectuality, and to remember the simple virtues of courage, honesty, fidelity, discipline.

But is all of this a way of saying that Hemingway is really writing innocently, without calculation, crudely? Now, as a matter of fact, his style is a result of calculation, and is not, strictly speaking, spontaneous and naïve at all. His style is, then, a dramatic device, developed because of its appropriateness to the total effect which he intends to give. A writer who was in point of fact uninstructed and spontaneous would probably not be able to achieve the impression of spontaneity and immediacy which is found in Hemingway's best work, the work in which his basic attitude and subject matter can be truly and functionally co-ordinated.

In our comment on this story we have tried, among other and more obvious concerns, to relate the style of the story to the theme and then to relate the various qualities of this story to the general body of Hemingway's work and his attitude towards his world. Ordinarily we have been studying stories taken individually, but it is time for us to realize that the various (and often quite different) stories done by a good writer always have some fundamental unifying attitudes—for a man can be only himself. Since this is true, we can nearly always enter more deeply into a piece of fiction and understand it more fully when we are prepared to relate it to the writer's other work. A good writer does not offer us, for instance, a glittering variety of themes. He probably treats, over and over, those few themes that seem to him most important in his actual living and observation of life. For we can remember, too, that a good writer is not merely playing a game to amuse his readers or to make a living—though quite properly he may do these things in addition to what else he may do. The good writer is trying in his personal way to find and to say something that he regards as true about life.

A Little Light on Hemingway's "The Light of the World" / *James J. Martine*

Hemingway's short story "The Light of the World" is generally ignored, and roundly misinterpreted when it is noticed at all. The reason for the misunderstanding may be an esoteric trick or device central to an understanding of the story. One critic suggests that the story "becomes so over subtle as to be entirely lost to a reader, and the story drifts away into vignette or sketch."[1] Carlos Baker, in fact, confines himself to Hemingway's fondness for the story and notes several letters in which Hemingway compared "The Light of the World" to Maupassant's "La Maison Tellier."[2] Nicholas Canaday gives an interesting recapitulation but does not approach a satisfactory interpretation of the story.[3] Constance Montgomery identifies the real life prototypes of the characters in "The Light of the World," but in suggesting common points with "La Maison Tellier" does not examine the indebtedness of Hemingway to the Maupassant piece.[4]

For there is a relationship in the two works, as Hemingway strongly indicated. First, there is the same number of "girls" (five) taking a trip by rail. In each story the central scene is awash with the tears of maudlin sentimentality. Then there is the description of Mme. Tellier, very like that of big Alice: tall, stout, and affable. A very funny line spoken to Nick[5] about Alice

James J. Martine, "A Little Light on Hemingway's 'The Light of the World,' " *Studies in Short Fiction*, VII (Summer 1970), 465–67. Copyright, 1970, Newberry College, Newberry, S.C.; reprinted by permission of *Studies in Short Fiction*.

1. Earl Rovit, *Ernest Hemingway* (New York, 1963), p. 97.
2. Carlos Baker, *Ernest Hemingway: A Life Story* (New York, 1969), p. 606.
3. Nicholas Canaday, "Is There Any Light in Hemingway's 'Light of the World'?" *Studies in Short Fiction*, III (Fall 1965), 75.
4. Constance Cappel Montgomery, *Hemingway in Michigan* (New York, 1966), pp. 91–95.
5. The "I" narrator of this story is clearly Nick Adams.

("Must be like getting on top of a hay mow.") may have been suggested to Hemingway by another Maupassant story, "On Perfumes," in which a central character is described as "a very stout lady . . . she looked like a moving haystack, and exhaled an odor of hay around her."

Perhaps the most significant relationship of one story to the other is in authorial intention, the key to which lies in Hemingway's ironic title. Hemingway's title has been variously described as derived from Matthew 5:14 (Montgomery) and from Holman Hunt's famous picture (Baker). In describing Mme. Tellier's house, Maupassant is sacrilegiously comic: ". . . all night long a little lamp burned, behind wire bars, such as one still sees in some towns, at the foot of the shrine of some saint." Again after the girls return from their excursion: "The little colored lamp outside the door told the passers-by that the flock had returned to the fold." The light in Hemingway's title is the archetypal light on the archetypal houses of the oldest profession in the world. A profane and irreligious suggestion? There is a great deal of ironic use of religious imagery in Hemingway's story. In describing her boxer-lover, Peroxide says in three separate places: "I knew him like you know nobody in the world and I loved him like you love God. . . . He was like a god . . . My soul belongs to Steve Ketchel. By God, he was a man." This is not a religion of spirit, but the religion of Hemingway and Maupassant, both over-virile and assertively physical men.

It is Ketchel, the prizefighter about whom Alice and Peroxide argue, who serves as the device upon which the story turns. And this device is central to an understanding of the story. Never noted critically, the identification of Ketchel is the fulcrum upon which the story works. They key passage is:

"Steve Ketchel," one of the blondes said. . . .
"His own father shot and killed him. Yes, by Christ, his own father. There aren't any more men like Steve Ketchel."
"Wasn't his name Stanley Ketchel?" asked the cook.
"Oh, shut up," said the blonde. "What do you know about Steve? Stanley. He was no Stanley."

Ironically, it is the homosexual cook who correctly identifies the fighter, and big Alice and Peroxide claim as a lover someone neither of them knew. For Stanley Ketchel (real name Stanislaus Kiecal) was the White Hope from Grand Rapids, Michigan, who fought Jack Johnson on October 16, 1909, in Colma, California. Peroxide closely recounts the details of the middleweight champion's fight with Johnson, the heavyweight champ, but it is clear Ketchel did not *know* her in any sense of the word. There was a Steve Ketchel who, on July 31, 1915, fought Ad Wolgast (the Ad Francis of "The Battler") in Forest Park, Illinois, but he is not the boxer who is the crux of the argument here, for Stanley Ketchel was shot and killed on October 15, 1910, in Conway, Missouri, not by his father as Peroxide claims, but by a ranchhand, Walter A. Dipley, in an argument over a girl.[6] The details of the Johnson-Ketchel fight in the story clearly establish that it is Stanley Ketchel about whom the ladies are arguing. Note further that they always describe him in terms of "white" and "whitest": Stanley Ketchel was the greatest Hope in the quest for a White Hope. The identification is really not so esoteric that the device, to Hemingway's mind at least, would go unnoticed, for the fight he describes was one of the high spots of American ring history. Preserving his renowed economy, Hemingway, in a single line by the cook, establishes that both Peroxide and big Alice are lying. For finally, it is a story about the male-female relationship, in a series of stories of Nick Adams' growth from innocence to experience.

What is the nature of the specific lesson to be learned here? Writing of "The Light of the World" and "La Maison Tellier," Mrs. Montgomery says that "both stories show that a woman's sense of truth and reality is not a true reality."[7] Maleness and the sense of a male world create quite special "realities" throughout the Hemingway canon. Here specifically, the ironic use of the title and the cook's identification of Ketchel suggest that what Hemingway is writing about, the point of the story if one will, is the unreliability of what a woman, any woman, says. Still Nick is attracted to Alice. How subtle (or universal) a phenomenon is this? The integrity of what big Alice says has gone unquestioned by everyone, astute critics included, for thirty-six years.

Hemingway's "Fifty Grand": The Other Fight(s) / James J. Martine

One point on which Carlos Baker is mistaken in *Ernest Hemingway: A Life Story* concerns Hemingway's short story "Fifty Grand." Baker contradicts an article by P. G. and R. R. Davies that seeks to establish the Jack

James J. Martine, "Hemingway's 'Fifty Grand': The Other Fight(s)," *Journal of Modern Literature*, II (September 1971), 123–27. Reprinted by permission of the *Journal of Modern Literature*.

6. It has recently been brought to my attention that Matthew J. Bruccoli in "'The Light of the World': Stan Ketchel as 'My Sweet Christ'" (included in *Fitzgerald/Hemingway Annual 1969*) proposes a thesis that is irreconcilable with a point of my essay. Mr. Bruccoli claims that Stanley and Steve Ketchel are the same man. Steve Ketchel fought Ad Wolgast in 1915; Stanley Ketchel was shot and killed in 1910. A very neat trick for Stan Ketchel, who "seems to have preferred being addressed as Steve" (Bruccoli, p. 128)—unless Ketchel as "My Sweet Christ" has greater messianic powers than even Mr. Bruccoli has given him credit for.

7. Montgomery, p. 95.

Britton–Mickey Walker fight, Madison Square Garden, November 1, 1922, as the one on which Hemingway based his story.[1] Baker indicates that "Fifty Grand" is based on a welterweight championship bout between Benny Leonard, the world lightweight king, and Britton, the welterweight champion, at New York Hippodrome on June 26, 1922.[2]

Baker's choice of the Leonard-Britton fight as *the* source for "Fifty Grand" can not be supported in light of one of the many recent discoveries of Philip Young in a bank in New York. (For an account of his findings see "In The Vault With Hemingway," *The New York Times Book Review*, September 29, 1968, 2, 28.) In the vault, Young discovered the first three pages of typescript of "Fifty Grand" (working title "Jack") that Hemingway deleted at the suggestion of Scott Fitzgerald. The story of the deletion was known but until recently the full content of the missing pages of typescript was not. Reproductions of some pages of typescript are included in Philip Young and Charles W. Mann's, *The Hemingway Manuscripts: An Inventory* (University Park, Pa., 1969). The first two and one-half pages of the discarded typescript lead directly into the story as we have it now. The story begins with Jack telling his colleagues, Soldier Bartlett and Jerry Doyle, how he defeated Leonard:

> Up at the Garden one time somebody says to Jack, "Say Jack how did you happen to beat Leonard anyway?" and Jack says, "Well you see Benny's an awful smart boxer. All the time he's in there thinking and all the time he's thinking I was hitting him."

It is quite clear, then, in the omitted pages that the Benny Leonard fight has already taken place. Thus, it is hard to imagine the Britton-Leonard fight as the source of "Fifty Grand": a fighter does not go to camp to prepare for a bout he has already fought.

The new evidence prompts a closer examination of the Davies' article, which claims to have *the* source. There is, first of all, one rather blatant error of commission. The Davies identify Jack Britton in the story as Jack Brennan, and Mickey Walker as Walcott, but they are too far from ringside when they say that Walcott is given no first name. The Walker to Walcott transmutation seems an obvious one and is very like Hemingway's practice, but when the signal for the foul is given, Walcott's manager calls him "Jimmy."

While Baker is mistaken, the Davies only have a part of it. The rest of it is that Hemingway had another fight in mind as well when he composed "Fifty Grand." The Davies' article mentions that Hemingway did not witness the Britton-Walker fight and suggests that perhaps Hemingway read about it in the papers. What the article does not mention is that five weeks

---

1. The Davies' article is "Hemingway's 'Fifty Grand' and the Jack Britton-Mickey Walker Prize Fight," *American Literature*, XXXVII (November 1965), 251–258.
2. Carlos Baker, *Ernest Hemingway: A Life Story* (New York, 1969), p. 157.

before the Britton-Walker fight, Hemingway was witness to one of the most famous prize fights of the century, and this fight influenced the composition of "Fifty Grand." On September 24, 1922, before leaving Paris for Constantinople to cover the Greco-Turkish War, Hemingway attended a murderous fight between Battling Siki and George Carpentier for the lightheavyweight championship of the world. The Davies' article suggests that the foul in "Fifty Grand" is the artistic imagination's reshaping of the facts, for there was none in the Britton-Walker fight, but such imaginative reshaping was not necessary, for a foul occurred in the Siki-Carpentier fight. The "disquieting reports," as the papers had it, of shady dealing are unsubstantiated in the Walker-Britton contest. The double-cross in the Siki-Carpentier fight was blatant and so controversial that it shook the foundations of the French Government.

Battling Siki was a Senegalese lightheavyweight of some small renown, and in 1922 Hemingway wrote to his brother that he and Ezra Pound had seen Siki, who Hemingway believed would become world champion if he would stop training in cafes. Siki, indeed, trained on absinthe. He must have made quite an impression on Hemingway, as he did on everyone else, as Siki regularly made the rounds of the Paris bistros with a lion in tow. (After the Carpentier fight Siki added a monkey, which perched on his shoulder.)

This was the fighter that Hemingway saw enter the ring at the new Mont Rouge arena in Paris, to meet Georges Carpentier, the lightheavyweight champion of the world. (Certain elements of the Siki-Carpentier fight may also have been in Hemingway's mind in the story of Bill Gorton's Negro fighter in *The Sun Also Rises*). Suffice to say that Siki was supposed to lose the fight, and decided in the ring to pull a double-cross. He fairly battered Carpentier into oblivion. Then, at the moment of the crucial knockdown, the referee stepped in suddenly and stopped the fight, awarding it to Carpentier on a foul. The referee's act started the hundreds of Americans at ringside to shouting "robber." (If a man standing at ringside in a photo of the knockdown is not Hemingway, one critic has offered to eat the *New York Times* September 26, 1922, p. 14, and the rest of the paper.) The crowd at the arena became so threatening that the fight officials rescinded the decision of the referee and awarded the bout to Siki. Later Siki himself related how the bout was framed. The Siki-Carpentier battle, which was designed to be "the frame-up of the century," became the greatest double-cross in fight history, and it is difficult to think that so famous a fight, with a double-cross, that Hemingway attended, played no part in the plot of "Fifty Grand."

The incidents of "Fifty Grand" were common occurrences and really representative of the era. Hemingway may have drawn his fictional characters from real people connected with the Britton-Walker fight. Perhaps he excised the fouling and the double-cross from the fight he saw at Mont Rouge. One thing is certain, however: the fictional Jack Brennan-Jimmy Walcott fight is an amalgamation of at least two real-life bouts. Hemingway is actually presenting the times. Fouls and the rather peculiar aroma of gambling arrangements pervaded more prize fights, both in Europe and the United States, than aficionadoes care to recall. It was at this very time that boxing commissions were trying to fight control of the sport by gambling interests. The growing frequency of unsatisfactory endings to boxing contests brought a proposal from the New York State Athletic Commission that boxers who lost on a foul be deprived of their share of the purse. It had reached the stage where boxers were disqualified for fouls on an average of once a week.

Today, prize fighting is virtually dead, at least as the progeny of what boxing was in the period that Hemingway preserves for us—the Golden Age of the prize ring. What has Hemingway captured in "Fifty Grand"? A country between wars, a period when our heroes came less from the world of diplomacy and statesmanship and more and more from the world of sports. Athletes were our folk heroes. This period reached its peak with the Carpentier-Dempsey fight in 1921. Boxing had begun to attract new fans, including women and intellectuals. It was the era of the first million dollar gate. The decade from 1919 to 1929 was when prize fighting was in transition to a relative legitimacy of sorts—in transition from swindling managers and fouls aplenty and referees of dubious credentials, and instructed fighters who knew in which direction the tank lay. It was the age of Dempsey, of Tunney, of low taxes; an age when prize fighters were more important (and better known) than presidents. Hemingway was recording faithfully a portrait of the American disposition. Did he portray the lost generation abroad? He, not a bit less, captured the essence of the times in America. When Morgan and Steinfelt are serving up drinks from the bottle, Jack cautions them to save some for their ride back to town. Morgan tells him not to worry, that they have plenty. Preserving the precious Hemingway economy, the author has captured the attitude and peculiarities of a generation in the period of the Volstead Act. The incidents of "Fifty Grand" are truly representative of their epoch, and this is one reason why the story is more important than heretofore realized.

Another reason for placing the story higher in the Hemingway canon is that it is an early working out of the tenets, that would remain unchanged, of the code. Critics of "Fifty Grand" call Jack Brennan "parismonious" and say that his action is undercut by very obvious monetary motives. What Hemingway is doing in this story is showing the very humanity of our folk heroes. And our folk heroes are our folk heroes because they are personifications of very human traits and desires. It is fallacious to say, as the Davies do, that the Hemingway code hero can only exist removed from the sordid, everyday world where money and success count. "Fifty Grand" shows that this kind of heroism exists especially in, and in spite of, the "sordid, everyday world." What is the nature of this code heroism? Writing of "Fifty

Grand," Carlos Baker says that Hemingway was interested in athletes "not so much because they are athletes as because they are people."[3] This is not so. It is precisely because they *are* athletes that Hemingway is interested in them. Athletes are a very special brand of people. And Hemingway was interested in a very special brand of athlete: the professional. One must understand what the decision Jack Brennan makes means to him: an understanding of what winning means to a professional. Jerry Doyle, the narrator, and Hogan, the operator of the training camp, are the experts. Hemingway portrays them as detached and objective because it is essential to his point that his reader trust their judgment. They establish at the outset that Brennan will get beaten. This is important to an understanding of Brennan's motive—it is not just for the money that he makes the bet. It is Jerry who states what may well be the underlying philosophy of the code: "Everybody's got to get it sometime." Everyone loses, of course; it is *how* that matters. Contrary to what some critics believe, Hemingway goes to great lengths to create reader sympathy for Brennan. The drinking scene with Morgan and Steinfelt, the trip to mail the letter, the drunken confession to the narrator, are melodramatic, almost hackneyed portraits of a man in a quandry. But there is nothing hackneyed about the dilemma. Brennan does not think he can beat Walcott, and when a professional *thinks* he can not win, he can not.

The reader must be cautious not to equate the professional Brennan with "tutor" and the first person narrator with "tyro" in this story, as one critic has done. Jerry Doyle is no innocent: *he* is the one who suggests that fifty thousand dollars is a lot of money, and that the syndicate might have *Walcott* throw the fight. The experienced Brennan naively dismisses the possibility of what is actually going to happen. Jerry is wiser than Brennan. He is wiser because Brennan, like all good code heroes, is not a thinker. Brennan is very explicit about his intellectual limitations when he chides Collins, his manager, for not being there when the press came to the camp for a prefight interview. Contrary to Charles A. Fenton's suggestion that "thinking" is what distinguishes the professional,[4] the opposite is true. In the ring Brennan reacts instinctively. He is a skilled and trained professional who does not have to think. The code relates to grace under pressure, in pain, and is consistent with the way in which Hemingway viewed himself, his art. When he covered the Baer-Louis fight in 1935, he had nothing but contempt for Max Baer, the nonprofessional fighter. The ultimate insult was "Max Baer had never bothered to learn his trade."[5] It was the same accusation Hemingway made against many of his colleagues, including Scott Fitzgerald.

3. Carlos Baker, *Hemingway: The Writer as Artist* (Princeton, 1963), p. 157.
4. Charles A. Fenton, "No Money for the Kingbird: Hemingway's Prizefight Stories," *American Quarterly*, IV (Winter 1952), 347.
5. Fenton, p. 349.

Jack Brennan is the consummate professional. Thus, learning the trade well insures a measure of victory in a life that spells defeat. He faces his greatest test in the late stages of his career, alone; alone in the oppressive confines of a crowded arena. Conditioning is everything, it is what prepares man for the supreme effort: physically for the athlete, morally and ethically for the code hero. When the moment occurs, there is not time for thinking, only action. This is the point of the deleted anecdote. One just does not reach for an ethical reserve in time of crisis, it must be there, built through conditioning. Thus, at the moment of losing the fight, Brennan is victorious. The last line of the story, "It was nothing," is the epitome of the code hero's stoicism. The code hero, like the king of old, has *hybris*. Brennan's *hybris* will not allow him to be knocked out. The defeat must be on his terms. Brennan, though not in "good shape"physically, is in peak condition morally—in that curious ethic that comprises the code.

Brennan has sacrificed *all* he had, his integrity, in the face of insurmountable odds: the odds that time, and life, impose upon a man. If life must beat you, and it does in Hemingway's cosmos, there is nothing "unethical" about getting some small consideration for participating in the game; a game, the definition of which, the very ground rules of which, can only go against you.

Hemingway's "The Gambler, the Nun, and the Radio": A Reading and a Problem / *Marion Montgomery*

Mr. Frazer, the central character of Hemingway's "The Gambler, the Nun, and the Radio," is a man about whom the reader learns few biographical facts. There are certain bits of information carefully seeded through the story: Frazer is a writer; he is in the hospital with a broken leg received when thrown by a horse; the injury has caused him considerable pain. And of prime concern is the fact that he is in a private room and has a radio which helps him avoid thinking. But Hemingway seems interested, not in the facts of Frazer's being, but in his emotional and intellectual response to people and situations around him. Frazer at first appears aloof, detached, even bitter. Nevertheless, his accident has brought him into personal relationships which he cannot avoid. He is forced by circumstance, then led by desire, to know the nun, Sister Cecilia, the gambler, Cayetano, and the other characters

Marion Montgomery, "Hemingway's 'The Gambler, the Nun, and the Radio': A Reading and a Problem," *Forum*, III (Winter 1962), 36–40. Reprinted by permission of *Forum*.

in the story; he warms from detachment to humanness, is drawn (in his mind at least if not in body) from his private room into the ward of common humanity.

This is not to say that Frazer's attitude, his perspective on the world, is one which changes from an initial pessimism to optimism. He is as aware in the end as in the beginning that nature—particularly human nature—is out of joint. There is the police sergeant, blindly at odds with humanity, intent on his duty to find out Cayetano's assailant, even if his questioning kills the seriously wounded gambler. There is the simple, naive Sister who prays for Notre Dame's gridiron victory because of the name of the school, who has dedicated her life to the ambition of sainthood with the intellectual simplicity of the child who dedicates himself to the Lone Ranger and Merita Bread for a tin star. There is the quietly determined gambler who is convinced that sooner or later his luck will change and he will become rich. There are the three unnamed Mexicans whom only bad music holds together. Frazier sees clearly the blindness of these persons but in the course of his increasing involvement he discovers that even his withdrawal—his attachment to his radio and the private room which help to hold the world of man at a proper distance for his thinking to control is itself a blindness. Frazer comes to see that, as prayer is to Sister Cecilia and gambling to Cayetano, so the radio is to him. [1] He is forced, then to see himself as he has seen others, and though his recognition that the radio is his personal form of opium (along with the private room and liquor) does not gain him a happy insight into man's place in the world, it does lead to stoical perseverance. He finally admires the warm human concern of Sister Cecilia and adopts as his own the quiet determination of Cayetano so that he can weather physical and intellectual pain. He seems to understand the pain no more than Cayetano does chance or Sister Cecilia sainthood; but he does understand that with a limited view which a faith in sainthood or in luck affords one, chance, religion, or pain may be endured to the ennoblement of the endurer.

We have stated that in this story Hemingway is interested primarily in his character's state of being, his emotional and intellectual attitude toward the people around him. The story is particularly effective in the modulation of the character's attitude through the use of the related point of view. The people and events are closely screened through Frazer, and the tone derives from this modulation and is Frazer's rather than Hemingway's. That is to say, Hemingway has so closely identified himself with Frazer that the story in tone gives the effect of first person narrative. To appreciate the dramatic transformation in Frazer (the actions and scenes are external, but the dramatic action is within Frazer), the technical handling of the point of

1. The surprise of this self-discovery is predicted in the title where the parallelism of the series of nouns is broken by an unparallel third term. One would expect *writer* to balance *gambler* and *nun* rather than *radio*.

view needs to be examined. Approximately three-fourths of the story (14 pages) is dialogue and of the remaining four pages of exposition, long passages of which are sandwiched by the dialogue, part is devoted to a summary of incident, part to indicating passage of time, and some to direct reflection of Frazer's attitude. But both the dialogue of the story's scenes (seven in all) and the exposition emphasize the particular state of mind Frazer experiences at the moment. The first of the nine distinct sections of the story (each separated from the other by white space) is dialogue and shows Frazer as a detached observer. The beginning paragraph, a single sentence, reads: "They brought them in around midnight and then, all night long, everyone along the corridor heard the Russian." The *they* and *them* tease the curiosity, and by calling attention to the screaming Russian Hemingway prepares for the contrast for the silent Cayetano, who in turn calls attention to the silent Frazer, both trying to hide pain from everyone.[2] As important as the vague identification of the wounded men through impersonal pronouns is the routine, detached interest reflected by Mr. Frazer's questions about them. The wounded men are objects of bored curiosity. Frazer asks where each is shot, a point of more interest to him than that they are shot. His detachment is further reflected by his casual notice of the facts of the shooting in a newspaper. The short passages of exposition in the scene are carefully paced to show Frazer's unhurried interest. Frazer's dissociation is developed further through the episode of the police sergeant's attempted questioning of Cayetano. Frazer becomes involved, accidentally, when the sergeant calls upon him to interpret since he mistrusts the interpreter he has. The frustrated sergeant laments his inability to speak "spick" and Frazer retorts sarcastically that he might learn. Frazer sees that the language barrier is the least formidable one. Both sardonic and sarcastic, he is temporarily safe in the detachment which allows him to see the futility of the situation without having to think about it. The first scene then, the entry of the wounded men into the hospital, is written in such a way that one knows Frazer's attitude toward his fellows though one does not understand its cause in terms other than those of the immediate situation. That his original detachment is undergoing a change is indicated by his shift to more obvious sarcasm in the second section, a scene outside Cayetano's room. Frazer, angry because of the sergeant's unfeeling treatment of Cayetano in the name of justice, fires a final dart as the sergeant leaves: "Don't let anybody shoot you in the back."

The third section of the story is, at first sight, exposition in which one is introduced to Sister Cecilia. But this is exposition closely strained through Frazer's ruminative mind by the device of indirect quotation with the primary purpose of reflecting his evaluation of the nun, not of showing her as

2. The setting is given indirectly and gradually. From unadorned nouns such as *corridor* and *night nurse* the reader fills in the setting. There is no description independent of the action just as there is no action which is not aimed at reflecting Frazer's attitude.

she is. Frazer sees her as a typical professional do-gooder, concerned for Cayetano because he smiles despite his pain, but even more concerned because he is a bad one and "I always like the bad ones." The paragraph of indirect quotations changes, as the quoted line indicates, into the direct words Frazer recalls to mimic Sister Cecilia. It ends "Oh, that poor Cayetano! I'm going right down and pray for him." It is followed by oblique derision in the direct statement, "She went right down and prayed for him." The mimicry and sarcasm of this short section reveal Frazer's suspicions of the professional saint, just as his sarcastic barbs at the sergeant reflect his suspicion of that professional seeker of justice.

A dramatic relationship has been established in these last two sections in preparation of Frazer's final self-understanding. His anger and contempt are aroused by the abuse of Cayetano by the professional saint of mercy and officer of justice. Thus aroused, he sees that Cayetano, like himself, is withdrawn, self-contained, and Frazer senses their kinship. Drawn to Cayetano now, he will later learn from him compassion for the professionals, compassion even for himself.

The fourth section consists of four paragraphs of exposition which explore the hospital world as seen by Frazer. The first paragraph concerns his dependence on the radio during the sleepless night (he seems never to sleep). He tunes stations westward, Seattle, Washington, being the most distant one and hence his favorite of the western stations; when Seattle signs off, he switches east to pick up the early morning program at Minneapolis, his favorite of the eastern stations, and works west till the hospital's x-ray machines make reception impossible at mid-morning. Through the radio he manipulates the outer world, keeping it in comfortable perspective. Thus he is saved confusion of thought, safe from intrusion by the outside world. But the outside world will not be kept at a distance, and the next paragraph shows the complications of intrusion. The doctor attempts to move Frazer's bed toward the window to show him pheasants in the snow. Frazer's bed lamp is dislodged, hitting him on the head, because the doctor (and everyone else) is looking out the window. The doctor is obviously trying to cheer his patient, get him interested in the existence of the outside world, but the result "seemed the antithesis of healing or whatever people were in the hospital for." This antithesis makes the incident funny, "a joke on Mr. Frazer and on the doctor," and though Frazer is in a less serious predicament than Cayetano, the irony of the two incidents is identical; the sergeant almost causes Cayetano's death in his intense desire to bring the assailant to justice, the doctor gives Frazer a slight bump in his efforts to encourage him to rejoin the human race. "Everything is much simpler in a hospital," which exists, Frazer seems to feel, so that some may intrude upon others to hurt them. Frazer appreciates the ironies involved in man's attempt to be his brother's keeper.

The next paragraph of this fourth section concludes that the limited view from a private bed is best if one has to be in a hospital; the sick man can best control a *portion* of reality. This central idea of the story, which Frazer later generalizes and justifies in the final section, is set forth here as objective statement concerning Frazer's actual physical situation, clearly with metaphorical implications:

> two views, with time to observe them, from a room the temperature of which you control, are much better than any number of views seen for a few minutes from hot, empty rooms that are waiting for someone else or just abandoned, which you are wheeled in and out of.

He is not to be forced into the hot room which the over anxious sergeant or doctor or the revolutionary Mexican (whom we shall presently consider) would wheel him into. He has time to appreciate Sister Cecilia's and Cayetano's views in the course of the story and his reaction harks us back to a sentence in this section: "If you stay long enough in a room, the view, whatever it is, acquires a great value and becomes very important and you would not change it, not even by a different angle."

Frazer, then, objects to being forcibly wheeled in and out of rooms to see other's views. He wishes to control the view or the temperature of the room as he controls the radio. The final paragraph of this fourth section turns attention back to the radio and to Frazer's habit of modulating the outer world, through the radio, to a simplicity which relieves thought.

But the world will not be so controlled, and subsequent sections are concerned with a series of invasions of his world which force him to modify his position as recluse. His early recognition of Cayetano as spiritual brother is understood instinctively by Sister Cecilia. She is as interested in Frazer as in his bad brother, and keeps him informed of Cayetano's progress, thus drawing Frazer out of himself. In the process Frazer becomes interested in Sister Cecilia and in the humor of her frenzied concern for Notre Dame's football victory. Though he still sees her concern as an ironical commentary on human nature, he has abandoned sarcasm. He becomes so friendly, in fact, that he is anxious that Sister Cecilia be kept posted on the progress of the game, though he teases about her superfluous prayers for victory. Later, in section eight, when Sister Cecilia confesses her ambition to be a saint, he insists with a repetition that threatens to break the story that she will become a saint, that "Everybody gets what they want." Frazer moves then from detachment to sarcasm to humorous acceptance to concerned respect for Sister Cecilia.

This humanizing of Frazer is furthered in part by his perception of the irony which brings the three Mexicans to sing for Cayetano. At Sister Cecilia's instigation the police have forced the players to visit the enemy of their friend. Each of the three has an obsession, two of them music and drink, the third music and violent reform.[3] It is the devotion of each to his view that has made oppression by life bearable. They even enjoy life, with the exception of the "thin" Mexican who refuses drink and conviviality and who finds occasion to scoff at Sister Cecilia and religion. The first two are stoics; the thin one is a hard man, intent on remaking the world. This thin one is a key character in the story, one who gives Frazer the most telling insight into himself. The unsmiling man would by revolution and "education" destroy all individual perspective that makes human commitment and individuality possible. Frazer can no longer maintain sufficient detachment to be sarcastic toward such innocents as Sister Cecilia or scoff at religion, whether it take the form of Sister Cecilia's or of Cayetano's faith in luck. He meets and talks with Cayetano, discovering that his obsession with gambling allows him to forgo revenge. Cayetano can laugh at the bad music his visitors play, but not in their presence any more than he can express his own pain through tears in the public ward. He is a respecter of persons in a way that the thin Mexican is not and in a way that Frazer has not been. Frazer, moved by this insight, says "I wish you luck, truly, and with all my heart."

Cayetano, then, is a "poor idealist," just as Sister Cecilia is, and in the midst of the accidents of human relationships he has learned forbearance and sympathy—for the poor fool of a beet worker who shot him for thirty-eight dollars, for the Russian who happened to be in the way when the shooting started. He does not impose upon his fellows by cynical aloofness as Frazer has; he accepts a stiff leg, as apparently Frazer must. Cayetano's quiet stoicism and Sister Cecilia's ebullient faith contrast sharply with the thin Mexican's devotion to remaking man in the Marxist image. The contrast leads Frazer to reflection and to a climax in which he comes to some decisions about himself. He hears men singing in a common ward (the final section of the story), men "laughing and merry with music made by the Mexicans who had been sent by the police." He thinks of the bronco-buster with the broken back who must now learn to work in leather, the fallen carpenter with broken ankles and wrists; there is the boy whose misset leg must be rebroken and there is Cayetano with his stiff leg. Frazer sees that by his own refusal to think about his relationship to the rest of mankind, he has managed to keep himself uncommitted, to enjoy his private misfortune as unique or, at most, shared by a few like souls such as Cayetano. His radio has been a handy device to this end of not thinking, where Cayetano has had only the courage of his blind devotion to chance. And now Frazer cannot forget the thin Mexican's scoffing at religion as an opium nor his own observations of private opiums: music, religion, economics, patriotism, sex, drink, gambling, radio,

3. They are distinguished by their obsessions and by the adjectives *big, smallest, thin*. That they are Mexican and somewhat inarticulate is indicated by distorted syntax and a limited and repetitious vocabulary.

ambition, belief in a new form of government. The political opium of the thin Mexican shocks him into serious thought and actions because that particular opium is destructive, intolerant of other opiums. Mr. Frazer sends for the thin Mexican who would "operate on the people without an anesthetic" (i.e., do away with whatever ideal makes life tolerable) and demands of him: "Why are not all the opiums of the people good? What do you want to do with the people?" "They should all be rescued from ignorance." "Don't talk nonsense," says Mr. Frazer. For such, "Education is an opium of the people," one that Frazer is prepared to oppose since it is not the same as "knowledge." Of this distinction between education and knowledge the Mexican says, "I do not follow you." And Mr. Frazer answers, "Many times I do not follow myself with pleasure."

It is at this point in the final section of the story that the reader also becomes unable to follow Mr. Frazer. One could hazard the guess that Frazer (and Hemingway) means to say that education is knowledge imposed upon others willy nilly, that it is tolerant knowledge which makes Cayetano and Sister Cecilia appealing, which leads them to accept an involvement with mankind in the accidents of existence. But though Frazer seems quite positive of the distinction, one doesn't understand from the story itself as he does. And at this crucial point in the story questions are raised concerning the relationship of this insight into the necessary balm of multiple opiums and Frazer's rather unexpected outburst against the Marxist Mexican. Specifically one wishes to know the real cause of Frazer's initial withdrawal. One needs to know because the story has taken a turn. We have, before this point, witnessed the emotional responses of Frazer as he sought to understand himself, and with his understanding and appreciation of Sister Cecilia and Cayetano (aided by the catalytic thin Mexican), he does reach an understanding and justifies his return to the radio and "giant killer." The justification is that, having experienced some painful revolution, a soothing opium is necessary. But what is the revolution that Frazer has experienced? We know that he has received a severe blow which caused his withdrawal, but is the blow the actual physical one which will leave him a cripple (so he tells Cayetano), as Cayetano and the bronco-buster, the carpenter, the farm boy will be? Is Frazer's initial bitterness directed against Nature's caprice? Or is Frazer a failure as a writer and does that account for his withdrawal? Are we to understand that he discovers a parallel between himself as artist, Sister Cecilia as saint, and Cayetano as gambler, and is his attachment to the radio intended as an ironical commentary on his lack of courage and creativity? He is too positively active in the final paragraphs to satisfy this view even though he does go back to his radio. Or is one to understand from the discussion with the Marxist Mexican, whose politics so disturb Frazer, and from Frazer's thoughts on the difference between the effects of cartharsis and of opium, developed in relation to political revolution, that he has undergone some bitterly disillusioning political experience? When Frazer confronts the Mexican he seems to be confronting a ghost of himself, a confrontation foreshadowed by his argument with the police sergeant. Is Frazer a liberal disillusioned by the Spanish Civil War or some less conspicious exposure to the extreme Marxist intent? Frazer seems certain that he has experienced a cartharsis through revolution, but it is ambiguous whether the revolution which brings the cartharsis is the pain of a broken leg, failure in art, or political disillusionment. And the indication of the concluding section is that Frazer has undergone a spiritual rehabilitation after having been spiritually destroyed, but we do not feel certain of this conclusion because we do not understand what pain the opium of the radio helps him bear. Sister Cecilia, the nun, has the dream of sainthood as an opium to help her bear the drudgery of her devotion; Cayetano, the gambler, has his dream of money, of changed luck, to help him bear the misfortunes of chance. But Mr. Frazer—the writer (?), bronco-buster (?), revolutionary (?)—has whiskey and radio to help him bear what pain?

Ernest Hemingway's "The End of Something": Its Independence as a Short Story and Its Place in the "Education of Nick Adams" / Horst H. Kruse

Interpretation of the seven Nick Adams stories of *In Our Time* and of the Nick Adams stories of Hemingway's later collections has always been drawn between two extremes. On the one hand they have been taken as individual works of art; on the other they have been found to constitute integral chapters in "a scrupulously planned account of [Nick Adams'] character,"[1] or rather in what has come to be called his "education." Interpretation of "The Killers" and the drawn-out debate over "whose story it is"[2] demonstrate the difficulty; and Hemingway's statement to Edmund Wilson that *In Our Time* "has a pretty good unity" does not resolve the dilemma, for at the same time that he thus asserts the essential unity of his first book, he also refers to it as

Horst H. Kruse, "Ernest Hemingway's 'The End of Something': Its Independence as a Short Story and Its Place in the 'Education of Nick Adams,' " *Studies in Short Fiction*, IV (Winter 1967), 152–56. Copyright, 1967, Newberry College, Newberry, S. C.; reprinted by permission of *Studies in Short Fiction*.

1. Philip Young, *Ernest Hemingway* (London, 1952), p. 2.
2. Cf. esp. Cleanth Brooks and Robert Penn Warren, *Understanding Fiction*, 2nd ed. (New York, 1959), pp. 303–312, and Oliver Evans, "The Protagonist of Hemingway's 'The Killers,' " *MLN*, LXXIII (December 1958), 589–591.

consisting of fourteen *stories*. In explaining the arrangement of the stories and the so-called interchapters, he not only speaks of "the picture of the whole" but also of an examination of it "in detail."[3]

The dispute over whose story "The Killers" is and, by implication, whether it can be understood independently of the rest of the Nick Adams stories, would seem to be the result of the author's technique, of his decision to relegate Nick to the role of little more than a spectator of the action. In this respect "The Killers" is like several stories of Hemingway's first collection, "Indian Camp," "The Doctor and the Doctor's Wife," and, to some extent, like "The Battler." In "The End of Something," however, Hemingway uses a different technique by making Nick the protagonist. Surely there can be no doubt that it is Nick's story. But this does not at all seem to imply that the story will yield its full meaning when interpreted as an individual work of art. Quite to the contrary, Philip Young asserts that

> the real difficulty in finding the meaning of this story of *In Our Time* is the same difficulty that has been encountered with "Indian Camp": the story is like a chapter of a novel (the book has Roman numeral chapter headings in addition to the usual story titles); it is like a chapter of a novel in that it by no means has all of its meaning when taken in isolation.[4]

Even so, Young explains, people are not justified in complaining that it has no "point." But taking the story in isolation, its point is "subtle and slight": "Things can suddenly go all wrong with the pleasantest of love affairs."[5] The real point of "The End of Something," Young maintains, is provided in "The Three-Day Blow," the next story of *In Our Time*. It is Bill who here interprets Nick's experiences for him and for the reader, and it is only now that the reader learns "why it was that Nick forced that break with Marjorie: she was of the 'wrong' class for a doctor's son." "It is not until this point," Young concludes, "that we can really understand why he was 'out of sorts' in 'The End of Something.' "[6]

I feel that Young's eagerness to prove his overall thesis has led him to misinterpret "The End of Something" and that the general validity of his thesis has apparently precluded an exhaustive evaluation of one of Hemingway's finest stories. The following suggestions for an interpretation aim mainly at establishing its independence as a short story and do not claim to be exhaustive. But it will soon become evident that to attempt to establish its indepen-

3. EH to EW, Paris, October 18, 1924; quoted in Edmund Wilson, *The Shores of Light* (New York, 1952), p. 123.

4. *Ernest Hemingway*, p. 6. I am not sure Young is right in taking the Roman numerals as "chapter headings"; they seem to refer to the interchapters only. Young also does not mention here that not all of the stories of *In Our Time* deal with the experiences of Nick Adams.

5. Ibid.   6. Ibid., p. 7.

dence also involves a reassessment of its place and its function in Hemingway's development of Nick Adams.

Formally, "The End of Something" shows a traditional three-part arrangement. A brief opening describes the history of the lumbering town of Hortons Bay, the setting of the subsequent action. The main scene opens when Nick and Marjorie appear, and it closes when Marjorie leaves after their final break. The conclusion introduces Bill, a new character. Nick's behavior, particularly his brief conversation with the friend, shows the impact of the action on the protagonist. Beginning, middle, and end are clearly marked, and their proportion (20–124–11 when expressed in the number of lines devoted to them) also meets traditional criteria. But formal arrangement alone is no more than a *conditio sine qua non* for an attempt to establish the independence of "The End of Something"; the *conditio per quam*, as Young's criticism would seem to suggest, involves meaning. Form, however, contributes significantly to the emergence of meaning in this story, and the formal arrangement deserves more than passing notice. Since it suggests Aristotle's criteria for the construction of epic poetry, it seems appropriate to ask whether the brief beginning, the extended middle, and the brief end do in fact make a whole. For the purposes of establishing that "The End of Something" is an independent story rather than a chapter in a larger work, the first crucial question we must ask is whether the beginning meets Aristotelian criteria in that it "does not itself come after anything else in a necessary sequence."

The question is an easy one to answer. In the twenty lines of its two paragraphs, the beginning provides more information than seems necessary for a delineation of the setting. Rather than start with the description of its concrete details, Hemingway combines its presentation with information about its history. The reader is taken back to the very beginning of Hortons Bay and follows the brief course of its development. Hortons Bay originated as a lumbering town. When "one year there were no more logs to make lumber," the two saws and other equipment were taken out of the mill and hoisted on board a schooner. It then "moved out of the bay toward the open lake, carrying with it everything that had made the mill a mill and Hortons Bay a town."[7] All that remained were empty buildings and "acres of sawdust." Hemingway gives a description of the present condition of Hortons Bay, the actual setting of the story, only in the first sentence of the third paragraph: "Ten years later there was nothing of the mill left except in broken white limestone of its foundations showing through the swampy second growth as Nick and Marjorie rowed along the shore." While by definition

---

7. These and the following quotations from "The End of Something" and "The Three-Day Blow" are taken from *The Short Stories of Ernest Hemingway* (New York, 1955). Page references have not been included since the stories are short and quotations can easily be located. Italics that occur in the passages quoted from these two stories are mine.

the opening is a real beginning in that it presupposes nothing, it seems
doubtful, however, that it is the beginning of Nick's story. The transitional
sentence clearly raises the question of natural sequence. Nick's story, it appears, is deliberately cut off from the history of Hortons Bay. It begins ten
years after the flush times of the town, and those flush times are not part of
Nick's experience.[8] But some tenuous connection exists even in the transitional sentence: the limestone foundations of the mill are still there, and
they have a very tangible function in the story. They serve as the first object
to present the contrasting sentiments of Nick and Marjorie. Mention of the
second-growth timber both in the transitional sentence and again twice
afterwards in the story also serves as a link between the opening paragraphs
and the main story. Its presence presupposes the history of Hortons Bay. A
third connecting link points to a far more important function of the opening.
When Marjorie asks, "Can you remember when it was a mill?" Nick answers,
"I can just remember." Indirect as it is, this statement of Nick's age is essential to an understanding of the story. The point needs to be made that contrary to Philip Young's assertion that Nick's age is never mentioned in the
stories devoted to him,[9] "The End of Something" comes close to giving a
precise statement: Nick is shown to be between sixteen and eighteen years
of age. The point also needs to be made that the reader need not turn to the
next story, "The Three-Day Blow," to find that Nick is old enough to have
thought about getting married.

While the indirect statement of Nick's age will be shown to be the most
important of these three functions of the introductory paragraphs, none of
them justifies the extent of the vignette of the history of Hortons Bay. Significant details in the sketch are not related to the subsequent story. Quite
to the contrary, Hemingway gives the real beginning of the story of Nick
and Marjorie, the exposition proper, analytically in the course of the story
itself. Marjorie's reference to the dilapidated mill as "our old ruin" indicates
that there indeed was a time when the plural of the possessive pronoun was
justified. The assumption that Nick has been going with Marjorie for some

8. I disagree with Austin McGiffert Wright, who, apparently also faced with the
problem of unity, assumes that "the old mill and the old days [of Hortons Bay] are
clearly on Nick's mind as he rows, although it is Marjorie who makes the connection
explicit: 'There's our old ruin, Nick,' " (*The American Short Story in the Twenties*
[Chicago, 1961], p. 318). The fact that Nick can only "just remember" the mill seems to
preclude the possibility that Nick is thinking about the old days of the town. Marjorie's
reference to "our old ruin" most likely evokes no associations other than those of the
far more recent "love among the ruins" episode of their common history. Another
critic, George Hemphill, has similarly been worried by the question of unity. He finds
that the story "fails because no necessary connection (other than biographical, perhaps)
between the end of the boy-and-girl affair between Nick and Marjorie and the end of
the old lumbering days in Michigan is suggested." ("Hemingway and James," *Ernest
Hemingway: The Man and His Work*, John K. M. McCaffery, ed. [Cleveland and New
York, 1950], p. 333.)

9. *Ernest Hemingway*, p. 2.

time is corroborated in other ways; there is the statement that "she loved to fish with Nick," and at the climax of the story Nick says, "I've taught you everything. . . . What don't you know, anyway?" The final piece of expository information comes almost at the very end of the story; Bill's first question reveals that the break had been planned beforehand for that particular night. The presence of a distributed exposition leaves us to conclude that what formally poses as the beginning of the story is a beginning in a very limited sense only. Since its importance for the plot is but slight, though not altogether negligible, we must seek, and shall easily find, elsewhere its functional relation to the rest of the story.

The above synopsis of the opening paragraphs, inadequate as it must needs be for conveying all of the meaning of Hemingway's text, clearly indicates the author's attempt to present the history of Hortons Bay as having described a cyclical movement. One cannot fail to perceive that its cycle is meant to be an analogue for the subsequent plot, which also deals with the completion of a cycle, that of Nick's love for Marjorie. The introduction thus prefigures the story. It also elucidates and interprets the story, a necessary function, as the story itself does not detail the whole course of Nick's love affair. Rather than present its whole history in chronological order, Hemingway starts close to the climax and, by means of implication and revelation, eventually evokes the totality of the cycle while at the same time presenting its conclusion. The analogy provided in the introduction can be and must be carried beyond the mere exteriors of a cyclical movement. In that it is taken from nature it implies that the course which Nick's love for Marjorie has taken is a natural one and as relentless as it is inevitable. The introduction, in fact, elucidates the lesson that the story has for the protagonist: all things run their natural course, and submission and acceptance are the only sensible responses.

An apparent inconsistency between introduction and main story, however, appears to be incompatible with the thesis that both are analogous. One can easily argue that while the cyclical course of the history of Hortons Bay is conditioned by natural events, the cyclical conclusion of the story of Nick and Marjorie is solely the result of Nick's decision to force a break and that it thus lacks the inevitability which characterized the rise and fall of the town. But to distinguish between exterior motivation of the introduction and interior motivation of Nick's story is to miss the essential point of the story. Hemingway demonstrates that the distinction is futile. When the supply of logs at Hortons Bay is exhausted, the mill workers accept the situation *and* they know how to cope with it; the machinery is taken out of the mill and hoisted on board the schooner "*by the men who had worked in the mill.*" Nature thus conditions man's decisions. Nick's case precisely parallels this. His decision to force a break with Marjorie is not at all momentary, and it is clearly not the result of an accidental quarrel. The concluding conversation with Bill reveals it to have been of some standing, and Hemingway's further use of analogues—as remains to be shown—reveals that it also proceeds from what must be called natural causes. It is this insight into the inevitability of the course of nature and its influence on the destinies of man that provides the real lesson of the story. It is the realization that a break should become necessary, rather than the fact that he has actually broken with Marjorie, that leaves Nick a wounded man at the end of the story. If the analogy between introduction and main story is at all inconsistent, then it is inconsistent only in so far as the mill workers unflinchingly accept the course of nature while Nick is still learning to do so. The workers provide the moral norm of the story from which the protagonist (as yet) deviates.

The conclusion demonstrates that the lesson is clearly a new one for Nick: it hits him with considerable impact. It is clear that the wound will be permanent, but it is also clear that he will survive it: he asks Bill to go away, then adds, "Go away *for a while*." This reading is supported by many details in the introductory analogue. The spoliated landscape of Hortons Bay also has begun to recover. Nature has reclaimed the scene, covering swamp and sawdust with second-growth timber. A more significant prefiguration of Nick's eventual response to the lesson occurs in an image with Freudian overtones. While "the sails of the schooner filled and it moved out into the open lake," it contained the odds and ends "that had made the mill a mill and Hortons Bay a town." The open hold where these things are stored is *"covered with canvas and lashed tight."* This image, while it symbolizes Nick's future attitude, does not at all rely on subsequent stories to reveal its meaning, though one need not argue that the symbolic meaning may be extended to encompass his responses to the incidents described in later works, his experiences and his responses there being different in kind, not in character.

Obviously the analogy may be pursued still further. If the schooner symbolizes Nick, then the spoliated landscape and the deserted buildings stand for Marjorie. She, too, has learned a lesson. The focus of the story, however, is not on her responses. But in desisting from all argument, she seems to demonstrate passive acceptance and thus functions, as she does throughout the story, as a foil to Nick. Applying the analogy in this manner, the second growth is primarily a symbol of Marjorie's future. Such a reading would leave the machinery in the schooner's hold, the tools of destruction, a symbol for Nick's disruptive influence rather than for experiences repressed in his personality to the level of the unconscious. Different interpretations of the introduction are obviously possible; but far from confusing the meaning of the story, they give to the introductory analogue the complexity of a true symbol. Its meaning and its function, however, are somewhat narrowed by another kind of analogy which operates in the story itself. Though working on a different and totally unrelated level, it further elucidates the meaning of the action and similarly establishes the independence of the story.

Philip Young has summarized the action of "The End of Something" as follows: "[Nick] takes the girl trolling for trout, demonstrates some knowledge of fish and fishing, and finally gets the girl to leave, perhaps for good."[10] Inadequate as any summary must be in view of Hemingway's careful handling of materials, this statement of the contents of the story does not even attempt to find any significance below its perfectly credible, realistic surface. To accept the summary as rendering the action of the story is to accept the possibility of an absolute break between style and technique of the beginning and those of the middle. Such a possibility cannot be rejected altogether. The beginning, as has been shown, is not the actual beginning of Nick's story; and it is quite conceivable that in its function as an analogue it can be trusted to provide the terms in which we are to take the subsequent story and to point to a significance that the story itself is unable to convey.

But even if we are to ignore Hemingway's avowed principles of composition, this interpretation is hard to accept, since the introduction does not outspokenly proclaim its interpretative function: it is a part of the whole also in that it contributes necessary details to the surface reality of the story. To take this surface reality—the detailed account of trolling for trout and planting handlines, the abortive picnic, and mainly its conversation—as the end of Hemingway's description is either to approach the story very naïvely, or to approach it from its sequel, "The Three-Day Blow," where the surface, indeed the "skillful representation of the conversation of adolescent boys" that Young calls it,[11] does seem to be more of an end in itself.

Apart from the nature analogue of the opening scene, the first and most important key to an understanding of what really happens to Nick is provided in the oblique statement of his age. While it is not very precise, it is still precise enough to indicate that Nick is at the verge of maturity and that his affair with Marjorie is not "a puppylove affair with a 'nice' girl," as one critic asserts.[12] While the nature analogue of the opening scene merely suggests that Nick's love affair involves sexual relations, this implication is elaborated when Nick, having told Marjorie once that "It isn't fun any more," repeats the same words and then adds, "*Not any of it.*" Immediately before, another phrase that occurs in Nick's talk is repeated and amplified in a similar manner. Apparently trying to pick a quarrel, he tells Marjorie, "You know everything," then continues, "You do. You know everything. That's the trouble. You know you do." When Marjorie does not answer, Nick resumes once more, "I've taught you everything. You know you do. What don't you know, anyway?" The immediate cause of this outburst seems negligible (When Nick observes, "There's going to be a moon tonight," Marjorie answers happily, "I know it."), and quite obviously Marjorie's knowledge in this particular case merely triggers Nick's reproaches.

10. *Ernest Hemingway*, p. 5.   11. Ibid., p. 7.
12. Earl Rovit, *Ernest Hemingway* (New York, 1963), p. 57.

As his wording indicates, his concern is far more general. Marjorie knows too much of a number of things because he, Nick, has taught her too much. This may be construed to mean that Nick is dissatisfied with the state of things because his love for Marjorie has been, first and foremost, a mere satisfaction of his tutorial instinct.[13] What few indications the story contains of the nature of their relationship seem to support this. Nick instructs Marjorie in the proper preparation of bait, and Marjorie quite naturally assumes the role of pupil. Her obvious usefulness in fishing and the care which she takes in doing things in the right, that is in Nick's, manner indicate that the teacher-pupil relationship has existed for some time, probably for as long as both have been going with each other. What is thus demonstrated with regard to fishing and boating, both in the action of the story and in its dialogue, has led Austin McGiffert Wright to conclude that "Nick has tired of [Marjorie] because she has learned too well the boyish things he has taught her; she has become too much of a 'pal,' thus losing her romantic appeal."[14] Wright apparently failed to note that the same facts also demonstrate that Marjorie's insecurity is as yet quite pronounced, that she does need instruction and that she will continue to need it. It is quite clear that the progress she has made in learning the "boyish things" her tutor has taught her and its demonstration in action and dialogue, if taken as mere fact, must fail to yield a plausible motive for Nick's eventual outburst and his break with Marjorie.

To find the true reason for Nick's break it is necessary and, in fact, inevitable to take both action and dialogue as another explicative analogue, and it is also inevitable to observe the sexual implications of this commentary on the meaning of the story. Again the analogue functions as a portent. Rowing away from the old mill (to Marjorie "our old ruin" and "more like a castle," references to which Nick does not respond in kind), Marjorie "was intent on the rod all the time they trolled, even when she talked," and she "did not reel in until the boat touched the shore." She remarks that the fish are feeding and obviously expects that they will strike, but Nick emphatically asserts that they "aren't striking" and that they "won't strike."

Although the analogue is incomplete, there is a correspondence between this scene and the subsequent picnic in Nick's eating from Marjorie's basket of supper, but refusing to "strike" and instead breaking away from her "hook" for good. If it is not possible to establish an absolute analogy between conversation and actions in the boat and those on the shore, this does not mean that the analogue as such is not intended. It merely confirms that here, as elsewhere, Hemingway did not "violate realism for the sake of his metaphor."[15] Recurrence and accumulation, furthermore, sufficiently counter-

13. Cf. Alice Parker, "Hemingway's 'The End of Something,'" *The Explicator*, X (1951/52), Item 36.
14. *The American Short Story in the Twenties*, p. 94.
15. E. M. Halliday, "Hemingway's Ambiguity: Symbolism and Irony," *American Literature*, XXVIII (March 1956), 14.

balance the absence of allegorical equations. So far, however, the function of the analogue has been shown to be merely that of portent rather than explication. It foreshadows what will happen and in doing so it also elucidates the significance of the following events/It has failed, however, to provide a motivation for such events, unless the opening analogue and its affirmation of the operation of natural cycles be deemed sufficient as a motivation/for Nick's break with Marjorie.

But man is not conscious of being a victim and a tool. Subject as he is to the laws of nature, he normally acts without insight into these laws. Rather than recognize the law and then act accordingly, Nick first responds accordingly and only afterwards is led to a recognition of the law he has followed in doing so. The plot of the story, therefore, must provide a specific cause for his break with Marjorie, a cause that leads to action and then to insight, which insight constitutes the lesson proper of the story. "The End of Something" provides the specific cause in an oblique statement made by Nick concerning the preparation of bait: " 'You don't want to take the ventral fin out,' he said. 'It'll be all right for bait but it's better with the ventral fin in.' " When read as an analogue and interpreted as having physiological implications, the statement contains a perfectly satisfactory and plausible motivation for Nick's behavior. It exemplifies at the same time that it demands that the love affair between Nick and Marjorie has involved sexual relations and that Nick's teaching extended to initiating Marjorie into sex. Reproaching her for knowing too much implies that Nick reproaches her for having lost her virginity. Thus, the analogy implies, she has lost her attraction for her lover, and therefore Nick concludes, "It isn't fun any more. Not any of it." Having found the action and the dialogue to function as explicatory analogues of the sexual implications of Nick's and Marjorie's love, one can easily find supporting evidence within the story that suggests these implications even on the very surface of plot and dialogue. After all, Nick and Marjorie are out at nightfall and prepared to stay out well into the night, neither apparently having stolen away from home.

To pursue the problem of the unity and the independence of "The End of Something" in terms of Aristotle's definition of a whole in epic poetry, we still must find whether the end naturally proceeds from the events described in the middle and, more importantly, whether it has nothing else following it. Both questions seem easy to answer as long as the attention remains focused on the individual story. The end describes Nick's response to the break with Marjorie; it shows the impact of the action on the protagonist. But it also contains an important revelatory detail in a very subtle punch line assigned to Bill. His question "Did she go all right?" suddenly illuminates the preceding events in that it reveals Nick to have planned the break beforehand. This explains why Nick's reason for terminating the love affair, while truthfully stated in Marjorie's knowing too much, nevertheless proceeds somewhat indirectly from the dialogue. His first "You know everything" implies irony and even sarcasm, but gradually his remarks reach the level of subjective truth. But Bill's revelatory question poses still another problem. Since Nick's plan to force a break precedes the events as narrated in the story, are those portentous analogues as are provided in his statements, specifically his remarks that the fish "won't strike" and that perch is better bait "with the ventral fin in," to be taken as consciously ambiguous on the speaker's part? Despite Nick's youth, we canot wholly exclude the possibility as long as we see the story only in its surface action. The ending, however, demonstrates that Nick himself has as yet but imperfectly understood the true nature and the importance of the lesson that this experience provides for him. His own fumbling attempt to explain to Marjorie the reasons for his break forms the beginning of such realization: "I feel as though everything was gone to hell inside of me. I don't know, Marge. I don't know what to say." It is here, when he first addresses Marjorie by name, that he actually exempts her from blame and also perceives himself to be subject to forces outside his own control. What these forces are, however, remains rather dimly recognized for Nick. For Hemingway it is sufficient to have shown Nick's progress toward such an understanding. What it will be is perfectly clear for the reader since the author has utilized both the nature analogue and Nick's own words to communicate the reason for the break as well as the nature and the meaning of the lesson. The end of the story thus is suggestive of future comprehension of the lesson by the protagonist; for the reader, however, it is a real end in so far as it "has nothing else following it" and leaves no questions unanswered.

To some readers the introduction of Bill in the concluding scene of the story has suggested that Nick is, at least latently, a homosexual.[16] The above interpretation, however, does not permit such a reading. Even to imply that Nick prefers male company to female does not coincide with the meaning of the main scene. Despite Hemingway's technique of implication and the density of symbolism and metaphor in this story, one feels no compulsion to postulate that Bill should have any function beyond that of providing another foil for Nick. Although the friends have discussed the possibility of Nick's break with Marjorie and although Bill attempts to show his sympathy, his main interest is to find out whether there was a scene. He selects a sandwich from the supper basket and goes to have a look at the fishing rods and in doing so clearly demonstrates that he fails to grasp what has actually happened to Nick.

A final test for both our interpretation and our thesis that "The End of Something" will indeed yield its full meaning when taken in isolation is to relate it to the other Nick Adams stories, particularly to "The Three-Day Blow." Not only must we find that the other stories do not contradict the de-

16. See Joseph Whitt, "Hemingway's 'The End of Something,' " *The Explicator*, IX (1950/51), Item 58.

tails of our interpretation, but it is also important that they should not uncover additional levels of meaning. The sexual implications of "The End of
Something" are not at all called in question by the following stories. "The
Three-Day Blow" shows Nick to be indeed old enough seriously to have
thought about marrying Marjorie; "Fathers and Sons," moreover, reveals
him to have received his initiation into sex at a much earlier age by an Ojib-
way Indian girl named Trudy who "did first what no one has ever done
better." [17] "The Three-Day Blow" also plainly excludes the possibility of
homosexual relations between Nick and Bill. Homosexuals are first observed
by Nick at a later time in "The Battler"; and homosexuality, as Philip Young
asserts on the basis of the evidence of further stories, normally functions as
"a kind of ultimate evil." [18] Finally, "The Three-Day Blow" shows that Nick
has not yet fully accepted the lesson contained in the earlier story. Again,
this does not contradict our interpretation of "The End of Something," since
what Hemingway communicates to the reader concerning the true nature of
the lesson is clearly shown to be but imperfectly perceived by Nick. To stress
the significance for him of the lesson described in the earlier story, realism
furthermore demands that in view of the short span of time that intervenes
between the events described in the two stories (shorter than that between
any other two Nick Adam stories) the break with Marjorie should occupy
him on what probably is the very next day.

Corroboration of our interpretation by means of further details in "The
Three-Day Blow" clearly runs counter to Philip Young's reading of the
story. If the thesis that "The End of Something" reveals its full meaning
when interpreted independently of the other Nick Adams stories is right, then
Young's thesis that "['The Three-Day Blow'] reveals the lesson Nick learned
from the preceding episode," [19] must be wrong. Once we no longer see "The
End of Something" and "The Three-Day Blow" as closely interrelated chapters, and once we interpret these two stories either as individual stories or
in the order in which they are presented in *In Our Time*, we shall perceive
that the supposed points of the second story have different meanings from
those given by Young. Bill's suggestion that Nick has broken with Marjorie
because "she was of the 'wrong' class for a doctor's son" [20] meets with no
response on the part of his listener: "Nick said nothing." This is repeated
several times in the course of Bill's discussion of his friend's love affair and
occasionally varied with rather monosyllabic assent, clearly noncommittal.
It seems highly improbable, therefore, that Bill's interpretation furnishes the
true motive for Nick's behavior in "The End of Something." It is more likely
that Hemingway is exploiting a favorite theme of his, that of failure of communication. The divergence between the views of the friends soon becomes

17. *The Short Stories of Ernest Hemingway*, p. 497.
18. *Ernest Hemingway*, p. 11.
19. Ibid., p. 7.   20. Ibid.

overt when Nick falls to thinking: "Bill wasn't there. He wasn't sitting in front of the fire or going fishing tomorrow with Bill and his dad or anything. He wasn't drunk. It was all gone. All he knew was that he had once had Marjorie and that he had lost her. . . ." Thematic exploitation of the contrast becomes still more obvious when Nick's imagination desperately clutches at Bill's advice—"You don't want to think about it. You might get back into it again."—and inadvertently reverses its intent:

> Nick hadn't thought about that. It had seemed so absolute. That was a thought. That made him feel better.—"Sure," he said. "There's always that danger."—He felt happy now. There was not anything that was irrevocable. He might go into town Saturday night. Today was Thursday.—"There's always a chance," he said—"You'll have to watch yourself," Bill said.—"I'll watch myself," he said.—He felt happy. Nothing was finished. Nothing was ever lost. He would go into town on Saturday. He felt lighter, as he had felt before Bill started to talk about it. There was always a way out.

The divergence between his thoughts and his words establishes more than an amusing irony; it exemplifies the essential contrast between the friends and thus corroborates our interpretation of the role of Bill in the final scene of "The End of Something."

The second point of the story, according to Young, lies in Nick's coming to see that "there was not anything that was irrevocable." This interpretation fails to show that the story, though indeed as many-sided as Young finds it to be, still primarily deals with Nick's introduction to alcohol. Before Bill takes up the subject of Nick's break with Marjorie, the story meticulously records the quantity of whisky consumed and the responses it produces in Nick. Beyond all doubt, and notwithstanding the subjective statements that "He wasn't drunk" and that "He was still quite drunk but his head was clear," Hemingway establishes—again by means of direct communication with the reader through realistic detail in the story—that Nick is indeed quite drunk when he reaches the understanding that "there was always a way out." The author thus demonstrates the function of the "giant killer" on the physical as well as on the psychic level, but it is from the latter that the true lesson that the episode has for Nick actually proceeds: the "giant killer" produces illusions and renders the lessons of life more acceptable. Again, as in the preceding story, Hemingway only implies the impact of the lesson on the protagonist. Again, as in the preceding story, the author enters into direct communication with the reader and reveals to him the nature of the lesson as yet unperceived by the protagonist. The resulting dramatic irony is an important part of Hemingway's technique of implication; it obviates another story, one devoted to the dissolution of the illusion and a detailed explication of the lesson of "The Three-Day Blow."

When interpreted in this sense, "The Three-Day Blow" does not contradict our reading of "The End of Something." It is important to add, however, that this interpretation of the second story does not proceed from, nor depend on, our interpretation of the first story. The later story, too, will yield its full meaning when read in isolation. But while the two stories are not interrelated, the interpretation of each can still be used to control that of the other; and details in each, though not essential to an understanding of the meaning of the other, still tend to emphasize certain of its points. Hemingway obviously devoted as much care to establishing the independence of the individual story as he did to relating it to the larger context of the education of Nick Adams. It is not necessary, therefore, to approach "The End of Something" from its supposed "points" in the subsequent story. To do so, in fact, not only robs the earlier, but also the later, story of what we find to be their independently developed and independently stated "true points."

In attempting to establish the independence of "The End of Something," we have discovered what we find to be its true point and its true lesson, and we have thus indicated a necessary reassessment of the function of the story in the biography of Nick Adams. But we have also shown the story to possess a far greater complexity and power than it has previously been credited with. Even if considered alongside those of the Nick Adams stories whose frequent presence in anthologies proclaims their independence as short stories, "The End of Something" would occupy a prominent place, for to isolate it does not require us to postulate the existence of two unrelated levels; the very point which makes it an independent story also relates it meaningfully and significantly to the education of Nick Adams.

Hemingway and the Fisher King ("God Rest You Merry, Gentlemen") / *Peter L. Hays*

Malcolm Cowley and Carlos Baker are among those critics who have remarked about the similarities between the Fisher King and Jake Barnes, wounded in the genitals and residing in sterile post-World War I Paris.[1] Yet no one, to my knowledge, has noticed the presence of a pair of characters re-

Peter L. Hays, "Hemingway and the Fisher King," *The University Review*, XXXII (1965–66), 225–28. Reprinted by permission of *New Letters*. Reprinted in Peter L. Hays, *The Limping Hero: Grotesques in Literature* (New York University Press, 1971).

1. Malcolm Cowley, ed., *Hemingway* (New York, 1944), p. xxi. Carlos Baker, *Hemingway: The Writer as Artist* (Princeton, 1952), p. 90.

lated to the Fisher King legend in one of Hemingway's stories most neglected by critics, "God Rest You Merry, Gentlemen."[2]

This morbid tale takes place in Kansas City on Christmas Day and is probably based on an incident Hemingway learned of while covering Kansas City General Hospital for *The Kansas City Star*.[3] It is narrated by a character called Horace, a newspaper reporter, and it concerns a boy of about sixteen who considers his erections sins against purity. The boy pleads with two doctors, Fischer and Wilcox, asking that they castrate him. They refuse, and the boy, not actually knowing what castration is, amputates his penis with a razor. He is brought to the hospital, but bungling Dr. Wilcox cannot stanch his loss of blood, and so the boy bleeds to death on Christmas Day.

Several points, especially a full comprehension of the nature of each character, are essential to an understanding of the story's meaning. Wilcox insists on his full title (possibly reflecting his lack of confidence in his own ability): Horace never refers to him except as Doctor Wilcox, whereas Fischer is always the more familiar "Doc." Not only is Wilcox incompetent, he is also harsh and insensitive to others. When the boy makes his request, Wilcox replies crudely:

"You're just a goddamned fool. . . . Oh, go and ———— [sic]."
"When you talk like that I don't hear you," the boy said with dignity to Doctor Wilcox . . .
"Get him out of here," Doctor Wilcox said. (pp. 47–48)

When Fisher mentions that it is "the day, the very anniversary, of our Saviour's birth," Wilcox's prejudiced reply is *"Our* Saviour? Ain't you a Jew?"* (p. 49). And, besides his inability to save the boy's life, Wilcox drinks on duty (p. 45) and relies entirely on *The Young Doctor's Friend and Guide*. As Horace says, "Doctor Wilcox was sensitive about this book but could not get along without it. . . . He had bought it at the advice of one of his professors who had said, 'Wilcox, you have no business being a physician and I have done everything in my power to prevent you from being certified as one. Since you are now a member of this learned profession I advise you, in the name of humanity, to obtain a copy of *The Young Doctor's Friend and Guide* and use it, Doctor Wilcox. Learn to use it' " (p. 44).

Horace[4] is a perfect Hemingway persona, an accurate but impartial ob-

2. Ernest Hemingway, *Winner Take Nothing* (New York, 1933) pp. 43–50. All subsequent references to GRYMG will be to this edition and will be paginated in my text.
3. Charles A. Fenton, *The Apprenticeship of Ernest Hemingway* (New York, 1954), p. 49. Baker, p. 303.
4. Only Doc Fischer addresses the reporter by name; he once says, "You don't mind my calling you Horace, do you?" (p. 45). He might be asking for permission to use the reporter's first name, or, in his sensitive way, asking if the nickname he has applied to the reporter is offensive. And if "Horace" is a nickname, did Fischer take it from Horace Greeley, Horatius Flaccus, or some comic, horse-faced character?

server, although none too intelligent. He believes that *Dans Argent* means silver dance or silver dancer and is pleased with his linguistic ability (p. 43). Fischer cautions him against too much intelligence: "Avoid it, Horace. You haven't much tendency but sometimes I see a gleam" (pp. 49–50).

Fischer is a Christ figure. He is a slim, blond Jew, he is a "fisher of men," he heals men with his hands and has suffered for it (p. 49), and he has ridden an ass:

> "It was an amputation the young man performed, Horace."
> "Well, I wish you wouldn't ride me about it," Doctor Wilcox said. "There isn't any need to ride me."
> "Ride you, Doctor, on the day, the very anniversary, of our Saviour's birth?"
> "*Our* Saviour? Ain't you a Jew?" Doctor Wilcox said.
> "So I am. So I am. It always is slipping my mind. I've never given it its proper importance. So good of you to remind me. *Your* Saviour. That's right. *Your* Saviour, undoubtedly *your* Saviour—and the ride for Palm Sunday." (p. 49)

He suffers, not only from Wilcox's prejudice, but also because of his own compassion. A "willingness to oblige" and a "lack of respect for Federal statutes" (p. 49), perhaps those which forbid doctors to aid fugitive criminals without reporting that aid, had caused him great trouble earlier, "on the coast." His compassion is obvious from his tender and sympathetic treatment of the boy, who responds by begging Fischer in particular to help him.

Fischer's education is also obvious. Besides the "certain extravagance of [his] speech which seemed to . . . [Horace] to be of the utmost elegance" (p. 45), there are his attempt to speak to the boy in the latter's own religious vernacular and the quality of his irony, his puns based on Biblical and medical metaphors. I have quoted the Wilcox-as-ass passage above; in another instance, Fischer satirically alludes to St. Luke by referring to Wilcox as "the good physician" (p. 48), and, when Wilcox continues to stress Fischer's separateness from the rest of humanity because of his religion, Fischer replies, "You hear him? Having discovered my vulnerable point, my achilles tendon so to speak, the doctor pursues his advantage" (p. 50).[5]

However, Fischer's "education" does not of itself fully describe him or adequately indicate his likeness to Christ. Fischer's superiority in ability, intelligence, self-confidence, and compassion irritates Wilcox and provokes

5. From the standpoint of myth criticism, let me suggest that Achilles, Christ, and Anfortas are all sacred kings, fertility figures sacrificed at full virility. The boy's self-mutilation at the winter solstice corresponds with that of Attis and Adonis (Lord), and if Robert Graves is correct in identifying mistletoe with Uranus' severed testicles (*The Greek Myths* [Baltimore, 1955], I, 37–38, 41), then the day of the boy's death gains additional significance.

him to a sarcastic comment—"You're too damned smart" (p. 50)—that both reflects Wilcox's own inadequacies and, ironically, defines Fischer's distinctions. And the same epithet could well have been hurled at Christ by his scorning contemporaries. Finally, both Christ and Fischer have visited hell—one to harrow, one to be harrowed:

> "The hell with you," Doctor Wilcox said.
> "All in good time, Doctor," Doc Fischer said. "All in good time. If there is such a place I shall certainly visit it. I have even had a very small look into it. No more than a peek, really. I looked away almost at once." (p. 50)

The ironic tone of the entire story, in fact, is established at the outset by the title, "God Rest You Merry, Gentlemen," especially we recall the full context of that line:

> . . . Let nothing you dismay,
> Remember Christ our Saviour was born on Christmas Day,
> To save us all from Satan's power when we were gone astray,
> O tidings of comfort and joy . . .

As Harry Levin has remarked, "The ironic contrast—romantic preconception exploded by contact with harsh reality—is basic with Hemingway. . . .[6]" And instead of the pleasant home scene such a carol might suggest, where men might indeed rest themselves merry, we have the harsh carbolic-tainted atmosphere of a hospital where there is much to cause dismay, where Satan's power (here ignorance of bodily functions and a too-strict religious fundamentalism) has caused a boy's death, and where tidings are far from comfortable and joyous.

Perhaps this perversion of the spirit of Christmas owes something to more ancient rituals. As Malcolm Cowley has said, "Hemingway . . . seems to have a feeling for half-forgotten sacraments; his cast of mind is pre-Christian and pre-logical. Sometimes his stories come close to being adaptations of ancient myths."[7] I think this is the case in "God Rest You Merry, Gentlemen." Cowley also believes that Hemingway did not read Jessie Weston's *From Ritual to Romance*, but I think it likely that he did, for the following reasons. If he had not, his choice of Fischer as a name is highly coincidental, for if he chose it for no other reason than to indicate the doctor's religion, he could easily have chosen a more distinctly "Jewish" one.

In Miss Weston's book, he would have learned the story of the Fisher King (Anfortas, in some versions), and he would have learned its ritual significance. He would also have read about the literary device of doubling, of dividing the ritual tasks of a hero between two characters who are usu-

6. Harry Levin, *Contexts of Criticism.*   7. Cowley, p. xxi.

ally related. Thus in "God Rest You Merry, Gentlemen," the roles in the tale of a fisher king wounded in the genitals, and healed by a young, pure knight, have been divided and reassigned: it is the young innocent who is wounded, and it is the fis(c)her who is the healer. But the age of romance is over, and miraculous cures are no longer effected, especially when helpful dwarfs and kindly uncles become, instead, bungling doctors. In *From Ritual to Romance*, Hemingway would have read about the vital and honored role of the healer, the medicine man, in the fertility cycle of life, death, and rebirth—and Miss Weston's statements might well have impressed a young doctor's son who had himself been brought back from near death by medical skill. Finally, he would have learned about the key role of fish in ritual and in religious symbolism—fish as symbols of divine life, of fertility, of wisdom. And, of course, fishing has meant many things in Hemingway's stories, from peace and renewal of vitality for Nick Adams to an affirmation of his selfhood and skill for Santiago.

Cowley and Baker both disclaim any direct dependence on Hemingway's part upon modern incarnations of ancient myth:

> I don't mean to imply that Hemingway owes a debt to *The Waste Land*. And yet when he wrote his first novel he dealt with the same legend Eliot had discovered by scholarship; recovering it himself, I think, by a sort of instinct for legendary situations.[8]

> [Hemingway employs] not so much literary myth-adaptation as psychological symbol-building.[9]

I certainly do not want to say that Hemingway had no such instinct or psychological sensitivity; to the contrary. But as each of the critics above has seen fit to defend Hemingway's careful, conscious craftsmanship against charges of primitivism, so I think we might also consider that he may have read more than he is usually credited with. Admittedly, the evidence which I cite for his having read Miss Weston's book is all circumstantial, but it is an unusually long string of coincidences. If he did not read *From Ritual to Romance* and if no friend like Ezra Pound communicated to Hemingway much of the information that appeared in Miss Weston's study, then Hemingway's sensitivity is very sharp indeed, and we must consider giving more credence than is fashionable in scholarly circles at present to the spontaneous appearance of Jungian archetypes.

If the story is not based on archetypes, it is at least based on universals. As Hemingway said in its first paragraph, Kansas City is much like Constantinople: the story need not have been located in Missouri. The setting is not important; the human relations are. The health of a land is related to the health of its king—materially to Anfortas, spiritually to Christ, symbol-

8. Cowley, pp. xxi–xxii.   9. Baker, p. 88.

ically to the boy and Fischer. The isolation that the vocation of the Grail imposed on its keepers has been transposed. In the story, the boy is set apart from a normal life by abnormal sensitivity and religiosity; Fischer is set apart by his compassion and his religion. Both feel too much and recognize the sensitivity of the other—their spiritual kinship—and both are separate from cruel Wilcox and impassive Horace. The harsh treatment they receive from the Horaces, and especially the Wilcoxes, of the spiritually sterile land they inhabit emphasizes the isolation of the sensitive, of those who feel too much. It emphasizes their separateness and their persecution by the unfeeling.

Ironic Action in "After the Storm" / *Anselm Atkins*

Hemingway's "After the Storm" has received little attention, although it not only is a highly successful example of his technique of understatement, but also exhibits another very effective ironic device: irony of action. In this brief story the main action stands in sharp contrast to a secondary action in the background. On the stylistic level, the flat, feelingless narration is ironic with respect to the emotion which the story generates. On the structural level, the main action is ironic with respect to the secondary action. These two sources of irony reinforce each other since they are brought together and focused by one person, the narrator-hero.

In the aftermath of a hurricane, an unnamed sponge fisherman—a "sponger" in a double sense—scavenges the Florida keys for flotsam. He tries to break into a sunken liner, but fails when the ship's nearest porthole, twelve feet deep, resists the blows of his wrench grapple. A fresh wind forces him to retire, leaving his trophy to a later, more successful band of "Greeks" (p. 376).[1] This action is typical of Hemingway's stories: the hero pits himself against an obstacle, but, handicapped by the loss of tools (weapons), misses victory by a pitifully narrow margin. In this story there are two actions of this kind; for the liner, forced by circumstance to put to sea in a hurricane,

Anselm Atkins, "Ironic Action in 'After the Storm,' " *Studies in Short Fiction*, V (1967–68), 189–92. Copyright, 1967, Newberry College, Newberry, S. C.; reprinted by permission of *Studies in Short Fiction*.

1. Ernest Hemingway, "After the Storm," in *The Short Stories of Ernest Hemingway* (New York, 1953), pp. 372–378. Edmund Wilson calls it one of his "finest," but sees nothing more in it than the usual hero's "keeping up a code or decency": *The Wound and the Bow* (Boston, 1941), pp. 224–225. See also Joseph DeFalco, *The Hero in Hemingway's Short Stories* (Pittsburgh, 1963), pp. 212–214; John Gardner and Lennis Dunlap, eds., *The Forms of Fiction* (New York, 1962), pp. 48–50.

drives blindly before the storm, strikes a sand bar at the very edge of open water, and thus misses its own goal by a scant "hundred yards" (p. 377). The ship's captain, like the sponger, is a loser. However, the loss of a ship, together with four hundred and fifty passengers, crew, and perhaps five million dollars' worth of goods (pp. 374, 377), far outweighs the paltry frustration of the sponger. The secondary action of the ship's misfortune contrasts dramatically with the main action. The story derives its force from Hemingway's careful handling of this contrast.

The massive suppression of the emotional significance implicit in the secondary action results in supreme irony. The reader sees the wrecked ship through the eyes of the sponger, for whom that underwater graveyard is nothing but a fortuitous jackpot. The sponger's first impression when he takes in the situation is simply the size of the ship—"the biggest boat I ever saw in my life" (p. 373). "It made me shaky to think how much she must have in her" (p. 374). What, for him, *was* in her? Not bodies, but treasure: "five million dollars worth" (p. 374). In the next two paragraphs Hemingway runs together a description of his diving and hammering on the porthole with the image of a floating woman's body visible through the glass. The sponger's matter-of-factness eliminates—or rather suppresses—the horror of the scene: "I could hold on for a second to the edge of the port hole and I could see in and there was a woman inside with her hair floating all out. I could see her floating plain and I hit the glass twice with the wrench . . ." (p. 374). Scavenger birds, which swarm above the wreck, dive for "pieces of things" (p. 374) that float to the surface from a rupture in the hull. The sponger-scavenger never tells what the pieces were, but the reader knows. The sponger's "you couldn't tell what they were" (p. 374) only means, "you couldn't identify them exactly," *i.e.*, anatomically; for, the second time he mentions seeing them, he immediately adds, "I looked for sharks" (p. 375); and, thinking about the pieces afterwards, he says, "it was funny there weren't any sharks though" (p. 377). The pieces obviously were parts of bodies mangled when the boilers exploded (p. 377). Seen in this light, the last sentence of the story—"First there was the birds, then me, then the Greeks, and even the birds got more out of her than I did"—takes on a terrible meaning. The sponger has put himself on a level with the birds, thus dissolving the staggering contrast between the petty loot he sought and the human remains on which the birds were feasting.

Hemingway evokes and smooths over the contrast between the sponger's loss and the ship's destruction in still more subtle ways. In the diving scene, the breathing of the sponger is opposed to the suffocation of the drowned woman; and her trapped, motionless floating stands out starkly against his constant diving up and down. But these contrasts are nullified by the even flow of the narrative. Again, in the last paragraph, the word *fast* is twice applied to the settling of the ship in quicksand, and, immediately, to the coming of the Greek looters (pp. 377–378). The same word thus contains opposed connotations. Another opposition occurs near the end of that paragraph: "They must have took it inside. Well, the Greeks got it all" (p. 378). "They" —the captain and the mate—"took" *death*; the Greeks "got" a safe and some valuables. The word "it" in these two sentences is loaded with the whole burden of the story's contrast of the story. But, by being compressed into that one innocent word, the poles of the contrast are, at the narrative level, merged and neutralized. More succinctly still, Hemingway puts the full ironic contrast of the story into the next one-word sentence, "Everything" (p. 378). As far as the sponger is concerned, the Greeks, in taking the valuables, got "everything" on the ship. The dead men that the birds and later (though Hemingway leaves this gruesome conclusion unstated) the jewfish got are excluded from his tally as irrelevant.

And now the apparently unimportant opening of the story becomes intelligible. The first sentence finds the sponger in a choke-and-knife fight. He disengages himself, flees, gets to his boat, and begins his search for treasure. According to him, the fight "wasn't about anything, something about making punch" (p. 372). Yet for this *nothing* he is quite willing to fight and kill. There is a gigantic disproportion between the provocation and the subsequent fight, but the sponger is not bothered by it. He equates the importance of the two events by minimizing the significance of one of them. Just as he can consider the loot of the ship its "everything," so he can say of a deadly serious fight, "it wasn't about anything." The harmless "anything" of the beginning of the story really prefigures and strengthens the pregnant "everything" of its ending. Hemingway has carried through to the last stylistic detail his program of creating and then concealing a contrast.

A brief comparison with "The Killers" will illustrate further the dialectic of flattened contrast in "After the Storm." As Cleanth Brooks and Robert Penn Warren point out, the final episode of that story is meaningful only in terms of the irony of Nick's "return to the normal scene, but the normal scene conscious of the impingement of horror."[2] In "After the Storm," the irony is greater. Hemingway makes the horror more graphic by the actual presence of a corpse—one of over four hundred and fifty. Likewise, the normality is more pervasive, since the sponger's equalizing vision dominates the story throughout. The polar contrasts and their ironic flattening have both been carried to greater extremes in "After the Storm." It is interesting to note, moreover, that whereas both George (in "The Killers") and the sponger say "it was a hell of a thing" (p. 433), the former, like many of Hemingway's people, doesn't want to think any more about Ole's fate, but the latter (a week later, to be sure) does indeed meditate on the ship's disaster. In a re-

---

2. "The Discovery of Evil: An Analysis of 'The Killers,' " in *Hemingway: A Collection of Critical Essays* (Englewood Cliffs, 1962), p. 117.

markable stretch of thinking, quite unlike that of Robert Jordan and Hemingway's other ruminators, the sponger assembles from odd pieces of observed fact ("I saw that wrench go into the sand"), reliable report ("they say she was just outside of Havana harbor"), and reasonable guess ("they must have opened the tanks") a coherent though fully concrete mental picture of how the ship foundered—and of the "scenes inside" (pp. 376–378). The undercurrent of death barely ripples the even surface of the sponger's casual, factual meditation. In effect, the closing passage, like the story as a whole, increases the sense of horror by smothering it with the calculating, objective everydayness of the sponger.

"After the Storm" shows Hemingway at his best. Its language of understatement fuses with ironic action to block the reader's emotion and suspend his usual valuations. The words and movement of the story lead the reader one way, while his unconscious feelings want to go the other. The maimed, subhuman viewpoint of the narrator-hero precludes the reader's experiencing the impact of the story until he has swallowed the whole dose of available stimulus. The story then bursts inside him like a little time bomb—a time bomb without a tick. Rarely does any writer, including Hemingway himself, achieve effects like these with such economy and cleanliness.

Symmetry in "Cat in the Rain" / *John V. Hagopian*

After an introductory paragraph that sets the scene and mood, "Cat in the Rain" is as formally and as economically structured as a classic ballet. It is probably Hemingway's best made short story. Every detail of speech and gesture carries a full weight of meaning.

In the opening paragraph we are told that the two Americans are isolated people: "they did not know any of the people they passed . . ." and their hotel room looks out on an empty square. In this isolation they are about to experience a crisis in their marriage, a crisis involving the lack of fertility, which is symbolically foreshadowed by the public garden (fertility) dominated by the war monument (death). "In the good weather there was always an artist," but the rain, ironically, inhibits creativity; there are no painters here, but the war monument "glistened in the rain."

There follows a movement of departure and return in five symmetrically

John V. Hagopian, "Symmetry in 'Cat in the Rain,' " *College English*, XXIV (December 1962), 220–22. Copyright © 1962 by the National Council of Teachers of English. Reprinted by permission of the publisher and John V. Hagopian.

arranged scenes: the hotel room, the passage through the lobby, outdoors in the rain, return through the lobby, and back in the hotel room.

In the first scene, the American wife standing at the window sees a cat crouched under an outdoor table to avoid the rain and her compassion is aroused: "the poor kitty . . . I'll get it." At this stage of the story her under-lying motives are not yet clear, but significant is the fact that she refers to the cat as a "kitty," sees it as a diminutive fluffy creature needing help and pro-tection. The husband, lying on the bed reading a book, offers to get it for her, but does not rise.

As she passes through the lobby, the hotel-owner, an old man and very tall, rises and bows. There is obviously a great contrast between him and the husband, and seven times the narrator repeats "She liked . . ." followed by attributes of the old man that powerfully appealed to her—he was serious, he had dignity, he wanted to serve her, he enjoyed his work, and he had an old heavy face and big hands. It would appear that these are traits lacking in her husband, but an explicit comparison does not occur to her. The story is told from her point of view, and only that which she is consciously aware of finds expression. Nevertheless the great attraction of this man is indicated by the repetitions of *she liked*. Since Hemingway is preeminently the artist of implications, we must try to discover what is implied here, a process which involves considerable speculation. We note that the old man is probably old enough to be her father and presumably arouses in her at a time of distress the feelings of comfort and protection that her father did. More immediately, he rises while her husband remained supine; he expresses himself with a gesture of masculine service that her husband had denied her. The further implications of this contrast become clear in the final scenes.

As she looks out into the wet empty square, she sees a man in a rubber cape crossing to the cafe in the rain. The critical reader seeking significance for every detail (as he must when working with a story so short and so eco-nomical as this) is encouraged again to speculate on possible meanings. The rubber cape is protection from rain, and rain is a fundamental necessity for fertility, and fertility is precisely what is lacking in the American wife's marriage. An even more precise interpretation is possible but perhaps not necessary here. At the moment she discovers that the cat is gone, she is no longer described as "the American wife," but as "the American girl"; it is almost as if she were demoted in femininity by failing to find a creature to care for.

But it is not the girl's fault. "Oh," she says to the maid sent by the padrone to assist her, "I wanted it so much. I wanted a kitty." Disappointed, she again enters the lobby and again the padrone rises to bow to her, a gesture which makes her feel "very small and tight inside . . . really important . . . of supreme importance," all phrases that might appropriately be used to de-scribe a woman who is pregnant. The conscious thought of pregnancy never enters her mind, but the feelings associated with it sweep through her.

As she returns to her room, her husband takes a moment to rest his eyes from reading to talk with her, but only briefly. He certainly does not rise or bow. The intensity of the repetitions of "she liked . . ." in the lobby scene is here replaced by the even greater intensity of "I wanted" and "I want," phrases which occur no less than sixteen times in this very short story. And again what she really wants never reaches consciousness, but the sum total of the wants that do reach consciousness amounts to motherhood, a home with a family, an end to the strictly companionate marriage with George. She wants her hair, which is "clipped close like a boy's" to grow out, but George says, "I like it the way it is." Since the close-cropped hair styles of the twenties was preceded by matronly buns, it would appear that the American girl wants to be like her mother when she says, "I want to pull my hair back tight and smooth and make a big knot at the back that I can feel." Interwoven with this symbol of maternal femininity is her wish for a kitty, now an obvious symbol for a child. But George apparently prefers the world of fiction to the real world of adulthood: "Oh, shut up and get something to read." Darkness descends and the rain continues to fall.

The story might have ended here, but Hemingway adds a final, ironic coda. The girl's symbolic wish is grotesquely fulfilled in painfully realistic terms. It is George, and not the padrone, by whom the wife wants to be fulfilled, but the padrone has sent up the maid with a big tortoise-shell cat, a huge creature that swings down against the maid's body. It is not clear whether this is exactly the same cat that the wife had seen from the window —probably not; in any case, it will most certainly not do. The girl is willing to settle for a child-surrogate, but the big tortoise-shell cat obviously cannot serve that purpose.

Hemingway has succeeded in rendering an immensely poignant human experience with all the poetry that pure prose can achieve. The simple language and brittle style simultaneously conceal and reveal a powerful emotional situation without the least trace of sentimentality. The delicacy and accuracy of the achievement are magnificent.

"A Canary for One": Hemingway in the Wasteland / Julian Smith

I

Although "A Canary For One" (1927) is one of Hemingway's most technically perfect stories and one of his most explicit portrayals of the post-World War I European wasteland, most critics have ignored it completely or dismissed it as a "lesser achievement."[1] Perhaps this is because "A Canary for One" seems at first glance confusing and full of apparently pointless details. Take, for instance, the second paragraph: " 'I bought him in Palermo,' the American lady said. 'We only had an hour ashore and it was Sunday morning. The man wanted to be paid in dollars and I gave him a dollar and a half. He really sings very beautifully.' " Who or what has she bought in Palermo, the impatient reader asks, an Italian urchin with a good voice? Or does she mean the canary of the title? If so, what does the title mean? "A Canary for Monica" might make sense, but what is a "canary for one"? As the story progresses we learn that the action takes place on a train passing through southern France and that the American lady does a number of apparently unimportant things: she pulls down the window blind, buys a London paper and a bottle of mineral water, stays close to the train when it stops in Marseilles, looks after "the canary from Palermo" (which explains the second paragraph, finally), lies awake at night waiting for a wreck, and goes to breakfast in the morning.

Not until almost halfway through the story does Hemingway reveal that the narrator is not a consciousness removed from the action: "For several minutes I had not listened to the American lady, who was talking to my wife." We learn very little about the narrator and his wife other than that they are Americans. Nor do they seem important, for half of the second part of the story consists of the American lady's speeches and a long summary of one of her speeches, and most of the remainder consists of responses to her

Julian Smith, " 'A Canary for One': Hemingway in The Wasteland," *Studies in Short Fiction*, V (1967–68), 355–61. Copyright, 1967, Newberry College, Newberry, S. C.; reprinted by permission of *Studies in Short Fiction*.

1. There is a helpful but sometimes impressionistic short study by Martin Dolch, John V. Hagopian, and W. Gordon Cunliffe in a collection of essays for German students of American literature: *Insight I: Analyses of American Literature*, Hagopian and Dolch, eds. (Frankfurt-am-Main, 1962), pp. 96–99. In addition, the following devote two, three, and four paragraphs, respectively, to "A Canary for One": Carlos Baker, *Hemingway: The Writer as Artist* (Princeton, 1956), pp. 137–138; Joseph DeFalco, *The Hero in Hemingway's Short Stories* (Pittsburgh, 1963), 174–176; John S. Rouch, "Jake Barnes as Narrator," *Modern Fiction Studies*, XI (Winter 1965–66), 361–363.

and descriptions of her actions. It is only in the very last sentence, when the narrator says he and his wife are "returning to Paris to set up separate residences," that we see that the story is not about the American lady but about a husband and wife whose last hours together are punctuated by the inane babbling of an insensitive, foolish, selfish, and opinionated woman who has, ironically, prevented her daughter from marrying the man she loved.

Professors Dolch, Hagopian, and Cunliffe, writing jointly, object to Hemingway's technique of withholding information: ["A Canary for One"] is not a complete success. The major flaw is the fact that until almost the middle of the story everything is presented as an objective third-person narrative. Then suddenly . . . everything is reoriented to the perspective of a subjective narrator. And the purpose of this unexpected reorientation is by no means clear, nor the reason for the delay." I would say the purpose of the "reorientation" and "delay" is very clear. First, Hemingway wants us to see the American lady as the narrator sees her, and he wants her at the center of the stage. Had he introduced all three characters in the first paragraph, he would not have been able to push the narrator and his wife aside without weakening our interest in them as well as distracting us from the American lady. Secondly, the sudden introduction of the two new characters in the middle of the story begins a pattern of refocusing that is completed with the last sentence; thus, we progress from interest in the American lady alone to interest in the American lady *and* the American couple to interest in the American couple alone.

II

"A Canary for One" is that rare bird, a *good* short story that one should re-read immediately. Unlike O. Henry's conclusions, which agreeably titillate the reader and reward him for paying attention, the ending of Hemingway's story is not so much a surprise ending as a surprise meaning, and with the meaning in mind we should start the story again.

As the story opens, the narrator is looking out the window at a pleasant scene full of color and variety. The arrangement of details in the first paragraph betrays a sensitive, selective eye: "The train passed very quickly a long red stone house with a garden and four thick palm trees with tables under them in the shade. On the other side was the sea. Then there was a cutting through red stone and clay, and the sea was only occasionally and far below against the rocks." Suddenly the American lady pulls down the blind. Does she do this because the hot afternoon sun is shining through the window, or because she does not want to see how fast the train is travelling, or because she wants the narrator to pay attention to her, or is she symbolically rejecting Europe? In any case, her rude action cuts off the narrator's

view of the Mediterranean. His response is an impassive statement of fact—
"and there was no more sea, even occasionally"—which establishes the sense
of quietly accepted loss that permeates the story. Forced to look in the other
direction, the narrator suddenly loses the ability to "compose" pictures he
demonstrates in the first sentence and becomes, instead, a "camera eye"
capable of focusing on only one thing at a time. First he sees the glass in the
door of his compartment, "then the corridor, then an open window, and outside the window were dusty trees and an oiled road and flat fields of grapes,
with graystone hills behind them." There is no selection of detail here, no
emotional or intellectual response to stimuli, only an objective, almost obsessive, report of what is visible and the order in which it is visible. Just as
the American lady's speeches are boring and trivial, the narrator's description becomes monotonous and apparently incapable of distinguishing between
the important and the trivial.

The American lady has forced the narrator to contemplate a wasteland to
which he can only apply a series of adjectives that are, taken together, drab
and unpleasant: *dusty, oiled, flat,* and *gray.* Gone symbolically is the possibility of seeing the likes of that red stone house or a distant sea breaking on
rocks; almost everything he now sees from the train is either a sign of the
urban wasteland of metropolitan Europe, a sign of violence, an ironic comment on his own plight, or just plain unpleasant. In the first sentence of the
fifth paragraph, for instance, he sees the industrial squalor of the Marseilles
"switch-yards and . . . factory smoke"; by *looking back,* however, he can see
what is probably an attractive sight; the panorama of "the town of Marseilles
and the harbor with stone hills behind it and the last of the sun on the water."
But because he is heading toward Paris and away from the Mediterranean,
this is a sign of what he is leaving, what he is losing. When the American lady
pulled down the blind, he lost the sea and found dust; looking back at Marseilles he sees the last of the sun (life?) and the sea (fertility?) as he heads
toward night and Paris, where his marriage will end.

In the second sentence of the fifth paragraph the oncoming darkness and
loss are foreshadowed in an image relevant to all three Americans in the
compartment: "As it was getting dark the train passed a farmhouse burning
in a field." Instead of the cozy, safe domesticity of the red stone house with
its garden, palm trees, and shaded tables, we have a home being destroyed
and the violation of the intimacy of marriage and family life objectified in
the "*bedding* and things from inside the farmhouse" that have been exposed
to the curious eyes of a crowd of gawking motorists. The destruction of the
farmer's house looks forward to the middle of the story, where the American
lady reveals she has violated the "domestic" privacy of her daughter by pre-
venting her from marrying the man she loved, and to the final revelation that
the American couple are about to set up "separate residences." Notice that

Hemingway does not say they are about to be separated or divorced but that they will live under different roofs.[2]

III

"A Canary for One" is a story of traps and cages. The American couple are trapped in the compartment with the American lady, they are trapped by their memories and exposed nerves and by the train itself, a *rapide* rushing toward Paris—not the Paris of romantic fiction, but the city where they must separate:

> ... coming into Marseilles. . . . The train left the station in Marseilles. . . . After it was dark the train was in Avignon. . . . The train left Avignon. . . . In the morning the train was near Paris. . . . The train was much nearer Paris. . . . The train passed through many outside of Paris towns. . . . The train was now coming into Paris. . . .

Then the train was in the dark of the Gare de Lyons. "At the end was a gate," the narrator tells us in the penultimate sentence as he describes his journey's end in Paris. Does this gate release them from an old way of life, is it the gate of a new cage, or is it both?

The canary is trapped in its cage, the American lady's daughter (for whom the canary is a present) is trapped by her mother's prejudices and her own weakness. The daughter had been in love with a young man of good birth and ambition. Though the American lady admits " 'He was from a very good family. . . . He was going to be an engineer,' " she broke up the romance because he was Swiss: " 'I couldn't have her marrying a foreigner. . . . Someone, a very good friend, told me once, "No foreigner can make an American girl a good husband." ' " So now she is bringing her daughter a canary for one, for a spinster, not for a man and wife.

But the strongest cage is reserved for the American lady. It is a cage of deafness, pettiness, intolerance, ignorance, and fear, chiefly fear—fear of foreigners, of missing trains, of train wrecks. The futility of this last fear is revealing: "all night the train went very fast and the American lady lay awake and waited for a wreck." She gains no safety by staying awake: there would be no warning of a wreck, even if she could hear such a warning; were she awake or asleep the effect would be the same. Perhaps it is this futility and fear that makes her unwilling to give up her daughter—adrift, lonely, and helpless in a dangerous world, she feels stronger and less empty in proportion to her ability to "protect" her daughter and the canary.

---

2. I cannot avoid biographical criticism when I point out that "A Canary for One" was published in 1927, the year Hemingway's first marriage broke up.

We see her cage of habit, self-interest, and parsimony even in the narrator's summary of her monologue about her clothes:

> The American lady admired my wife's travelling coat, and it turned out that the American lady had bought her own clothes for twenty years now from the same maison de coutoure in the Rue Saint Honoré. They had her measurements, and a vendeuse who knew her and her tastes picked the dresses out for her and they were sent to America. . . . Before the present vendeuse, named Thérèse, there had been another vendeuse, named Amélie. Altogether there had been only these two in the twenty years. It had always been the same couturier. Prices, however, had gone up. The exchange, though, equalized that.

Notice the way she turns the compliment on the wife's travelling coat into a discussion of trivia of interest only to herself. But the trivia itself is important to our understanding of the American lady: by not picking her own clothes, she shows her readiness to allow others to make decisions for her, a trait mirrored in her last action, putting herself under the care of a Cook's agent who finds her name "on a typewritten page in a sheaf of typewritten pages which he replaced in his pocket." Her last cage is the cage of anonymity—just as she is only one name on a list of names to the man from Cook's, she is no more than a set of measurements to the vendeuses (who, significantly, have the only names in the story).

The last two sentences in the paragraph show her preoccupation with what she has done to her daughter as well as the sterile result of her management of her daughter: "They had her daughter's measurements now too. She was grown up and there was not much chance of their changing now." Like Prufrock, who measured out his life with coffee spoons, the daughter is defined and thus trapped by these measurements; in her mother's mold now, there can be no change for the daughter, neither spiritual (by giving in to her mother she has entered the canary's gilded cage) nor physical (she will not need maternity clothes).

IV

Trapped in their individual cages, the characters cannot communicate successfully with one another. This failure of communication is objectified in the American lady's physical deafness and in the fact that not once do the narrator and his wife speak to each other in the story. They even say good-by to the American lady separately: "My wife said good-by and I said good-by to the American lady." And oddly enough, though the narrator communicates the story to us, he does not communicate with his fellow travellers; the first time he speaks, the American lady does not hear him; the second time, he speaks only to disrupt a conversation; the third time is to say good-by. His isolation is established in his very first reference to himself in the middle of the story: "I had not listened to the American lady, who was talking to my wife."

Strangers cannot talk *with* each other, only *to* or *at* each other, Hemingway implies. As the train pulls into Paris, the American lady opens a conversation by making two generalizations about Americans as husbands. The narrator's wife, in an apparent *non sequitur*, asks " 'How long ago did you leave Vevey?' " either to change the topic from American husbands (she is losing one) or because she is remembering her own honeymoon in Vevey. Instead of talking about Vevey, the American lady switches the conversation to her daughter. When the narrator's wife mentions that they had been in Vevey on their honeymoon, the American lady again switches back to herself and her daughter: " 'Were you really [in Vevey]? That must have been lovely. I had no idea, of course, that she'd fall in love with him.' " When the narrator's wife changes the topic back to Vevey a *third* time, the American lady, who has dominated this and earlier conversations, finally sees that the younger woman wants to talk about Vevey and her honeymoon, not about a broken romance. As the narrator's wife begins to reminisce about her honeymoon, the American lady forgets her own problems and begins to ask questions that show she is interested. For the first time in the story, a genuine conversation develops, but the narrator, who doesn't want to be reminded of happier days, breaks in to point out a wrecked train—which causes the American lady to launch a monologue concerning her fear of train wrecks.

The last things the narrator notices before he arrives at the Paris station, the wrecked passenger cars symbolize what has happened in the story: three people are traveling on a train and pass three wrecked cars—the narrator and his wife are heading toward the wreckage of their marriage, the American lady toward an empty life and emptier death. Significantly, the American lady, whose moral vision is self-centered and thus incomplete, sees only the last of the wrecked cars. If life in the wasteland is a train trip, the end is a wreck. And even if there is no wreck, there is no turning back, for in the last sentence but one the narrator tells us "At the end was a gate and a man took the tickets."

The Short Happy Life of Macomber / *Virgil Hutton*

Despite Mark Spilka's defense of Wilson at the expense of Warren Beck,[1] critics are catching up with the red-faced white hunter. For instance, William Stein sees the "degrading identification of Wilson's principles with the ruthless and selfish philosophy of British imperialism, in particular with the affectation of humanitarian interest in the fate of the regimented natives," and cites as evidence Wilson's lashing of the natives and his upholding of the myth that "no white man ever bolts."[2] Mr. Spilka, however, brushes aside Mr. Beck's similar response to the lashing by implying that Wilson's illegal practice is more humane than fining the natives. But to uphold Mr. Spilka's position one must, like the Americans who lashed Negroes, believe that the natives are not members of the human race.

It is time for Robert Wilson to be exposed and for Hemingway's unrelenting satire of Wilson to be recognized. Throughout the story, Wilson represents an unwitting hypocrite who harshly judges others on the basis of various strict and false codes that he himself does not follow.

To start, let us observe Wilson's appearance. "He was about middle height with sandy hair, a stubby mustache, a very red face and extremely cold blue eyes with faint white wrinkles at the corners that grooved merrily when he smiled." After this opening description, only two features are stressed: the very red face and the extremely cold blue eyes. Francis Macomber's attempted joke about his face being red that day calls attention to the implicit shamefulness of a red face, and Margaret pointedly remarks that Wilson's face "is always red." It remains to be seen how Wilson, as a hypocrite, merits his perpetual badge of shame, but for the moment we can notice that a red face is an unusual mark for a hero.

"Extremely cold blue eyes" suggest the deficiency of human warmth one finds in the technicolor movie stereotype of a specialist in torture. To reinforce this suggestion, Hemingway later adds not only the adjective "flat," but also the devastating tag of "machine-gunner's eyes." Wilson is not the detached observer with perceptive and discriminating insight. Such precision belongs to the marksman, not to the machine gunner, who indiscriminately blasts down whatever appears within range of his gun. Wilson's great talent is neither, as Mr. Beck says, for "great physical courage," nor, as Mr. Spilka

Virgil Hutton, "The Short Happy Life of Macomber," *The University Review*, XXX (June 1964), 253–63. Reprinted by permission of *New Letters*.

1. Mark Spilka, "The Necessary Stylist: A New Critical Revision," *Modern Fiction Studies*, VI (Winter, 1960–61), 283–297.
2. William Bysshe Stein, "Hemingway's 'The Short Happy Life of Francis Macomber,'" *The Explicator*, XIX (April, 1961), No. 47.

says, for "order, health, dignity, and *moral* courage." Wilson's great talent, the talent Margaret acutely perceives, is simply his talent for killing. Shortly after the machine-gunner tag, Margaret, who, in addition to baiting her husband, consistently satirizes the imperceptive red-faced hunter, makes pointed use of her recognition.

> "What importance is there to whether Francis is any good at killing lions? That's not his trade. That's Mr. Wilson's trade. Mr. Wilson is really very impressive killing anything. You do kill anything, don't you?"
> "Oh, anything," said Wilson. "Simply anything."

A few lines later, Margaret again jabs Wilson.

> "You're not coming," Wilson said.
> "You're very mistaken," she told him. "And I want *so* to see you perform again. You were lovely this morning. That is if blowing things' heads off is lovely."

It is remarkable that critics have stressed Wilson's bravery, in contrast with Macomber's supposed cowardice, since Hemingway's text nowhere calls attention to the bravery of Wilson. Instead, the text perpetually emphasizes the force of Wilson's gun—his "short, ugly, shockingly big-bored .505 Gibbs," which becomes a "cannon"; its tremendous roar that at the end drowns out the noise of Macomber's rifle; and the horrible effects of its power. The lion hunt furnishes an example.

An obvious question first strikes the mind: If Hemingway is trying to dramatize a contrast between Macomber's cowardice and Wilson's bravery, why does he take us into the lion's consciousness, which provides many irrelevant details? Furthermore, tne lion's viewpoint arouses sympathy for the animal rather than for the hunter. Ordinarily one would not, for instance, attempt to impress an audience with the bravery of the atomic bombardier over Hiroshima by dwelling on the horrible experiences undergone by the people below. To account for Hemingway's curious technique, we must assume either that he bungled (as critics have unhesitatingly done when analyzing this story) or that his aim differs from the traditional interpretation. Once one overcomes the tendency to idolize Wilson, the persistent pattern of details becomes plain: Hemingway is stressing the ugliness, the brutality, and the horror of the kill.

> . . . and turning saw the lion, horrible-looking now, with half his head seeming to be gone, crawling toward Wilson in the edge of the tall grass while the red-faced man worked the bolt on the short ugly rifle and aimed carefully as another blasting *carawong!* came from the muzzle, and the crawling, heavy, yellow bulk of the lion stiffened and the huge, mutilated head slid forward . . .

Macomber did not know how the lion had felt before he started his rush, nor during it when the unbelievable smash of the .505 with a muzzle velocity of two tons had hit him in the mouth, nor what had kept him coming after that, when the second ripping crash had smashed his hind quarters and he had come crawling on toward the crashing, blasting thing that had destroyed him.

The lion is depicted as magnificent, but essentially helpless because of the horrendous power of Wilson's big rifle. Thus we witness no vignette of bravery; we witness a slaughter. And upon seeing Wilson in action, we can appreciate Margaret's satiric classification of him as a lovely killer.

During the lion hunt, Wilson lives up to his "machine-gunner's eyes"; now we must see how fully he deserves his clownish red face. In connection with the already mentioned unwitting hypocrisy of Wilson, it must be noted that whenever Wilson is most serious he is most likely to be mistaken; but when he is not serious, when he says what he does not think, he is most likely to be correct.

Wilson's first harsh judgment comes early in the story when Macomber indirectly asks him not to tell what happened during the lion hunt.

Wilson looked at him now coldly. He had not expected this. So he's a bloody four-letter man as well as a bloody coward, he thought. I rather liked him too until today. ". . . It's supposed to be bad form to ask us not to talk though."

Incidentally, through Wilson's mechanical harping on what is supposed to be good form, Hemingway satirizes the Britisher's reverence for decorum. But the chief importance of this passage lies in its contrast with a similar incident towards the end of the story when the situation is reversed. After Margaret questions the legality of Wilson's chasing the buffalo from cars, Wilson asks her not to tell on him: "Wouldn't mention it to anyone though." This time, however, he fails to perceive that his request may be "bad form." Wilson sees the splinter in his neighbor's eye, but overlooks the beam in his own.

Soon after his judgment of Macomber, Wilson passes judgment on the cruelty of Margaret. "She's damn cruel but they're all cruel. They govern, of course, and to govern one has to be cruel sometimes. Still, I've seen enough of their damn terrorism." Here Wilson's theory that to govern one must be cruel fits Mr. Stein's point that British imperialistic attitudes are being satirized through Wilson. But we must also recognize that Wilson criticizes Margaret for what he himself practices on the native boys, despite Mr. Spilka's opinion that Wilson is being humane rather than terroristic when he threatens a native boy with fifteen lashes for the universal crime of curiosity.

Shortly afterwards comes a clear example of the periodic splits between what Wilson thinks and what he says. "I should think it would be even more unpleasant to do it, Wilson thought, wife or no wife, or to talk about it having done it. But he said, 'I wouldn't think about that any more. Any one could be upset by his first lion. That's all over.' " Wilson's thoughts harshly condemn Macomber's supposed act of cowardice; his words treat Macomber's act lightly. The point is that Wilson's insincere reassurance represents the truth: any one could be upset by his first lion. It is not by accident that only one-and-a-half paragraphs later the narrator gives the Somali proverb, "a brave man is always frightened three times by a lion; when he first sees his track, when he first hears him roar and when he first confronts him." An earlier instance of Wilson's inadvertent deviation into truth comes when he tells Macomber, "Forget the whole thing. Nothing to it anyway."

During the lion hunt, Macomber again outrages Wilson's moral sensitivity by innocently asking, "Why not leave him there?" Hemingway goes on: "Robert Wilson . . . suddenly felt as though he had opened the wrong door in a hotel and seen something shameful." How righteous. How prim, proper, and puritanical for one who that night sleeps with another man's wife and who, "to accommodate any windfalls," sports a spacious double cot. Whether or not one condemns Wilson's sexual habits, one can at least smile at his high and mighty attitude.

But let us see how he justifies his participation in Margaret's revengeful adultery. "What does he think I am, a bloody plaster saint? Let him keep her where she belongs. It's his own fault." In his customary manner, Wilson excuses himself and pins the guilt on somebody else. And why is not Wilson partially responsible? Because he is made of flesh and blood. When judging others, however, he fails to consider that they too are mere flesh and blood, and that fear as well as lust arises from flesh and blood. While pondering his own frailty, he looks at the Macombers with "his flat, cold eyes": other people are objects that should act like plaster saints; only to himself does he grant the luxury of human weakness.

One begins to wonder whether Wilson has any personal standards other than the opportunistic requirements of his flesh. Surely one must look to his hunting as a last resort. To Mr. Beck's contention that even here Wilson has no rigid code because of his illegal chasing of the buffalo from cars, Mr. Spilka justifiably replies that Wilson's code was never one of mere legality. But if it can be shown that in the buffalo hunt Wilson breaks not only legal standards but also what he believes to be his own standards, then Mr. Spilka's answer no longer suffices. The text says: "They were his standards in all except the shooting. He had his own standards about the killing and they could live up to them or get some one else to hunt them. He knew, too, that they all respected him for this." A paragraph and a half earlier, however, Wilson's planning of the buffalo hunt reveals the hypocrisy of his pride in his shooting standards: ". . . if he could come between them and their swamp with the car, Macomber would have a good chance at them in the open. He did not want to hunt buff with Macomber in thick cover."

Here legality or illegality is not the issue. Wilson plans the kill in accordance not with his own supposed standards but with the standards he thinks Macomber can meet. Wilson's standards are simply his clients' standards, even in the shooting. And Wilson abandons his mythical shooting standards for a simple and selfish reason: "He did not want to hunt buff with Macomber in thick cover."

In case the reader has somehow missed the steady devastation of Wilson, Hemingway inserts during the buffalo hunt his most obvious and most crushing blow at the cold, egotistical, opportunistic, red-faced white hunter. Macomber, in his newly-found foolhardiness that is far removed from bravery, delivers the straight line when, after expressing his lack of fear of lions, he asks, "After all, what can they do to you?" Wilson eagerly rises to the challenge. " 'That's it,' said Wilson. 'Worst one can do is kill you.' " The irony is fierce, for few people consider death a triviality, but Wilson evokes the magic name of Shakespeare to buttress his assertion, and offers a quotation from the fountain of truth. " 'By my troth, I care not; a man can die but once; we owe God a death and let it go which way it will, he that dies this year is quit for the next.' "

An examination of this quotation will, I think, show its paucity of significant content. Most people already know that men "can die but once," but few, apparently, find this obvious fact as comforting as the quotation implies they should. On the contrary, the finality of death makes people fear it. Nor, because "we owe God a death," do many people, even the most devout Christians, hasten to pay off this debt any sooner than necessary. Finally, it is evident that dying this year will eliminate worry about next year; but again, a slight lack of profundity mars the thought.

Now who is the fool: Shakespeare, Hemingway, or Wilson? The answer may quickly be found by resorting to Shakespeare's text. The quotation comes from *Henry IV, Part II*, Act III, Scene ii, 250–55, and is spoken by one of Shakespeare's clowns, Francis Feeble, a woman's tailor, who belongs to the ragged band of recruits that Falstaff helpfully rounds up for the King's army. Clearly, the fool is neither Shakespeare nor Hemingway but Robert Wilson, who damns himself not only by framing the quotation with witless "damned goods" and "damned fines," but also by accepting the quotation as a sufficient guide for one's life. Indeed, Wilson has reason to be "very embarrassed" after supremely illustrating how little he can be relied upon, when most serious, as a purveyor of truth.

But Hemingway's satire also cuts in other directions. He is satirizing the juvenile practice of clinging to some emotionally satisfying quotation that one can supposedly live by: the simple-minded worship of Shakespeare as an infallible god, and the critical fallacy of accepting all Shakespearian characters as equally trustworthy spokesmen for Shakespeare's own sentiments. Further, as a colleague of mine, Mr. Carrol Cox, suggested, Hemingway may thus be warning the reader not to accept Wilson as the spokesman for his creator.

Wilson professes to live by this quotation, but his acts belie him. He shows his concern over dying this year instead of next, for example, when he hopes that the back of his head won't be blown off by Macomber, and when he ducks aside from the charging buffalo "to get in a shoulder shot." Wilson simply does not know himself, and he lacks self-knowledge because he never takes the trouble to examine himself—he fears mouthing things up too much. Such a man is hardly acceptable as a moral guide along the tortuous path to manhood; and indeed, following directly after his tribute to Feeble, Wilson's glib summing up of American men and Macomber's change becomes pompous nonsense.

That a man of Wilson's habits fails as a moral guide should cause no surprise, but a shock of surprise does hit when we realize that Wilson is not even a competent hunting guide. The final directions he gives for shooting the buffalo illustrate his bungling. "The only shot is straight into the nose. The only other shot is into his chest or, if you're to one side, into the neck or the shoulders. After they've been hit once they take a hell of a lot of killing. Don't try anything fancy. Take the easiest shot there is." At this crucial point with a novice hunter on his hands, Wilson should not even have mentioned the tricky nose shot, and certainly he should not have implied that it was "the only shot." Having recognized Macomber's fire-eating condition, Wilson should have realized that Macomber, in trying to prove himself, would be content with nothing but the most difficult shot. Wilson's ranking of the shots according to their difficulty lures Macomber to his death.

The ending of the story continues to heap coals of fire on Wilson's head through the simple device of having the omniscient narrator tell what happened before Wilson reveals his cruel and distorted judgment of Margaret Macomber. Critics and readers have performed ingenious juggling acts with Margaret's conscious and subconscious motives in order to reconcile the explicit statement that she "had shot at the buffalo" with Wilson's view that she had shot at her husband, but such attempts become unnecessary and pointless once we recognize Wilson as the butt rather than the spokesman of Hemingway. Right to the end, the satire on Wilson follows the patterns established throughout the story. When he says what he does not think—"Of course it's an accident"—he speaks the truth; and his comical British reverence for good form slips out when he asks Margaret, "Why didn't you poison him? That's what they do in England." Even his pleasure over Margaret's use of "please" continues the assault on his lack of concern for anything but appearances in the actions of others. Finally, Wilson's confession, "I'd begun

to like your husband," which might appear to be an understatement of genuine feeling, is worthless because throughout the story Wilson intermittently
likes or despises Macomber in accordance with the American's most recent
display of good or bad form. That Wilson liked some of the clientele when
they paraded through his double cot though he despised them later reinforces
the insignificance of his liking Macomber or anyone.

But all these bits of grim humor at Wilson's expense are minor backdrops
to the dramatic exposure of Wilson as a bully who unleashes against Margaret the sarcastic terrorism that earlier he had condemned her for using.
And part of Margaret's horror, as one of my students acutely suggested, is
that she must recognize, now that she has become the victim, the extent of
her cruelty towards her husband. To stress Wilson's role as bully, Hemingway
changes the designation of Margaret from "Mrs. Macomber" to "wife" to
simply "the woman." Thus, it is over a hysterically crying woman that
"Feeble" Wilson, who as usual places the blame on someone else without
perceiving his own share in the guilt, enjoys his petty triumph.

If Wilson's triumph is hollow, what about Macomber's purported triumph?
Traditionally, Macomber has been seen as a man who dramatically replaces
ineffective cowardice with masterful bravery. This reading, however, largely
rests on an acceptance of Wilson as a reliable interpreter; and once doubt is
cast on Wilson's credibility, doubt must also undermine the accepted view
of Macomber. But Ronald Crane's perceptive analysis demonstrates that the
very structure of the story, aside from one's attitude towards Wilson, does
not support the traditional interpretation. Mr. Crane's discussion of the
flashback is especially pertinent.

> Now I think we do become more or less convinced during the opening
> scene that Macomber is "less of a man and more of an object than ever
> before" and that Wilson, if not Margot, is probably right in judging him
> as severely as he does. But then we learn for ourselves what has actually
> happened earlier in the day, and I think he would be a rather excep-
> tional reader who could feel quite sure that, if he were put into the same
> fearsome circumstances as Macomber, and with no more previous ex-
> perience with African lions, he would not, like Macomber, suddenly
> find himself "running wildly, in panic in the open, running toward the
> stream." It may be, as you suggest, that Hemingway wishes us to think
> of Macomber, in this situation, as "less . . . even as an *object*, than the
> lion itself"; and this may be the reason for the otherwise somewhat
> arbitrary glimpses he gives us into the lion's thoughts. But if so, the
> device surely misses the mark, with the result that so far from thinking
> that Wilson's previously indicated contempt has been warranted by
> the facts, we now tend to feel that he and his professional code are
> below humanity in a sense in which Macomber's regrettable but wholly
> natural "cowardice" is not. I repeat that I don't think this is a part of

the plot as Hemingway conceived it; about that you seem to me to be right. But certainly to the extent that you are right, Hemingway is wrong! [3]

This passage beautifully pinpoints the main purpose of the flashback, but because he does not see through Wilson, Mr. Crane concludes that Hemingway has blundered. Another look at the lion hunt will show how carefully it is contrived to produce the effect that Mr. Crane finds fault with.

The episode is structured around Macomber's crescendo of fear up to his climactic running from the lion. Almost every detail serves to increase his fear; nothing allays it. The opening of the flashback emphasizes Macomber's isolation with his fear. His wife is asleep. "There was no one to tell he was afraid, nor to be afraid with him . . ." And he does not know what the Somali proverb makes clear: that his fear instead of indicating cowardice, is a natural reaction for even the bravest of men. In the morning he is even more alone. Wilson's offhand comments on the size of the lion and the range at which it must be shot offer little help, and Margaret's unawareness of the danger involved again isolates Macomber from any understanding he might have expected to receive from his wife. She cannot help him because she, like Macomber, believes that fear automatically betrays cowardice.

"You're not afraid, are you?"
"Of course not."

Macomber cannot reveal his fear for fear of being called a coward, but ironically this forced bottling up of his fear leads to the act for which he is labeled a coward.

After Macomber's unsuccessful try at the lion, his courage is inexorably broken down by a string of ominous details: the gun-bearers' fear; the lion's being in a bad place because you "can't see him until you're right on him"; the lion's dark blood; and the fact that it would be "murderous" to send in beaters because they are "bound to get mauled." Wilson, after mentioning these details without considering their effect on Macomber until too late, comically advises, "Don't worry about anything." Before Wilson recognizes his oversight, he has already shut off Macomber's chance to escape.

"I don't want to go in there," said Macomber . . .
"Neither do I," said Wilson very cheerily. "Really no choice though."

Only after making Macomber believe he has no choice does Wilson reveal that Macomber actually does have a choice, and that, in such situations, it

3. Ronald S. Crane, "Observations on a Story by Hemingway," in Louis G. Locke, William M. Gibson, and George Arms, *Introduction to Literature* (New York, 1962), pp. 482–83.

is quite acceptable for the professional hunter to finish the kill by himself. But Macomber interprets Wilson's retraction as a concession to his client's fear, and stays in order not to be thought a coward.

The flashback indicates neither the bravery of Wilson nor the cowardice of Macomber, whose flight seems natural and inevitable. Rather, the flashback allows us to perceive how unjustified are the harsh judgments of Margaret and Wilson, and serves to illustrate both Wilson's ineptness as a hunting guide and his refusal to accept any responsibility for his mistakes. Plainly, Wilson should share the guilt, but he thrusts all the shame onto Macomber in order to preserve the heroic image of the infallible guide. And naive faith in the "infallible" judgment of a fallible guide leads Macomber to his destruction during the buffalo hunt.

Mr. Crane urges that during the buffalo hunt Hemingway's technique becomes so clumsy and obvious that Hemingway seems to have suddenly remembered he was writing for *Cosmopolitan* readers. Particularly objectionable for Mr. Crane are Macomber's "reiterated assertions" of his happiness over being without fear, which should have been left "to the reader's inference." If one accepts the traditional interpretation of Macomber's change— an interpretation obvious enough for any schoolgirl to grasp—one must accept Mr. Crane's charge that here Hemingway falls to his crudest level. But upon examination, the buffalo hunt reveals, I think, not crudity but extreme subtlety.

As usual, the standard view of Macomber largely rests on the acceptance of Wilson as a reliable chorus (the term "chorus" seems to enhance Wilson's position until one remembers that Greek choruses are often unreliable interpreters of the dramatic action), and particularly on Wilson's stereotyped notions concerning bravery: fear denotes a coward; lack of fear denotes a brave man. The Somali proverb in the flashback shows, however, that fear does not necessarily indicate cowardice; conversely, the buffalo hunt shows that the absence of fear does not necessarily indicate bravery.

For a starting point, we again turn to Mr. Crane. ". . . there is a certain jarring incongruity, too, between the commonplace flavor of Macomber's thoughts as the narrator states them and the relatively heroic quality of his action." The commonplace quality of Macomber's thoughts, however, indicates no weakness in Hemingway; it warns us not to accept Wilson's analysis of Macomber. Hemingway insists on the fatuity of Macomber's joy by linking his insight—that lions need not be feared because they can only kill you— with the inane philosophy of Feeble that Wilson professes. Hemingway's own viewpoint slips in through Margaret: " 'You're both talking rot,' said Margot."

The "commonplace flavor of Macomber's thoughts" does not jar with his heroic actions, because his acts are not presented as heroic. Wilson, the professional killer, sensibly ducks aside for a shoulder shot; Macomber, the novice, foolishly and futilely keeps attempting the almost impossible nose shot. This final contrast between the two men presents Macomber's needless courting of death as not bravery but rash foolhardiness. Macomber's moment of "heroism" resembles that of the soldier who temporarily goes berserk in battle.

Wilson's share in the destruction of Francis Macomber looms large, but Macomber's own weaknesses betray him into Wilson's hands. Basically, Macomber is a good fellow whose instinctive shock at Wilson's treatment of the native boys serves as a foil for Wilson's own inhuman attitude (Hemingway's technique here echoes Twain's use of Huck Finn). Being a good fellow, however, cannot save Macomber either from death or from Hemingway's satire, which strikes not at his cowardice but at his ignorance. His knowledge of life is wholly superficial. "He knew . . . about motor cycles . . . about motor cars, about duck-shooting, about fishing, trout, salmon and big-sea, about sex in books, many books, too many books, about all court games, about dogs, not much about horses, about hanging on to his money, about most of the other things his world dealt in . . ." And this superficiality, which, of course, reflects the segment of American society from which he comes, prevents him from perceiving the vacuity in his guide, Wilson. Through accepting, during the buffalo hunt, Wilson's false creeds concerning bravery and death, Macomber becomes an eager victim of Wilson's inept shooting instructions.

Macomber, then, illustrates no dramatic change from boyish cowardice to heroic manhood. He is a man betrayed by his own society, which failed to give him the wisdom needed to stave off disaster when he was transplanted into the deadly world of big game hunting. The bond between Macomber and his wife epitomizes the American values of money and physical beauty, and the destruction of Macomber implies the collapse of any society that places its highest values on external things.

Though arguing from faulty premises, Mr. Crane is correct, I think, in denying Macomber the status of tragic hero. Macomber undergoes no basic character change, does not fall from a position of eminence, and achieves no meaningful insight about himself or about the pattern of action that destroys him. Oddly enough, the most tragic figure is Margaret, who, excepting Mr. Beck, has almost universally been damned as a classic example of the dominating American bitch. Margaret remains the most elusive and most subtly drawn character in the story; but once freed from the view that Wilson is Hemingway's spokesman, one can give adequate weight to the clues Hemingway provides to show not only that she is no stereotyped bitch, but that she is the only character who achieves any insight concerning both herself and the tragic action that destroys her husband.

Despite Mr. Beck's attention to these clues, a few points deserve mention. If Margaret so strongly desired to be the dominating female, it is remarkable that she should have been so upset over her husband's display of weakness, which would only reinforce her domination. Furthermore, Margaret's having "done the best she could for many years back" (which means that from a point many years back up to the present she had been trying her best to make her marriage work) contradicts the image of a dominating bitch. And to insert this comment, which tends to arouse sympathy for Margaret, just before the climax of the action is an odd way to prepare the reader for adopting Wilson's belief that she is not only a bitch but also a murderess.

The trouble is that Margaret's bitchery has too often been accepted as her characteristic behavior, whereas the story frames her bitchery as a special reaction to a specific event. Wilson's surprise over her sudden change from a fine, understanding woman to an "enamelled" sadist, and his momentary surmise that she might simply be trying to put up "a good show" stress the fact that Margaret is putting on an act to repay her husband for failing her through his supposed cowardice. Though recognizing this possibility, Wilson cannot integrate the seemingly contradictory facts of Margaret, and finally accepts the ostentatious display of bitchery as her whole character. The reader should not make the same mistake.

Margaret's extreme reaction of committing adultery with Wilson indicates how deeply she feels that her years of effort have been betrayed. This reaction is unjustified, but Margaret, a product of upper class American society, is, like her husband, a victim of Wilson's stereotyped notions of fear and bravery. The structure of the story depicts a fundamental change in Margaret's attitude—a change leading not to murder but to understanding.

Many have pointed out the symbolic shifting of the characters' positions in the motor car, and traditionally the reversal from Macomber's being the outsider has been seen as a triumph for Macomber. Actually, the pattern reveals Macomber's seduction by a hypocritical fool as opposed to Margaret's dissociation from the fool's blighting influence. She gains new awareness by participating in the buffalo hunt, which transforms her attitude toward big-game hunting.

Before the lion hunt, Macomber remains alone with his fear because his wife sees no reason for anyone to be afraid. Like the American society columnist, Margaret regards the hunt as an adventurous game. She feels "marvellous" and "very excited"; she thinks the lion's roar "very impressive" and reassures her husband that she knows he will kill the lion "marvellously," and she is "awfully anxious to see it." Macomber, who thinks the lion's roar "frightful," exposes the fatuousness of his wife's comments by answering, "It sounds easy, doesn't it?"

Immediately following the automobile chase of the buffalo, however, Margaret's inner turmoil cracks her enamelled affectation of gaiety. She is "very white faced," and says, "It was frightful. I've never been more frightened in my life." Significantly, she uses the word that Macomber used to describe the lion's roar. But the reversal in their positions, the peripety, appears only after they examine the dead buffalo. Macomber views the buffalo "with delight"; whereas, Margaret says, "He's hateful looking." Now, in addition to her white face, she looks "ill." But Macomber, full of his unwarranted sense of power, rattles on in terms that are commonplace because they echo Margaret's earlier fatuities.

> "Wasn't it marvellous, Margot?"
> "I hated it."
> "Why?"
> "I hated it," she said bitterly. "I loathed it."

The reversal is then symbolized by Margaret's "sitting far back in the seat" while Macomber is "sitting forward talking to Wilson." She has no part in the fools' chatter about the insignificance of lions that can only kill you.

Her thoughts are quite the opposite, for the peripety has occurred because of Margaret's discovery—through experiencing fear, and through looking at the dead buffalo that "bulked blackly in the open" with its "massive horns swung wide"—of the ugliness and the potential deadliness of the hunt. And upon seeing the change in her husband, she becomes "very afraid" not that Macomber will leave her, as Wilson, who realizes nothing of her change, thinks, but that her husband may be killed.

The ending establishes the hysterically crying Margaret, whose fatal attempt to save her husband leaves her with nothing but the recognition that her earlier lack of understanding helped drive her husband to his death, as the central tragic figure in this tragedy of ignorance and misunderstandings. Wilson, tightly sealed from the actual course of events by his smug self-righteousness, performs a horrifyingly ironic concluding chorus over the weeping woman. In this story, the fool indeed triumphs.

Some final observations concerning Wilson's red face. On the political level, behind Wilson's red face lies the red coloring once used on maps to designate areas of the world under British rule. Through Wilson, Hemingway exposes these areas as blots of hypocrisy and shame, where human laws (against lashing, for example) are preached but not practiced. On the literary level, behind Wilson's red face leers the red face of Molière's archetypal hypocrite, Tartuffe, who, like Wilson, passes puritanical judgments on others' actions but pleads the frailty of flesh and blood to excuse his own lust for his friend's wife. Despite the wife's exposure of the hypocrite, the force of evil is presented as so great that the duped husband can escape ruin in Molière's comic world only through the intervention of an omniscient, omnipotent king. In Hemingway's tragic world, however, no such all powerful figure exists to insure the downfall of evil and to rescue Francis and Margaret Macomber.

The Dark Snows of Kilimanjaro / *Gennaro Santangelo*

Hemingway's "iceberg" theory has often caused critical confusion in readings of the short stories. Although their narrative line has appeared firm, the omissions have tended to obscure their thematic implications. What precisely is the degree and kind of initiation in "The Killers," or to what extent might the reader, looking at "Big Two-Hearted River" as a self-contained story, agree with Mr. Young's theory that its hero is trying to overcome a traumatic experience?[1] "The Snows of Kilimanjaro" conversely has embarrassed the critic by its riches—the author himself commented on the plethora of material which he claimed used up four novels in this one rich short story. Ironically this abundance has also caused confusion about details and overall meaning. The major unresolved issue centers on Harry's salvation or non-salvation, whether the plane ride represents a symbolic raising above the stinking plain, a journey earned by a true death-bed repentance, or the ride is only a dream, an ironic counterpart to his wasted life. The symbolic significance of the details are then clustered around these divergent assessments, the most significant being the interpretation of the leopard. Does he symbolize Harry's striving for salvation, or is he an ironic counterpart to Harry? Do the mountains represent clean salvation and the plains stinking damnation? This apparent confusion has irritated some perceptive critics to retort with testy impatience that the confused symbolization blurs the ending.[2]

The larger theme of self-realization is also problematic. Some argue that although Harry has failed as a writer because of moral delinquencies, and there is no longer any chance for professional redemption, he is morally redeemed and has finally reasserted the full force of his talented and superior personality. Conversely, there are serious doubts about the quality of this self-realization and the moral worth of his life style.

These polarized interpretations have encouraged a proliferation of dichotomies with the critics emphasizing those which best formulate their respective thesis. The most obvious has been the cluster of mountain-cold-

---

1. Philip Young, *Ernest Hemingway: A Reconsideration* (University Park, Pa.: The Pennsylvania State University Press, 1966), 43–48.

2. Caroline Gordon and Allen Tate, "The Snows of Kilimanjaro: Commentary" in *Hemingway's African Stories*, ed. John M. Howell (New York: Charles Scribner's Sons, 1969), 142. There are useful essays in this anthology that represent the general line of criticism of "Snows of Kilimanjaro." Especially interesting is the essay of Marion Montgomery. Invaluable is the essay of Oliver Evans, "The Snows of Kilimanjaro: A Revaluation," *PMLA*, LXXVI (December, 1961) which presents some standard arguments, many that I do not accept. The references to the story are taken from Ernest Hemingway, *The Snows of Kilimanjaro and Other Stories* (New York: Charles Scribner's Sons, 1936).

leopard versus plain-heat-hyena, possibly the former representing a type of moral rectitude and the later decay. There is the contrast between death and life—the former in the concrete images of death which surround the dying Harry and the latter in the review of his life. Allied to this pair is the contrast between life-in-death and death-in-life: the writer was dead morally while he lived, his wife representing death in life, but by dying honestly he finds a life in death (this contrast is of course based on a debatable critical position). I believe the contrast between projected art and accomplished art just as significant. Corollary to the observed reflections on his personal life is the contrast between love and sex: love involves pain and misunderstanding, sex a tool for financial ease and superficial harmony. Possibly these dichotomies can be infinitely multiplied, based as they are on the fundamental movement of the story by contrast. Other pairs have not been noted or largely neglected. The startling difference between projected experiences and accomplished art is as significant as any other fundamental contrast. The concrete manifestation of the distance between fantasy and reality is revealed by the vivid vision of Harry's gangrened leg. The contrast between the euphoria of the journey with its comforting snows and the reality of the green rot exposes the futility of Harry's apparent last minute repentance—the leg expresses the ultimate meaning of the action. The Hemingway reader will remember very well Jake Barnes's acceptance of reality when he retorts to Brett's plea for a life together, "Isn't it pretty to think so." So also the leg reveals the sham of what has not been and is not now. Harry has lost both this world and the next because he had neither character nor faith. His art and life are not vitalized by any insight into experience. His failure is caused by a lack of soul, not will, nor talent—he is not someone who could have been better and is now saved.

I

Such a portrait of failure both moral and professional perplexes the Hemingway student. Almost all critics agree that the story is among Hemingway's most autobiographical with its clearly veiled allusions to personal events in his own life.[3] Most cogent is Carlos Baker's statement that the portrait presents Hemingway as he might have been, and one may add as he feared he might be. The story presents an "ur" image of Hemingway—of the mistakes he could have made and might make, of the fears he had, at the time of the writing, that he might have lost his art and his soul.

After the first flush of critical acceptance and the very few reservations about *A Farewell To Arms*, Hemingway in the early thirties was nettled by

3. Carlos Baker, *Ernest Hemingway: A Life Story* (New York: Charles Scribner's Sons, 1969), 289.

the inevitable second-look attack from friends such as Gertrude Stein and unknowns such as Wyndham Lewis in his famous dumb-ox attack. Although basically self-confident, he resented and was hurt by these attacks. Also, he wasn't writing all that well in spite of his blustering. *Winner Take Nothing* does not reach the standard of his other collections, and *Death in the Afternoon* was severely criticized, while the Henry Morgan story which he set great store by was not that well received. It was already five years since his last full fictional work, and he did not seem to have the handle for a long work.[4]

Beyond these professional preoccupations were personal problems which naturally affected his writing career. Although at the time he wrote "The Snows of Kilimanjaro" his marriage to Pauline looked solid, Hemingway may have had some reservations about accepting her uncle's money, a blow to his touchy pride, and a feeling of being bought. This is a knotty and speculative problem, but the somber vision of the period from 1933–37 has obviously some illuminating causes. The resentments both in "Snows" and "The Short Happy Life of Francis Macomber" point to a fear of the debilitating effect of money. His life in Key West with the rich sporting set, as much as he seemed to enjoy it, obviously aroused some reservations about his own ability to resist the pressures of leisure. His scorn at this time for the nonproducers increased. Scott Fitzgerald for whom he had both admiration and contempt was suffering from alcoholism and emotional fatigue. I think it more than coincidence that Hemingway had him first in mind when he wrote the story, not merely because he remembered what he said about the rich, but because Harry's lost career certainly had a close application to Fitzgerald—who recognized the slur immediately and asked Hemingway to delete it.[5] I do not wish to imply that Fitzgerald was the prototype for Harry because their respective circumstances are entirely different—the physical memories of Harry are light years away from the sensibility of the Jazz-Age historian. Yet the situations present similarities—loss of talent through drink, money, and women.

This contempt for those who "are going to write" has its origins in Paris. In an early attack on "bohemians," the young Hemingway berates "the phonies" in a heavy-handed way. Incrusted in these hard chestnuts is a serious attitude toward art: "They [the Rotonde Crowd] are nearly all loafers expending the energy that an artist puts into his creative work in talking

4. Ibid., Chapter V, VI for many of these details.
5. Ibid., 290. The letter might be interesting in its entirety, "Please lay off me in the print. If I choose to write de profundis sometimes it doesn't mean I want friends praying aloud over my corpse. No doubt you meant it kindly, but it cost me a night's sleep. And when you incorporate it in a book would you mind cutting my name? It's a fine story—one of your best— even though Poor Scott Fitzgerald rather spoiled it for me. Ever your friend, Scott. Riches have never fascinated me, unless combined with the greatest charm or distinction."

about what they are going to do. . . . By talking about art, they obtain the same satisfaction that the real artist does in his work." Then he goes on to mention that even if Baudelaire had led a lobster on a leash he probably" . . . parked the lobster with the concierge down on the first floor, put the chloroform bottle corked on the washstand and sweated and carved at the *Fleurs du Mal* alone with his ideas and his paper as all artists have worked before and since."[6] Hemingway on creation and noncreation is very clear. You cannot talk about what you're going to write because there is literally *nothing* to talk about—nor can you conjecture on what might make a good story because the story hasn't been made until the act of creation takes place. Any attempt to find salvation in what one might have done is meaningless. Such fears about his own life style and its effect on his artistic integrity influenced the way he perceived his problem in "The Snows of Kilimanjaro," for Harry can be connected with the failed artist such as Fitzgerald and the phony Rotonde Crowd.

In this context the content and quality of Harry's recollections bear comparison to the vignettes of *In Our Time* in terms of artistic integrity and achievement. Hemingway made a fascinating statement about art that applies to the Nick Adams stories and Harry's predicament:

> The only writing that was any good was what you made up, what you imagined. . . . That was the weakness of Joyce. Daedalus in Ulysses was Joyce himself, so he was terrible. Joyce was so damn romantic and intellectual about him. He'd made Bloom up. Bloom was wonderful. He'd made Mrs. Bloom up. She was the greatest in the world. That was the way with Mac [McAlmon]. Mac worked too close to life. You had to digest life and then create your own people. . . . Nick [Adams] in the stories was never himself. He had made him up. Of course he'd never seen an Indian woman having a baby. That was what made it good. . . . He'd seen a woman having a baby on the road to Karagatch and tried to help her. That was the way it was.

> [Nick] wanted to be a great writer. He was pretty sure he would be. . . . It was hard to be a great writer if you loved the world and living in it and special people. It was hard when you loved so many places. . . . There were times when you had to write. Not conscience. Just peristaltic action. It was really more fun than anything. . . . It had more bite to it than anything else. . . . He, Nick, wanted to write about country so it could be there like Cézanne had done it in painting. You had to do it from inside yourself. . . . He felt almost holy about it. It was deadly

6. Ernest Hemingway, *By-Line: Ernest Hemingway*, ed. William White (New York: Charles Scribner's Sons, 1967), "American Bohemians in Paris A Weird Lot," *Toronto Star Weekly*, March 25, 1922, 23–25.

serious. You could do it if you would fight it out. If you'd lived right with your eyes. It was a thing you couldn't talk about. . . .[7]

Such a statement, deleted obviously for esthetic reasons from "Big-Two-Hearted River," defines Harry's esthetic and moral failures. The criticism of McAlmon, that he worked too close to life, applies concisely to Harry. You had to digest life and then create your own people. When Nick had seen the woman having a baby, he used it creatively in an entirely different setting. The act of creation itself made the art and talent—without these one is left with vague reminiscences. Harry's memories record experiences, not art. Nick was "deadly serious." You had to fight it out. These qualities are not found in Harry. These observations appear more apt here than the more famous statements in *Death In the Afternoon* and *Green Hills of Africa*, but all three say the same thing, only this one is more applicable to the problem of "Snows."

The achievements of *In Our Time* contrast with the sterility of Harry's memories. Taking one of the simplest vignettes, the scene of Nick and Rinaldo, the reader responds to the terseness of Nick's statement, " 'Senta Rinaldo; Senta. You and me we've made a separate peace.' Rinaldo lay still in the sun, breathing with difficulty. 'We're not patriots.' "[8] Such an artistic ordering acts as a charging agent to infuse with meaning the rest of the vignette, the fallen pink wall of the house, the two Austrian dead, etc.

Harry's memories explore an earlier stage of realization, the raw material that needs the infusion of art. Two of his most vivid memories, the affair in Constantinople and the gunning of the Austrian officers on leave, utilize the same kind of vivid details as the Adams story. The vivid recall of the ". . . hot Armenian slut, that swung her belly against him so it almost scalded." and, "That was the day he'd first seen dead men wearing white ballet skirts and upturned shoes with pompons on them," or, ". . . that cold, bright Christmas day with the mountains showing across the plain that Barker had flown across the lines to bomb the Austrian officers' leave train, machine-gunning them as they scattered and ran. He remembered Barker afterwards coming into the mess and starting to tell about it. And how quiet it got and then somebody saying, 'You bloody murderous bastard.' "

The most Hemingway could do with such material is place it as inter-chapters in *In Our Time*, and many of these are not singularly successful. When he found meaning, he created a story that transcended memory and experience as the young Nick so aptly observed. When he could not adequately organize memory and experience, Hemingway wrote a series of disorganized, uncharged stills. The rejected and unfinished "The Last Good

7. Baker, 131–132. He quotes from the unpublished deleted conclusion to "Big-Two-Hearted-River."
8. Ernest Hemingway, *In Our Time* (New York: Charles Scribner's Sons, 1958), 81.

Country" recently published in *The Nick Adams Stories* portrays vividly the experiences of the senses and the working of memory, but Hemingway could make nothing of it because he "worked too close to life"[9]—he had not written about country ". . . so it would be there like Cézanne had done it." With his excellent critical sense, Hemingway rejected this fragment. Others he had not rejected, like "Out of Season" and "A Day's Wait" which were too close and unrealized.

Harry knows, too, that fragments are not art, but surely such an insight does not constitute some kind of redemption. Unlike his creator, Harry has not gone beyond the stage of the minor Nick Adams vignettes. In one respect one might say that Harry's artistic development is more primitive—since the title *In Our Time* tends to fuse all the diverse elements into one vision. The projection by Hemingway of what he might have been or might become is clear in the contrast between Harry's fragmented memory and the consummated art of the Nick Adams stories.

Possibly the ultimate revelation of Harry's spiritual bankruptcy may be in the lack of coherent structure in the memories and Harry's pessimistic preoccupation with a meaningless death. The flashbacks are essentially chaotic beginning with thoughts of snow, which is not necessarily a preservative because there are messy deaths in snow just as there are on the plain. These memories reveal Harry's preoccupation with death and his moral failings, but he himself sees no meaning in his death. Of course there are "still moments" such as the skiing incident which contrast with this preoccupation. His last memory recalls death without redemption, the soldier caught in the wire begging for death. God can send one more pain than he can endure. The plane journey should be seen too as another fragment. While all the other interludes explored Harry's memory of the past, this one projects another fantasy into the future. Although it is not placed in italics like Harry's thoughts, the narrator reports what Harry projects. The flashbacks reveal not only a failed life, but a chaotic death.

The narrator has not been objective in describing Harry's death on the plains of Africa. Previously he had criticized him, "He slipped into the familiar lie he made his bread and butter by." The critical narrator has passed a value judgment. So too at the end the narrator doesn't present what is in Harry's mind, but a satiric report of what might pass through his consciousness. The journey becomes another of Harry's unrealized experiences, another one of Harry's failures—the narrator comments on the unrealized act which takes on ironic implications by contrast with other unrealized experiences. Throughout, the narrator cleverly contrasted Harry's return from undigested experience to the reality of dying: so too does the reader come back from the fantasy of salvation to the reality of the green leg. The incidents

9. Ernest Hemingway, *The Nick Adams Stories* (New York: Charles Scribner's Sons, 1972).

indicate the futility of the trip unrealized. As the raw experiences turn into fantasies which replace the consummation of art, the trip is a fantasy without the consummation of salvation. The leopard, too, in this context is an ironic counterpart to point up the futility of the journey—he is everything Harry is not. The author did not strive and brave the snows of neglect and poverty and exert self-discipline, but rather had rested in safety with his final trip a gentle lark, flying over the plains and mountains to reach the top comfortably.[10]

In presenting the chaotic life of a failed artist, Hemingway tackled a special problem (on the same order of making a boring character interesting). Harry's reminiscences had to hold the reader's attention at the same time that they could be evaluated as raw experience rather than imaginative, artistic reconstructions. In presenting vivid recollections of experience (the province of those who are not artists) he gives the reader experiences still not vitalized by the selectivity of art, but still interesting in the vividness of the senses as unrealized experiences. Hemingway can maintain the reader's interest, but still give an inchoate jumble of jigsaw pieces which do not codify.

II

What the experiences reveal is not Harry's sensibility or artistry, but illuminate his character and failure of vision. Harry confirms this observation, "Now he would never write the things that he had saved to write until he knew enough to write them well. Well, he would not have to fail at trying to write them either. Maybe you could never write them, and that was why you put them off and delayed the starting." He affirms his talent, but here he recognizes his problem as a lack of vision and possibly of soul. He reveals too that his marriages and easy life had possibly been a screen for his lack of vision, a further excuse for not writing because essentially he had nothing to say.

At this time Hemingway was fascinated with the professional and personal problems of the artist. In a conversation with an improbable Austrian in the middle of the African plain, he responded to a question of what it takes to write honest prose. Hemingway said there must be great talent and, "Then there must be discipline. The discipline of Flaubert. Then there must be the conception of what it can be and an absolute conscience as unchanging as the standard meter in Paris, to prevent faking. Then the writer must be intelligent and disinterested and above all he must survive."[11] Obviously Harry

10. Jackson Benson, *The Writer's Art of Self Defense* (Minneapolis: University of Minnesota Press, 1969) has some useful ironic observations on the last journey, ". . . Harry is provided with a slick-magazine exit which comes just in time, like the cavalry, and wafts him over pink clouds and a picture landscape to his own Shangri-La."

11. Ernest Hemingway, *Green Hills of Africa* (New York: Charles Scribner's Sons, 1935), 27.

had no discipline, and he became a fake. The artist can fake his personal life for the sake of his art, but when he plays the "artist" to fake his personal life, he is a total sham. His lying is not a screen to protect his art, but a way to avoid his art. He never had an "absolute conscience," for he was ready to sell himself quickly. Curiosity, his last line of defense, proves itself simply that. A voyeur has curiosity as well, but Harry's has not been disciplined. Rather than representing a great soul and imagination striving to integrate experience and the human sense of comedy and tragedy, based on concrete reality, his curiosity has been the reflex action of a well developed sensitive organism—certainly a requirement for artistic talent, but it must be transcended by his own vision. One need only to compare the disciplined vision and talent of the esthetic Flaubert with the fake Harry—one the man of integrity, the other a sham. Here then the problem of Harry is defined not merely as a lack of talent, but lack of soul.

Lack of commitment has led to a loss of selfhood. In the same conversation with the Austrian, Hemingway says concerning lack of accomplishment in American writers, "Others are ruined by the first money, the first praise, the first attack, the first time they find they cannot write, or the first time they cannot do anything else, or then they get frightened and join organizations that do their thinking for them." Hemingway has presented here a program of the things Harry did not and did do. Harry had been ruined by the first money. But before that he had not known where his true self could be found. He sent a love letter to his first wife which he dishonestly seeks to hide from his second. When he copulates his way into the world of the rich, he lies to himself claiming he is a spy, but actually he cannot find the locus of his personality. He is of them and against them at the same time. A man who has lacked vision, integrity, and greatness of soul, and one who has disintegrated morally to the point of losing his self-orientation finally finds death boring:

> "No, he thought, when everything you do, you do too long, and do too late, you can't expect to find the people still there. The people all are gone. The party's over and you are with your hostess now.
>
> I'm getting as bored with dying as with everything else, he thought."

The finale then does not justify his curiosity. Even the one great journey of everyman has escaped the possibilities for creative thought on his part. The dying scene merely sums up the man he was. The memories instead of defining a great talent present a man consumed by selfish sensuality rather than a passionate interest in the meaning of experience. The experiences are either pointless fragments of memory well presented, or scenes from his life which show neither love, devotion, nor charity but rather aimless sensuality, self-indulgence, or deception.

These negative qualities are very evident in his relations with women. In addition to the memories and his thoughts on dying, the most important element in the fictive action of the story is the relation to his wife. These last scenes rather than pointing to a man on the way to redemption as he rejects the wife who represents death in life, confirm us in the type of man he was and is. Surely one is tempted to condemn her superficiality, and the syndicated clichés put the teeth on edge—he looks like a hero when he retorts to her bland, wealthy suburban banalities. But his fretful, testy opposition does not qualify for redemption. She married him not only to bask in his glory, but out of a profound need based on a normal but fairly unhappy life of a rich woman. She is what she is—there is nothing false, or cruel, or unkind about her. She is a fairly good-natured, bland woman who likes to please her husband. She is no emasculator, etc. If Hemingway had wished to present such, he could do so very well. She herself is not death in life, but the death in life he chooses to make her. His realization of his offense does not mitigate his guilt or save him. Through most of the story he treats her with unwarranted cruelty: surely the action speaks to the reader and helps formulate the theme. She is the object of the scorn which he finally turns on its proper object: himself.

His relations with women reveal a life without glory or honesty. He says that he is loved more when he lies. Possibly this is true because his true self is not very lovable, and/or he can lie better than he can love. He is callous in the essential life of the heart. He leaves a dull companion alone for the Armenian whore. He betrays his second wife. And finally he does not love this wife who has approached him with fundamental honesty. One often hears of Hemingway's chauvinistic treatment of women, but such an evaluation is based on a one-sided reading of his works such as *A Farewell To Arms*. Often the women are the victims of callous indifferent men such as can be found in "Hills Like White Elephants" or "Cat in the Rain." Women in Hemingway can be flawed and decent, as this woman is. Possibly she deserves some of his scorn, but the marriage to such a shallow but clinging and devoted woman indicates his lack of soul, not hers, and his behavior at the end indicates not conversion but nasty petulance.

The critic should not be impressed by his self-flagellation, nor should the analogy to the dying sinner with his death-bed confession lead one astray. Has Harry finally achieved greatness of soul, vision, compassion, or even honesty? I don't think so. Harry views his life in despair much as the characters in Dante's hell reveal themselves with honesty, but they are lost.

The death images confirm this reading. Death to Harry can be two policemen, but it is the hideous animal, the hyena with the stinking breath. A man gets the death he deserves, and the rotted leg and the repulsive animal sum up a life. One thinks of Svidrigaylov in *Crime and Punishment* who thinks of death and eternity as a dirty bath house with spiders. He too had some honesty, but there is no redemption. Harry is bored with death, and he dies on the plain with the heat, vultures, and hyena.

Within the context of this analysis the problem of the symbols can more easily be solved. The leopard has caused more problems and spilled more ink than his changing spots warrant. More fruitful might be to observe the symbols embedded in a narrative structure, as reinforcing rather than determining theme.

The cluster of mountain-snow-leopard might lose much of its confusing ambiguity if it is seen as reinforcing specific meanings of a particular incident rather than determining overall meaning. Surely the death in the snow of the Austrians on leave cannot represent a life in death theme or the snows-in-the-mountains preservative theme. Rather we see it as another example of Harry's sensate memory and fragmented sensibility. The question at the end of Hemingway's epigraph presents difficulties. He had read about the leopard incident in travel books where it was reported as actually seeking big-horned sheep, but the narrator asks a question. The narrator who had satirized Harry and reported his plane journey, throws out at the beginning an enigma, but the question has negative relevance. The image of grace, control, and courage in the leopard (see *The Green Hills of Africa* for Hemingway's classification of noble and ignoble animals) could not possibly apply to Harry: the narrative movement and moral incidents contradict such a reading. The man who has morally and professionally failed, who has little sense of identity, who has taken the easy way is properly dying on the plain. The airplane trip contrasts in its ease with the difficult ascent of the leopard. One thinks of Hawthorne's "Celestial Railroad" with Mr. Smooth-it-Away's scorn of the pilgrims who go on foot, for now we have the railroad, but the train plummets to hell and the pilgrims continue their ascent. Harry knows he is going to the top, but nothing justifies this. It is another of his self-deceptions, reinforced by the vivid contrast with the striving, dead leopard. There is no shift to salvation in the story. The journey and the leopard-snow-mountain contrast rather than fuse with Harry's life.

To reinforce such a reading of the symbolism, a glance at Hemingway's most successful stories written at the time might be illuminating. In "A Clean, Well-Lighted Place" the old man's integrity which defies the enclosing darkness contrasts nicely with Harry's petulance and fragmented memory. The old man has defined the area of his courage and dignity, Harry has not. In "The Short Happy Life of Francis Macomber" the hero does not live until he proves himself. He has met his own highest expectations by doing the difficult thing, by facing himself honestly. The bitchy wife refuses to redeem herself by dedication to her rejuvenated husband. In the "Snows" the wife becomes victim. Hemingway may have written his most pessimistic story of the three. A moral redemption is real in the other stories, but in

"Snows" the redemption is spurious. The story reflects as Mr. Carlos Baker hinted not only a vision of what Hemingway might be, but a nightmare vision of what he might have been and still might be.

The ultimate irony of course is that the achieved story itself denies its possible premises. The high achievement, the profusion of material, and the suggestiveness as well as the great moral honesty which infuses the narrative result in a great work. The encounter with the projected self comes out honestly and triumphantly—here Hemingway does not fake. He reached into the well and pulled out a fascinating spore, full of disease and real.

Character, Irony, and Resolution in "A Clean, Well-Lighted Place" / *Warren Bennett*

Interpretation of Hemingway's short story "A Clean, Well-Lighted Place" has always been confronted with the illogical dialogue sequence between the two waiters. Since analysis probably became stalled on the question of which waiter knew about the old man's attempted suicide, interpretation has tended to center on either the older waiter's *nada* prayer or the problem of the illogical sequence itself.[1] The result seems to be a partial misinterpretation of the character of the younger waiter, a failure to see the wide play of irony in the story, and the absence of any interpretation of the story's ironic resolution.

However, before these latter matters can be successfully dealt with, the story's troubled dialogue must still be preliminarily considered. Scribner's claims that the dialogue inconsistency occurred when a slug of type was evidently misplaced in the first printing of the story in *Scribner's* magazine in

Warren Bennett, "Character, Irony, and Resolution in 'A Clean, Well-Lighted Place,' " *American Literature*, XLII (March 1970), 70–79. Reprinted by permission of the publisher. Copyright © 1970, Duke University Press.

1. See Robert Penn Warren, Introduction, *A Farewell to Arms* (New York, 1949), pp. xv–xvi; Mark Schorer, ed., *The Story: A Critical Anthology* (New Jersey, 1950), p. 427; Carlos Baker, *Hemingway: The Writer as Artist* (New Jersey, 1952), p. 124; F. P. Kroeger, "The Dialogue in 'A Clean, Well-Lighted Place,' " *College English*, XX (Feb., 1959), 240–241; William E. Colburn, "Confusion in 'A Clean, Well-Lighted Place,' " *College English*, XX (Feb., 1959), 241–242; Otto Reinert, "Hemingway's Waiters Once More," *College English*, XX (May, 1959), 417–418; Edward Stone, "Hemingway's Waiters Yet Once More," *American Speech*, XXXVII (Oct., 1962), 239–240; Joseph F. Gabriel, "The Logic of Confusion in Hemingway's 'Clean, Well-Lighted Place,' " *College English*, XXII (May, 1961), 539–546; John V. Hagopian, "Tidying Up Hemingway's 'Clean, Well-Lighted Place,' " *Studies in Short Fiction*, I (Winter, 1964), 140–146.

1933, and since reprint plates were made from that printing and not from the original manuscript, which is no longer extant to anyone's knowledge, the error was perpetuated until 1965.[2] At that time Scribner's issued a new edition of *The Short Stories of Ernest Hemingway* and made an "editorial" correction in the illogical sequence because the dialogue dictated it.

All texts from 1933 to 1965:

> "His niece looks after him."
> "I know. You said she cut him down."

The 1965 text and all subsequent printings:

> "His niece looks after him. You said she cut him. down."
> "I know."[3]

This solved the problem of the illogical sequence, but because it gives the knowledge of the old man's attempted suicide to the older waiter instead of the younger waiter, it is contrary to some critical opinion and compatible with others. The correction, therefore, traded one kind of question for another kind: since Hemingway did not correct his own story during his lifetime, does that make the old text Hemingway's story and the new text his publisher's story? Should the critic use the old text or the new text?

In order to put my own interpretation on a firm footing, I hope to demonstrate, first of all, that even though no corrections were made in the story, it is still possible to determine that the older waiter is the one who knows about the old man's attempted suicide.

The structure of the story is based on a consistent polarity: "despair," characterized by depth of feeling and insight into the human condition, in opposition to "confidence," characterized by a lack of feeling and, therefore, a lack of insight. Each pole is seen as an attitude, or stance, in relation to Hemingway's *donnée*, which is a nihilistic concept of life: nothingness or *nada*. The spark which ignites the conflict of stances is the deaf old man who has tried to commit suicide and needs a clean, well-lighted cafe in which to stay late. The denouement is an irony of fate, presented by image and understatement, which will shatter "confidence" against the hard truth that "it [is] all a nothing and a man [is] nothing too."

The tension of the conflict is rendered almost exclusively through the dialogue of the two waiters, who are said to be of "two different kinds," and we can identify one waiter by tracing the use of the word "kill." When the

---

2. Information concerning the correction is in letters to the author from Mr. L. H. Brague, Jr., editor, Charles Scribner's Sons, and from Professor Philip Young of Pennsylvania State University. I would like to express my appreciation to Mr. Brague and Professor Young for their help.

3. *The Short Stories of Ernest Hemingway* (New York, 1965), pp. 379–383. All subsequent references will be to this text.

younger waiter returns from taking the old man's brandy order, he says to the older waiter, " 'I'm sleepy. I never get into bed before three o'clock. He should have *killed himself* last week' " (italics mine). Then when the younger waiter takes the brandy out to the old man, he says to him, " 'You should have *killed yourself* last week' " (italics mine). Since there is no textual basis for transferring the younger waiter's mode of expression to the older waiter, the text clearly establishes that it is the younger waiter who asks for further information: " 'What did he want to *kill himself* for?' " (italics mine). Consequently, it is the older waiter who knows the history of the old man and speaks the first line of dialogue in the story: " 'Last week he tried to commit suicide.' "

This is supported by a structural pattern, utilizing verbal irony, which is repeated in three separate scenes—two formerly in question and one not in question. For the pattern to emerge clearly, it is necessary to look at the scenes in reverse order, beginning with the scene where the lines are not in question. The scene is the bodega where the older waiter stops for a drink.

"What's yours?" asked the barman. [Serious question.]
"Nada." [Verbal irony: the older waiter.]
"Otro loco mas," said the barman and turned away. [Dropping the subject.]
"A little cup," said the waiter. [Serious reply.]

The bodega barman, of course, must be equated with the younger waiter because he has an "unpolished" bar, equivalent to the younger waiter pouring into the old man's brandy glass until it "slopped over and ran down the stem." Also, the barman calls the older waiter "another crazy one," as the younger waiter has accused the older waiter of "talking nonsense." But for our purposes, the important aspect is the pattern: serious question, verbal irony by the older waiter, a dropping of the subject, and then a serious reply. The significant factor in the pattern is the older waiter's use of verbal irony in response to a serious question.

The complete pattern appears earlier in the story, in that exchange concerned with why they cut the old man down.

"Why did they do it?" [Serious question.]
"Fear for his soul." [Verbal irony: the older waiter.]
"How much money has he got?" [Dropping the subject; serious question.]
"He's got plenty." [Serious reply.]

The third scene is the first exchange between the two waiters, near the beginning of the story. The pattern here is abbreviated, repeating only the older waiter's use of verbal irony in response to a serious question. One waiter says the old man was in despair, and the other waiter asks,

"What about?" [Serious question.]
"Nothing." [Verbal irony: the older waiter.]
"How do you know it was nothing?" [Serious question.]
"He has plenty of money." [Verbal irony: the older waiter.]

In this last scene, the reply, "nothing," and the reply, "he has plenty of money," both carry an undertone of irony, regardless of which waiter speaks the lines.⁴ The irony is inherent in them as answers to the serious questions asked. For example, if the younger waiter answered that the old man was in despair about "nothing," the reply still carries the charge of double meaning, i.e., a serious meaning: there was, in fact, no apparent reason; *and* a malicious meaning: the reason seems ridiculous and unimportant to me: he was only feeling sorry for himself.

Since verbal irony is employed, we must look to the text for hard evidence of which waiter employs it as a mode of speaking, and that evidence is in the scene with the bodega barman. It is the *older* waiter who uses verbal irony; he even thinks ironically: "After all, he said to himself, it is probably only insomnia. Many must have it." There is no definite evidence, anywhere in the story, that the younger waiter has mastered such a manner of speaking, or thinking. On the contrary, the younger waiter is consistently serious and changes his form of address only once, "speaking with that omission of syntax stupid people employ when talking to drunken people or foreigners."

Once it has been established that the older waiter is the one who knows about the old man, it is then possible to see the characters of the two waiters in correct perspective.

Essentially, the younger waiter is not a "materialist," as critics, explicitly or implicitly, have tried to make him. Expressing interest in money and sex does not automatically relegate one to the pigeonhole labeled "materialist," which critics like to use in a pejorative sense, although it should not be so used. Materialism denotes a complex set of ideas, and to the extent that the story is held to have philosophical import, the philosophical senses of "materialism" must be recognized.

Briefly, a materialist is one who affirms matter as the only reality, or one who gives it an effective priority. Looking at the two waiters in this light, it is the older waiter who holds the view which is most compatible with philosophic materialism, not the younger waiter.

It is better, undoubtedly, to avoid classifying the younger waiter at all,

4. It is interesting to note that the line, "He has plenty of money," is reminiscent of the famous exchange between Hemingway and F. Scott Fitzgerald which Hemingway recorded in "The Snows of Kilimanjaro": "He remembered poor Julian and his romantic awe of them and how he had started a story once that began, 'The very rich are different from you and me.' And how some one had said to Julian, Yes, they have more money" (p. 72). The story was "The Rich Boy," which appeared in *Red Book Magazine* in January and February, 1926.

than to misclassify him. The most we can do with the younger waiter is describe him, an effort which results in showing him to be something of a "type," the average individual, "in a hurry." He is self-interested and indulges himself with believing an hour is " 'more to me than to him [the old man].' " He does not especially like work, and accuses the old man of having " 'no regard for those who must work' "; nevertheless, he seems to accept it as economically necessary and is quite an efficient waiter, making sure the shutters are closed before he leaves. He is satisfied with his marriage and is eager to get home to his wife "waiting in bed" for him. He is a legalist in his attitude toward the soldier, although even when refusing to serve the old man, he does not "wish to be unjust. He was only in a hurry." He is no Christian zealot but accepts the church with its transcendent values, illustrated by his changing the subject to money when told the niece cut the old man down because of "fear for his soul." In short, he is one of those who have "confidence," or faith, in the established system in which they live. He has " 'youth, confidence, and a job . . . everything.' " His job gives him a sense of economic success within the community. The institution of marriage has provided him with a "waiting" wife who satisfies the biological drive and gives him a sense of male effectiveness. His youth gives him a sense of life as infinite continuum, and the institution of the church confirms such immortality for him. " 'I have confidence,' " he says, " 'I'm all confidence,' " and as long as he has this confident faith in the value and permanence of these cultural structures, he has "everything."

The older waiter, on the other hand, is unable to muster such faith or confidence. He *is* a materialist and beyond the material there is "nothing." "Some lived in it and never felt it but he knew it all was nada y pues nada y nada y pues nada." The individual "cannot find anything to depend upon either within or outside himself."[5] There is no a priori order or value system, either providential, natural, or social, on which man may intelligently depend and predict a future. " 'No. I have never had confidence and I am not young.' " The material world, which includes the mental processes, is the only reality and has priority, but it is found lacking: life is a net of illusions. " 'And what do you lack?' " asks the younger waiter. " 'Everything but work,' " replies the older waiter. And even the ability to "work" has been taken from the old man, as it evidently was from Hemingway by July 2, 1961.

This profound, but masked "difference" between the two waiters is imbedded in the casual-appearing conversation about the old man. When the younger waiter asks, " 'How do you know [the old man's despair was about] nothing,' " the reply, " 'He has plenty of money,' " is more philosophically precise than an entire chapter of discursive contortions. *Nada* can be de-

5. Jean Paul Sartre, "Existentialism Is a Humanism," *Existentialism from Dostoevsky to Sartre*, ed. Walter Kaufmann (Cleveland, 1956), p. 295.

scribed only in terms of an opposite because to make some-thing out of no-thing is not only incomprehensible but impossible.[6] And "plenty of money" provides the most nearly perfect polar opposite to "nothing." The holes in a fish net are perceptible because of the net. When a man has the power of money and the plenty which it makes possible, it also makes the "lack," *nada*, that much more apparent and unbearable. "Plenty" intensifies what is lacking to the psychological breaking point. The old man's severe despair, and the serious despair of the older waiter, are not caused by some-thing, and are not *about* anything. Despair is a negation, a lack. The lack of life after death, the lack of a moral order governing the universe, the lack of trustworthy interpersonal relations, the lack of an ordering principle in the individual consciousness, the lack of the ability to work, and the lack, there-fore, of even self-respect and dignity. The old man lacks any-thing to live *for*. " 'It was a nothing he [the older waiter] knew too well.' "

However, to quit the story on the philosophical level is to leave the pri-mary question of "confidence" or "despair" artistically unanswered. The younger waiter would go confidently home to his "waiting wife" and live happily ever after: a winner who takes everything.[7] The older waiter's *nada* is "probably only insomnia" and will pass with daylight, which, if not a happy ending, is at least a very tolerable ending. This is essentially an uncommitted balance, which is where interpretation to date has left it.

But this is to understand only the "literal" ending of the story; that is, what happens to the older waiter after *he* leaves the cafe. It does not reveal what happens when the younger waiter arrives home. For this insight, which Hemingway refers to as the "real end," which may be "omitted" on the basis of his "new theory," it is necessary to go back into the story.[8]

6. Jean Paul Sartre seems to fall into this linguistic trap when he describes nothing-ness in *L'Etre et le néant*: "c'est au sein même de l'être, en son coeur, comme un ver" (Paris, 1943, p. 57).

7. "A Clean, Well-Lighted Place" was included by Hemingway in a collection of rather bitter stories, *Winner Take Nothing* (New York, 1933), pp. 17–24.

8. Ernest Hemingway, *A Moveable Feast* (New York, 1964), p. 75. The complete statement is as follows:

It was a very simple story called "Out of Season" and I had omitted the real end of it which was that the old man hanged himself. This was omitted on my new theory that you could omit anything if you knew that you omitted and the omitted part would strengthen the story and make people feel something more than they understood.

Well, I thought, now I have them so they do not understand them. There can-not be much doubt about that. There is most certainly no demand for them. But they will understand the same way that they always do in painting. It only takes time and it only needs confidence.

Professor Philip Young refers to the passage in his book *Ernest Hemingway: A Re-consideration* (New York, 1966), p. 285, and cites three stories for which we already have an answer: "Out of Season," "Fathers and Sons," and "Big Two-Hearted River." Suicides are omitted from the first two stories, and the fact that Nick Adams has just returned from the war is omitted in the third.

In the silence that takes place immediately following the older waiter's ironic " 'He has plenty of money,' "

A girl and a soldier went by in the street. The street light shone on the brass number on his collar. The girl wore no head covering and hurried beside him.

Y.W. "The guard will pick him up," one waiter said.
O.W. "What does it matter if he gets what he's after?"
Y.W. "He had better get off the street now. The guard will get him. They went by five minutes ago."

The younger waiter emphasizes the military guards because to him they represent guardians of a culture in which one may be confident of success. He is not concerned about the soldier. Individual needs, whether they are the need of a girl or the need of a drink for a lonely old man, must be sacrificed to the punctualities of the job, the ignorant securities of rule and routine. The younger waiter wants everyone off the street, as he wants the old man out of the cafe. He wants to be off the streets himself, and is, in fact, also a kind of guard. " 'No more tonight. Close now,' " he says to the old man and begins "pulling down the metal shutters."

But the older waiter does understand that agonizing lack in an individual: " 'What does it matter if he gets what he's after?' " Company punishment will be minor compared to the anguish of being alone. Everything is a temporary stay against despair: a light for the night, another drink, relations with a girl. " 'You can't tell,' " even the old man " 'might be better with a wife.' "

The soldier's kinship with the older waiter and the old man is illustrated by the metaphor of light and something clean or polished. "The street light shone on the brass number of his collar." They are all of a "kind," the soldier as disillusioned with the military machine as the older waiter and the old man are disillusioned with the machine of the world. The soldier is not concerned about curfew as the older waiter is not concerned about closing the cafe on time, and the old man is not concerned about letting the cafe close. The soldier needs the sexual intoxication of this girl as the older waiter and the old man need a drink. The soldier is no more concerned about military regulations than the old man is concerned about financial regulations, and "would leave without paying" if he became too drunk. "As Hemingway once put it, 'There is honor among pickpockets and honor among whores. It is simply that the standards differ.' "[9]

The scene—a prostitute and a soldier—is the epitome of a meaningless and chaotic world full of loopholes: an interwoven fabric of ironies punctured by nothingness. Everything is possible through love or aggression, but

9. Young, p. 64.

268 The Short Stories of Ernest Hemingway

paradoxically nothing is permanent. There is a constant, desperate struggle against the coefficients of adversity. Living becomes a deadly affair, or conflict, essentially devoid of humor because everything is ultimately a "dirty trick."[10]

This is the basis for the older waiter's not so funny "joke" later in the story. The younger waiter has just suggested that the old man could buy a bottle and drink at home, to which the older waiter replies, " 'It's not the same.' "

> "No, it is not," agreed the waiter with a wife. He did not wish to be unjust. He was only in a hurry.
> "And you? You have no fear of going home before your usual hour?"
> "Are you trying to insult me?"
> "No, hombre, only to make a joke."
> "No," the waiter who was in a hurry said . . . "I have confidence. I am all confidence."

The joke is crucial and hinges directly on the scene with the girl and the soldier. Structurally and texturally they establish the love wound motif which is so dominant in Hemingway that it becomes the other side of the same psychic coin as the war wound. Through either the death of one of the partners or the inability of one partner to fulfill the promise of love—satisfy the other's needs—an individual is isolated and pushed to despair by the failure of the love alliance.

The complete working out of this motif is the "real end" which Hemingway omitted, and the phrase "waiter with a wife" preceding the joke, functions as a lens to bring into focus the catastrophe which the younger waiter will face. When the younger waiter goes home before his "usual time," his wife will be gone, or perhaps, though at home in bed, engaged in another desperate relationship. The girl and the soldier appear again like ghosts, only this time the girl without a "head covering," ironically "hurrying," is suggestive of the younger waiter's wife.

The story now becomes superbly charged with dramatic as well as verbal irony. The younger waiter's confidence dissolves into tragic hubris, and his statements, such as " 'I'm not lonely,' " are imbued with an impending doom that is near classic. Situations become ironically transferred. The old man's despair and loneliness without a wife, the older waiter's insomnia and need of light, the soldier's risk for temporary sexual meaning—all are now the younger waiter's future. At the very moment that he is playing the heartless and uncompromising judge, he is also reality's dupe and victim. Whatever he has said about the others may soon be said about him. And with equal

---

10. Ernest Hemingway, *A Farewell to Arms* (New York, 1957), p. 331. Shortly after Frederic Henry has prayed "Please, please, dear God, don't let her die," Catherine says "I'm not a bit afraid. It's just a dirty trick."

irony, he has "hurried" to his own undoing. His all-confident intentions will be reversed. His recognition of another truth is imminent. The radical contingencies of life will have taught him the absurdity of the human condition, and the twist of events will topple him from his pinnacle of confidence into the phantasmagoria where the older waiter and the old man cling despairingly to their clean, well-lighted place. The younger waiter will become a new member of Hemingway's collection: *Winner Take Nothing*.

4. An Overview of the Short Stories

Ernest Hemingway as Short Story Writer / *Jackson J. Benson*

The real mastery of the Hemingway stories lies in a delicacy of touch, a subtlety of minute shadings. Malcolm Cowley, in his famous *Portable* introduction, pointed out that Hemingway was not simply or even primarily a realist or naturalist, but more closely related in his work to the dark writers out of our literary Renaissance, to Poe and the terror of incipient violence, to Hawthorne and psychological outrage, and to Melville and the questions of identity, innocence, and guilt. Such a relationship as described by Cowley says more, however, about Hemingway's themes, than it does about the texture of the stories. In texture they can be more profitably compared to the stories of Henry James—although they would seem at first to be quite different in conception.

The great thing in much of Hemingway's short fiction, as in James's, is not so much what happens, but what doesn't happen. Although he uses symbols, Hemingway is not a Symbolist nor is he a Romantic; his best work shows the care, restraint, and control more often associated with the Classical tradition. In the manner of James, Hemingway is a master of rhythm and of structure, and the essence of what he is saying often lies in what is suggested or left unsaid. Thus, as I have suggested elsewhere, Hemingway works as an architect, carefully constructing a classic arch, moving from a finely wrought definite center to suggest dimensions operating in all directions to the "outside."

Although Hemingway's central figures characteristically try not to think about things, they always do. Like so many James characters, they are worriers who react to very subtle clues in a world tinted in an array of potential significance, and whose conflicts are carried on in the ghostly reflections of their psyches in their environment. The world of "Big Two-Hearted River" has a rough proximity to the world of "The Turn of the Screw" and "The Beast in the Jungle." Both worlds are paradoxically very detailed and immediate in terms of experience, yet very abstract—nearly anonymous people have intense experiences in a sort of mental envelope which excludes both the necessities of everyday life and the remedies we all count on.

While the similarities can be illuminating, the comparison eventually breaks down, for essentially, the James story is but a modification of the traditional form, whereas the Hemingway story marks a significant advance in a new direction. What makes the difference, I think (and as I will subsequently try to show), was that while Hemingway acquired an extensive knowledge of the literature of fiction, he was never literary. And the fact that he was not literary, that like Jay Gatsby he sprang from his Platonic conception of himself,[1] made him modern in a way that no other major writer would become modern.

In an essay on Pound, Joyce, and Flaubert, Forest Read makes a statement about Joyce's contribution to the short story that might be applied with even more justice to Hemingway:

> In 1914, Joyce appeared as a prose imagist who invented a new form for short prose fiction; based on the form of an emotion rather than the form of the short story, it was perfectly adapted to register modern life both objectively and as it struck the sensitive individual.[2]

Hemingway may, of course, have taken some of his cues from Joyce (as well as from a number of other writers, as I shall bring out in a moment). But in any case, it was the Hemingway manner which carried the new form into the position of dominant influence which it has held for nearly a half century, since Joyce could not carry the form into the truly modern. Both his style and his sense of man's condition were too closely linked to the past. For Joyce, as well as for Ezra Pound, T. S. Eliot, and Henry James, modern man's problem was that he was cut off from the past. For Hemingway, the past didn't really matter for itself; it only mattered as it was sensed as a part of present experience.

Those writers which I have mentioned above were all highly educated men. Hemingway had an advantage that enabled him alone among his contemporaries to become the true modern: he was not well educated and his concern, directed by his seminal experiences as a journalist, was concentrated on the contemporary. Those elements from the past which appear in his stories, Catholicism and the ritual of the bullfight for example, are inevitably viewed (and ultimately evaluated) as components of the immediate. He was, in short, the true existentialist, interested in the ongoing emotional condition of man within his immediate environment. As all our textbooks tell us, James, Pound, and Eliot went to Europe in order to embrace a richer tradition, to find a climate more accommodating to the artist, and to absorb that sense of the past so abundant abroad, but so often lacking in the United States. Hemingway carried that lack with him. He went to Europe to live more cheaply and to improve his technical skill. To caricature the difference

1. I have borrowed this application of *The Great Gatsby* from an essay by George Wickes, "Sketches of the Author's Life in Paris in the Twenties," in *Hemingway in Our Time*, ed. Richard Astro and Jackson J. Benson (Corvallis: Oregon State University Press, 1974), p. 32.

2. Forrest Read, "Pound, Joyce, and Flaubert: The Odysseans," in Eva Hesse, ed., *New Approaches to Ezra Pound* (Berkeley and Los Angeles: University of California Press, 1969), p. 131.

—and it is an extremely important difference—Hemingway was a newspaperman, whereas Joyce, Pound, and Eliot were scholars. Hemingway could never wear the mask of the artist or of the man of letters; it was inimical to his whole personality. His primary mask, particularly in the early years, was that of reporter: the young man whose sensibilities encounter the "times," registering shock and dismay at each discovery of human callousness and his own vulnerability, yet managing, like a good reporter, to suppress his emotions and set aside any overt emotionalism in order to file his reports from the "front."

The reporter's mask is at once both Huck Finn on shore and Henry James's American in Europe. There is resilient, he-man fiber at the heart of each, as in the reporter, and in the heart of all of them is the rustic and the moralist. As rustic, the reporter takes nothing for granted and looks carefully at everything. As moralist, the reporter is always concerned, sometimes shocked at what he sees; he hides his bias, but tends to focus his stories on those things which upset him the most. He must be on the scene, and he must search out where the action is. But he seldom participates. His role is the observer, even if what he observes is primarily himself. He is not actor, but reactor. As Earl Rovit has expressed it, "Hemingway's exceptional forte was not to describe what he saw, but to describe himself *seeing*, to convey the complex of feeling which was evoked in him or an invented character."[3] One might add that he described himself seeing, while *seeming* to describe what he saw. This misdirection, if it can be called that, is at the heart of the Hemingway technique.

Hemingway's concern, in newsreporter fashion, was "to get it right" and to get it down in words so that it was true. To worry about how other people had in the past viewed things was to be trapped by "what you were supposed to feel, and had been taught to feel."[4] The position of the reporter is to be on the scene "away from," sending reports "back to." He is the modern transparent eyeball, completely alienated—not only from home, family, and country, not only from the past, but from any *consciousness* of the past. He finds truth not in conventions, nor traditions, nor books, but in the justice of feelings in response to experience. In rendering these experiences truly, the reporter is the modern source of truth: he will be the instruments by which we may read our weather. He does not tell "stories"; he gives you the "straight story." Any dispatch sent is a bond of honor—every story seems by its tone to tell us that—and it is the bond of a professional who takes his work very seriously, even when he is joking.

Hemingway tapped dozens of sources and shaped them with his own peculiar personality to create, with great skill, the perfect style to match our

3. *Ernest Hemingway* (New Haven: College and University Press, 1963) p. 51.
4. *Death in the Afternoon* (New York: Charles Scribner's Sons, 1932), p. 2.

cynical, literal-minded, modern sensibility, a style that appeared to be completely devoid of artifice, completely devoid of emotion, and completely devoid of the dramatic, the rhetorical, and the decorative. Such a style was really a new application of an old approach that goes back to the "true accounts" of Defoe and the early novelists. Fiction, the history of fiction tells us, must never be fiction, never "made up," but always presented as something that really happened—either history, a discovered "document," or biography, a discovered "diary." But the modern temper demands more immediacy, more authenticity, more impersonality. Dispatches are written by tough, cynical men in shirtsleeves; they are not written by Bohemians, "artists" dressed in velvet, lisping about aesthetic values at the tables of outdoor cafes. A dispatch comes out of a typewriter, into a cable, and is dispensed from a printing press. This style as a product of a personality—in marked contrast to the style of his literary friends—is clearly defined in a scene from Hemingway's Chicago days, as described by Charles A. Fenton:

> While the others discussed art and the artistic verities, and urged Hemingway to concern himself more with the permanent values of literature, he was actually subjecting himself to a rigid professional discipline. He was dismayed and angered, however . . . by too much talking in large, vague terms about writing. "Artist, art, artistic!" he would shout. "Can't we ever hear the last of that stuff!" While they talked about art, with the rather easy intensity of dilettantes, Hemingway talked about story markets, and about the fighters he was watching in Kid Howard's gym; and above all, his friends remembered, he talked about soldiering.[5]

A writer's "apprenticeship" is often used simply to indicate a period at the beginning of his career in which he writes a number of stories which are rejected for publication. In Hemingway's case, however, the term must be used literally. In fact, his apprenticeship has become *The Legend of the Writer* for all of us. In addition to writing stories and reading them to friends for comment, he set out a series of exercises for himself. During a day's activities, he would try to identify the sensations that he experienced—the smells, the color, the movement. Then at night he would try to get them down on paper. He set out to write a series of sentences, the truest sentences he could write. He wrote short scenes, and pared them down, rearranged them, and worked them over, time and time again, until he was satisfied that they were as close to the real thing as he could make them. He apprenticed himself to several of the best writers of his time and set out systematically to learn as much from them as he could. When they criticized his work, he went back and rewrote it. When accomplished writers talked, he listened. When others played,

5. *The Apprenticeship of Ernest Hemingway: The Early Years* (New York: Viking Press, 1954), p. 102.

he worked. The curious split, so characteristic of the modern temper, is well illustrated in Hemingway's character itself: he pursued his anti-Victorian rebellions with an intense Victorian energy and application.

His vision of the literary artist was the "craftsman." Behind the reporter's mask was a craftsman who set out to learn all there was to know about his "trade" of creative writing. He would beat them all. Every sentence would be a three-cushion shot, every story an iceberg, and eventually he would go on to achieve that fifth dimension in writing that had never been achieved before. In writing for a newspaper, with one trick or another, you could communicate "a certain emotion" which could be given "to any account of something that has happened on that day." [6] But he was after "the real thing," that sequence of motion and fact that made the emotion and which, if it were rendered by the craftsman purely enough, would be valid always. Behind the reporter was the craftsman, and behind the dispatch was an artifact, which had been measured true, and tooled and polished with precision:

> He wanted to be a great writer. He was pretty sure he would be. He knew it in lots of ways. He would in spite of everything. It was hard, though. . . . He felt almost holy about it. It was deadly serious. You could do it if you would fight it out. If you lived right with your eyes.[7]

I

The modern writer has often approached fiction first through experience with the short story form. His struggles with the more demanding short forms have often served to teach him his craft, and from the short story, he has moved on to the novel. Hemingway's progress as a writer in its various stages matches the typical story of the writer in our time, at least the story as it is dreamed of by creative writing students and journalists around the country. To support himself, during his apprenticeship, the writer turns to a job related to writing—newspaper work or advertising—and presumably, learns something more about writing as he writes commercially, spends his evenings attacking the magazine-rejection-slip barrier, and saves his money for the time when he can take a year off to write the great American novel. Whereas most give up the fight after the dreams of fame fade in the reality of bone-weary evenings with crying children, a wife who deserves some attention, and the price of shoes, Hemingway, with a little help from his wife's patrimony, made it work.

Hemingway knew in high school, if not earlier, that he was going to be a

6. *Death in the Afternoon*, p. 2.
7. "On Writing" in *The Nick Adams Stories* (New York: Charles Scribner's Sons, 1972), pp. 238–39.

professional writer. From the beginning, perhaps because of his early admiration for Ring Lardner, writing was associated in his mind with newspaper work. His "pre-apprenticeship" to the short story began in high school with the publication of three stories in the school literary magazine and extensive work on the school newspaper. When he had a chance to go to college, he turned it down for a job as a cub reporter on one of the nation's great newspapers at that time, the Kansas City *Star*. As nearly everyone who cares must know by now, it was on the job with the *Star* that Hemingway's style gained its basic elements. Every young reporter was expected to master the elements of the newspaper's famous style sheet:

> The *Star* included several rules which went far beyond the conventional instruction in spelling, punctuation, and grammar. These were the rules that made a *Star* training memorable. The style sheet's first paragraph . . . might well stand as the First Commandment in the prose creed which is today synonymous with the surface characteristics of Hemingway's work. "Use short sentences. Use short first paragraphs. Use vigorous English. Be positive, not negative."[8]

Hemingway did not pay much attention to the instruction in spelling, punctuation, and grammar, but this first paragraph became one of the major lessons of his apprenticeship.

Hemingway left the *Star* for service with the Red Cross as an ambulance driver on the Italian front in World War I. When he returned to Oak Park early in 1919, he took up his life again slowly, spending much of his time recuperating from his wounds, physical and emotional. A few weeks after his return, he began to work on his first professional stories. He had the usual experiences. No one wanted his stories. He carried the traditional stack of battered manuscripts with him from place to place, his only audience a victimized friend who listened while he read aloud from them. He sought the advice of a writer, an ex-newspaperman and novelist, who lived near the Hemingway summer home in Michigan.[9] But after a year of writing, he had not been able to place a single story.

In his anxiety to sell a story, Hemingway had apparently taken to studying the slick fiction of the time, for the story fragments which have survived since that period display the smart-alecky tone and the psuedo-cosmopolitan diction of the magazine fiction of that day. (Hemingway had an incredibly acute ear and a talent for mimicry—there are any number of passages in his stories and novels which parallel passages in things he must have been reading at the time.) From what little we know of his fiction of the 1919–20

8. Fenton, pp. 30–31.
9. Carlos Baker, *Ernest Hemingway: A Life Story* (New York: Charles Scribner's Sons, 1969), p. 62.

period, it has little in common with his newspaper articles written at just about the same time. There is the same kind of compartmentalization in his use of models: Hemingway tended to look only to newspaper articles for his newspaper work, only magazines and collections by short story writers for his short stories, and only novels for his novels. For his high school literary magazine, he imitated Jack London. Later, while writing his first two novels, he was heavily influenced by his reading of the novels of Laurence Sterne and Henry Fielding,[10] but there is no indication that his reading of the novels influenced the short stories that were written at nearly the same time. Each type of writing was apparently held completely separate in his mind, and it was not until he was able to break this pattern and bring his newspaper skills to his short story writing that he was able to develop his own version of the short story.

What helped Hemingway to bridge the gap from reporter to creative writer, so that the creative writer became a "reporter," was his next four years as a feature writer for the Toronto *Star Daily* and Toronto *Star Weekly*. He looked upon this writing as hack work, and complained that it took all his time and energy, yet his newspaper prose was usually better than his short story prose, and his best Toronto articles have more in common with his first important stories ("Big Two-Hearted River," "Indian Camp," "The Doctor and the Doctor's Wife") than with his previous fiction, including not only "Wolves and Doughnuts" (1919), but "Up in Michigan" (1921–22). Fortunately, Hemingway had the imposed discipline of his Kansas City training under his belt (*"Gott Mit Uns"*) when he began his work for the twin Toronto newspapers. For in Toronto he was not on the payroll, but a feature writer paid by the word, and rather than being assigned to stories or to a particular beat as he had been in Kansas City, he was largely on his own to find his subjects as he could, to approach them as he saw fit, and to set his own deadlines. The only restrictions were rather general limits on appropriate topics and style. Although Hemingway apparently didn't realize it, he was fortunate in the kind of writing he was doing, in that his entertainment articles, even his more serious foreign dispatches, were very close to the sort of writing he really wanted to do. Many of the Toronto pieces were very nearly short stories, and several later in one way or another contributed to his first published short fiction.[11] Within the loose restrictions that governed his journalism, he was free to experiment with narrative devices, tone, and style

---

10. See my article "Literary Allusion and the Private Irony of Ernest Hemingway," *Pacific Coast Philology*, IV (April 1969), 24–29.

11. For an analysis of how one dispatch is transformed into fiction, see Charles A. Fenton, "Revision of Chapter III from *In Our Time*" in this collection. See also Robert O. Stephens, *Hemingway's Nonfiction: The Public Voice* (Chapel Hill: University of North Carolina Press, 1968), and John Alexander Shtogren, Jr., "Ernest Hemingway's Aesthetic Use of Journalism," unpublished dissertation, University of Michigan 1971.

—all this, and have the pleasant certainty that the piece would be published.

But from the point of view of directly advancing Hemingway's career as a short story writer, the first two years of his association with the Toronto *Star Weekly* were as disappointing as the year of his return from the war. His disability payments had run out and the income from the few *Weekly* articles that he submitted was meagre. In the fall of 1920, he went to Chicago to look for a job. After several months he finally found a writing job with the *Cooperative Commonwealth*, a monthly slick-paper journal that publicized the activities of the Cooperative Society of America. The best that can be said of his work there was that it gave him a steady job when he needed one, and as in his work for the *Star Weekly* (which he continued to write for), he was required to write forceful, appealing prose. Hemingway quit after only a few months, however, when he learned in the spring of 1921 that the society was the front for a fraudulent stock scheme.

During these months Hemingway was writing almost constantly, for the *Cooperative Commonwealth* during the day and on his own at night. One of those with whom he shared an apartment remembered later that he "was trying any and every kind of writing at the time—he even fired out satirical rewrites of the world news to *Vanity Fair*, to no avail."[12] Only one item of fiction written during this period was published, a short, satirical sketch which was published the following year in the New Orleans *Double Dealer*. It was the first appearance of his fiction in an American magazine, and the last for several years.

In September of 1921, jobless and with no encouraging signs which forecast literary success, Hemingway was married to Hadley Richardson. She had a small income, and with that and what little Hemingway had managed to save from his *Cooperative Commonwealth* job and his occasional *Star Weekly* pieces, they resolved to go to Europe. Hemingway wanted to return to Italy, but Sherwood Anderson, whom Hemingway had come to know through his Chicago friends, talked him into Paris—the "place for a serious writer."[13] It is not entirely clear why Hemingway wanted so badly to go to Europe at this point. Part of the reason was a nostalgia for the scenes of his wartime experiences and for the freedom that he had felt in Europe. And part, no doubt, was the need for a new start—he had been making so little progress toward publication of his fiction, that it had become an obsession. "Do you think it will sell?" he invariably asked his friends in Chicago after reading one of his stories aloud to them.[14] Of course, there was also the favorable exchange rate, twelve francs for a dollar (it had been fifteen the year before). With a letter of introduction to Gertrude Stein furnished by Sherwood Anderson, the Hemingways sailed for Europe right after Thanksgiving, 1921, on the French Line's *Leopoldina*.[15]

12. Fenton, *Apprenticeship*, p. 101.   13. Baker, p. 82.
14. Fenton, p. 102.   15. Baker, p. 82.

II

We don't know exactly what or how much Hemingway's tutors taught him, since most of the instruction was private and never reported in any detail, either by Hemingway or the teachers themselves. But we do know that he had a series of them, starting with Sherwood Anderson in Chicago, and continuing with Gertrude Stein and Ezra Pound in Paris. We do know also some of the things that Hemingway's tutors were interested in at the time Hemingway was influenced by them, and we can detect changes in Hemingway's work which appear to have some relationship to the writings of his tutors.

Sherwood Anderson's influence was the only influence that Hemingway denied. Until he wrote "Out of Season" in 1923, Hemingway's fiction was highly imitative. With the publication of *Three Stories and Ten Poems* in 1923, critics immediately spotted one of the stories, "My Old Man," as an Anderson imitation. Hemingway, who had always been both vain and highly competitive, turned his embarrassment into anger against Anderson. What made Hemingway's embarrassment even more acute was that he really didn't approve of Anderson's theories of writing.

Anderson's ideas about methods of writing couldn't have been more divergent from those held by Hemingway. Whereas Anderson believed and expounded (but did not necessarily practice) a theory of spontaneous writing and talked a good deal about the role of the "artist" in society, Hemingway already was firmly committed to consciously formed and carefully revised prose and thought of himself as learning a "trade." On the other hand, Anderson's ideas and themes as subject matter could not have met more sympathetic ears, particularly at this time in Hemingway's life. In Europe during the war, Hemingway had fallen deeply in love, and had been seriously wounded and had seen death and grievous suffering. He also had had the personal freedom to eat, drink, and talk pretty much as he pleased. When he returned home, it was like casting off his mantle of manhood to assume the duties of a child again. His parents prayed and fretted over his behavior, and finally at the end of the summer before he met Anderson, they "kicked him out" over the trivial incident of a midnight beach party. Anderson was the first major writer of Hemingway's acquaintance, and he felt very much the same way about his background as Hemingway felt about his. The stories that Anderson told in the Chicago apartment about his rebellions in the repressive provinciality of small-town Ohio probably pushed Hemingway toward verbalizing his own feelings of rebellion, feelings which are so strongly expressed in his first few published stories.[16]

In his short stories of that period, Anderson repeatedly dramatized several

16. In *Winesburg, Ohio* most of the stories document the need for freedom of emotional expression within the repressive atmosphere of the small town. Several stories describe characters, such as the Reverend Curtis Hartmen and Alice Hindman, who at

attitudes that Hemingway no doubt already had, but had not yet articulated and brought into his own fiction. Two of them were later to become recurring themes in Hemingway's own work: the importance and naturalness of sex, and the destructive repression of respectability and sanctimoniousness. Until he was caught imitating Anderson, Hemingway talked about Anderson to nearly everyone he met in Paris, and for more than a year after he left Chicago, he was reading Anderson's fiction (Hemingway dutifully made it a practice to read carefuly and in depth the writings of all of his tutors). As a number of Hemingway critics have discovered, if one reads the Anderson stories of that period, those collected in *Winesburg, Ohio* and *The Triumph of the Egg*, alongside the early Hemingway stories, many parallels become immediately apparent. The parallels are evident in the first two stories Hemingway wrote in Paris in the months right after he left Chicago, "Up in Michigan" (1921–2) and "My Old Man" (1922). Both stories are so clearly derivative of Anderson's work in both theme and manner that they seem out of place when brought together with stories that Hemingway wrote only a year later.[17] The Michigan story has many characteristics which tie it to Anderson's work in general, but it is perhaps most specifically related to "Nobody Knows." Hemingway's "My Old Man" reminds one of "I'm a Fool," and even more particularly, of "I Want to Know Why."

Tying together "My Old Man" and "I Want to Know Why" are similarities in point of view, subject, plot, tone, and diction. Both stories are about boys in a race track setting. Both boys admire an older man, are influenced by him, and then find their admiration betrayed. Both boys are left puzzled and hurt by the experience. Each story is told in the first person by the boy who is characterized by slightly broken grammar and the use of adolescent slang: "Gee," "Gosh," and "swell." In "I Want to Know Why" the boy says, "I'm crazy about thoroughbred horses," and talks about the "niggers" working around the stables, whereas the boy in "My Old Man" says, "I was nuts about the horses," and talks about the "wops" at the track in Italy. In the Anderson story the boy "aches" inside at the sight of a beautiful horse, while the other boy, in similar circumstances, "felt all hollow."

Hemingway quickly jettisoned Anderson's most prominent mannerisms, but Anderson's prose texture, a mixture of the semiformal with touches of

---

one point explode as a result of their containment of emotional pressure. Others, such as Wing Biddlebaum and Elizabeth Willard, are severely crippled by the lack of understanding and compassion which characterizes their "respectable" environment. See the first part of my book, *The Writer's Art of Self-Defense* (Minneapolis: University of Minnesota Press, 1969) for a reading of the Nick Adams stories as reactions to respectability.

17. See John T. Flanagan, "Hemingway's Debt to Sherwood Anderson," *Journal of English and Germanic Philology*, LIV (October 1955), 507–20. See also Paul Preston Somers, Jr., "Sherwood Anderson and Ernest Hemingway: Influences and Parallels," unpublished dissertation, Pennsylvania State University, 1970. Particularly relevant to the discussion here is chapter 2, "A Matter of Style," pp. 37–65.

colloquial rhythm, no doubt made a permanent impression on the prose that Hemingway used in his fiction, a prose that had been stilted and artificial. The precise influence of Anderson's prose style on Hemingway's work is hard to determine, because Anderson's own style was influenced by Gertrude Stein, who later herself influenced Hemingway. Furthermore, both Stein and Anderson were influenced, in turn, by Twain, and both emphasized the importance of *Huckleberry Finn* to Hemingway, who very possibly was influenced by Twain's style directly.[18]

As the story of earliest composition among Hemingway's published short stories, "Up in Michigan" is an interesting example of the transition of a style and the interplay of stylistic influences. Carlos Baker indicates that the story was written after Hemingway arrived in Paris (winter of 1921–22), but the story itself suggests that it had been subject to a number of revisions and that the first version may have been written as early as 1919–20. A substantial part of the final version shows the influence of Anderson. The opening sentences are typically Andersonesque—beginning with the name of a character, introducing him with flat understatement, and focusing on grotesque, identifying features linked together with "and's":

> Jim Gilmore came to Hortons Bay from Canada. He bought the black-smith shop from old man Horton. Jim was short and dark with big mustaches and big hands. He was a good horseshoer and did not look much like a blacksmith even with his leather apron on.

Compare Anderson's "Paper Pills": "He was an old man with a white beard and huge nose and hands," or "Mother": "Elizabeth Willard, the mother of George Willard, was tall and gaunt and her face was marked with smallpox scars," or "The Philosopher": "Doctor Parcival was a large man with a drooping mouth covered by a yellow mustache." Then there are the indefinite adverbs and adjectives, a device used also by Twain, which are sprinkled through the Hemingway story: "Liking that made her feel funny"

18. There is no question that Hemingway was influenced by Twain's themes—see Philip Young's chapter "Adventures of Huckleberry Finn" in *Ernest Hemingway: A Reconsideration* (University Park: Pennsylvania State University Press, 1966), pp. 211–41; and Wright Morris's *The Territory Ahead: Critical Interpretations in American Literature* (New York: Atheneum, 1963), pp. 133–46.
Although I agree completely with Young's analysis and approve the justice of his comparison with Twain, I feel that there is something fundamentally misleading in the comparison as well. Twain's vision is essentially a nineteenth century one, and despite the blood and violence and shock that underlies Huck's experience (paralleling, as Young points out, the experience of Nick Adams), there is still something Norman Rockwellesque about Huck's experience also. This Rockwellesque quality is seldom reflected in the stories about Nick Adams. The stories are haunted in a way completely foreign to Twain's work, even foreign to the earlier American "writers of darkness." If one keeps the comparison with Twain too much in mind, it tends to blind us to Hemingway's essential modernity and the radicalism of his vision, a radicalism—as I point out later in this essay—which is best exposed by comparison with a writer such as Kafka.

and "When she saw the wagon coming down the road she felt weak and sick sort of inside." The indefinite modifier became, of course, a Hemingway trademark. "Up in Michigan" also shows touches of Anderson (barely) suppressed emotionalism. Except for the name, this sentence could have been lifted right out of Anderson's "Adventure": "Liz was terribly frightened, no one had ever touched her, but she thought, 'He's come to me finally. He's really come.' "

There are echoes in the story, too, of Twain's prose, whether directly from Twain or through Anderson. In addition to the "She felt weak and sick sort of inside" noted above, there is the Huckism of "he liked her face because it was so jolly" and the Twain-like diction and rhythm of the following:

> "Ain't there something left in that crock, Jimmy?" D. J. Smith asked, and Jim went out to the wagon in the barn and fetched in the jug of whiskey the men had taken hunting with them. It was a four-gallon jug and there was quite a little slopped back and forth in the bottom.

III

In addition, the third paragraph of "Up in Michigan" contains one of the two most commonly referred to examples of Gertrude Stein's influence on Hemingway's prose (the other example is in "Mr. and Mrs. Elliot" which really parodies Stein). "Up in Michigan" was written before Hemingway met Stein and it was one of the first stories that he showed her. It is unlikely that this paragraph was written until after Hemingway had read Stein's *The Making of Americans* (sometime in April or May of 1922—he had met her for the first time in March[19]) and it was added sometime before the publication of *Three Stories and Ten Poems* in July of 1923. Charles A. Fenton has discussed this paragraph in some detail as a lesson learned from Stein:

> "Liz liked Jim very much." Here, in the lead sentence, it says no more than one says casually about a dozen people each day. Then, by repetition, Hemingway strengthened and qualified it. He showed the variety and sensation of her liking. He displayed its immediacy. This was the quality Gertrude Stein had attempted to imbed in *The Making of Americans*. Hemingway also indicated his grasp of her declaration that the twentieth century was not interested in events. Midway through the paragraph, as his tutor herself did constantly, he gave the repetition a new element by using "like" as a different part of speech. Finally, as the paragraph ended, Hemingway conceived another variation, again as echo of Miss Stein's own susceptibility to it. This was "liking," the gerund.[20]

19. Fenton, p. 152; Baker, p. 86.   20. p. 153.

Repetition, of course, became another—along with the indefinite modifier, mentioned above—of the most famous characteristics of Hemingway's prose style. When critics deal with Stein's influence on Hemingway, they usually pass over the topic rather quickly with a reference to "repetition" and let it go at that. There are two problems with such a treatment: one, Stein's influence went far beyond just the use of repetition, and two, the use of repetition by Hemingway is an exceedingly complex subject, worthy of an extended study in itself.

Just to note some of the dimensions of the problem briefly—repetition in Hemingway's work is used in a number of different ways and often very subtly. His sources for the technique did not just include Stein, but probably Twain, Anderson, Joyce, and Ezra Pound as well. One technique which Twain, Anderson, and Stein share with Hemingway employs repetition to give a natural or colloquial sound to speech (and sometimes to narrative). Formal writing discourages the repetition of a noun, requiring that a pronoun or synonym be used instead; but ordinary conversation is replete with repetitions which tend to give it structure and provide unity and transitions.[21] Stein realized that normal speech does not follow the logical patterns imposed by formal writing, but is full of digressions, circular movements, and banal repetitions of introductory phrases, time-fillers and habitual expressions. Hemingway dialogue, which is based on these Stein assumptions, uses the natural rhythms of speech, for which Hemingway had an unequalled ear, and often makes conversation an undulating poem. Hemingway also uses this same kind of banal repetition for ironic purposes, as the echoing and re-echoing phrases of the opening of "The Killers" and in the repetitions "I don't want you to do it" and "it's perfectly simple" in "Hills Like White Elephants."

The other general category of repetition is that used to achieve secondary meaning. In this kind of repetition, the work of James Joyce may well have served as the primary model for Hemingway, reinforced by lessons in "Imagism" served up by Ezra Pound and lessons in nonintellectual association served up by Gertrude Stein. Pound formulated for poetry what Joyce had already been doing in prose when he stated that there are three ways that words can be charged with meaning: "You use a word to throw a visual image on to the reader's imagination, or you charge it by sound or you use groups of words to do this."[22] Hemingway seldom uses symbol in his stories; instead, he achieves secondary meaning primarily through the use of image and image patterning and various kinds of irony. (As will be argued later

21. Frank O'Conner, "A Clean Well-Lighted Place" in his collection of essays, *The Lonely Voice: A Study of the Short Story* (Toronto: Macmillan, 1965), p. 159; see also Somers, pp. 53–55.
22. *ABC of Reading* (New York: New Directions, 1960), p. 37.

in this essay, Hemingway was an "Imagist," by Pound's definition, throughout most of the period during which the bulk of his short stories was written.) Instead of using figurative language, Hemingway usually brings his language to the intensity of image through ironic use of context and through presentation in repetitive patterns. Hemingway's technique does not involve much symbolism, as we normally define it, because he works with the verbal equivalents of sensation, rather than with the association of ideation. He brings the Imagist's concept of presenting the thing to evoke the emotion together with Gertrude Stein's concept of tapping the prelogical reservoir of associations in the mind through sound and reiterative stimulation.

To take an obvious example first, from "Chapter V" of *In Our Time*, the six cabinet ministers are shot "against the wall of a hospital" and "all the shutters of the hospital were nailed shut." Aside from the glaring ironies of location (the hospital) and condition (the sick minister being shot outside the hospital with the shutters nailed closed), there is a sense of barrier (isolation, separation, and refusal) that transcends the intellectually apprehended irony to the level of sensation. This is reinforced by three repetitions of "wall," preceded by "against the"—evoking associations of hardness, unyieldingness, inescapability, inevitability. The effort here is to bring "barrier" away from its denotation as a thing into the realm of "barrier" as a set of interconnected sensations (vicarious nerve responses) and feelings (commonly shared emotional responses to certain sensations). This translation of subjective processes into objective explanation is necessarily both inadequate and incomplete. When it works, this kind of repetition achieves, like poetry, a meaning that goes beyond mere statement.

At the beginning of "In Another Country" Hemingway sets up a precise emotional analogue to the substance of the story, a theme which concerns the inevitability of "loss." The cold so permeating in the first paragraph leads us to the limbs stiffened in the war which the young narrator and the major are required to try to reanimate through the use of therapy machines. It also leads us to the pneumonia which kills the major's wife. But these connections are secondary to the feelings produced by repetition of words like "cold," "wind," "blew," and "fall." In the statement "the war was always there," "war" becomes almost a generic term for all those forces in opposition to life, which mutilate and kill, which take that which is animated and make it "stiff, heavy, and empty," either hung stiff or blown about at the will of force unopposable and inevitable.

In the fall the war was always there, but we did not go to it any more. It was cold in the fall in Milan and the dark came very early. Then the electric lights came on, and it was pleasant along the streets looking in the windows. There was much game hanging outside the shops, and the snow powdered in the fur of the foxes and the wind blew their tails. The deer hung stiff and heavy and empty, and small birds blew in the wind and the wind turned their feathers. It was a cold fall and the wind came down from the mountains.

In his essay, "A Clean Well-Lighted Place," Frank O'Connor equates this paragraph with a paragraph from Joyce, stating that "when you really know *A Portrait of the Artist as a Young Man* you recognize exactly where the beautiful opening of Hemingway's 'In Another Country' came from."[23] Perhaps—although there are probably several sources for the technique used in the passage. O'Connor does, however, put his finger on the workings of this kind of prose in a discussion of the Joyce parallel that he cites. The comments apply equally well to the Hemingway passage above (specific references to the Joyce paragraph are deleted here):

> This . . . seems to me a development of Flaubert's "proper word," a word proper to the object, not to the reader; and as well as imposing on the reader the exact appearance of the object in the manner of an illustrator, seeks also to impose on him the author's precise mood. By the repetition of key words and key phrases . . . it slows down the whole conversational movement of the prose, the casual, sinuous, evocative quality that distinguishes it from poetry and is intended to link author and reader in a common perception of the object, and replaces it by a series of verbal rituals which are intended to evoke the object as it may be supposed to be. At an extreme point it attempts to substitute the image for the reality.[24]

The point is, of course, that with such a technique as this we are no longer dealing with reality as a collation of things, but reality as experience, not "cold" as a physical phenomenon, but "cold" as a key to a complex of sensation-emotion. The modulated rhythm of such a passage is indeed a verbal ritual, almost an incantation to call up a shudder from the Jungian unconscious.

Commencing with "Indian Camp" and "Big Two-Hearted River" in 1924, Hemingway's prose takes a new direction in which repetition plays an important part. The foundation is newspaper prose—short sentences, direct statement, and simplified diction. But working from this foundation, the prose has been hardened and sharpened: it is both more intense and more formal, as well as more abstract. The formality is not that of literary prose, but that of oral literature. The emphasis is on simple words with a history, words that are haunted with associations which date back to man's earliest experiences with nature. Every Hemingway story, even the story with comic

23. p. 157.   24. p. 157.

elements, is tragic.²⁵ The tragedy of a modern event is given a timeless, mythic quality as the flat, impersonal, simplified prose, punctuated and structured by repetition, recounts the inevitable doom that overtakes nearly anonymous people in nearly anonymous settings.

Much of this ritualistic, mythic quality, which is particularly evident in the Hemingway stories of the mid-twenties, is the result of a deliberate effort by the author to achieve a literary currency which could not be dated, a mode so fundamental to human experience that like the folk epic, the fable, and the fairy tale, it would remain uneroded by the passing of literary fashions. There is little doubt, by the way, that Gertrude Stein is the primary influence in leading Hemingway in this direction, for Stein was deeply involved in Jungian theories of language and their relation to the "collective unconscious."²⁶ (The declaration on page two of *Death in the Afternoon* which talks about Hemingway's effort to transcend the kind of timelessness that can be produced by tricks in newspaper prose in order to achieve the "real thing" which will be valid "always"—usually compared to T. S. Eliot's "objective correlative"—is almost pure Stein, from beginning to end.) But from the repetition which is the result of deliberate craftsmanship, there ranges a repetition on a larger scale, from story to story, which would appear so obsessive in its emphasis on certain image relationships, that it appears to be the product of the author's own unconscious predilections. Such obsessive patterning is particularly evident in the collection of stories and vignettes, *In Our Time*, wherein we are brought back again and again to pain, mutilation

---

25. It is perhaps a mistake to use *tragic* or *tragedy* at all in such a context as this, since the grief of the historical argument probably outweighs any benefits in communication. Nevertheless, *tragic* may be the best way to describe both the mood and the central mechanism of the stories as a whole. In Richard B. Sewall's "The Vision of Tragedy" (as reprinted in *Tragedy; Vision and Form*, ed. Robert W. Corrigan, [San Francisco: Chandler Publishing Company, 1965]), the tragic vision is described as that which "recalls the original terror, harking back to a world that antedates the conceptions of philosophy, the consolations of the later religions, and whatever constructions the human mind has devised to persuade itself that its universe is secure. It recalls the original un-reason, the terror of the irrational. It sees man as questioner, naked, unaccommodated, alone, facing mysterious, demonic forces in his own nature and outside, and the irreducible facts of suffering and death" (p. 37). This describes very well, I think, the world of the short stories, even the world that lies behind such slight efforts as "A Day's Wait" and "A Very Short Story." In opposition to this world, the Hemingway "protagonist of courage" brings to bear a "greatness of spirit" (as used by D. D. Raphael in *The Paradox of Tragedy* [Bloomington: Indiana University Press, 1960], p. 26) which, no matter how meagerly maintained, is maintained with a dignity that elevates him within the artistic context of Hemingway's language. The elevated tone and narrowness of conception which have irritated so many critics (qualities which are certainly inappropriate to naturalistic and realistic writing) make an appropriate frame for the tragic tension between chaos and man's will which informs so many of the stories. Although the protagonist of courage does not meet death, literally, in every story, some kind of confrontation with death figures prominently in most of them.

26. As developed in Jung's *Studies in Word Association*, 1918.

and death in connection with birth, sex, and the female. Thus, style brings us to the man, repetition to the dark channels of Hemingway's personality.

IV

The young ambitious writer devoured what Sherwood Anderson had to offer, swallowed what he needed to go on his own way, and spit out the rest— the subject matter, the diction, the tone, and most of Anderson's rhetorical devices. What Hemingway kept was an approach to fiction. The first part of that approach is illustrated in the emotional terms of "My Old Man," wherein the adolescent, with a capacity for love and a need for justice, is confused, frustrated, and hurt by adult behavior and values. This mode gradually extends in Hemingway's work from the initiation stories, such as "Indian Camp" (1924) and "The Killers" (1926), to the grim necessity of any individual, young or old, to maintain courage and dignity in the face of nothingness, as in "A Clean, Well-Lighted Place" (1933). Following "My Old Man," the majority of Hemingway stories are strongly tied, in one way or another, to Hemingway's own life and emotions. Previously, his very early stories had been contrived and artificial—he did not, directly or indirectly, risk himself in them.

The second part of the approach that Hemingway learned from Anderson was how to combine his imagination with his own experiences, not just the things that he had seen and the names of places, but the way he felt, and the relationships that he had had with others. The real power of the stories he was to write after his emulation of Anderson comes from a new ability to involve his deepest emotions in his fiction. The two parts of the approach come together: the adolescent who faces the complexities and contradictions of an adult world (and by extension, the individual who faces a hostile or indifferent universe) is animated by the hurts, shocks, pleasures, and rebellions of Hemingway's own emotional history.

The constant flow of biographical criticism has made it clear that few writers of fiction have used so much material so directly and so consistently from their own lives as Hemingway. Most of the short stories contain material based on autobiographical events or situations; many contain characters closely modeled after people Hemingway had known. In the first half of 1924, approach, style, and technique all jelled, and he produced nine stories, making this one of the most productive periods of his career. Eight of the nine stories were drawn in some measure from Hemingway's own experiences, during childhood, adolescence, and as a young man. Six of the nine were Nick Adams stories. Hemingway eventually published sixteen stories with Nick Adams as the protagonist (eight others have been published posthumously, and a half a dozen other stories published in Hemingway's lifetime had nameless or differently named protagonists who could be placed in the Nick Adams chronology).[27] Although the Nick Adams stories were written and published without strict regard to chronology, they do, when arranged chronologically, trace the development of a consistent character in his growth "from child to adolescent to soldier, veteran, writer, and parent—a sequence closely paralleling the events of Hemingway's own life."[28] Nick Adams thus becomes the first of a series of Hemingway fictional characters who resemble their creator: Jake Barnes, Frederic Henry, Richard Cantwell, and Thomas Hudson. All these were to have behind them, as Philip Young points out, "part of Nick's history and, correspondingly, part of Hemingway's."[29]

Thus, the pattern of semi-autobiographical correspondence in a great many of Hemingway's short stories is but a part of a large pattern of correspondence throughout most of Hemingway's fiction. As helpful as it can be on occasion to approach Hemingway's fiction through autobiographical correspondence, however, the approach, as many have found, can also be treacherous. Like all writers of fiction, Hemingway enlarged, subtracted, combined, transposed, and added whole cloth to his underlayment of memory. For example, it is true that the father in "Indian Camp" acts consistently with what we know of Hemingway's actual father, that "Uncle George" was in fact the name of Hemingway's uncle, and that Hemingway traveled with his father, probably by boat, to the Indian camp which was down the lake from the Hemingway summer home. And we know also that Doctor Hemingway frequently ministered to the Indians at times of emergency during his summers at Walloon Lake. But no one in the Hemingway family remembers the doctor delivering an Indian baby by Caesarean section.[30] Furthermore, talking about the story himself, Hemingway states that he never witnessed an Indian childbirth, but brought in this part of the story (the central incident) from having witnessed a refugee trying to have a baby on the road to Karagatch during the Greco-Turkish war of 1922.[31] (This incident is described more literally, interestingly enough, in "Chapter II," which immediately follows "Indian Camp" in *In Our Time*.)

Although the process is impossible to trace precisely, many stories appear

---

27. *The Nick Adams Stories* (New York: Charles Scribner's Sons, 1972) contains the posthumously published Nick Adams stories and fragments. Some of the stories with unnamed or differently named protagonists which might be placed in the Nick Adams chronology are "A Very Short Story," "Soldier's Home," "Cat in the Rain," "Out of Season," "Hills Like White Elephants," and "A Canary for One." See Philip Young's essay in this collection, " 'Big World Out There': The Nick Adams Stories" for a discussion of the interrelationship of the Nick Adams stories. See also Julian Smith's suggestion (in "Hemingway and the Thing Left Out," this collection) that there may be more than one "Nick Adams."

28. Preface, by Philip Young to *The Nick Adams Stories*, pp. 5–6.

29. Ibid., p. 6.

30. Constance Cappel Montgomery, *Hemingway in Michigan* (New York: Fleet Publishing Corp., 1966), pp. 59–60.

31. "On Writing," *The Nick Adams Stories*, p. 238.

to have begun with a small emotional seed—a moment of great excitement or fear, an incident arousing resentment, a black mood of self-doubt, self-pity, or guilt—which is magnified and dramatized by the use of the situation and characters drawn from the emotion-creating event itself, transposed from a different context, or created from something heard or observed (there are hardly any other alternatives). In ordinary conversation with others, Hemingway had a tendency to enlarge upon past experiences and fabricate others in order to make people believe that his boyhood and adolescence was far more independent and dangerous than it actually was.[32] As a young man he would tell tales of how he had to carry a knife as a boy, and know how to use it, to protect himself from hoboes.[33] Such a self-dramatization is probably the basis for "The Battler," wherein an ex-boxer and his Negro companion are encountered by young Nick Adams at a hobo camp. The story is loaded with the atmosphere of perversion and potential violence—reflecting the actual fears, if not the actual events, of a Hemingway teen-age trip across country. At one point the punch-drunk ex-boxer asks if he can take Nick's knife, and the Negro quickly tells Nick not to let him have it. To give flesh to this adolescent fantasy, Carlos Baker tells us that Hemingway brought in two characters modeled after people he had heard about—the ex-boxer was based on a combination of traits of two fighters, Ad Wolgast and Bat Nelson, and the Negro based on a Negro trainer who looked after Wolgast in his decline.[34]

The whole relationship of Hemingway's biography to his fiction is complicated by this fantasy mechanism. Gradually, he could not distinguish in his memory what he imagined from what actually had happened, so that in a sense, he created a fictional life for himself. (For example, he insisted throughout his life that he had run away from home on numerous occasions—he never did.) And it is this fictional life, more elaborate and more compulsively created than the fictions most of us make up for ourselves, that is so often the basis for the consciously created fiction of the stories. The best way I can sum up the complexity of factors at work here is to put it this way: the act of creative writing, when Hemingway became successful, was an act of self-dramatization which justified his emotional history and gave substance to a created identity. He began to identify very closely with his protagonists as he wrote about them, thinking of them as himself. Evidence for this may be found in the early manuscript of *The Sun Also Rises* wherein "Hem" is used rather than "Jake," and in stories like "Three-Day Blow" and "Summer People" wherein Hemingway's own nickname "Wem*edge*" is used as a *nick*-name for Nick. (Can the whole thing be an elaborate pun?)[35]

32. For several examples of such fabricated stories, see Baker, pp. 22, 28–29, 63, 70.
33. *A Moveable Feast* (New York: Charles Scribner's Sons, 1964), p. 18.
34. Baker, p. 141.
35. One of the meanings for "wem" given in the *Webster's Third International* is "a

The circumstances surrounding the semi-autobiographical protagonist may vary to suit the direction of the self-dramatization, but the emotional seed which sets the basic pattern (self-glorification, self-justification, self-pity) usually has a firm biographical foundation, if it can be discovered. The climactic scene of "Soldier's Home" seems, in regard to the actual sequence of events involving Hemingway and his mother, an unlikely biographical occurrence, but the mother's attitude and her relationship with her son is biographically accurate. Harry, in "The Snows of Kilimanjaro," is an exaggerated personification of Hemingway's "black ass" view of his career and his relationship with his wife at the time he wrote the story. "Get Yourself a Seeing Eye Dog" is a dramatization of Hemingway's fear that he might be losing his sight.

This emotional-psychological underpinning of Hemingway's fiction leads most readers to the realization eventually that there is a rather consistent psychological pattern, sometimes consciously and sometimes unconsciously expressed, in the bulk of the stories. The pattern has roughly three parts: (1) assertion of the self, (2) fear of failure, and (3) attacks on those things which threaten the successful assertion of the self. Assertion of the self in the stories usually takes the form of the assertion of the masculine principle. A great part of this might be called the "male brag." It is the dramatization of power, courage, achievement, and virility-life. We find the male brag in "A Very Short Story" wherein the protagonist implies frequent intimacy with the nurse, Luz (an affair which in life, if we accept Baker's research here, did not get beyond the kissing stage). A similar announcement of virility may be found in "Summer People." We find other rather frequent assertions of maleness, as skillfulness, as superiority, or as courage. In "On Writing" Nick is a more skillful writer than others. We encounter Nick as the skillful woodsman and fisherman ("The End of Something," "Big Two-Hearted River," "The Last Good Country"), and we see him as a skillful skier ("Cross-Country Snow," "An Alpine Idyll"), as a dominant male ("The End of Something," "Summer People"), and as a boy of rather remarkable courage ("The Killers," "The Battler").

Fears of failure, of cowardice, of incompetence, and of failing masculine prowess are expressed through Harry in "The Snows of Kilimanjaro," through Nick in "Three Shots" and "Now I Lay Me," and through Frazer in "The Gambler, the Nun and the Radio." And these fears, in these same stories and many others, are in turn connected to fears of weakness, sickness, mutilation, death, and fear itself. As already mentioned, there is a commonly repeated verbal formula throughout many of the stories: "He tried to

---

flaw or stain in something material." In regard to the nickname "Wemedge," see Sheridan Baker, *Ernest Hemingway: An Introduction and Interpretation* (New York: Holt, Rinehart and Winston, Inc., 1967), p. 123.

stop himself from thinking," or "He didn't want to think about it." In "Big Two-Hearted River" sleep comes as a triumph over the thoughts that keep one awake; in "Now I Lay Me" Nick is afraid to go to sleep in the dark for fear his soul will go out of him; and in "A Clean, Well-Lighted Place" the older waiter must go home to another sleepless night, lying awake and braced against the dark nothingness.

Targets for Hemingway's attacks on those things which threaten the successful assertion of the self include parents and parental figures, certain kinds of women, marriage, Victorian morality, and competing writers. During his late adolescence and early manhood, Hemingway had an increasing antipathy toward his parents which went beyond the usual mixed emotions of the adolescent trying to gain independence. In the several Nick Adams stories in which the parents appear, their characteristics match very closely those of Hemingway's own parents. The fictional treatment is invariably hostile—of Mrs. Adams, in particular. In such stories as "The Doctor and the Doctor's Wife" and "Now I Lay Me," she is seen as selfish, self-centered, and self-righteous. As every reader quickly learns after reading the first few stories, she is the prototype for the recurring figure of the castrating female in Hemingway's fiction. Girls and young women may be seen as sexually desirable or as good companions, as Marjorie was both, until the affair is broken off in "The End of Something." As per Philip Wylie's *Generation of Vipers*, however, Cinderella turns into "Mom" once she takes off the wedding gown. Poor Marjorie is cut off on just the possibility, as Nick sees it, that the affair may become serious. On his wedding day, Nick wonders "if it would be this way if he were going to be hanged" (in "Wedding Day"). Once you were married, you were "absolutely bitched" and the biological trap closes in on you. For the next step, as in "Cross-Country Snow," is for your wife to get pregnant, and with each step you lose all those things that had made life worthwhile (the self-image of the independent, dominant, virile male) the hunting, the fishing, the skiing, and all the male friends to do them with. This kind of thinking did not endear him to many of his readers, some calling him a chauvinist, others finding evidence for alleged sexual abnormality.

When several of these psychological motifs combine, as they do in "The Short Happy Life of Francis Macomber," a powerful web of tension is the result. Masculine assertion reaches its apex in Hemingway's professional, in this case, the white hunter Wilson. Casually courageous, coolly competent, and completely independent of domestic tyranny, he hunts lion and seduces the willing wives of his customers with equal skill. By comparison, in Macomber we have the nadir of being "absolutely bitched" from the Hemingway point of view. In him are dramatized the terrible possibilities of courage failed, manhood weakened, independence gone, and competition lost. The third part of the scheme, the "attack," is of course centered on the woman,

wife-Mom, Mrs. Macomber. She spends most of her time figuratively castrating her husband—needling him, cuckolding him, and finally shooting him
at the moment that he gains courage, manhood, and independence. The fact
that the men come together in comradeship, so to speak, at the end to stand
together against the destructive woman completes the circle of the story. This
is one of the few Hemingway stories with a happy ending—although not
traditionally so, of course: the only way that Macomber can "live happily
ever after" is by dying. "The Short Happy Life of Francis Macomber" is a
definition of "happiness." (An early title was "Happy Ending.") "Happiness" is the escape from fear to courage, the moment of change from a wom-
an-dominated man to a man's man. Regardless of its relative virtues and
faults as a short story, "Francis Macomber" has value for the student of
Hemingway's short stories as an almost perfect compendium of the major
recurring elements of the Hemingway psychological pattern.

V

If Hemingway's stories were primarily concerned with manners and mor-
als, his emphasis on masculinity would date the stories and eventually make
them unbearable. But with what appears to be a measure of both conscious
and unconscious intent, masculinity is transformed into larger questions of
contemporary concern, of the sanctity of the individual, whether man or
woman, and of the individual's struggle to maintain his identity against those
forces, both natural and social, which would rob him of individuality, freedom, and integrity. For Hemingway, the preservation of identity rested primarily on courage—not in Hemingway's work an exclusively masculine
exercise, although it is most frequently seen as exercised within traditionally
masculine activities. A story like "The Undefeated" deals with man gener-
ically; that this is a male and that he is involved in a male activity are the
exterior circumstances of the central struggle: to paraphrase Emerson, society everywhere is in conspiracy against the man-woman-hood of every one
of its members. Hemingway's paranoia is one that we must all share in part
in order to maintain our freedom and defend our integrity.
    In the eccentricity and narrowness of his view of life, Hemingway might
best be compared to Kafka. Out of a personal neurosis produced by the circumstances of his own history and psychological characteristics, Hemingway
produces a metaphor for modern life which transcends the personal. Hemingway's mothers take on roughly the same position as Kafka's fathers,
naturally enough, since the setting is American matriarchy, rather than
European patriarchy.
    An examination of Hemingway's stories in regard to certain basic themes

of Kafka's work (I am not going to attempt a detailed comparison)[36] can be useful to us here in several ways. First, such a focus sets the stage for viewing Hemingway's stories in a far more radical light than they are ordinarily seen. What I want to suggest here is that not only is Hemingway not primarily a realist or naturalist, but that Cowley's comparison with Hawthorne (useful as it might have been at the time) is both anachronistic and far too tame. Hawthorne's doom is ultimately Christian; Hemingway's doom is a darkness beyond hell, unthinkable and omnipresent. We have come to associate this kind of total darkness (beyond the pessimism glibly assigned to the "dark early stories") with its most direct presentation in one story, "A Clean, Well-Lighted Place," whereas it is nearly pervasive, touching most of the stories, early and late. Second, such an examination of the stories forms a natural transition from the psychological patterns which have generated Hemingway's themes to the techniques by which they have been so indirectly presented. Third, I would like to suggest, pressing forward with a thesis I have proposed elsewhere that the wound of war (the Philip Young thesis) which is so pervasive in Hemingway fiction is not Hemingway's primary concern, but rather a metaphor which expresses a Kafka-like obsession with parental authority.[37] In Hemingway's case, the prototype figure is the emasculating mother who in her various forms is most conveniently referred to as the "woman-with-power."

Hemingway was in several respects a more complex personality than Kafka. Kafka was a very private person who pursued his writing privately and did not wish his work to be published. Hemingway was the introvert who forced aside his insecurity, his oversensitivity, and his shyness to assume a public role of expansiveness and bravado. He consciously evolved a mask behind which he could approach his work and wrote with conscious regard for his reader—a conscious regard that was often a conscious duplicity. Although both writers employed a misdirection by which they lead the reader to believe that they are writing about one thing, when they are actually writing about something else, Hemingway's misdirection was more profound and constant. Behind the public "story," however, Hemingway, like Kafka, was ultimately writing about himself, for himself. Kafka decided to keep his problems to himself by not publishing his work; Hemingway evidently decided to keep his problems to himself by applying as much skill as possible in keeping them hidden. The complexity of Hemingway's technique can no doubt be traced to this necessity to hide or disguise what he was compelled to express.

36. For a detailed comparison (which in my opinion does not do justice to either Hemingway or Kafka) see Caroline Gordon, "Notes on Hemingway and Kafka," *Sewanee Review*, LVII (April–June 1949), 215–26.

37. Philip Young has, independently, come to a somewhat similar conclusion regarding the importance of the mother figure in Hemingway's work. See his essay in this collection, " 'Big World Out There': The Nick Adams Stories."

A familiar character in the fiction of both Hemingway and Kafka is the lonely figure who is distraught and dislocated, but in a very matter-of-fact way is attempting to adapt to circumstances beyond his control. As we might recall, Gregor Samsa in Kafka's best known story, "Metamorphosis," wakes up in the morning to find that he is a giant insect. As the story unfolds, we realize that this new form is but the outward manifestation of Gregor's self-disgust and desire for punishment—he has secretly aspired to take his father's place. His transformation does not astonish him; he is too occupied in the moment by moment struggle to get off his hard-shelled back and adjust to his new situation. This radical metaphor expresses very directly Kafka's own emotions. By contrast, Hemingway could never overtly adopt such a fantastic metaphor (covertly, he did, as we shall see in a moment), but in his need to hide his obsessions was forced to maintain a surface realism which is seldom, if ever, violated. (If realism is breached, it is breached on a realistic premise, such as a blow to the head or a head wound.) But, several situations in Hemingway's stories do parallel this, and other similar Kafka stories, and a close reading reveals that Kafka-like Hemingway which the author has taken such pains to conceal.

"Now I Lay Me" begins much like a Kafka story, with the same matter-of-fact acceptance of peculiar circumstances: "That night we lay on the floor in the room and I listened to the silk-worms eating." (Compare the beginning of Kafka's "The Burrow": "I have completed the construction of my burrow and it seems to be successful.") The story's position in the Nick Adams chronology lead us to believe that Nick is still in a state of shock several months following his wounding—and the story has usually been interpreted along these lines.[38] Yet, the two obsessively recurring elements of the story are the noises of the silk worms eating and the subject of women and marriage. Like Gregor, Nick is psychologically and physically immobilized. Is he victimized by the war and by fear, as is John, his companion in the dark of the make-shift barracks? Perhaps, but the central scene of the story is a memory of mother, who, while smiling sweetly, tells her husband that she has just burned his most treasured possessions while he was gone on a hunting trip. It is a traumatic experience for the young Nick, who watches his father's specimen jars "popping in the heat" and "the snakes burning in the fire." He remembers his father, humiliated, stooping to pick out from the ashes the blackened and chipped arrowheads and pottery. The father trans-

38. Julian Smith in "Hemingway and the Thing Left Out" (included in this collection) sees the Nick Adams protagonist in "Now I Lay Me" as a possible extension of Jake Barnes and suggests that the basis of Nick's problem is physical rather than psychic —that Nick has a wound similar to Jake's. I don't see how Smith's thesis explains the deep *fear* of marriage which is at the center of the story. Smith does not approve of Richard B. Hovey's phychoanalytical approach, an approach similar to the one I have taken here. See Hovey, *Hemingway: The Inward Terrain* (Seattle and London: University of Washington Press, 1968), pp. 47–53.

fers his shotgun to Nick to carry into the house, but it is too heavy and Nick finds that "it banged against my legs." The father comments, "Don't try and carry too much at once." The pattern of imagery suggests that what Nick learns here is that what happened to his father may happen to him: mothers castrate fathers, and when it is his turn to carry the masculine load, he too will be vulnerable.

Ironically, John suggests repeatedly to Nick that the cure for his "condition" lies in marriage. For a while, instead of concentrating on the masculine reassurance of remembered fishing, Nick lies in the dark thinking of "all the girls he had ever known and what kind of wives they would make," but finds finally that "they all blurred and *all became rather the same*" (my emphasis). At the beginning of the story, Nick explains that he does not want to sleep, because if he shuts his eyes and lets himself go, his "soul would go out of his body." Clearly, however, it is not gunfire, but something else eating at him, threatening to rob him of his identity. The wound of war has been transposed here, as it often is in Hemingway, to represent the threat of what a woman can do to a man. The archetype representing this transposition in Hemingway's work is Jake Barnes, in *The Sun Also Rises*, whose crotch wound suggests the power that Brett has to emasculate him. She turns out to be far more damaging to the integrity of his manhood than his physical wound. What mothers can do to fathers has its earlier counterpart in the sexual lure which incapacitates the lover. Along these lines, when Frederic Henry, in *A Farewell to Arms,* escapes from war by jumping into the river, he is not "baptized" and cleansed of war in order to enter the "purer" realm of love. On the contrary, he jumps from the mud of the retreat into the biological trap of the feminine principle itself, lured there, by his images of lust.

The transposition in "Now I Lay Me" occurs when the introductory passage of being blown up and losing his soul is connected in the center of the story with Nick's memory of the jars blowing up and belching forth their burning snakes. One fear merges with another. The beginning of the story states the danger, the central incident discovers its real nature and its source, the following conversation between Nick and John about marriage develops the danger as theme, and the conclusion certifies that theme.

The certification at the end of the story is found in Nick's recollection (some time after the events of the story proper) that John visited him later in the hospital and "was very disappointed that I had not yet married, and I know he would feel very badly if he knew that, so far, I have never married. He was going back to America and he was very certain about marriage and knew it would fix up everything." The important words, spoken some time later, are "so far, I have never married." The thread is the threat, and the thread of Nick's condition is interminable. No happy ending to his problem, no "getting married and living happily ever after," is possible. In fact, that happy ending spells disaster.

Nick's life, as we perceive it in the framework of the story, consists almost entirely of waking dreams created in his mind as he lies in the darkness. The continuous filament of threat is countered by a series of rituals in which memories of fishing, of people, places, animals, and things are strung together like rosary beads, memories which are in fact punctuated by Hail Marys and Our Fathers. Nick must touch these beads and hold on to them as if they were life itself, for to let go would allow his soul, his identity, to be pulled away from him. The filament of threat and the rosary of life are bound together in the constant activity of the silk worms. Their eating and dropping in the darkness become, like the ticking of a clock, the tangible substance of his sleepless anxiety and the conflict at the heart of that anxiety. Nick strives to hold on in a state approximating death, but a death which recognizes the identity of separate things (a death with the memories of people and a God who can look after those people), as against that other death which, without selfhood or identity, leads into nothingness. The ever-present chewing of the worms is an early appearance of the *nada* of "A Clean, Well-Lighted Place." Their interminable activity elevates the threat of the wound into the omnipresent shroud of darkness.

The metaphor suggests that Nick's state is akin to that of being in the grave, listening to the worms and praying for the salvation of the soul. The prayers are not, however, prayers to a God to be answered, but statements which in themselves, forming a thread of consciousness, assert life. The central ritual is fishing, the assertion of the masculine self, which sometimes can offset the pain of the inadvertent memories of father being destroyed by mother. Not only is "maleness" connected with life and identity, but the mental life Nick clings to is a combination of memory and imaginative creation based on memory ("some nights too I made up streams") which forms an interesting parallel to Hemingway's position here as writer—to write, or to create from memory and imagination, is to live, but to give into the temptation not to write (to sleep, or give way to the danger of a "normal" life) is to die. One can only conclude that there is a coldness in this grotesque iceberg which is several degrees centigrade lower than even Kafka was able to reach.

A similar argument can be made for Harry in "The Snows of Kilimanjaro" and Nick in "A Way You'll Never Be" as immobilized victims in a dislocated, often surreal, environment. Both are physically wounded, but in each case the physical wound is but the exterior sign of deep emotional problems. Harry has sold out to the "wife-mother," allowing women and their money to subvert his manhood, so that he can no longer function as a writer. (In "Now I Lay Me" John suggests, "Why don't you pick out some nice Italian girl with plenty of money?") Harry's self-disgust and guilt are nearly as intense as Gregor Samsa's—he has become king of the dunghill, rather than the leopard at the top of the mountain, and he was led there, as he says, by his "cock."

Nick's case in "A Way You'll Never Be" is not nearly so clear as Harry's. The story parallels the structure of "Now I Lay Me" in that both stories are ostensibly stories of a man trying to deal with the shock of physical wounds, whereas the imagery of the stories suggests that the real cause of suffering and dislocation is elsewhere. Again, a transposition occurs in which a physical wound of war merges with the damage done by the woman-with-power, and fear comes in response to sexuality rather than gunfire. The image which signals this transposition in the previous story is the popping jars and burning snakes; whereas in "A Way You'll Never Be," the transposition is suggested by the recurring image of the "low house painted yellow" which, because of Nick's fear of it, has usually been interpreted as the traumatic scene of his wounding. However, a central passage in the story (somewhat equivalent to the central passage concerning mother in "Now I Lay Me") of rather opaque stream-of-consciousness suggests that the house is also associated with the scene of sexual activity.

The terms of Nick's "peril," as he calls it, which frightens him more "than he had ever been in a bombardment," are outlined in the imagery of the opening passages. The story begins with a view of the dead on a battlefield. The *dead* are surrounded by images, literally, of *sex* and *marriage*—a common combination in Hemingway's work which draws its own connections. More specifically, around the dead are scattered papers: prayer books, group picture postcards showing a unit "standing in ranked and ruddy cheerfulness," letters from home, and pictures of children—all these mixed grotesquely with propaganda postcards "attractively" showing the enemy raping women, and smutty postcards by village photographers.

This dichotomy between healthy and unhealthy is later echoed in one of Nick's satiric speeches. In an attempt, perhaps, to cleanse himself, Nick has donned an American uniform for "propaganda" purposes, and declares himself the representative of the cleancut, all-American boy image that is the opposite of the propaganda postcards:

> "Do you think they will send Americans down here?" asked the adjutant.
> "Oh, absolutely. Americans twice as large as myself, healthy, with clean hearts, sleep at night, never been wounded, never been blown up, never had their heads caved in, never been scared, don't drink, faithful to the girls they left behind them, many of them never had crabs, wonderful chaps. You'll see."

The tone suggests that these Americans, clean, healthy, and sexually pure, will be in every respect the antithesis of Nick in his present condition.

The connection between wounding-death and sex juxtaposed once again in his speech suggests a connection not only between Nick and the danger of war, but between Nick and the unhealthy pornographic images of sex which surround the dead. Hemingway slyly reinforces these connections through puns. When telling the Captain that he had been at the scene of the recent battle (the dead surrounded by postcards designed to incite the troops to anger toward the enemy, but the rape so "attractively depicted" that the cards serve another purpose), Nick says that he had just come from "Fornaci." When Nick asks the Captain if he seems all right to him, the Captain replies that Nick seems in "top-hole shape" (a three-cushion shot: "top-drawer" or "good," Nick's head wound, and sex).

Throughout the story image and pun suggest that Nick is haunted by sexual experiences which he considers illicit and unhealthy. His trip back to the lines appears to be motivated by a need to sort out his feelings of guilt and fear, since the occasions for his feelings have become submerged and confused in his mind. The apparent cause of his confusion is his physical wound, but the constant undertone of unhealthy sexuality suggests that his problems are emotional, and that these emotions have either blocked or disguised the memory of those experiences which caused them in the first place. Nick also seems motivated by the need to perform some vaguely conceived act of penitence by taking on the appearance which would fulfill the expectations of his middle-class, Middle Western upbringing. He has come back to the lines to pass out chocolate bars rather than dirty postcards.

The blocked or disguised memories which are the occasions for Nick's emotional difficulties are grouped together into a rather opaque stream-of-consciousness passage in the center of the story. Twice in the section we explicitly see Nick's "girl," and twice she is associated with fear and guilt. Both times Nick remembers her as with him or sometimes with someone else—suggesting that she may be a prostitute. Both times she is associated with doing something wrong, jumping out of a taxi in order to avoid paying the fare (he is frightened by the possibility "that they might take the same driver twice").

In reviewing his fears in the passage, Nick shifts from war to woman, to war, and back to woman. The transposition of one danger to the other is indicated in Nick's comment on his own stream of memory: "If it didn't get so damned mixed up he could follow it all right." But the danger that bothers him most, the danger he insists on, is not the danger of war: "He never dreamed about the front now any more but what frightened him so that he could not get rid of it was that long yellow house and the different width of the river."

From clues throughout the story it seems certain that Nick was wounded near a river, but it also seems certain that "river" has come to mean something else to him at this point. (The river at the front and the river near the yellow house appear to be two different locations which Nick transposes.) In the stream-of-consciousness passage the emotions Nick has in regard to the attack—fear, and guilt in response to his necessity for getting drunk—

seem identical to those attached to his visits to the yellow house. What happens during these visits with an Italian prostitute (who is associated in Nick's mind with "his girl" in Paris) is coded in the topography of the description:

> Outside of Fossalta there was a low house painted yellow with willows all around it and a low stable and there was a canal, and he had been there a thousand times and never seen it, but there it was every night as plain as the hill, only it frightened him. That house meant more than anything and every night he had it. That was what he needed but it frightened him especially when the boat lay there quietly in the willows on the canal.

One apparently goes by boat through the canal surrounded by willows into the yellow house. If this, as the context strongly suggests, is a description of a sexual act, then that yellow house (when one lies there "quietly in the willows" and stops to think about it after the passion of the moment) carries the possibility of disease and death. If Nick's fear and guilt in response to having intercourse with a prostitute seem exaggerated, remember this is the same Nick who is told by his father (in "Fathers and Sons") that "masturbation produced blindness, insanity, and death, while a man who went with prostitutes would contract hideous venereal diseases and that the thing to do was to keep your hands off of people."

Immediately following the passage which describes the house, the willows, and the canal is a description of a similar canal-river, where soldiers came "wallowing across the flooded ground holding the rifles high until they fell with them in the water." (Compare the rifles here to the shotgun carried by Nick in "Now I Lay Me" or the shotgun held by the father in "The Doctor and the Doctor's Wife" from which he pumps yellow shells in frustrated anger.) To the soldiers gathered around him at one point in the story, Nick, in a moment of hysterical oratory, repeatedly advises, "Gentlemen, either you must govern—or you must be governed." Like Harry in "The Snows of Kilimanjaro," Nick has been governed by the need for a woman which in turn has given her power over him—and like Harry, as a result of what a woman can do to a man, he is rotting out his insides. The "yellow" poison on his brain should have been "trepanned" out, as the Captain suggests, but has been left, instead, to "absorb."

As in Kafka wherein the father may appear without being literally present in the story, the woman-with-power and the danger she represents may be present in the Hemingway story as suggested only in the imagery. Like the soldiers carrying their rifles over the flooded ground and falling wounded into the water, as noted above, Nick in "Big Two-Hearted River" carries his pole to the swamp, but cannot enter for "the fishing would be tragic." Deciding to put off fishing the swamp, Nick takes the "male trout" that he has just caught and whacks its head against a log so that it "quivered rigid." Then

Nick takes out his knife, opens it, and sticks it in the log. In contrast to the female swamp which would require "deep wading with the water deepening up under his armpits," "log" is asserted eight times in the course of a page, and after cleaning his male fish, he finds "his knife was still standing, blade stuck in the log." This is the first time that I have ever seen a trout identified as male or female in a fishing story.

When the primary or prototype figure does appear in Kafka or Hemingway—the Kafka father and the Hemingway mother—his or her power is awesome and compelling beyond reasonable explanation. One of the stories most used to discuss the relationship of son to father in Kafka's work is "The Judgment." The complete lack of understanding between the two, the continual suspicions of the parent, the ultimate knowledge of the parent (he always knows more or has known all along), and the capricious uses of anger and authority make this story a nightmare, in extremis, of our deepest childhood fears, guilts, and wounds.[39] At the end of the story, the father sentences the son to death by drowning, and the son, compelled as if on strings by the hand of the father, is driven to the water, crying out as he jumps, "Dear parents, I have always loved you, all the same." Even at the moment of destruction, he fulfills his filial duty and declares his love.

In less expressionistic terms, Hemingway's Harold Krebs in "Soldier's Home" is forced to perform a similar act of self-immolation, while declaring his love for his parent. (Krebs's declaration is less spontaneous and probably less sincere, so that there is a far deeper sense of pathos in the Kafka story.) Mrs. Krebs, however, uses the same levers of guilt, of personified societal judgment, of complete lack of understanding but secret and superior knowledge. Krebs has come home from the war, filled with lassitude and nausea. He wants a girl, but he "did not want to have to work to get her" and he "did not want any *consequences*" (my emphasis). Thus, what would be a "normal" adjustment to life—to meet a girl, get a job, and get married—is stalled. The mother feels (as does John about Nick in "Now I Lay Me") that the solution to all of her son's problems lies in marriage. What the "consequences" are of such a normal course of affairs, however, are illustrated in the pattern set by the mother's relationship to the father. When she says that his father has decided to let him use the family car (as a means of getting Krebs into a position to date girls), Krebs replies, "I'll bet you made him."

Before breakfast one morning, the mother, representing the force of both father and mother, puts the pressure on Harold to conform to the "normal" pattern he has been resisting. "God has some work for everyone to do," she admonishes him with irresistable authority. She pursues her connection with God further, indicating her secret knowledge of his temptations overseas has led her to pray for him. She points out that "Charley Simmons, who is just

39. A similar treatment of these themes can be found in Harold Pinter's *The Birthday Party*.

your age, has a good job and is going to be married. The boys are all settling down. . . . on their way to being really a credit to the community." Thus having bludgeoned with all possible authority except the last one, she brings that out too: "Don't you love your mother, dear boy?" Krebs says "No." She starts to cry and "went on crying" as Krebs begs her to believe that he didn't mean it: "Please, please mother. Please believe me." Sick and vaguely nauseated, Krebs is pressed by her tears into becoming a little boy again, as she says, "I'm your mother. . . I held you next to my heart when you were a tiny baby," and he replies, "I know, Mummy . . . I'll try and be a good boy for you." She finally brings him, literally, to his knees with her tears. Pushing him inexorably toward a figurative self-immolation, she insists that they pray to her God, her source of guilt-power, together.

The lonely figure who is distraught and dislocated; the recurring emotions of fear, guilt, and even self-disgust; and the obsessive concern for the woman-with-power—the emasculating mother, the wife with money, the sexually attractive girl—these are all common ingredients in Hemingway's stories which have some kinship with the pathology of Kafka's fiction. Equally important, however, in exploring the manifestations of these characteristics in the stories, we have certified, along the way, the details of a writing technique which can be extremely subtle and complex.

As we have seen, "Now I Lay Me" and "A Way You'll Never Be" are by no means simple stories by any definition. Yet, simplicity remains one of the main misconceptions about the stories, persisting among critics and general readers alike.[40] This misconception has denied many of the stories the kind of close reading they deserve—a reading we automatically give to Joyce and too often just as automatically refuse Hemingway. While Hemingway's style has often been imitated, few writers have ever approached the sophistication of the Hemingway technique behind that style. Again, the difference lies in the mask of the reporter—easily simulated in its obvious features—and the carefully executed touches of the accomplished craftsman behind the mask— a craftsmanship which can be so fine that it has been often overlooked by the expert. If, roughly speaking, the reporter was made in Kansas City, the writer who could risk his own emotions in his work, in Chicago, then the craftsman was made in Paris. The heart of what Hemingway was talking

40. A fairly typical comment made in passing is this one by William Peden in *The American Short Story: Front Line in the National Defense of Literature* (Boston: Houghton Mifflin Company, 1964), p. 6: "Over the years, the contemporary short story in America has proved itself large enough to include the sparse simplicities of Hemingway's 'Indian Camp' and the more leisurely complexities of Katherine Anne Porter's 'Flowering Judas.'" If there are "sparse simplicities" in this story, they are bobbing on the surface of richer broth than Peden apparently has stomach for. For other examples, consult John A. Jones, "Hemingway: The Critics and the Public Legend," *Western Humanities Review*, XIII (Autumn 1959), 387–400, and *The Literary Reputation of Hemingway in Europe*, ed. Roger Asselineau, (New York: New York University Press, 1965)—see particularly, D. S. R. Welland's essay, "Hemingway's English Reputation."

about can be located through his personality, but the center of his technique must be discovered in terms of what happened to the newspaperman when he met the poet.

VI

Early readers were simply not prepared to deal with Hemingway's short fiction. Looking back, with characteristic self-dramatization, Hemingway recalled his initial reception after a period of serious writing in Paris:

> Those first years here when I made my run . . . and I quit my foreign correspondent job with the Toronto *Star* to put myself on the line, I suffered a lot. I had finally shucked off the journalism I had been complaining about and I was finally doing all the good writing I had promised myself. But every day the rejected manuscripts would come back through the slot in the door of that bare room where I lived over the Montmartre sawmill. They'd fall through the slot onto the wood floor, and clipped to them was that most savage of all reprimands—the printed rejection slip. The rejection slip is very hard to take on an empty stomach and there were times when I'd sit at that old wooden table and read one of those cold slips that had been attached to a story I had loved and worked on very hard and believed in, and I couldn't help crying.[41]

Hemingway's frustration came because the writing was good, and he knew it was good, but the form and technique did not fit the preconceived ideas about short fiction held first by the editors and then later by the reviewers and critics:

> All of the stories back in the mail that came in through a slit in the saw mill door, with notes of rejection that would never call them stories, but always anecdotes, sketches, contes, etc. They did not want them.[42]

What "they" were that the editors didn't want can probably be best described as "prose pieces written in the manner of modern poetry." The editors and critics would have been better advised to look to the work of Pound and Eliot, than back to the well-made story. Even in the early days, without the techniques acquired and developed in Paris, Hemingway's "conception of what constituted a salable short story was not in line with prevailing editorial opinion. To a considerable extent he would have to create the taste by which his stories would eventually be judged."[43] To create a taste for their

41. A. E. Hotchner, *Papa Hemingway* (New York: Random House, 1966), p. 57. Either Hotchner or Hemingway has made a mistake here. The apartment over the sawmill was not near Montmartre, but on the rue Notre-Dame-des-Champs near the Boulevard Montparnasse.
42. *Green Hills of Africa* (New York: Charles Scribner's Sons, 1935), p. 70.
43. Baker, p. 69.

own work is precisely what Eliot, Pound, and Joyce had to do. In their case, their work was obviously different, obviously challenging and over a period of years their work has been self-educating. But Hemingway's vehicle had such an attractively utilitarian look, once one got used to it, that no one could believe that it really had any horsepower. What eventually captured both the general reader and critic alike was the manner—the dry, hard finish without decoration. But this acceptance led to a second disaster almost equal to the earlier one of rejection: the manner made such an impression that the substance and the finer details of the mechanism were overlooked.

It is hard to conceive of the work by a Hemingway that didn't go to Paris, for there seems to be little doubt that his immersion into a group of what became some of the most accomplished writers of the century affected his work profoundly. He was changed from a young man who wanted to sell short stories into a young man who wanted to write the best short fiction that had ever been written and to do things with prose that had never been done before. Although there was already in Hemingway an impulse toward the controlled use of language and already an intense concern for technique before the Paris years, the suggestions, criticism, and the example—even the general flow of talk about writing—fed those interests and gave them direction and substance. In Paris, and largely because of Paris, Hemingway became an accomplished artist.

Many of those who have dealt with the Pound-Lewis-Ford-Joyce-Stein-Eliot "group" in Paris during the early twenties have tended to treat Hemingway a bit like the idiot country cousin, who hung about, gnashing his pearl white teeth and shadow boxing with statues—a seriocomic footnote to great literature. This treatment is in some degree justified, for the flow of ideas and influence was almost entirely toward Hemingway—these people were important to Hemingway's development, but only in rare instances did the help or advice go the other way. Hemingway was younger than the others, and although the only really established literary figure among them (on a widely-known basis) was Ford Madox Ford, all of them had written, published, and suffered in the literary wars far more than Hemingway, who, in 1922, had really done nothing of any literary consequence. He also was by far the least educated, formally and informally, of all the group, most of whom were scholars.

"Group," of course, is only a convenient label for a number of literary figures who happened to be on the Paris scene at the same time (Eliot was actually not on the scene very much—his influence on Hemingway came by proxy through Pound's recommendation of his work). Each did not necessarily know, like, or influence each of the others. The two key figures in the further education of Ernest Hemingway were, of course, Ezra Pound and Gertrude Stein—Hemingway has told us about Pound and Stein has told us, repeatedly, about Stein. As already noted, Stein influenced Hemingway's uses of language and philosophy of composition profoundly; nevertheless, on the whole Ezra Pound's friendship and tutelage were even more valuable, for Pound not only helped with the advancement of the writing, but helped the writer advance. He was, far more than Stein, the center of activity, introducing Hemingway not only to numerous other artists, but to literature Hemingway should know, both past and present. And Hemingway was ambitious enough by this time to want to learn, intelligent enough to learn quickly and well, and perceptive enough to pick and choose among those things that came to him, keeping what he needed to adapt to his own purposes and discarding the rest.

Pound seems to have had his finger on everything important that was going on in literature in Paris, England, and even on the other side of the Atlantic. He was the gadfly, the stimulator, the explainer and definer, and most of all, the benefactor. In 1925, Hemingway wrote a tribute to Pound which was published in *This Quarter*, a little magazine, the first issue of which had been dedicated to Pound:

> So far, we have Pound the major poet devoting, say, one fifth of his time to poetry. With the rest of his time he tries to advance the fortunes, both material and artistic, of his friends. He defends them when they are attacked, he gets them into magazines and out of jail. He loans them money. He sells their pictures. He arranges concerts for them. He writes articles about them. He introduces them to wealthy women. He gets publishers to take their books. He sits up all night with them when they claim to be dying and he witnesses their wills. He advances them hospital expenses and dissuades them from suicide. And in the end a few of them refrain from knifing him at the first opportunity.[44]

Pound had been the "foreign editor" for *The Little Review* when it had been located in New York, and it was through Pound that Hemingway met the editors, Margaret Anderson and Jane Heap, resulting in Hemingway's first major publication, the six vignettes which led off the Exiles number of *The Little Review* for May, 1923.[45] Through Pound, Hemingway came to know Ford Madox Ford and his ideas (most of which seem to have come through Pound, rather than from Ford directly), and it was Pound who touted the works of Eliot and Joyce to Hemingway. It was Pound who talked Ford into making Hemingway his assistant editor on the *Transatlantic Review*. Hemingway's real start as a short story writer came through his publication in the little magazines and private "little presses" of Paris. Ezra

44. As quoted in Charles Norman, *Ezra Pound* (New York: The Macmillian Co., 1960), p. 275. On the topic of Pound's influence on Hemingway, see Harold M. Hurwitz, "Hemingway's Tutor, Ezra Pound," *Modern Fiction Studies*, XVII (Winter 1971–72), 469–82.

45. Nicholas Joost, *Ernest Hemingway and the Little Magazines* (Barre, Mass.: Barre Publishers, 1968), pp. 51–52.

Pound contributed a good deal to that start. Not until after his successes with *In Our Time* and *The Sun Also Rises* was Hemingway able to place a short story in a quality American periodical: "The Killers" appeared in *Scribner's Magazine* in March of 1927.

Probably because of Pound's influence, Hemingway embarked upon an extensive reading program during his Paris years (Pound was famous for his reading lists). The works of four writers that Pound thought were particularly important were Flaubert, Stendhal, Fielding, and Henry James—and all contributed one way or another to Hemingway's development. Pound took the time to sit down and work with Hemingway on his manuscripts, much in the same way that he had worked on Elliot's *The Waste Land*. He crossed things out. Pound's views on this matter were set down later in the *ABC of Reading*:

> The reader's first and simplest test of an author will be to look for words that do not function; that contribute nothing to the meaning OR that distract from the MOST important factor of the meaning to factors of minor importance.[46]

As the passage indicates, Pound was also greatly concerned with the matter of intensity—a concern we will consider in some detail in a moment. Although Pound thought Joyce to be *the* great prose writer of the time, the heir to Pound's version of the "prose tradition" in Western literature, he was equally generous in his praise of Hemingway. He recommended Hemingway to Ford as "the finest prose stylist in the world" and said of the vignettes which were published as *in our time* that they contained the best prose he had read in forty years.[47]

No doubt Pound admired Hemingway's prose as it developed during the period of 1922–24 because it was almost a perfect demonstration of Pound's doctrine of writing, as it had evolved during the previous decade. (This is true also of *The Waste Land*, explaining in part why the Eliot poem and Hemingway's *In Our Time* have so much in common.) Pound's doctrine was the major factor in liberating those instincts and skills that Hemingway had developed as a newspaperman and which, up to this point, he had tended to keep separate from his creative writing: brevity, clarity, austerity, and directness. Through Pound's influence too, Hemingway began to bring the intensity and depth characteristics of poetry to his prose. Roughly speaking, while Pound was working to bring the virtues of prose to his poetry, Hemingway was working to bring the virtues of the new poetry to his prose.

During the years of his own apprenticeship, Pound had gathered together material and techniques from many sources, out of a variety of languages

46. P. 63.
47. Baker, pp. 121, 123. Pound was born in 1885, indicating pregestation reading ability.

and traditions, ancient and modern. Two main, interconnected concerns within the Pound doctrine (that is, Pound's ideas about writing, circa 1922) may be singled out as particularly relevant to Hemingway's writing as it developed during his first years in Paris. The first has to do with certain qualities of prose within what Pound called the "prose tradition," and the second has to do with a particular kind of image technique associated with the movement called "Imagism."

In London, during the years from 1908 to 1914, Pound became convinced that good modern poetry must evolve out of the prose of nineteenth century French fiction, out of Stendhal, Flaubert, and de Maupassant. This conviction came to him out of his association with Ford Madox Hueffer (later Ford Madox Ford). Pound had gone to England largely because he considered W. B. Yeats the greatest living poet, but it was Hueffer, who had been friend to Henry James and who had collaborated with Joseph Conrad, who turned out to be the greatest influence on Pound, and Pound who influenced Yeats. Although at first Pound argued with Hueffer and resisted his ideas, by 1914 he had been converted enough to say, in an essay called "Mr. Hueffer and the Prose Tradition in Verse,"

> It is he who has insisted, in the face of a still Victorian press, upon the importance of good writing as opposed to the opalescent word, the rhetorical tradition. . . . I find him significant and revolutionary because of his insistence upon clarity and precision, upon the prose tradition; in brief, upon efficient writing—even in verse.[48]

Along with this insistence on clarity and precision, Hueffer also emphasized two other related principles: the language of speech as a basis for the new literature, and the necessity for the modern writer of poetry or prose to present, rather than comment. It is at this point that the "prose tradition" as found in the French writers, but also carried out in the work of Henry James and Joseph Conrad, touches on the Imagist technique of modern poetry (here defined by Richard Aldington in "Modern Poetry and the Imagists"):

> We convey an emotion by presenting the object and circumstances of the emotion without comment. For example, we do not say "O how I admire that exquisite, that beautiful, that—25 more adjectives—woman" . . . but we present that woman, we make an "Image" of her, we make the scene convey the emotion.[49]

We are inclined to think, even today, of image as a "picture word," but for Pound and the Imagists, such a concept involves the use of words as decora-

48. As quoted in Herbert N. Schneidau, *Ezra Pound: The Image and the Real* (Baton Rouge: Louisiana, 1969), p. 25.
49. Ibid., p. 27.

tion. For the Imagists, an image is functional; it says itself; as Pound pointed out, "emotional force gives the image" and "the natural object is always the adequate symbol."[50]

Add to these ingredients the Poundian concept of *intensity*, which originates, perhaps, with Flaubert as interpreted by Hueffer, and is further enhanced by Pound's association with the work of the Oriental scholar, Ernest Fenollosa. By "intensity" Pound means two things: language that is condensed and language that is at the same time charged with meaning. In his *ABC of Reading* Pound defines literature as "language charged with meaning," and "great literature" as "simply language charged with meaning to the utmost possible degree."[51] In this recipe, taken as a whole, we have if not the basis for—the lines of cause and effect are blurred—at least very strong parallels with, Eliot's "objective correlative," Joyce's "epiphany," and Hemingway's "the sequence of motion and fact which made the emotion."

Hemingway's work during his first year in Paris can be graphed in terms of two curves, a falling line representing the influence of Anderson, and a rising line representing the influence of the Pound doctrine in conjunction with certain key concepts derived from Gertrude Stein and the reading of Joyce and Eliot. One thing both Stein and Pound agreed on was the necessity for "discipline," reinforcing the approach to writing that Hemingway began to take as he struggled to begin over, beginning with the "simplest things," in the hotel room that he had rented to get away from the confusion of his apartment:

> "All you have to do is write one true sentence," he told himself. "Write the truest sentence that you know." It must be above all a "true simple declarative sentence" without scrollwork or ornamental language of any sort. It must deal with something he knew from personal experience. Stories like "The Passing of Pickles McCarty" or "Wolves and Doughnuts" had been largely invented. They grazed his own experience in Italy and Illinois without keeping the central facts in focus. Now he wanted to place his faith in the direct transcription of what he saw. That and no more. Somehow the emotion that he wanted to convey would filter through the reported facts.[52]

This, of course, is the central element of the Pound doctrine which, in a sense, permeated the atmosphere of literary Paris as Hemingway perceived it in those first few months. In short, his method could be summed up in the Poundian motto obtained from a German-Italian dictionary, "Dichten = condensare."[53]

50. Schneidau, pp. 48, 72.   51. P. 28.
52. Baker, p. 84.
53. *ABC of Reading*, p. 36: "Basil Bunting, fumbling about with a German-Italian dictionary, found that this idea of poetry as concentration is as old almost as the German language."

During his first year or so in Paris, Hemingway still talked of Anderson, and it was during this time that he produced "Up in Michigan" and "My Old Man" in the Anderson manner. But at the very same time, he began with "one true sentence" to rebuild his skills along other lines. Strangely enough, it was the reportorial skills that Hemingway now began to employ in his creative work that led him to writing prose in the manner of modern poetry. His effort involved looking carefully, getting at the essential facts of the situation he observed, putting these facts down in a straight-forward, economical fashion, and then letting this "condensed essence" speak the emotion for itself. When he wrote these sentence exercises, he wrote them first in his blue exercise books and then, significantly, copied them down in longhand on three telegraph blanks and headed them "Paris 1922," as if they had been dispatches to the *Star*.[54]

Each of the sentences he wrote is a "presentation," to use a word favored by the Imagists, of an event which implicitly carries within the terms of the event itself a complex of emotion. Each one is declarative, straightforward, highly condensed, and without rhetoric or decoration:

> I have seen the favourite crash into the Bulfinch and come down in a heap kicking, while the rest of the field swooped over the jump . . . and the crowd raced across the pelouze to see the horses come into the stretch. . . . I have seen the one-legged street walker who works the Boulevard Madelaine between the Rue Cambon and Bernheim Jeune's limping along the pavement through the crowd on a rainy night with a beefy red-faced Episcopal clergyman holding an umbrella over her.[55]

Each of the six sentences he wrote is really a short story in miniature, in that each contains a setting, characters, and an implicit conflict. In the first of the two sentences cited above, the horse which is the "favourite" is quickly forgotten, as the crowd runs across the turf of the infield to see the stretch run. While the horse "crashes" down into a "heap kicking," both horses and men continue without pause; the crowd, motivated by its wagers, "raced" as surely as do the horses to the finish line. In the second sentence cited above, we again view the individual as victim, ignored as an individual, in contrast to an indifferent crowd and a consuming personal motivation. The "beefy red-faced" clergyman herds his captive soul like a policeman (souls are hard to come by for an Episcopalian in a Catholic country). The tension is achieved in the contrast between large and small, hard and soft, competence and incompetence. Here, as in all six of the sentences, there is a sense of timelessness: the vision of an instant and all its internal stresses, isolated and captured, yet speaking for itself. The matter-of-factness is journalistic, but it is also poetic. These sentences are very much like Pound's "In a Station of the Metro" which he called "a *hokku*-like sentence":

54. Baker, p. 90.   55. Baker, pp. 90–91.

> The apparition of these faces in the crowd;
> Petals on a wet, black bough.

Again, the suspended tension. The illumination of the beauty of the faces suddenly realized, fragile, temporary—subject to forces which are gross, inevitable, dark, and threatening. There is a similar tension in the first two lines of Pound's "The Garden":

> Like a skein of loose silk blown against a wall
> She walks by the railing of a path in Kensington Gardens

Soft, loose, disconnected, she moves in marked contrast to the stability, hardness and durability of the wall and the railing.

From these "Paris 1922" sentences, Hemingway turned, with the same discipline, the same basic ingredients, to the vignettes of *In Our Time* and then to the first great stories, "Indian Camp" and "Big Two-Hearted River." During the years 1922–24 in Paris, listening, reading, writing, and rewriting, he was able to find his identity as a writer of prose fiction, his mask for creation, and from that identity develop a method for work and create a technique for expression, an expression which gave a new definition to short fiction and a new direction to prose style in the English language. These were the ingredients, then, of that expression, the presentation and condensation of what is accurately and minutely observed (from the root of journalism) and the intensity and illumination of language (from the root of Imagism). Journalism and poetry may seem unlikely partners, but it was Pound who said, "Literature is news that STAYS news."

5. A Comprehensive Checklist of Hemingway Short Fiction Criticism, Explication, and Commentary

I. Books on Hemingway's Work Containing Discussion of the Short Stories

NOTE: Discussions of individual stories in the following books are listed separately for each story in Section VI of the checklist. Items reprinted in critical collections listed below are listed in Sections III, IV, and VI in their original publications as articles or book segments. Items which appear for the first time in a collection (as in the Astro and Benson collection) and which deal with several stories or the stories generally are listed in this section only.

Astro, Richard, and Jackson J. Benson, eds. *Hemingway in Our Time*. Corvallis: Oregon State University Press, 1974.
    Pp. 13–23: "Posthumous Hemingway, and Nicholas Adams" by Philip Young.
    Pp. 53–65: "Internal Treachery and the Last Published Short Stories of Ernest Hemingway" by Delbert E. Wilder.
    Pp. 113–143: "Hemingway's Sense of Place" by Robert W. Lewis.
    Pp. 145–157: "A Sometime Great Notion: Ernest Hemingway's Roman Catholicism" by John Clark Pratt.
    Pp. 159–173: "Rectitude in Hemingway's Fiction: How Rite Makes Right" by John Griffith.
    Pp. 175–189: "Hemingway and the Modern Metaphysical Tradition" by Michael Friedberg.
Atkins, John. *The Art of Ernest Hemingway: His Work and Personality*. London: Spring Books, 1952.
Baker, Carlos. *Hemingway: The Writer as Artist*. Princeton, N.J.: Princeton University Press, 1952. [Referred to below as "Baker (*Artist*)".]
Baker, Carlos. *Ernest Hemingway: A Life Story*. New York: Charles Scribner's Sons, 1969. [Referred to below as "Baker (*Life*)".]
Baker, Carlos, ed. *Hemingway and His Critics: An International Anthology*. New York: Hill and Wang, 1961. [Referred to below as "Baker (*Critics*)".]
    Pp. 71–79: "Hemingway's Short Stories" by H. E. Bates, reprinted from *The Modern Short Story*. London: Thomas Nelson & Sons, Ltd., 1942, pp. 167–78.
    Pp. 245–58: "Hemingway: The Matador and the Crucified" by Melvin Backman, reprinted from *Modern Fiction Studies*, I (August 1955), 2–11.
Baker, Sheridan. *Ernest Hemingway: An Introduction and Interpretation*. New York: Holt, Rinehart & Winston, Inc., 1967.
Bakker, J. *Ernest Hemingway: The Artist as Man of Action*. Assen, N.V.: Van Gorcum & Company, 1972.

Benson, Jackson J. *Hemingway: The Writer's Art of Self-Defense*. Minneapolis: University of Minnesota Press, 1969.

DeFalco, Joseph. *The Hero in Hemingway's Short Stories*. Pittsburgh: University of Pittsburgh Press, 1963.

Fenton, Charles A. *The Apprenticeship of Ernest Hemingway: The Early Years*. New York: Farrar, Straus & Young, 1954.

Grebstein, Sheldon Norman. *Hemingway's Craft*. Carbondale: Southern Illinois University Press, 1973.

Gurko, Leo. *Ernest Hemingway and the Pursuit of Heroism*. New York: Thomas Y. Crowell Company, 1968.

Hovey, Richard B. *Hemingway: The Inward Terrain*. Seattle: University of Washington Press, 1968.

Howell, John M., ed. *Hemingway's African Stories: The Stories, Their Sources, Their Critics*. New York: Charles Scribner's Sons, 1969.

Pp. 55–59: "The Slopes of Kilimanjaro" by Carlos Baker, reprinted from *American Heritage Magazine*, XIX (August 1968), 40, 42–43, 90–91; first published, in different form, as "The Snows of Kilimanjaro: A Biographical Perspective," in *Novel: A Forum on Fiction*, I (Fall 1967), 19–23.

Pp. 93–94: "Hemingway's Riddle of Kilimanjaro: Idea and Image" by Robert O. Stephens, reprinted from *American Literature*, XXXII (March 1960), 84–87.

Pp. 101–09: "Vivienne de Watteville, Hemingway's Companion on Kilimanjaro" by Robert W. Lewis, Jr., reprinted from *The Texas Quarterly*, IX (Winter 1966), 78–85.

Pp. 113–15:"Dangerous Game" by Carlos Baker, reprinted from *Hemingway: The Writer as Artist*. Princeton, N.J.: Princeton University Press, 1963, pp. 186–91; reprinted as the first part of "The Two African Stories" in Weeks, Robert P., pp. 118–21.

Pp. 116–18: "The Hero and the Code" by Philip Young, reprinted from *Ernest Hemingway: A Reconsideration*. University Park, Penn.: The Pennsylvania State University Press, 1966, pp. 69–74.

Pp. 119–28: "The Shorter Happy Life of Mrs. Macomber" by Warren Beck, reprinted from *Modern Fiction Studies*, I (November 1955), 28–37.

Pp. 129–36: "Ernest Hemingway: 'The Short Happy Life of Francis Macomber' " by R. S. Crane, reprinted from *The Idea of the Humanities and Other Essays Critical and Historical*. 2 vols., Chicago: The University of Chicago Press, 1967, II, pp. 315–26; originally published in *English "A" Analyst* (Department of English, Northwestern University), XVI (November 1, 1949).

Pp. 137–41: "Macomber and the Critics" by Robert B. Holland, reprinted from *Studies in Short Fiction*, V (Winter 1967), 171–78.

Pp. 142–44: " 'The Snows of Kilimanjaro': Commentary" by Caroline Gordon, and Allen Tate, reprinted from *The House of Fiction*. New York: Charles Scribner's Sons, 1950, pp. 419–23.

Pp. 145–49: "The Leopard and the Hyena: Symbol and Meaning in 'The Snows of Kilimanjaro' " by Marion Montgomery, reprinted from *The University of Kansas City Review*, XXVII (Summer 1961), 277–82.

Pp. 150–57: " 'The Snows of Kilimanjaro': A Revaluation" by Oliver Evans, reprinted from *PMLA*, LXXVI (December 1961), 602–07.

Pp. 158–61: " 'The Snows of Kilimanjaro': Harry's Second Chance" by Gloria R. Dussinger, reprinted from *Studies in Short Fiction*, V (Fall 1967), 54–59.

Joost, Nicholas. *Ernest Hemingway and the Little Magazines: The Paris Years*. Barre, Massachusetts: Barre Publishers, 1968.

Killinger, John. *Hemingway and the Dead Gods: A Study in Existentialism*. Lexington: University of Kentucky Press, 1960.

Lewis, Robert W., Jr. *Hemingway on Love*. Austin and London: University of Texas Press, 1965.

Longyear, Christopher R. *Linguistically Determined Categories of Meanings: A Comparative Analysis of Meaning in "The Snows of Kilimanjaro."* The Hague: Mouton, 1971.

McCaffery, John K. M., ed. *Ernest Hemingway: The Man and His Work*. New York: Cooper Square Publishers, Inc., 1969.

Pp. 76–108: "Ernest Hemingway: A Tragedy of Craftsmanship" by J. Kashkeen, reprinted from *International Literature*, V (1935), (U.S.S.R.).

Pp. 130–42: "Farewell the Separate Peace" by Edgar Johnson, reprinted from *Sewanee Review*, XLVIII (July–September 1940), 289–300.

Pp. 143–89: "Ernest Hemingway: You Could Always Come Back" by Maxwell Geismar, reprinted from *Writers in Crisis*. Boston: Houghton Mifflin Company, 1942, pp. 39–85.

Pp. 236–57: "Hemingway: Gauge of Morale" by Edmund Wilson, reprinted from *The Wound and the Bow*. New York: Oxford University Press, 1947, pp. 214–42.

Pp. 329–39: "Hemingway and James" by George Hemphill, reprinted from *The Kenyon Review*, XI (Winter 1949), 50–60.

Pp. 340–51: "Hemingway's Women" by Theodore Bardacke.

Montgomery, Constance Cappel. *Hemingway in Michigan*. New York: Fleet Publishing Corporation, 1966.

Nahal, Chaman. *The Narrative Pattern in Ernest Hemingway's Fiction*. Rutherford: Farleigh Dickenson University Press, 1971.

Peterson, Richard K. *Hemingway: Direct and Oblique*. Paris: Mouton and Company, 1969.

Rovit, Earl H. *Ernest Hemingway*. New York: Twayne Publishers, 1963.

Sanderson, S. F. *Ernest Hemingway*. New York: Grove Press, Inc., 1961.

Scott, Nathan A., Jr. *Ernest Hemingway: A Critical Essay*. [Pamphlet] Grand Rapids, Michigan: William B. Eerdmans, Pub., 1966.

Shaw, Samuel. *Ernest Hemingway*. New York: Frederick Ungar Publishing Co., 1973.

Stephens, Robert O. *Hemingway's Nonfiction: The Public Voice*. Chapel Hill: University of North Carolina Press, 1968.

Wagner, Linda W., ed. *Ernest Hemingway: Five Decades of Criticism*. East Lansing: Michigan State University Press, 1974.

> Pp. 75–102: "Ernest Hemingway" by Robert Penn Warren, reprinted from *The Kenyon Review*, IX (Winter 1947), 1–28.

> Pp. 103–08: "The Other Hemingway" by Alan Holder, reprinted from *Twentieth Century Literature*, IX (October, 1963), 153–57.

> Pp. 188–200: "Hemingway and the Thing Left Out" by Julian Smith, reprinted from *Journal of Modern Literature*, I (1970–71), 169–82.

> Pp. 201–11: "The Marinating of *For Whom the Bell Tolls*" by Linda W. Wagner, reprinted from *Journal of Modern Literature*, II (1972), 533–46.

> Pp. 222–23: "Mr. Hemingway's Dry Points" by Edmund Wilson, reprinted from *Dial*, LXXVII (October 1924), 340–41.

> Pp. 224–40: "The Shock of Vision: An Imagist Reading of *In Our Time*" by Richard Hasbany.

Waldhorn, Arthur. *Ernest Hemingway: A Collection of Criticism*. New York: McGraw-Hill Book Company, 1973.

> Pp. 56–82: "The Snows of Ernest Hemingway" by Bernard S. Oldsey, reprinted from *Wisconsin Studies in Contemporary Literature*, IV (Spring–Summer 1963), 172–98.

> Pp. 112–26: "Hemingway and the Pale Cast of Thought" by Robert Evans, reprinted from *American Literature*, XXXVIII (May 1966), 161–76.

Waldhorn, Arthur. *A Reader's Guide to Ernest Hemingway*. New York: Farrar, Straus, & Giroux, 1972. [Referred to below as "RG."]

Watts, Emily Stipes. *Ernest Hemingway and the Arts*. Urbana, Illinois: University of Illinois Press, 1971.

Weeks, Robert P., ed. *Hemingway: A Collection of Critical Essays*. Englewood Cliffs, N.J.: Prentice-Hall, 1962.

> Pp. 93–94: " 'In Our Time': A Review" by D. H. Lawrence, reprinted from *Phoenix*. New York: The Viking Press, Inc., 1936, p. 365.

> Pp. 95–111: "Adventures of Nick Adams" by Philip Young, reprinted from *Ernest Hemingway*. New York: Holt, Rinehart and Winston, Inc., 1952, pp. 1–27.

> Pp. 112–13: "A Clean Well-Lighted Place" by Sean O'Faolain, reprinted from *Short Stories: A Study in Pleasure*. Boston: Little, Brown and Company, Inc., 1961, pp. 76–79.

Pp. 114–17: "The Discovery of Evil: An Analysis of 'The Killers' " by Cleanth Brooks, and Robert Penn Warren, reprinted from *Understanding Fiction*. New York: Appleton-Century-Crofts, Inc., 1959, pp. 303–12.

Pp. 118–26: "The Two African Stories" by Carlos Baker, reprinted from *Hemingway: The Writer as Artist*. Princeton: Princeton University Press, 1952, pp. 186–96.

White, William. *Guide to Ernest Hemingway: An Essay*. [Pamphlet] Columbus, Ohio: Charles E. Merrill Publishing Co., 1969.

Young, Philip. *Ernest Hemingway*. New York: Holt, Rinehart & Winston, 1952. [Referred to below as "Young, 1st."]

Young, Philip. *Ernest Hemingway: A Reconsideration*. University Park, Pennsylvania: Pennsylvania State University Press, 1966. [Referred to below as "Young, 2nd."]

Young, Philip and Charles W. Mann. *The Hemingway Manuscripts: An Inventory*. University Park, Pennsylvania: Pennsylvania State University Press, 1969. [In Section VI of this checklist, unpublished short fiction manuscripts are identified by reference to this catalog.]

II. Dissertations Containing Discussion of Hemingway's Short Stories

NOTE: Dissertations which became the basis for a book on Hemingway's work have not been listed. Except where indicated, only dissertations which are available through University Microfilms have been listed.

Alderman, Taylor. "Ernest Hemingway: Four Studies in the Competitive Motif." The University of New Mexico, 1970.

Bobb, Sydney Ralph. "Fighter Against Loss: The Hemingway Hero." Stanford University, 1954.

Bovie, Verne H. "The Evolution of a Myth: A Study of the Major Symbols in the Works of Ernest Hemingway." University of Pennsylvania, 1957.

Broer, Lawrence Richard. "The Effects of Ernest Hemingway's Identification with Certain Aspects of Spanish Thinking on His Rendering of Character." Bowling Green State University, 1968.

Byrd, Lemuel Brian. "Characterization in Ernest Hemingway's Fiction: 1925–1952, with a Dictionary of the Characters." University of Colorado, 1969.

Dean, Anthony Bruce. "Hemingway's Fiction: A Tragic Vision of Life." Temple University, 1971.

Dunn, Charles William Jr. "Ironic Vision in Hemingway's Short Stories." Kent State University, 1971.

Elliott, Gary Douglas. "The Hemingway Hero's Quest for Faith." Kansas State University, 1973.

Feeney, Joseph John, S.J. "American Anti-War Writers of World War I: A Literary Study of Randolph Bourne, Harriet Monroe, Carl Sandburg, John Dos Passos, E. E. Cummings, and Ernest Hemingway." University of Pennsylvania, 1971.

Gebhardt, Richard Coate. "Denial and Affirmation of Values in the Fiction of Ernest Hemingway." Michigan State University, 1969.

Gleaves, Edwin Sheffield. "The Spanish Influence on Ernest Hemingway's Concepts of Death, Nada, and Immortality." Emory University, 1964.

Grant, Naomi M. "The Role of Women in the Fiction of Ernest Hemingway." University of Denver, 1968.

Grimes, Sister Richard Mary. "Hemingway: The Years with Esquire." Ohio State University, 1965.

Hagood, Thomas Neal. "Elements of Humor in Ernest Hemingway." Louisiana State University and Agricultural and Mechanical College, 1968.

Josephs, Mary Jim. "The Hunting Metaphor in Hemingway and Faulkner." Michigan State University, 1973."

Kobler, Jasper Fred III. "Journalist and Artist: The Dual Role of Ernest Hemingway." The University of Texas at Austin, 1968.

Kvam, Wayne Eugene. "The Critical Reaction to Hemingway in Germany." The University of Wisconsin, 1969.

Laurence, Frank Michael. "The Film Adaptations of Hemingway: Hollywood and the Hemingway Myth." University of Pennsylvania, 1970.

Linderoth, Leon Walter. "The Female Characters of Ernest Hemingway." The Florida State University, 1966.

MacDonald, Scott M. "Narrative Perspective in the Short Stories of Ernest Hemingway." University of Florida, 1970. [Not available through University Microfilms.]

Matsuda, Sumio. "Symbolism and the Rhetoric of Fiction in Hemingway's Novels." University of Southern California, 1967.

Mikhail, Mona Naguib. "Major Existentialist Themes and Methods in the Short Fiction of Idris, Mahfouz, Hemingway and Camus." The University of Michigan, 1972.

Morrison, Robert William. "The Short Stories of Ernest Hemingway: A Search for Love and Identity." Washington State University, 1969.

Nelson, Jon Eric. "Religious Experience in the Fiction of Ernest Hemingway." University of North Carolina at Chapel Hill, 1969.

Nucci, Joseph Charles. "The Poetry of Time and Place in the Fiction of Ernest Hemingway." University of Pittsburgh, 1968.

O'Brien, Richard Michael. "The Thematic Interrelation of the Concepts of Time and Thought in the Works of Ernest Hemingway." New York University, 1969.

Oliver, Charles Montgomery. "Principles of 'True Felt Emotion' in Hemingway's Novels." Bowling Green State University, 1970.

Pendleton, Harold Edmen. "Ernest Hemingway: A Theory of Learning." University of Illinois, 1959.

Rodnon, Stewart. "Sports, Sporting Codes, and Sportsmanship in the Work of Ring Lardner, James T. Farrell, Ernest Hemingway and William Faulkner." New York University, 1961.

Rosen, Kenneth Mark. "Ernest Hemingway: The Function of Violence." The University of New Mexico, 1969.

Shtogren, John Alexander Jr. "Ernest Hemingway's Aesthetic Use of Journalism in His First Decade of Fiction." University of Michigan, 1971.

Silverman, Raymond Joel. *The Short Story Composite: Forms, Functions, and Applications.* University of Michigan, 1970.

Sniderman, Stephen Lee. "The 'Composite' in Twentieth Century American Literature." University of Wisconsin, 1970.

Somers, Paul Preston Jr. "Sherwood Anderson and Ernest Hemingway: Influences and Parallels." The Pennsylvania State University, 1970.

Stephens, Robert Oren. "The Escape Motif in the Works of Ernest Hemingway." The University of Texas, 1958.

Stephenson, Edward Roger. "Stephen Crane and Ernest Hemingway: A Study in Literary Continuity." Brown University, 1972.

Sylvester, Bickford. "Hemingway's Extended Vision: The Old Man and the Sea." University of Washington, 1966.

Toop, Ronald Glenson. "Technique and Vision in the Fiction of Ernest Hemingway: A Chronological Study." University of Toronto, 1969. [Not available through University Microfilms.]

Vandiver, Samuel Earl. "The Architecture of Hemingway's Prose." The University of Texas, 1967.

Wylder, Robert Clay. "An Investigation of Hemingway's Fictional Method, Its Sources, and Its Influence on American Literature." The University of Wisconsin, 1955.

Yokelson, Joseph Bernard. "Symbolism in the Fiction of Ernest Hemingway." Brown University, 1960.

Young, Leo Vernon. "Values of the Young Characters in the Fiction of Dos Passos, Hemingway, and Steinbeck." Stanford University, 1957.

III. General Books Containing Discussion of Several Hemingway Short Stories

NOTE: Page numbers in this section may refer (1) to the inclusive pages of a titled essay, titled chapter, or untitled segment in which discussion of the stories occurs here and there throughout, or (2) to part of a titled essay, titled chapter, or untitled segment which is totally devoted to a discussion of the stories.

Aldridge, John W. "Hemingway: Nightmare and the Correlative of Loss," in *After the Lost Generation: A Critical Study of the Writers of Two Wars.* New York: McGraw-Hill, 1951, pp. 26–29.

Ashley, Schuyler. *Essay Reviews.* Kansas City: Lowell Press, 1929, p. 67. [Review of *In Our Time* (1925) from Kansas City *Star.*]

Bachman, Melvin. "Hemingway: The Matador and the Crucified," in Litz, A. Walton, ed. *Modern American Fiction: Essays in Criticism.* New York: Oxford University Press, 1963, pp. 201–14.

Beach, Joseph Warren. *The Outlook for American Prose.* Chicago: University of Chicago Press, 1926, pp. 11, 277–78.

Beach, Joseph Warren. *American Fiction: 1920–1940.* New York: The Macmillan Company, 1942, pp. 108–10.

Booth, Wayne C. *The Rhetoric of Fiction.* Chicago: University of Chicago Press, 1961, pp. 151–52, 299–300.

Bridgman, Richard. "Ernest Hemingway," in *The Colloquial Style in America.* New York: Oxford University Press, 1966, pp. 195–230.

Brooks, Cleanth. *The Hidden God.* New Haven: Yale University Press, 1963, pp. 8–16.

Earnst, Ernest. *The Single Vision.* New York: New York University Press, 1970, pp. 144–50.

Fiedler, Leslie A. *Love and Death in the American Novel.* New York: Criterion Books, 1960, pp. 305–07, 351.

Fiedler, Leslie A. *The Return of the Vanishing American.* New York: Stein and Day, 1969, pp. 144–45.

French, Warren. *The Social Novel at the End of an Era.* Carbondale and Edwardsville: Southern Illinois University Press, 1966, pp. 91–93, 98–99, 108–09.

Geismar, Maxwell. "Ernest Hemingway: You Could Always Come Back," in *Writers in Crisis.* Boston: Houghton Mifflin, 1942, pp. 39–85. [Reprinted in M. Caffery, John K. ed. *Ernest Hemingway: The Man and His Work.* New York: Cooper Square Publishers, Inc., 1969, pp. 143–89.]

Grant, Douglas. "Men Without Women," in *Purpose and Place: Essays on American Writers*. New York: St. Martin's Press, 1965, pp. 175–82.

Grebstein, Sheldon N. "Hemingway's Dark and Bloody Capital," Topic: 12, VI, *New Perspectives in American Literature*. Washington, Pennsylvania: Washington and Jefferson College, 1966, pp. 21–30.

Grebstein, Sheldon Norman. "The Tough Hemingway and His Hard-Boiled Children," in Madden, David, ed., *Tough Guy Writers of the Thirties*. Carbondale: Southern Illinois University Press, 1968, pp. 18–41.

Gross, Theodore. *The Heroic Ideal in American Literature*. New York: Free Press, 1971, pp. 198–221.

Hassan, Ihab. *Radical Innocence*. New York: Harper and Row, 1961, p. 56.

Hays, Peter L. *The Limping Hero: Grotesques in Literature*. New York: New York University Press, 1971, pp. 70–77.

Heiney, Donald. *Recent American Literature*. Great Neck, New York: Barron's Education Series, Inc., 1958, pp. 162–65.

Howe, Irving. "The Quest for a Moral Style," in *A World More Attractive: A View of Modern Literature*. New York: Horizon Press, 1963, p. 69.

Huddleston, Sisley. *Paris Salons, Cafes, Studios: Being Social, Artistic and Literary Memories*. Philadelphia and London: J. B. Lippincott Co., 1928, pp. 121–23.

Kaplan, Harold. *The Passive Voice: An Approach to Modern Fiction*. Athens: Ohio University Press, 1966, pp. 93–110.

Kazin, Alfred. *On Native Grounds*. Garden City, New York: Doubleday & Company, 1956, pp. 253–56.

Lawrence, D. H. "*In Our Time*: A Review," in *Phoenix*. New York: The Viking Press, Inc., 1936, p. 365. [Reprinted in Weeks, Robert P., ed., *Hemingway: A Collection of Critical Essays*. Englewood Cliffs, New Jersey: Prentice-Hall, Inc., 1962, pp. 93–94.]

MacDonald, Dwight. *Against the American Grain: Essays on the Effects of Mass Culture*. New York: Random House, 1962, pp. 173–78.

Maloney, Michael F. "Ernest Hemingway: The Missing Third Dimension," in Gardiner, Harold C., S.J., ed., *Fifty Years of the American Novel: A Christian Appraisal*. New York: Charles Scribner's Sons, 1952, pp. 184–86, 188.

McCole, C. John. "Ernest Hemingway: Spokesman for His Generation," in *Lucifer at Large*. New York: Longmans, Green and Co., 1937, pp. 153–72.

Meaker, M. J. *Sudden Endings*. Garden City, New York: Doubleday & Company, 1964, pp. 1–25.

Mizener, Arthur. "The Two Hemingways," in Bode, Carl, ed., *The Great Experiment in American Literature: Six Lectures*. New York: Frederick A. Praeger, Publisher, 1961, pp. 145–51.

Mizener, Arthur. "The American Hero as Leatherstocking: Nick Adams,"

The Sense of Life in the Modern Novel. Boston: Houghton Mifflin, 1964, pp. 205–26.

Mosely, Edwin M. *Pseudonyms of Christ in the Modern Novel: Motifs and Methods.* Pittsburgh: University of Pittsburgh Press, 1962, pp. 111–13.

Noble, David W. "The Lost Generation: Winston Churchill, Ernest Hemingway," in *The Eternal Adam and the New World Garden: The Central Myth in the American Novel Since 1830.* New York: Braziller, 1968, pp. 146–51.

O'Brien, Edward J. *The Advance of the American Short Story.* New York: Dodd, Mead, 1931, pp. 269–75.

O'Connor, Frank. *The Lonely Voice: A Study of the Short Story.* Cleveland: World, 1963, pp. 156–69. ["A Clean Well-Lighted Place," an essay on Hemingway's short stories.]

O'Faolain, Sean. *The Vanishing Hero.* New York: Grosset & Dunlap, 1956, pp. 119–25.

Orvis, Mary. *The Art of Writing Fiction.* New York: Prentice-Hall, 1948, pp. 99–101, 129–32.

Rosenfeld, Paul. "Hemingway's Perspective," in *By Way of Art.* Freeport, N.Y.: Books for Libraries Press, 1928; reprinted 1967, pp. 151–63.

Savage, D. S. "Ernest Hemingway," in *The Withered Branch: Six Studies in the Modern Novel.* London: Eyre and Spottiswoode, 1950, pp. 24–26.

Schorer, Mark. *The World We Imagine: Selected Essays.* New York: Farrar, Straus, & Giroux, 1968, pp. 332–35.

Snell, George. *The Shapers of American Fiction.* New York: Cooper Square Publishers, 1961, pp. 159–60, 163, 170–71.

Stewart, Randall. *American Literature and Christian Doctrine.* Baton Rouge: Louisiana State University Press, 1958, pp. 35–36, 134–35.

Straumann, Heinrich. *American Literature in the Twentieth Century.* New York: Harper and Row, 1965, pp. 101–04.

Tanner, Tony. "Ernest Hemingway's Unhurried Sensations," in *The Reign of Wonder: Naivity and Reality in American Literature.* Cambridge: Cambridge University Press, 1965, pp. 228–57.

Walcutt, Charles C. *American Literary Naturalism, A Divided Stream.* Minneapolis: University of Minnesota Press, 1966, pp. 271–72, 275–76.

West, Ray B., Jr. *The Short Story in America: 1900–1950.* Chicago: Regnery, 1952, pp. 85–106. [Chapter IV: "Hemingway and Faulkner: Two Masters of the Modern Short Story."]

Wilson, Colin. *The Outsider.* Boston: Houghton Mifflin Company, 1956, pp. 31–39.

Wilson, Edmund. *The Wound and the Bow: Seven Studies in Literature.* New York: Oxford University Press, 1947, pp. 214–42. [Reprinted in McCaffery, John K. M., ed. *Ernest Hemingway: The Man and His Work.* New York: Cooper Square Publishers, Inc., 1969, pp. 236–61.]

Wilson, Edmund. *The Shores of Light: A Literary Chronicle of the Twenties and Thirties*. New York: The Noonday Press, 1952, pp. 115–24. ["Emergence of Ernest Hemingway," a review of *Three Stories and Ten Poems* and *in our time* (1924); reprinted in Baker (*Critics*), pp. 55–60.]

Witham, W. Tasker. *The Adolescent in the American Novel: 1920–1960*. New York: Frederick Ungar, 1964, pp. 34–35, 235.

Wright, Austin McGiffert. *The American Short Story in the Twenties*. Chicago: University of Chicago Press, pp. 33–34, 94–95, 370–73, 391–93, 400–02.

IV. General Articles Containing Discussion of Several Hemingway Short Stories

Adams, J. Donald. "Ernest Hemingway," *English Journal*, XXVIII (February 1939), 87–94.

Aldridge, John W. "Hemingway: The Etiquette of the Berserk," *Mandrake*, II (Autumn–Winter 1954–55), 331–41. [Reprinted in *In Search of Heresy*, New York: McGraw-Hill, 1956, pp. 149–65.]

Allen, Charles A. "Ernest Hemingway's Clean, Well-Lighted Heroes," *Pacific Spectator*, IX (Autumn 1955), 383–89.

Anderson, David D. "Ernest Hemingway, the Voice of an Era," *Personalist*, XLVII (Spring 1966), 234–47.

Backman, Melvin. "Hemingway: The Matador and the Crucified," *Modern Fiction Studies*, I (August 1955), 2–11. [Reprinted in slightly altered form in Baker, Carlos, ed., *Hemingway and His Critics: An International Anthology*. New York: Hill and Wang, pp. 245–58. Reprinted from *Hemingway and His Critics* in Baker, Carlos, ed., *Ernest Hemingway: Critiques of Four Major Novels*. New York: Charles Scribner's Sons, 1962, pp. 135–43.]

Bardacke, Theodore. "Hemingway's Women," in McCaffery, John K. M., ed., *Ernest Hemingway: The Man and His Work*. New York: Cooper Square Publishers, Inc., 1969, pp. 340–51.

Bell, Neil. "Of the Company," *Mark Twain Journal*, XI (Summer 1962), 18.

Benson, Jackson J. "Patterns of Connection and Their Development in Hemingway's *In Our Time*," *Rendezvous* (Special Hemingway Issue), (Winter 1970), 37–52.

Bluefarb, Sam. "The Search for the Absolute in Hemingway's 'A Clean, Well-

Lighted Place' and 'The Snows of Kilimanjaro,'" *Bulletin of the Rocky Mountain Modern Language Association*, XXV (1971), 3–9.

Bryan, James E. "Hemingway as Vivisector," *University Review*, XXX (Autumn 1963), 3–12.

Burhans, Clinton S., Jr. "The Complex Unity of *In Our Time*," *Modern Fiction Studies* (Ernest Hemingway Special Number), XIV (1968), 313–28.

Burnam, Tom. "Primitivism and Masculinity in the Work of Ernest Hemingway," *Modern Fiction Studies*, I (August 1955), 20–24.

Ciardi, John. "The Language of an Age" ("Manner of Speaking" Column), *Saturday Review*, XLIV (July 28, 1961), 32.

Clendenning, John. "Hemingway's Gods, Dead and Alive," *Texas Studies in Literature and Language*, III (Winter 1962), 489–502.

Colvert, James B. "Ernest Hemingway's Morality in Action," *American Literature*, XXVII (November 1955), 372–85.

Cowley, Malcolm. "Hemingway at Midnight," *New Republic*, CXI (August 14, 1944), 190–95. [Reprinted in expanded form as "Introduction," *The Portable Hemingway*, ed. Malcolm Cowley. New York: Viking Press, Inc., 1945, pp. VII–XXIV. "Introduction" to the *Portable* reprinted as "Nightmare and Ritual in Hemingway," in Weeks, Robert P., ed., *Hemingway: A Collection of Critical Essays*. Englewood Cliffs, N.J.: Prentice-Hall, Inc., pp. 40–51.]

Cowley, Malcolm. "The Middle American Style: Davy Crockett to Ernest Hemingway," *New York Times Book Review*, (July 15, 1945), pp. 3, 14.

Daiches, David. "Ernest Hemingway," *English Journal*. XXX (March 1941), 175–86. [Reprinted in *College English*, II (May 1941), 725–36.]

Dieckmann, Edward A., Jr. "The Hemingway Hypnosis," *Mark Twain Journal*, XI (Summer 1962), 3–4, 16.

Dillingham, W. B. "Hemingway and Death," *Emory University Quarterly*, XIX (Summer 1963), 95–101.

Drinnon, Richard. "In the American Heartland: Hemingway and Death," *The Psycho-Analytic Review*, LII (Summer 1965), 5–31.

Drummond, Ann. "The Hemingway Code as Seen in the Early Short Stories," *Discourse: A Review of the Liberal Arts*, I (October 1958), 248–52.

Eastman, Max. "The Great and Small in Ernest Hemingway," *Saturday Review*, XLII (April 4, 1959), 13–15, 50–51.

Egri, Peter. "The Relationship Between the Short Story and the Novel, Realism and Naturalism in Hemingway's Art," *Hungarian Studies in English*, IV (1969), 105–26.

Evans, Robert. "Hemingway and the Pale Cast of Thought," *American Literature*, XXXVIII (May 1966), 161–76. [Reprinted in Waldhorn, Arthur, ed., *Ernest Hemingway: A Collection of Criticism*. New York: McGraw-Hill Book Company, 1973, pp. 112–26.]

Fenton, Charles A. "No Money for the Kingbird: Hemingway's Prizefight Stories," *American Quarterly*, IV (Winter 1952), 339–50.

Ficken, Carl. "Point-of-View in the Nick Adams Stories," *Fitzgerald/Hemingway Annual 1971*, Matthew J. Bruccoli and C. E. Frazer Clark, Jr., eds., Washington, D.C.: N.C.R. Microcard Editions, 1971, 212–35.

Fitz, Reginald. "The Meaning of Impotence in Hemingway and Eliot," *Connecticut Review*, IV (April 1971), 16–22.

Fitzgerald, F. Scott. "How to Waste Material: A Note on My Generation," *Bookman*, LXIII (May 1926), 262–65. [Reprinted in *Afternoon of an Author*. New York: Charles Scribner's Sons, 1958, pp. 117–22.]

Flanagan, John T. "Hemingway's Debt to Sherwood Anderson," *Journal of English and Germanic Philology*, LIV (October 1955), 507–20.

Fredrick, Otto. "Ernest Hemingway: Joy Through Strength," *American Scholar*, XXVI (Autumn 1957), 470, 518–30.

Friedman, Norman. "What Makes a Short Story Short?" *Modern Fiction Studies*, IV (Summer 1958), 103–17.

Gifford, William. "Ernest Hemingway: The Monsters and the Critics," *Modern Fiction Studies*, XIV (Autumn 1968), 255–70.

Goldhurst, William. "The Hyphenated Ham Sandwich of Ernest Hemingway and J. D. Salinger: A Study in Literary Continuity," *Fitzgerald/Hemingway Annual 1970*, Matthew J. Bruccoli and C. E. Frazer Clark, Jr., eds. Washington, D.C.: N.C.R. Microcard Editions, 1970, pp. 136–50.

Gordon, Caroline. "Notes on Hemingway and Kafka," *Sewanee Review*, LVII (April–June 1949), 215–26.

Gordon, David. "The Son and the Father: Patterns of Response to Conflict in Hemingway's Fiction," *Literature and Psychology*, XVI (Summer 1966), 122–38.

Grebstein, Sheldon Norman. "The Structure of Hemingway's Short Stories," *Fitzgerald/Hemingway Annual 1972*, Matthew J. Bruccoli and C. E. Frazer Clark, Jr., eds. Washington, D.C.: N.C.R. Microcard Editions, 1973, pp. 173–93.

Griffin, Gerald R. "Hemingway's Fictive Use of the Negro: 'the curious quality of incompleteness,' " *Husson Review*, I (1968), 104–11.

Hale, Nancy. "Hemingway and the Courage to Be," *Virginia Quarterly*, XXXVIII (Autumn 1962), 620–39. [Reprinted in *The Realities of Fiction: A Book About Writing*. Boston: Little, Brown, 1962, pp. 85–112.]

Halliday, E. M. "Hemingway's Hero," *University of Chicago Magazine*, LV (May 1953), 10–14.

Halliday, E. M. "Hemingway's *In Our Time*," *Explicator*, VII (March 1949), Item 35.

Hamalian, Leo. "Hemingway as Hunger Artist," *Literary Review*, XVI (Fall 1972), 5–13.

Harrison, James M. "Hemingway's *In Our Time*," *Explicator*, XVIII (May 1960), Item 51.

Hauger, B. A. "First Person Perspective in Four Hemingway Stories," *Rendezvous*, VI (1971), 29–38.

Hemphill, George. "Hemingway and James," *Kenyon Review*, XI (Winter 1949), 50–60. [Reprinted in McCaffery, John K. M., ed., *Ernest Hemingway: The Man and His Work*. Cleveland: World, 1950, pp. 329–39.]

Hertzel, Leo J. "Hemingway and the Problem of Belief," *Catholic World*, CLXXXIV (October 1956), 29–33.

Hertzel, Leo J. "The Look of Religion: Hemingway and Catholicism," *Renascence*, XVII (Winter 1964), 77–81.

Hicks, Granville. "The World of Hemingway," *New Freeman*, I (March 22, 1930), 40–42.

Hoffman, Frederick J. "No Beginning and No End: Hemingway and Death," *Essays in Criticism*, III (January 1953), 73–84.

Holder, Alan. "The Other Hemingway," *Twentieth Century Literature*, IX (October 1963), 153–57. [Reprinted in Wagner, Linda W., ed., *Ernest Hemingway: Five Decades of Criticism*. East Lansing: Michigan State University Press, 1974, pp. 103–8.]

Hurwitz, Harold M. "Hemingway's Tutor, Ezra Pound," *Modern Fiction Studies*, XVII (Winter 1971–72), 469–82.

Johnson, Edgar. "Farewell the Separate Peace," *Sewanee Review*, XLVII (July–September 1940), 289–300. [Reprinted in McCaffery, John K. M., ed., *Ernest Hemingway: The Man and His Work*. New York: Cooper Square Publishers, Inc., 1969, pp. 130–42.]

Johnson, James. "The Adolescent Hero: A Trend in Modern Fiction," *Twentieth Century Literature*, V (April 1959), 3–11.

Jones, John A. "Hemingway: The Critics and the Public Legend," *Western Humanities Review*, XIII (Autumn 1959), 387–400.

Kashkeen, J. "Ernest Hemingway: A Tragedy of Craftsmanship," *International Literature*, V (1935), (U.S.S.R.). [Reprinted in McCafferty, John K. M., ed., *Ernest Hemingway: The Man and His Work*. New York: Cooper Square Publishers, Inc., 1969, pp. 76–108.]

Knieger, Bernard. "The Concept of Maturity in Hemingway's Short Stories," *College Language Association Journal*, VII (1964), 149–56.

LeBost, Barbara. " 'The Way It Is': Something Else on Hemingway," *Journal of Existentialism*, VI (Winter 1965–66), 175–80.

Lebowitz, Alan. "Hemingway In Our Time," *The Yale Review*, LVIII (March 1969), 321–41.

Levin, Harry. "Observations on the Style of Ernest Hemingway," *Kenyon Review*, XIII (Autumn 1951), 581–608.

Light, Martin. "Of Wasteful Deaths: Hemingway Stories About the Spanish War," *Western Humanities Review*, XXIII (Winter 1969), 29–42.

Lovett, Robert Moss. "Ernest Hemingway," *English Journal*, XXI (October 1932), 609–17.

Mai, Robert P. "Ernest Hemingway and Men Without Women," *Fitzgerald/Hemingway Annual 1970*, Matthew J. Bruccoli and C. E. Frazer Clark, Jr., eds. Washington, D.C.: N.C.R. Microcard Editions, 1970, pp. 173–86.

Marsden, Malcolm M. "Hemingway's Symbolic Pattern: The Basis of Tone," *Discourse*, XII (Winter 1969), 16–28.

Monteiro, George. "The Education of Ernest Hemingway," *Journal of American Studies*, VIII (April 1974), 91–99.

Motola, Gabriel. "Hemingway's Code: Literature and Life," *Modern Fiction Studies*, X (Winter 1964–65), 319–29.

Moylan, Thomas J. "Violence in Hemingway," *Catholic World*, CLXXXI (July 1955), 287–93.

Oldsey, Bernard S. "Hemingway's Old Men," *Modern Fiction Studies*, I (August 1955), 31–35.

Oldsey, Bernard. "Of Hemingway's Arms and the Man," *College Literature*, I (Fall 1974), 174–89.

Oldsey, Bernard S. "The Snows of Ernest Hemingway," *Wisconsin Studies in Contemporary Literature*, IV (Spring–Summer 1963), 172–98. [Reprinted in Waldhorn, Arthur, ed., *Ernest Hemingway: A Collection of Criticism*. New York: McGraw-Hill Book Company, 1973, pp. 56–82.]

Rao, K. S. Narayana. "Women, Violence and Darkness in the World of Hemingway's Short Stories," *Literary Criterion*, IV (Winter 1960), 32–38.

Reardon, John. "Hemingway's Esthetic and Ethical Sportsmen," *University Review*, XXXIV (October 1967), 12–23.

Rosene, M. R. "The Five Best American Books Published Since 1900," *Writer*, XLVI (October 1934), 370–71.

Rouch, John S. "Jake Barnes as Narrator," *Modern Fiction Studies*, XI (Winter 1965–66), 361–70.

Savage, D. S. "Ernest Hemingway," *Hudson Review*, I (Autumn 1948), 380–401.

Schmidt, Dolores Barracano. "The Great American Bitch," *College English*, XXXII (May 1971), 900–905.

Schneiderman, Leo. "Hemingway: A Psychological Study," *Connecticut Review*, VI (April 1973), 34–49.

Schokley, Martin S. "Hemingway's Moment of Truth," *Colorado Quarterly*, V (Spring 1957), 380–88.

Schwartz, Delmore. "Ernest Hemingway's Literary Situation," *Southern Review*, III (Spring 1938), 769–82. [Reprinted in McCaffery, John K. M., ed., *Ernest Hemingway: The Man and His Work*. New York: Cooper Square Publishers, Inc., 1969, pp. 114–29.]

Schwartz, Delmore. "The Fiction of Ernest Hemingway," *Perspectives U.S.A.*, XIII (Autumn 1955), 68–88.

Shelton, Frank W. "The Family in Hemingway's Nick Adams Stories," *Studies in Short Fiction*, XI (Summer 1974), 303–05.

Skipp, Francis E. "Nick Adams, Prince of Abyssinia," *Carrell*, XI (1970), 20–26.

Slabey, R. M. "The Structure of *In Our Time*," *South Dakota Review*, III (August 1965), 38–52.

Smith, Julian. "Christ Times Four: Hemingway's Unknown Spanish Civil War Stories," *Arizona Quarterly*, XXV (Spring 1969), 5–17.

Smith, Julian. "Eyeless in Wyoming, Blind in Venice: Hemingway's Last Stories," *Connecticut Review*, IV (1971), 9–15.

Smith, Julian. "Hemingway and the Thing Left Out," *Journal of Modern Literature*, I (1970–71), 169–82. [Reprinted in Wagner, Linda W., ed., *Ernest Hemingway: Five Decades of Criticism*. East Lansing: Michigan State University Press, 1974, pp. 188–200.]

Somers, Paul P., Jr. "The Mark of Sherwood Anderson on Hemingway: A Look at the Text," *South Atlantic Quarterly*, LXXIII (Autumn 1974), 487–503.

St. John, Donald. "Indian Camp Camp," *Carleton Miscellany*, IX (Winter 1968), 95–109.

Stavrou, C. N. "Nada, Religion, and Hemingway," *Topic: 12*, VI (Fall 1966), 5–20.

Stein, William Bysshe. "Love and Lust in Hemingway's Short Stories," *Texas Studies in Literature*, III (Summer 1961), 234–42.

Takigawa, Motoo. "A Study of Ernest Hemingway: *Men Without Women*," *Journal of the Society of English and American Literature*, IV (May 1962), 41–66.

Waggoner, Hyatt H. "Ernest Hemingway," *Christian Scholar*, XXXVIII (June 1955), 114–20.

Wagner, Linda Welshimer. "The Marinating of *For Whom the Bell Tolls*," *Journal of Modern Literature*, II (November 1972), 533–46. [Reprinted in Wagner, Linda W., ed., *Ernest Hemingway: Five Decades of Criticism*. East Lansing: Michigan State University Press, 1974, pp. 201–11.]

Warren, Robert Penn. "Hemingway," *The Kenyon Review*, IX (Winter 1947), 1–28. [Reprinted in Wagner, Linda W., ed., *Ernest Hemingway: Five Decades of Criticism*. East Lansing: Michigan State University Press, 1974, pp. 75–102.]

Weeks, Robert P. "Cleaning Up Hemingway," *Fitzgerald/Hemingway Annual 1972*, Matthew J. Bruccoli and C. E. Frazer Clark, Jr., eds. Washington, D.C.: N.C.R. Microcard Editions, 1973, pp. 311–13.

West, Ray B. "Ernest Hemingway: Death in the Evening," *Antioch Review*, IV (Winter 1944), 569–80.

West, Ray B. "Ernest Hemingway: The Failure of Sensibility," *Sewanee Review*, LIII (1945), 120–35.

White, William. "Father and Son: Comments on Hemingway's Psychology,"
    The Dalhousie Review, (1952), 276–84.
White, William. "Ernest Hemingway: Violence, Blood, Death," *Orient/
    West*, VI (November 1961), 11–23.
Wylder, D. E. "Hemingway's Satiric Vision—The High School Years,"
    Rendezvous (Special Hemingway Issue), V (Winter 1970), 29–35.
Wyrick, Green D. "Hemingway and Bergson: The *Élan Vital*," *Modern
    Fiction Studies*, I (August 1955), 17–19.
Yalom, Irving D. and Marilyn Yalom. "Ernest Hemingway—A Psychiatric
    View," *Archives of General Psychiatry*, XXIV (June 1971), 485–94.
Young, Philip. " 'Big World Out There': The Nick Adams Stories," *Novel:
    A Forum for Fiction*, VI (Fall 1972), 5–19.
Young, Philip. "Hemingway's *In Our Time*," *Explicator,* X (April 1952),
    Item 43.
Young, Philip. "Hemingway's Manuscripts: The Vault Reconsidered,"
    Studies in American Fiction, II (Spring 1974), 3–11.

V. Reviews of Hemingway Story Collections

NOTE: The following items are listed chronologically by date of first publication. The only newspaper reviews included are those from the *New York Times Book Review*, the *New York Herald Tribune Books*, and the *Times Literary Supplement*. A key to abbreviations for the Hemingway story collections appears at the beginning of Section VI. An exception to those abbreviations here is the use of *First 49* for the collected stories, referring to the title of first publication: *The Fifth Column and the First Forty-Nine Stories*.

"K.J." Review of *TSTP*, *Transatlantic Review*, I (April 1924), 246.
Reid, Marjorie. Review of *iot*, *Transatlantic Review*, I (April 1924), 247–
    48.
Wilson, Edmund. "Mr. Hemingway's Dry Points," review of *TSTP* and *iot*,
    Dial, LXXVII (October 1924), 340–41. [Reprinted as part of "Emer-
    gence of Ernest Hemingway" in Wilson, Edmund, *The Shores of Light:
    A Literary Chronicle of the Twenties and Thirties*. New York: Farrar,
    Straus & Young, 1952, pp. 115–24; also reprinted as part of "Emergence
    . . ." in Baker, Carlos, ed., *Hemingway and His Critics*. New York: Hill
    and Wang, 1961, pp. 55–60; also reprinted in Wagner, Linda W., ed.,
    Ernest Hemingway: Five Decades of Criticism. East Lansing: Michigan
    State University Press, 1974, pp. 222–23.]

Review of *IOT, New York Times Book Review* (October 18, 1925), p. 8.

Rosenfeld, Paul. Review of *IOT, New Republic*, XLV (November 25, 1925), 22–23.

"E.W." Review of *IOT, This Quarter*, I (Autumn–Winter 1925–1926), 319–21.

Review of *IOT, Time*, VII (January 18, 1926), 38.

Tate, Allen. Review of *IOT, Nation*, XCCII (February 10, 1926), 160–62.

Kronenberger, Louis. Review of *IOT, Saturday Review of Literature*, II (February 13, 1926), 555.

Wolf, Robert. Review of *IOT, New York Herald Tribune Books* (February 14, 1926), p. 3.

O'Brien, Edward J. Review of *IOT, Now & Then*, Number 21 (Autumn 1926), 30–32.

Review of *IOT, Times Literary Supplement* (November 4, 1926), p. 766.

Lawrence, D. H. Review of *IOT, Calendar of Modern Letters*, IV (April 1927), 72–73. [Reprinted in *Phoenix: The Posthumous Papers of D. H. Lawrence*, ed. Edward D. McDonald, London: Heinemann, 1936, p. 365. Also reprinted in Weeks, Robert P., ed., *Hemingway: A Collection of Critical Essays*. Englewood Cliffs, N.J.: Prentice-Hall, Inc., 1962, pp. 93–94.]

Rascoe, Burton. Review of *MWW, Bookman,* LXVI (September 1927), 90.

Woolf, Virginia. "An Essay in Criticism," review of *MWW, New York Herald Tribune Books* (October 9, 1927), pp. 1, 8. [Reprinted in *Granite and Rainbow: Essays*. New York: Harcourt, Brace, 1958, pp. 85–92.]

Hutchison, Percy. Review of *MWW, New York Times Book Review* (October 16, 1927), pp. 9, 27.

Review of *MWW, Time*, X (October 24, 1927), 38.

Review of *MWW, New Yorker*, III (October 29, 1927), 92–94.

Krutch, Joseph Wood. Review of *MWW, Nation*, CXXV (November 16, 1927), 548.

Dodd, Lee Wilson. Review of *MWW, Saturday Review of Literature*, IV (November 19, 1927), 322–23.

Connolly, Cyril. Review of *MWW, New Statesman*, XXX (November 26, 1927), 208.

Wilson, Edmund. "The Sportsman's Tragedy," review of *MWW, New Republic*, LIII (December 14, 1927), 102–03. [Reprinted in *The Shores of Light*. New York: Farrar, Straus, and Young, Inc., 1952, pp. 339–44.]

Curtis, William. Review of *MWW, Town and Country*, LXXXII (December 15, 1927), 59.

Rothman, N. L. Review of *MWW, Dial*, LXXXIV (April 1, 1928), 336–38.

Mencken, H. L. Review of *MWW, American Mercury*, XIV (May 1922), 127.

Redman, Ben Ray. Review of *IOT*, *New York Herald Tribune Books*, (November 16, 1930), p. 22.

Review of *IOT*, *Saturday Review of Literature*, VII (January 24, 1931), 548.

Fadiman, Clifton. "A Letter to Mr. Hemingway," review of *WTN*, *New Yorker*, IX (October 28, 1933), 74–75.

Canby, Henry Seidel. "Farewell to the Nineties," review of *WTN*, *Saturday Review of Literature*, X (October 28, 1933), 217. [Reprinted in *Seven Years' Harvest*, Port Washington, N.Y.: Kennikat Press, Inc., 1964, pp. 150–54.]

Gregory, Horace. Review of *WTN*, *New York Herald Tribune Books* (October 29, 1933), p. 5.

Kronenberger, Louis. Review of *WTN*, *New York Times Book Review* (November 5, 1933), p. 6.

Review of *WTN*, *Time*, XXII (November 6, 1933), 59–60.

Troy, William. Review of *WTN*, *Nation*, CXXXVII (November 15, 1933), 570.

Matthews, T. S. Review of *WTN*, *New Republic*, LXXVII (November 15, 1933), 24.

Rascoe, Burton. Review of *WTN*, *Esquire*, I (January 1934), 86.

Review of *WTN*, *Times Literary Supplement* (February 8, 1934), p. 90.

Garnett, David. Review of *WTN*, *New Statesman & Nation*, VII (February 10, 1934), 192.

Plomer, William. Review of *WTN*, *Now & Then*, Number 47 (Spring 1934), 22–23.

Davis, Elmer. Review of *First 49*, *Saturday Review of Literature*, XVIII (October 15, 1938), 6.

Kazin, Alfred. Review of *First 49*, *New York Herald Tribune Books* (October 16, 1938), p. 5.

Review of *First 49*, *Time*, XXXII (October 17, 1938), 75.

Fadiman, Clifton. Review of *First 49*, *New Yorker*, XIV (October 22, 1938), 94–95.

Jack, Peter Monro. Review of *First 49*, *New York Times Book Review* (October 23, 1938), p. 4.

Cowley, Malcolm. "Hemingway in Madrid," review of *First 49*, *New Republic*, XCVI (November 2, 1938), 367–68.

Burgum, Edwin Berry. Review of *First 49*, *New Masses*, XXIX (November 22, 1938), 21–24.

Wilson, Edmund. "Hemingway and the Wars," review of *First 49*, *Nation*, CXLVII (December 10, 1938), 628, 630.

Trilling, Lionel. "Hemingway and His Critics," review of *First 49*, *Partisan Review*, VI (Winter 1939), 52–60. [Reprinted in Baker, Carlos, ed., *Hemingway and His Critics*. New York: Hill and Wang, 1961, pp. 61–70.]

Review of *First 49, Times Literary Supplement* (June 17, 1939), p. 359.

Mellers, W. H. "Hollywooden Hero," review of *First 49, Scrutiny*, VIII (December 1939), 335–44.

Norton, Dan S. "Eclectic Hemingway," review of the Viking Portable *Hemingway, New York Times Book Review* (October 8, 1944), p. 3.

Hicks, Granville. "Twenty Years of Hemingway," review of the Viking Portable *Hemingway, New Republic*, CXI (October 23, 1944), 524, 526.

Hyman, Stanley Edgar. "A Hemingway Sampler," review of *The Hemingway Reader, New York Times Book Review* (September 13, 1953), p. 28.

Whicher, George F. Review of *The Hemingway Reader, New York Herald Tribune Book Review* (September 27, 1953), p. 21.

Review of *FUS, Times Literary Supplement*, (March 7, 1968), p. 219.

Bradbury, Malcolm. Review of *FUS, New Statesman*, LXXV (March 22, 1968), 386–87.

Paul, Kenneth. Review of *FUS, Newsweek*, LXXIV (September 8, 1969), 88.

Baker, Carlos. Review of *FUS, Saturday Review*, LII (September 20, 1969), 36–37.

Young, Philip. Review of *FUS, New York Times Book Review*, (September 21, 1969), p. 6.

Spender, Stephen. Review of *FUS, New York Review of Books*, XIII (September 25, 1969), 5.

McNamara, Eugene. Review of *FUS, America*, CXXI (October 18, 1969), 333.

Hughes, John W. Review of *FUS, The New Leader*, LII (November 24, 1969), 19–20.

Hollander, John. Review of *FUS, Harper's Magazine*, CCXXXIX (December 1969), 146.

Sale, Roger. Review of *FUS, Hudson Review*, XXII (Winter 1969–70), 709–10.

Alderman, Taylor. Review of *EHA, Hemingway Notes*, I (Fall 1971), 22–23.

Prescott, Peter S. Review of *NA, Newsweek*, LXXIX (April 17, 1972), 100, 104.

Stephens, Robert O. Review of *EHA, Resources for American Literary Study*, II (Spring 1972), 115–16.

Review of *NA, Time* XCIX (May 1, 1972), 81.

Abrahams, William. Review of *NA, Atlantic*, CCXXIX (June 1972), 98, 100–01.

Larson, E. Review of *NA, The Carleton Miscellany*, XII (Spring–Summer 1972), 76.

McSweeney, Kerry. "The First Hemingway Hero," review of *NA, Dalhousie Review*, LII (Summer 1972), 309–14.

Bruccoli, Matthew J. *"The Nick Adams Stories,"* *Fitzgerald/Hemingway Annual 1972*, Matthew J. Bruccoli and C. E. Frazer Clark, Jr., eds. Washington, D.C. N.C.R. Microcard Editions, 1973, pp. 397–98.

Davis, Robert M. *"The Nick Adams Stories*: A Review Essay," *Southern Humanities Review*, VII (Spring 1973), 215–19.

Wilson, Douglas. Review of *NA*, *Western Humanities Review*, XXVII (Summer 1973), 295–299.

VI. Criticism, Explication, and Commentary on Individual Stories, Listed by Story—Including Specific Articles, Segments From Books on Hemingway's Work, and Segments From General Books

NOTE: Each title for an item of short fiction in the list below is followed by parentheses containing the following information: (date of composition / date of first publication / place of first publication / abbreviations of Hemingway story collections in which the item has been reprinted).

The Hemingway story collections have been abbreviated as follows:

TSTP	*Three Stories and Ten Poems* (1923)
iot	*in our time* (1924)
IOT	*In Our Time* (1925)
MWW	*Men Without Women* (1927)
WTN	*Winner Take Nothing* (1933)
CS	(Collected Stories) *The Fifth Column and the First Forty-Nine Stories* (1938); *The Short Stories of Ernest Hemingway* (1954)
FUS	*The Fifth Column and Four Unpublished Stories of the Spanish Civil War* (1969)
NA	*The Nick Adams Stories* (1972) [Preface by Philip Young]
EHA	*Ernest Hemingway's Apprenticeship: Oak Park, 1916–1917* (1971) [Edited by Matthew J. Bruccoli]

Items below which consist of last names followed by page numbers refer to books solely devoted to a discussion of Hemingway's works. Complete publication information for such books is given in Section I of this checklist.

The page numbers which are incorporated in these entries differ from the pages listed for particular stories in the book indexes, in that pages listed here refer to something more than mention of the story title, a brief quotation from the story without comment, or brief summary of the story's subject or plot. (Page numbers also differ from index listings in that many such listings are inaccurate.) The only exception to the above restrictions are in the reference to Carlos Baker's *Ernest Hemingway: A Life Story*, wherein even the smallest reference may have some value for the scholar. References to the first edition of Philip Young's book ("Young, 1st") are given only when material has been reprinted from that edition. Complete references are given in "Young, 2nd" listings.

1. After the Storm
   (1932/May 1932/*Cosmopolitan*/WTN, CS)
   Atkins, Anselm. "Ironic Action in 'After the Storm.' " *Studies in Short Fiction*, V (Winter 1968), 189–92.
   Baker (*Life*), pp. 227, 241, 246, 597, 603.
   Bakker, pp. 142–3.
   DeFalco, pp. 212–14.
   Gardner, John and Lennis Dunlap, eds. *The Forms of Fiction*. New York: Random House, 1962, pp. 48–50.
   Gurko, p. 180.
   Hovey, p. 24.
   Wilson, Edmund. *The Wound and the Bow*. New York: Oxford University Press, 1947, pp. 224–25.

2. An Alpine Idyll
   (1926/September 1927/*American Caravan* [anthology]/MWW, CS, NA)
   Atkins, pp. 224, 237.
   Baker (*Artist*), pp. 119–21.
   Baker (*Life*), pp. 168, 171, 182, 184.
   Bakker, pp. 35–37.
   Benson, p. 55.
   DeFalco, p. 216.
   Fenton, pp. 167–68.
   Hattam, Edward. "Hemingway's 'An Alpine Idyll,' " *Modern Fiction Studies*, XII (Summer 1966), 261–65.
   Hovey, pp. 9–10.
   Killinger, pp. 70–71.

2. **An Alpine Idyll,** cont.
   Stephens ("Appendix B: More Sources, Analogues, and Echoes"), p. 370.
   Young, 2nd, pp. 59–60.

3. **The Autobiography of Alice B. Hemingway or Who Taught the Fifth Grade Then? Or Finally She Bit on the Nail Again, a Little** (Unpublished; burlesque) [See Young and Mann, Item 25.]

4. **Banal Story**
   (1926/Spring–Summer 1926/*Little Review*/MWW, CS)
   Baker (*Life*), p. 184.
   Baker, S., p. 56.
   DeFalco, p. 95.
   Joost, pp. 150–51.
   Magalaner, Marvin and Edward L. Volpe. *Teacher's Manual to Accompany "Twelve Short Stories."* New York: Macmillan, 1961, pp. 10–11.

5. **The Battler** ("Great Little Fighting Machine"; "The Great Man")
   (1925/October 5, 1925/*In Our Time*/CS, NA)
   Bache, William B. "Hemingway's 'The Battler,'" *Explicator*, XIII (October 1954), Item 4.
   Baker (*Life*), pp. 141, 143, 509, 588.
   Baker, S., p. 29.
   Bakker, 19–21.
   DeFalco, pp. 71–81.
   Gold, Herbert and David L. Stevenson, eds. *Stories of Modern America.* New York: St. Martin's Press, 1961, pp. 228, 236.
   Grebstein, pp. 96–98.
   Gurko, pp. 185–86.
   Hardy, John E. *Commentaries on Five Modern American Short Stories.* Frankfurt: Diesterweg, 1962, pp. 15–19. [Reprinted in his *The Modern Talent: An Anthology of Short Stories.* New York: Holt, Rinehart & Winston, 1964, pp. 32–36.]
   Hovey, p. 20.
   Killinger, pp. 22, 51.
   Lewis, p. 13.
   Montgomery, pp. 89–91.
   Stephens, ("Appendix B: More Sources, Analogues, and Echoes"), p. 363.
   Stewart, Randall and Dorothy Bethurum, eds. *Modern American Narratives.* Chicago: Scott, Foresman, 1954, pp. 68–70.

Waldhorn, RG, pp. 58–59.

Young, 1st, pp. 8–11. [Reprinted in Weeks, Robert P., ed. *Hemingway: A Collection of Critical Essays*. Englewood Cliffs, N.J.: Prentice-Hall, 1962, pp. 104–07.] Young, 2nd, pp. 36–40, 235–37.

6. Big Two-Hearted River
(1924/Spring 1925/*This Quarter*/IOT, CS, NA)

Anderson, Paul V. "Nick's Story in Hemingway's 'Big Two-Hearted River,' " *Studies in Short Fiction*, VII (Fall 1970), 564–72.

Andrews, Larry. " 'Big Two-Hearted River': The Essential Hemingway," *Missouri English Bulletin*, XXV (May 1969), 1–7.

Baker (*Artist*), pp. 125–28.

Baker (*Life*), pp. 63, 127, 131–32, 138, 140, 171, 219, 268, 574, 585–86.

Baker, S., pp. 31–33, 36–38.

Baker, Sheridan. "Hemingway's Two-Hearted River," *Michigan Alumnus Quarterly Review*, LXV (February 28, 1959), 142–49.

Bakker, pp. 31–34, 40, 252.

Benson, pp. 137–40.

Cantwell, Robert. "The River That Will Flow Forever," *Sports Illustrated*, XV (July 17, 1961), 52–59.

DeFalco, pp. 144–51.

Doxey, William S. "The Significance of Seney, Michigan, in Hemingway's 'Big Two-Hearted River,' " *Hemingway Notes*, I (Fall 1971), 5–6.

French, Warren. *The Social Novel at the End of an Era*. Carbondale: Southern Illinois University Press, 1966, pp. 98–99.

Green, James L. "Symbolic Sentences in 'Big Two-Hearted River,' " *Modern Fiction Studies*, XIV (Autumn 1968): Ernest Hemingway Spec. No., 307–12.

Gubstein, pp. 19–21, 82–84, 151.

Gurko, pp. 201–03.

Hovey, pp. 32–36.

Howard, Daniel F. *Manual to Accompany "The Modern Tradition: An Anthology of Short Stories*. Second Edition. Boston: Little, Brown, 1972, pp. 19–20.

Joost, pp. 86, 146, 147.

Kaplan, Harold. *The Passive Voice: An Approach to Modern Fiction*. Athens: Ohio University Press, 1966, pp. 97–98.

Kazin, Alfred. "Young Man, Old Man," *Reporter*, XXIX (December 19, 1963), 33–36. ["Big Two-Hearted River," pp. 35–36.]

Killinger, p. 71.

Korn, Barbara. "Form and Idea in Hemingway's 'Big Two-Hearted

6. Big Two-Hearted River, cont.

River,' " *English Journal*, LVI (October 1967), 979–981, 1014.

Larsen, Erling. "Making the Seney Scene," *Carleton Miscellany*, V (Fall 1964), 50–74.

Montgomery, pp. 20, 141–58.

Morris, Wright. "The Ability to Function: A Reappraisal of Fitzgerald and Hemingway," in *New World Writing, #13*. New York: The New American Library, 1958, pp. 34–51 ("Hemingway: The Function of Style," pp. 43–51). [Pp. 43–51 reprinted in *The Territory Ahead*, New York: Atheneum, 1963, pp. 133–46.]

Moseley, Edwin M. *Pseudonyms of Christ in the Modern Novel: Motifs and Methods*. Pittsburgh: University of Pittsburgh Press, 1962, pp. 205–06.

Nahal, pp. 101–08.

Peterson, pp. 45–47, 64, 191.

Rovit, pp. 25–26, 80–83, 164.

Sanderson, pp. 33–34.

Scott, pp. 16–18.

Shaw, pp. 32–36.

Simonson, Harold P. *Instructor's Manual to Accompany "Trio: A Book of Stories, Plays and Poems."* New York: Harper & Row, 1965, pp. 10–11.

Stein, William Bysshe. "Ritual in Hemingway's 'Big Two-Hearted River,' " *Texas Studies in Literature and Language*, I (Winter 1960), 555–61.

Stephens ("Appendix B: More Sources, Analogues, and Echoes"), pp. 365–67.

Stewart, Randall. *American Literature and Christian Doctrine*. Baton Rouge: Louisiana State University Press, 1958, pp. 135–36.

Traver, Robert. "Hemingway's Big Two-Hearted Secret," *Sports Afield*, CLXX (July 1973), 46–47, 82–84.

Twitchell, James. "The Swamp in Hemingway's 'Big Two-Hearted River,' " *Studies in Short Fiction*, IX (Summer 1972), 275–76.

Walcutt, Charles C. *Man's Changing Masks: Modes and Methods of Characterization in Fiction*. Minneapolis: University of Minnesota Press, 1966, pp. 307–09.

Waldhorn, RG, pp. 33–34, 65–67.

Watts, pp. 46, 95, 110, 111–12, 142–43, 163, 215–18.

Wells, Elizabeth. "A Comparative Statistical Analysis of the Prose Styles of F. Scott Fitzgerald and Ernest Hemingway," *Fitzgerald/Hemingway Annual 1969*, Matthew J. Bruccoli, ed. Washington, D.C.: N.C.R. Microcard Editions, 1969, pp. 47–69.

Young, 1st, pp. 15–20. [Reprinted in Weeks, Robert P., ed. *Heming-*

way: A Collection of Critical Essays. Englewood Cliffs, N.J.: Prentice-Hall, 1962, pp. 104–07.] Young, 2nd, pp. 43–48, 53, 285n.

7. The Butterfly and the Tank
(1938/December 1938/*Esquire*/FUS)

Baker (*Life*), pp. 337, 387.

Hughes, Langston. *I Wonder as I Wander.* New York: Rinehart, 1956, pp. 362–65.

[See Section IV: Martin Light, "Of Wasteful Deaths," and Julian Smith, "Christ Times Four."]

8. A Canary for One
(1926/April 1927/*Scribner's Magazine*/MWW, CS)

Atkins, pp. 88–89.

Baker (*Artist*), pp. 137–38.

Baker (Life), pp. 177, 184, 592.

Benson, p. 148.

Cunliffe, W. Gordon, Martin Dolch, and John V. Hagopian. "A Canary for One," in Hagopian, John V., and Martin Dolch, eds. *Insight I: Analysis of American Literature.* Frankfurt: Hirschgraben, 1962, pp. 96–99.

DeFalco, pp. 174–76.

Grebstein, pp. 19–21, 77.

Hovey, pp. 11, 42–43.

Killinger, p. 38.

Peterson, p. 178.

Smith, Julian. " 'A Canary for One': Hemingway in the Wasteland," *Studies in Short Fiction,* V (Summer 1968), 355–61.

9. The Capital of the World ("The Horns of the Bull")
(1936/June 1936/*Esquire*, as "The Horns of the Bull"/CS)

Atkins, pp. 136–37.

Baker (*Life*), pp. 284, 314, 492, 617.

Bakker, pp. 140–41.

DeFalco, pp. 88, 91–99, 122, 197.

Grebstein, p. 103.

Gurko, pp. 193–94.

Hovey, pp. 119–23.

McAleer, John F. "Christ Symbolism in Hemingway's 'The Capital of the World,' " *English Record,* XII (Spring 1961), 2–3.

Peterson, pp. 74–75.

Reid, Stephen A. "The Oedipal Pattern in Hemingway's 'The Capital of the World,' " *Literature and Psychology,* XIII (Spring 1963), 37–43.

Rovit, p. 72.

9. The Capital of the World, cont.

Schwartz, Delmore. "The Fiction of Ernest Hemingway," *Perspectives USA*, XIII (Autumn 1955), 85–86.

Stephens, ("Appendix B: More Sources, Analogues, and Echoes"), p. 373.

10. Cat in the Rain

(1924/October 5, 1925/*In Our Time*/CS)

Baker (*Artist*), pp. 135–36.

Baker (*Life*), pp. 107, 133, 580, 585.

DeFalco, pp. 158–61.

Grebstein, pp. 108–9.

Hagopian, John V. and Martin Dolch, eds. "Cat in the Rain," *Insight I: Analyses of American Literature*. Frankfurt: Hirschgraben, 1962, pp. 93–96.

Hagopian, John V. "Symmetry in 'Cat in the Rain,' " *College English*, XXIV (December 1962), 220–22. [Reprinted in Miller, James E. and Bernice Slote, eds. *The Dimension of the Short Story*. New York: Dodd, Mead, 1964, pp. 531–33.]

Hovey, pp. 10–11.

Magee, John D. "Hemingway's 'Cat in the Rain,' " *Explicator*, XXVI (September 1967), Item 8.

Srivastava, Ramesh. "Hemingway's 'Cat in the Rain': An Interpretation," *Literary Criterion* (Mysore), IX (Summer 1970), 79–84.

11. Chapter I (Vignette: "Everybody was Drunk")

(1923/Spring 1923/*Little Review*/iot, IOT, CS)

Baker, S., p. 20.

12. Chapter II (Vignette: "Minarets Stuck up in the Rain")

(1923/Spring 1923/3rd vignette in *Little Review* and iot/IOT, CS)

Baker (*Artist*), p. 10.

Benson, p. 113.

Fenton, pp. 229–36.

Joost, p. 54.

Peterson, pp. 115–16.

Stephens ("Appendix B: More Sources, Analogues, and Echoes"), pp. 362, 364.

Waldhorn, RG, pp. 47–49.

Watts, pp. 56–57, 59.

13. Chapter III (Vignette: "We Were in a Garden at Mons")

(1923/Spring 1923/4th vignette in *Little Review* and iot/IOT, CS)

Baker, S., p. 21.

Sanderson, pp. 8–9.

14. **Chapter IV** (Vignette: "It was a Frightfully Hot Day")
     (1923/Spring 1923/5th vignette in *Little Review* and iot/IOT, CS)
     Peterson, p. 78.

15. **Chapter V** (Vignette: "They Shot the Six Cabinet Ministers")
     (1923/Spring 1923/6th vignette in *Little Review* and iot/IOT, CS)
     Baker, S., pp. 20–21.
     Bakker, pp. 11–12.
     Benson, p. 120.
     Fenton, pp. 236–38.
     Joost, p. 55.
     Peterson, p. 65.
     Reynolds, Michael S. "Two Hemingway Sources for *In Our Time*," *Studies in Short Fiction*, IX (Winter 1972), 81–86.
     Rovit, pp. 46–50.
     Stephens ("Appendix B: More Sources, Analogues, and Echoes"), p. 363.
     Young, 2nd, p. 36.

16. **Chapter VI** (Vignette: "Nick Sat Against the Wall")
     (1923/Spring 1924/*in our time* as "Chapter VII"/IOT, CS, NA)
     Bakker, pp. 51–52.
     Killinger, pp. 18, 22.
     Shaw, pp. 27–29.
     Stephens ("Appendix B: More Sources, Analogues, and Echoes"), p. 363.
     Young, 2nd, pp. 40–42.

17. **Chapter VII** (Vignette: "While the Bombardment was Knocking the Trench to Pieces")
     (1923/Spring 1924/*in our time* as "Chapter VIII"/IOT, CS)

18. **Chapter VIII** (Vignette: "At Two O'Clock in the Morning Two Hungarians")
     (1923/Spring 1924/*in our time* as "Chapter IX"/IOT, CS)
     Fenton, p. 45.
     Reynolds, Michael S. "Two Hemingway Sources for *In Our Time*," *Studies in Short Fiction*, IX (Winter 1972), 81–86.

19. **Chapter IX** (Vignette: "The First Matador got the Horn")
     (1923/Spring 1923/2nd vignette in *Little Review* and iot/IOT, CS)
     Baker, S., p. 20.
     Fenton, pp. 238–39.
     Grebstein, pp. 141–43.
     Joost, p. 55.

19. **Chapter IX,** cont.
    Stephens ("Appendix B: More Sources, Analogues, and Echoes"), p. 364.

20. **Chapter X** (Vignette: "They Whack-Whacked the White Horse")
    (1923/Spring 1924/*in our time* as "Chapter XII"/IOT,CS)
    Peterson, p. 67.
    Stephens ("Appendix B: More Sources, Analogues, and Echoes"), p. 364.

21. **Chapter XI** (Vignette: "The Crowd Shouted All the Time")
    (1923/Spring 1924/*in our time* as "Chapter XIII"/IOT, CS)

22. **Chapter XII** (Vignette: "If it Happened Right Down Close in Front of You")
    (1923/Spring 1924/*in our time* as "Chapter XIV"/IOT, CS)
    Young, 2nd, p. 42.

23. **Chapter XIII** (Vignette: "I Heard the Drums Coming Down the Street")
    (1923/Spring 1924/*in our time* as "Chapter XV"/IOT, CS)

24. **Chapter XIV** (Vignette: "Maera Lay Still")
    (1923/Spring 1924/*in our time* as "Chapter XVI"/IOT, CS)
    Rovit, pp. 128–29.

25. **Chapter XV** (Vignette: "They Hanged Sam Cardinella")
    (1923/Spring 1924/*in our time* as "Chapter VII"/IOT, CS)
    Fenton, pp. 45–46, 239.
    Stephens ("Appendix B: More Sources, Analogues, and Echoes"), p. 367.
    Waldhorn, RG, p. 49.

26. **Che ti Dice la Patria?** ("Italy—1927"; second part also "A Meal in Spezia")
    (1927/May 18, 1927/*New Republic*, as "Italy—1927"/MWW, CS)
    Baker (*Artist*), pp. 200–01.
    Baker (*Life*), p. 184.
    Grebstein, pp. 10–13, 16, 190–91.
    Hovey, p. 16.
    Watts, p. 150.

27. **A Clean, Well-Lighted Place**
    (1933/March 1933/*Scribner's Magazine*/WTN, CS)
    Atkins, pp. 57–58, 144.
    Bache, William B. "Craftsmanship in 'A Clean, Well-Lighted Place,' " *Personalist*, XXXVII (Winter 1956), 60–64.

Baker (*Artist*), pp. 123–25.

Baker (*Life*), pp. 238, 241.

Baker, S., pp. 86–87.

Bakker, pp. 148–51.

Barnes, Daniel R. "Ritual and Parody in 'A Clean, Well-Lighted Place,' " *Cithara: Essays in the Judaeo-Christian Tradition*, V (May 1966), 15–25.

Barrett, William. *Irrational Man: A Study in Existential Philosophy*. Garden City, New York: Doubleday and Company, Inc., 1962, pp. 283–86.

Benert, Annette. "Survival Through Irony: Hemingway's 'A Clean, Well-Lighted Place'," *Studies in Short Fiction*, XI (Spring 1974), 181–87.

Bennett, Warren. "Character, Irony, and Resolution in 'A Clean, Well-Lighted Place,' " *American Literature*, XLII (March 1970), 70–79.

Benson, pp. 116–18, 121.

Booth, Wayne C. *The Rhetoric of Fiction*. Chicago: University of Chicago Press, 1963, pp. 8–11.

Brooks, Cleanth. *The Hidden God*. New Haven: Yale University Press, 1963, pp. 8–11.

Campbell, Harry M. "Comments on Mr. Stock's *Nada* in Hemingway's 'A Clean, Well-Lighted Place,' " *Midcontinent American Studies Journal*, III (Spring 1962), 57–59.

Colburn, William E. "Confusion in 'A Clean, Well-Lighted Place,' " *College English*, XX (February 1959), 241–42.

DeFalco, pp. 215–16.

Dietrich, R. F. and Roger H. Sundell. *Instructor's Manual for The Art of Fiction*. New York: Holt, Rinehart & Winston, 1967, pp. 55–57.

Dolch, Martin. "A Clean, Well-Lighted Place," in Hagopian, John V., and Martin Dolch, eds. *Insight I: Analyses of American Literature*. Frankfurt: Hirschgraben, 1962, pp. 105–11.

Ewell, Nathaniel M., III. "Dialogue in Hemingway's 'A Clean, Well-Lighted Place,' " *Fitzgerald/Hemingway Annual, 1971*, Matthew J. Bruccoli and C. E. Frazer Clark, Jr., eds. Washington, D.C.: N.C.R. Microcard Editions, 1971, pp. 305–06.

Gabriel, Joseph F. "The Logic of Confusion in Hemingway's 'A Clean, Well-Lighted Place,' " *College English*, XXII (May 1961), 539–46.

Grebstein, p. 105.

Gurko, pp. 186–87.

Hagopian, John V. "Tidying up Hemingway's 'A Clean, Well-Lighted Place,' " *Studies in Short Fiction*, I (Winter 1964), 140–46.

Hamilton, John B. "Hemingway and the Christian Paradox," *Renascence*, XXIV (Spring 1972), 141–54.

27. A Clean, Well-Lighted Place, cont.

Harder, Kelsie B. "Hemingway's Religious Parody," *New York Folklore Quarterly*, XXIV (March 1970), 76–77.

Heilman, Robert B., *Modern Short Stories: A Critical Anthology*. New York: Harcourt, Brace, 1950, pp. 390–92. [Reprinted in part in Stallman, Robert N. and Arthur Waldhorn, eds. *American Literature: Readings and Critiques*. New York: Putnam, 1961, pp. 786–87].

Hovey, pp. 24–25.

Kaplan, Harold. *The Passive Voice: An Approach to Modern Fiction*. Athens: Ohio University Press, 1966, p. 100.

Killinger, pp. 14–15.

Kroeger, F. P. "The Dialogue in 'A Clean, Well-Lighted Place,' " *College English*, XX (February 1959), 240–41.

LeBost, Barbara. " 'The Way It Is': Something Else on Hemingway," *Existentialism*, VI (1965), 179.

Lodge, David. "Hemingway's 'Clean, Well-Lighted,' Puzzling Place," *Essays in Criticism*, XXI (January 1971), 33–56. [Reprinted in Lodge, David. *The Novelist at the Crossroads and other Essays on Fiction and Criticism*. Ithaca, New York: Cornell University Press, 1971, pp. 184–202.]

May, Charles E. "Is Hemingway's 'Well-Lighted Place' Really Clean Now?" *Studies in Short Fiction*, VIII (Spring 1971), 326–30.

MacDonald, Scott. "The Confusing Dialogue in Hemingway's 'A Clean, Well-Lighted Place': A Final Word," *Studies in American Fiction*, I (Spring 1973), 93–101.

O'Faolain, Sean, ed. *Short Stories: A Study in Pleasure*. Boston: Little, Brown, 1961, pp. 76–78. [Reprinted in Weeks, Robert P., ed. *Hemingway: A Collection of Critical Essays*. Englewood Cliffs, N.J.: Prentice-Hall, 1962, pp. 112–13.]

Peterson, pp. 35–37.

Reinert, Otto. "Hemingway's Waiters Once More," *College English*, XX (May 1959), 417–18.

Ross, Ralph, John Berryman, and Allen Tate, eds. *The Arts of Reading*. New York: Crowell, 1960, pp. 231–35.

Rovit, pp. 110–16, 135.

Sanders, Thomas E. *The Discovery of Fiction*. Chicago: Scott, Foresman, 1967, pp. 304–16.

Schorer, Mark, ed. *The Story: A Critical Anthology*. Englewood Cliffs, N.J.: Prentice-Hall, 1967, pp. 323–25. [Also *The Story: A Critical Anthology*. New York: Prentice-Hall, 1950, pp. 425–28.]

Scott, pp. 20–22.

Shaw, pp. 80–81.

Stallman, R. W., and Arthur Waldhorn. *American Literature: Readings and Critiques.* New York: Putnam, 1961, pp. 786–88.

Stewart, Randall. *American Literature and Christian Doctrine.* Baton Rouge: Louisiana State University Press, 1958, pp. 134–35.

Stock, Ely. "*Nada* in Hemingway's 'A Clean, Well-Lighted Place,' " *Midcontinent American Studies Journal,* III (Spring 1962), 53–57.

Stone, Edward. "Hemingway's Waiters Yet Once More," *American Speech,* XXXVII (October 1962), 239–40.

Waldhorn, RG, pp. 27–28.

Warren, Robert Penn. "Ernest Hemingway," *Kenyon Review,* IX (Winter 1947), 1–28. [pp. 5–6 reprinted in *Horizon,* XV (1947), 159–60; in his *Selected Essays.* New York: Random House, 1958, pp. 91–92; reprinted as "Introduction" to Modern Standard Authors edition of *A Farewell to Arms.* New York: 1949; in Aldridge, John W., ed., *Critiques and Essays on Modern Fiction.* New York: Ronald, 1952, pp. 447–73; and in *Literary Opinion in America,* M. D. Zabel, ed., revised edition. New York: Harper, 1951, pp. 447–60.]

Watts, pp. 72, 74, 160–61.

West, Ray B. *The Short Story in America, 1900–1950.* Chicago: Regnery, 1951, pp. 97–98; Gateway edition, 1952, pp. 93–94.

Young, 2nd, pp. 67n, 195–96.

28. Crime and Punishment (Unpublished)
   [See Young and Mann, Item 32]

29. Cross Country Snow
   (1924/January 1925/*Transatlantic Review*/IOT, CS, NA)
   Baker (*Artist*), pp. 121, 133.
   Baker (*Life*), pp. 133, 580, 585.
   Baker, S., p. 27.
   Bakker, pp. 34–35.
   DeFalco, pp. 172–74.
   Hovey, pp. 13–14.
   Joost, pp. 118, 142.
   Stephens ("Appendix B: More Sources, Analogues, and Echoes"), p. 365.
   Waldhorn, RG, pp. 35–36.
   Wright, Austin McGiffert. *The American Short Story in the Twenties.* Chicago: University of Chicago Press, 1961, pp. 391–93.
   Young, 2nd, pp. 42–43.

30. The Cross Roads ("Black Ass at the Cross Roads," unpublished)
   (1956/ . . . / . . .)
   Baker (*Life*), p. 534.

31. Crossing the Mississippi (Fragment)
   (. . . /1972/*The Nick Adams Stories*/ . . .)

32. A Day's Wait
   (ca. 1932/October 27, 1933/*Winner Take Nothing*/CS)
   Atkins, pp. 144–45.
   Baker (*Artist*), p. 134.
   Baker (*Life*), pp. 236, 246.
   Bakker, pp. 40, 252.
   DeFalco, pp. 53–54.
   Dolch, Martin. "A Day's Wait," in Hagopian, John V. and Martin
      Dolch, eds. *Insight I: Analyses of American Literature*. Frankfurt:
      Hirschgraben, 1962, pp. 104–05.
   Grebstein, p. 8–10.
   Hovey, pp. 43–44.
   Killinger, p. 25.
   Mahoney, Patrick J. "Hemingway's 'A Day's Wait.'" *Explicator*,
      XXVII (November 1968), Item 18.
   Waldhorn, RG, pp. 70–71.
   Young, 2nd, p. 286n.

33. The Denunciation
   (1938/November 1938/*Esquire*/FUS)
   Baker (*Life*), p. 337.
   Grebstein, pp. 60–63.
   [See Section IV: Martin Light, "Of Wasteful Deaths," and Julian
      Smith, "Christ Times Four."]

34. A Divine Gesture (Fable)
   (1921/May 1922/*Double Dealer*/ . . .)
   Baker (*Artist*), p. 7, 7n.
   Baker (*Life*), pp. 80, 90.
   Baker, S., p. 15.
   Joost, pp. 18, 23, 26–30.
   Young, 2nd, p. 175.

35. The Doctor and the Doctor's Wife
   (1924/December 1924/*Transatlantic Review*/IOT, CS, NA)
   Arnold, Aerol. "Hemingway's 'The Doctor and the Doctor's Wife,'"
      Explicator, XVIII (March 1960), Item 36.
   Baker (*Artist*), p. 129.
   Baker (*Life*), pp. 132, 585.
   Baker, S., pp. 28–29.
   Bakker, pp. 15–17.

Benson, pp. 8–9.

Davis, Robert Murray. "Hemingway's 'The Doctor and the Doctor's Wife,' " *Explicator*, XXV (September 1966), Item 1.

DeFalco, pp. 33–40.

Fox, Stephen D. "Hemingway's 'The Doctor and the Doctor's Wife,' " *The Arizona Quarterly*, XXIX (Spring 1973), 19–25.

Grebstein, pp. 5–9.

Hovey, pp. 38–39.

Joost, p. 117.

Levin, Gerald. *The Short Story: An Inductive Approach*. New York: Harcourt, Brace & World, 1967, pp. 138–40.

Montgomery, pp. 53, 65–70.

Nahal, pp. 84–85, 90–93.

Waldhorn, RG, pp. 55–56.

Wright, Austin McGiffert. *The American Short Story in the Twenties*. Chicago: University of Chicago Press, 1961, pp. 205–08, 400–01.

Young, 2nd, pp. 32–33, 135.

36. The End of Something

(1924/October 5, 1925/*In Our Time*/CS, NA)

Atkins, pp. 12–13.

Baker (*Life*), pp. 64, 132, 574, 585.

Bakker, pp. 17–18.

Barba, Harry. "The Three Levels of 'The End of Something,' " *West Virginia University Philological Papers*, XVII, 1970, 76–80.

DeFalco, pp. 40–44.

Grebstein, p. 158.

Gurko, pp. 183–84.

Hovey, p. 7.

Killinger, p. 43.

Kruse, Horst H. "Ernest Hemingway's 'The End of Something': Its Independence as a Short Story and Its Place in the 'Education of Nick Adams,' " *Studies in Short Fiction*, IV (Winter 1967), 152–66.

Montgomery, pp. 128–34, 139.

Parker, Alice. "Hemingway's 'The End of Something,' " *Explicator*, X (March 1952), Item 36.

Waggoner, Hyatt. "Hemingway and Faulkner: 'The End of Something.' " *Southern Quarterly*, IV (Spring 1968), 458–66.

Waldhorn, RG, p. 68.

Whitt, Joseph. "Hemingway's 'The End of Something,' " *Explicator*, IX (June 1951), Item 58.

Wright, Austin M. *The American Short Story in the Twenties*. Chicago: University of Chicago Press, 1961, pp. 94–95.

36. The End of Something, cont.
> Young, 1st, pp. 5–6.[Reprinted in Weeks, Robert P., ed. *Hemingway: A Collection of Critical Essays.* Englewood Cliffs, N.J.: Prentice-Hall, 1962, p. 98.] Young, 2nd, pp. 33–35.

37. L'Envoi (Vignette: "The king was working in the garden")
> (1923/Spring 1924/*in our time* as "Chapter XVIII"/IOT, CS)
> Fenton, pp. 239–41.
> Stephens ("Appendix B: More Sources, Analogues, and Echoes"), p. 367.
> Waldhorn, RG, p. 50.

38. The Faithful Bull (Fable)
> (1950/March 1951/*Holiday*/ ...)
> Baker (*Life*), pp. 492, 653.
> Joost, p. 27.
> Stephens ("Appendix B: More Sources, Analogues, and Echoes"), p. 377.

39. Fathers and Sons ("The Tomb of My Grandfather")
> (1933/October 27, 1933/*Winner Take Nothing*/CS, NA)
> Baker (Artist), p. 134.
> Baker (*Life*), pp. 235, 241, 313.
> Baker, S., p. 39.
> Bakker, pp. 37–39.
> Benson, pp. 10–11, 13–14, 16–17.
> DeFalco, pp. 217–18.
> Grebstein, pp. 19–20, 143–45, 150–51.
> Hovey, pp. 44–47, 118.
> Montgomery, pp. 82–84, 86–88, 102–06.
> Peterson, pp. 42–43, 45.
> St. John, Donald. "Hemingway and Prudence," *Connecticut Review*, V (April 1972), 78–84.
> White, pp. 38–41.
> Young, 1st, pp. 32–34, 36–37. [Reprinted in Browne, Ray B., and Martin Light, eds. *Critical Approaches to American Literature, II.* New York: Crowell, 1965, pp. 279–80.] Young, 2nd, pp. 60–62.

40. Fifty Grand ("Jack")
> (1925/July 1927/*Atlantic*/MWW, CS)
> Baker (*Artist*), p. 122.
> Baker (*Life*), pp. 157, 168, 182, 184, 589.
> Baker, S., pp. 61–62.
> Bakker, pp. 82–85.
> Brooks, Cleanth. *The Hidden God.* New Haven: Yale University Press, 1963, pp. 13–14.

Davies, Phillip G. and Rosemary R. Davies. "Hemingway's 'Fifty Grand' and the Jack Britton-Mickey Walker Prize Fight," *American Literature*, XXXVII (November 1965), 251–58.

DeFalco, pp. 211–13.

Fenton, Charles A. "No Money for the Kingbird: Hemingway's Prize-fight Stories," *American Quarterly*, IV (Winter 1952), 342–47.

Grebstein, pp. 58–60.

Gurko, pp. 178–79.

Hovey, pp. 12–13.

Martine, James J. "Hemingway's 'Fifty Grand': The Other Fight(s)," *Journal of Modern Literature*, II (September 1971), 123–27.

Rovit, p. 61.

Stephens ("Appendix B: More Sources, Analogues, and Echoes"), p. 370.

Summers, Richard, ed. *The Craft of the Short Story*. New York: Rinehart, 1948, pp. 190–92.

Waldhorn, RG, p. 27.

Young, 1st, pp. 36–37. [Reprinted in Browne, Ray B., and Martin Light, eds. *Critical Approaches to American Literature, II*. New York: Crowell, 1965, p. 281.] Young, 2nd, pp. 64–65.

41. The Gambler, the Nun, and The Radio ("Give Us a Prescription, Doctor")

(1933/April 1933/*Scribner's Magazine*, as "Give Us a Prescription, Doctor"/WTN [revised], CS)

Atkins, pp. 22–23, 42.

Baker (*Artist*), p. 141.

Baker (*Life*), p. 238.

Baker, S., pp. 85–86.

Bakker, pp. 146–48.

DeFalco, pp. 214–15.

Doshiell, Alfred A. *Editor's Choice*. New York: Putnam, 1934, pp. 131–32.

Grebstein, pp. 194–98.

Hovey, pp. 27–28.

Kaplan, Harold. *The Passive Voice: An Approach to Modern Fiction*. Athens: Ohio University Press, 1966, p. 98.

Killinger, pp. 37–38.

Mizener, Arthur. *The Sense of Life in the Modern Novel*. Boston: Houghton Mifflin, 1964, pp. 222–23.

Montgomery, Marion. "Hemingway's 'The Gambler, the Nun, and the Radio': A Reading and a Problem," *Forum*, III (Winter 1962), 36–40.

41. The Gambler, the Nun, and The Radio, cont.

Peterson, pp. 35, 130.

Rodgers, Paul C., Jr. "Levels of Irony in Hemingway's 'The Gambler, the Nun, and the Radio,' " *Studies in Short Fiction*, VII (Summer 1970), 439–49.

Rovit, p. 70.

Schwartz, Delmore. "Ernest Hemingway's Literary Situation," *Southern Review*, III (Spring 1938), 769–82. [pp. 775–76 "The Gambler, the Nun, and the Radio."] [Reprinted in *Ernest Hemingway: The Man and His Work*, John K. M. McCaffery, ed. New York: Cooper Square Publishers, Inc., 1969, pp. 114–29 (p. 122, "The Gambler, the Nun, and the Radio").]

Soucie, Gary. "Reflections on Hemingway," *Carolina Quarterly*, XI (Spring 1960), 57–63. ["The Gambler, the Nun, and the Radio," p. 60.]

Stephens ("Appendix B: More Sources, Analogues, and Echoes"), pp. 372–73.

Stone, Edward. "Hemingway's Mr. Frazer: From Revolution to Radio," *Journal of Modern Literature*, I (March 1971), 375–88.

Waldhorn, RG, pp. 25, 26.

Young, 1st, pp. 38–41. [Reprinted in Browne, Ray B., and Martin Light, eds. *Critical Approaches to American Literature, II*. New York: Crowell, 1965, pp. 282–84.] Young, 2nd, pp. 66–68.

42. Get a Seeing-Eyed Dog ("Get Yourself a Seeing-Eyed Dog")

(1956/November 1957/*Atlantic*/ ...)

Baker (*Life*), p. 534.

DeFalco, pp. 216–17.

Rovit, p. 56.

[See Section I: Astro and Benson, Delbert E. Wylder, "Internal Treachery." See also Section IV: Julian Smith, "Eyeless in Wyoming."]

43. God Rest You Merry, Gentlemen

(1932/April 1933/*God Rest You Merry, Gentleman* [pamphlet]/ WTN, CS)

Baker (*Life*), pp. 36, 227, 237.

Baker, S., p. 85.

Benson, p. 60.

DeFalco, pp. 54–55.

Hays, Peter L. "Hemingway and the Fisher King," *University Review*, XXXII (Spring 1966), 225–28. [Reprinted in altered form in Hays, *The Limping Hero: Grotesques in Literature*. New York: New York University Press, 1971, pp. 72–76.]

Hovey, pp. 22–24.

Monteiro, George. "Hemingway's Christmas Carol," *Fitzgerald/Hemingway Annual 1972*, Matthew J. Bruccoli and C. E. Frazer Clark, Jr., eds. Washington, D.C.: N.C.R. Microcard Editions, 1973, pp. 207–13.

44. The Good Lion (Fable)

(1950/March 1951/*Holiday*/[*Hemingway Reader*])
Baker (*Life*), pp. 492, 653.
Joost, p. 27.

45. Good News from the Mainland (unpublished)
[See Young and Mann, Item 44]

46. Hills Like White Elephants

(1927/August 1927/*Transition*/MWW, CS)
Atkins, pp. 64–65, 163.
Baker (*Life*), pp. 184, 186, 227, 595.
Baker, S., pp. 58–59.
Bakker, pp. 10, 11–14, 143–44.
Bates, H. E. *The Modern Short Story: A Critical Survey*. London: Thomas Nelson, 1943, pp. 172–73.
Benson, p. 137.
DeFalco, pp. 168–72.
Friedman, Norman. "What Makes a Short Story Short?" *Modern Fiction Studies*, IV (Summer 1958), 107–08. [Reprinted in Rideout, Walter B. and James K. Robinson, eds. *A College Book of Modern Fiction*. Evanston, Illinois: Row, Peterson, 1961, pp. 552–65.]
Grebstein, pp. 21, 111–13.
Gurko, pp. 191–93.
Hovey, p. 14.
Jain, S. P. " 'Hills Like White Elephants': A Study," *Indian Journal of American Studies*, I (1970), 33–38.
Kraus, W. Keith. "Ernest Hemingway's 'Hills Like White Elephants': A Note on a 'Reasonable' Source," *English Record*, XXI (December 1970), 23–26.
Lid, Richard W. "Hemingway and the Need for Speech," *Modern Fiction Studies*, VIII (Winter 1962–1963), 401–07.
Maynard, Reid. "Leitmotif and Irony in Hemingway's 'Hills Like White Elephants,' " *University Review*, XXXVII (Summer 1971), 273–75.
Peterson, pp. 88–89.
Rodrigues, Eusebio L. " 'Hills Like White Elephants': An Analysis," *Literary Criterion*, V (1962), 105–09.
Stephens ("Appendix B: More Sources, Analogues, and Echoes"), p. 370.

46. Hills Like White Elephants, cont.

Trilling, Lionel, ed. *The Experience of Literature: Fiction.* New York: Holt, Rinehart, & Winston, 1967, pp. 729–32.

Waldhorn, RG, pp. 36–37.

Watts, p. 151.

Wright, Austin McGiffert. *The American Short Story in the Twenties.* Chicago: University of Chicago Press, 1961, pp. 370–73.

47. Homage to Switzerland

(1933/April 1933/*Scribner's Magazine*/WTN/CS)

Baker (*Artist*), pp. 138–39.

Baker (*Life*), p. 238.

Baker, S., p. 85.

Bakker, p. 145.

DeFalco, pp. 179–83.

Hovey, pp. 11–12.

Stephens ("Appendix B: More Sources, Analogues, and Echoes"), p. 372.

48. The Home Front (Unpublished; "The Stooges of Stalin")

[See Young and Mann, Item 50]

49. I Guess Everything Reminds You of Something (A story; unpublished)

[See Young and Mann, Item 51]

50. Ignorance or a Puritan Courtship (Unpublished)

[See Young and Mann, Item 52]

51. In Another Country

(1926/April 1927/*Scribner's Magazine*/MWW, CS, NA)

Baker (*Artist*), p. 137.

Baker (*Life*), pp. 177, 184, 190.

Baker, S., pp. 33–34, 42.

Bakker, pp. 27–29, 46–47.

Bartlett, Phyllis. "Other Countries, Other Wenches," *Modern Fiction Studies*, III (Winter 1957–58), 345–49.

Benson, pp. 144–45.

Brooks, Cleanth. *The Hidden God.* New Haven: Yale University Press, 1963, pp. 11–13.

Brooks, Cleanth, John T. Purse, and Robert Penn Warren, eds. *An Approach to Literature*, 3rd edition. New York: Appleton-Century Crofts, 1952, pp. 104–06; 4th edition (1964), pp. 135–37.

Davis, Robert Gorham. *Instructor's Manual for Ten Modern Masters.* New York: Harcourt, Brace, 1953, pp. 26–27.

DeFalco, pp. 129–36.

Grebstein, pp. 168–69.

Gross, Theodore, and Norman Kelvin, *An Introduction to Fiction*. New York: Random House, 1967, pp. 299–305.

Gurko, pp. 180–81.

Hall, James and Joseph Langland, eds. *The Short Story*. New York: Macmillan, 1956, pp. 456–57.

Heiney, Donald. *Recent American Literature*. Great Neck, N.Y.: Barron's Educational Series, Inc., 1958, p. 163.

Hovey, p. 9.

Irwin, Richard. " 'Of War, Wounds, and Silly Machines': An Examination of Hemingway's 'In Another Country,' " *Serif*, V (1968), 21–29.

Kaplan, Harold. *The Passive Voice: An Approach to Modern Fiction*. Athens: Ohio University Press, 1966, p. 102.

Ludwig, Jack Barry and W. Richard Poirier. *Instructor's Manual to Accompany "Stories: British and American."* Boston: Houghton Mifflin, 1953, pp. 12–13.

Rovit, pp. 61–64, 96–98, 129–31.

Short, Raymond W. and Richard B. Sewell. *A Manual of Suggestions for Teachers Using "Short Stories for Study,"* revised edition. New York: Holt, 1950, pp. 22–24; 3rd edition (1956), pp. 7–8.

Steinmann, Martin and Gerald Willen, eds. *Literature for Writing*. Belmont, California: Wadsworth, 1962, pp. 175–76.

Stephens ("Appendix B: More Sources, Analogues, and Echoes"), p. 369.

Stephens, Rosemary. " 'In Another Country': Three as Symbol," *University of Mississippi Studies in English*, VII (1960), 77–83.

Waldhorn, RG, pp. 68–70.

Wright, Austin McGiffert. *The American Short Story in the Twenties*. Chicago: University of Chicago Press, 1961, pp. 401–02.

Young, 1st, pp. 30–31. [Reprinted in Browne, Ray B., and Martin Light, eds. *Critical Approaches to American Literature, II*. New York: Crowell, 1965, p. 277.] Young, 2nd, pp. 58–59.

52. Indian Camp ("Work in Progress"; "One Night Last Summer") (1924/April 1924/"Work in Progress," *Transatlantic Review*/IOT, CS, NA)

Baker (*Life*), pp. 125, 127, 132, 171.

Baker, S., p. 28.

Bakker, pp. 14–15.

Bernard, Kenneth. "Hemingway's 'Indian Camp,' " *Studies in Short Fiction*. II (Spring 1965), 291. [For Philip Young's reply see *Studies in Short Fiction*, III (Fall 1965), ii–iii.]

52. Indian Camp, cont.
  DeFalco, pp. 27–33, 40, 48.
    Grebstein, pp. 17–18, 100–2.
  Guerin, Wilfred L., et al. *Mandala: Literature for Critical Analysis*
    (Manual). New York: Harper & Row, 1970, pp. 28–30.
  Hovey, pp. 15–16.
  Joost, pp. 84–86.
  Killinger, p. 17.
  Monteiro, George. "The Limits of Professionalism: A Sociological
    Approach to Faulkner, Fitzgerald, and Hemingway," *Criticism*, XV
    (Spring 1972), 145–55.
  Montgomery, pp. 56–64.
  Nahal, pp. 87–91.
  Orvis, Mary. *The Art of Writing Fiction.* New York: Prentice-Hall,
    1948, pp. 26–27.
  Rehder, Jessie, ed. *The Story at Work.* New York: Odyssey, 1963, pp.
    5–6.
  Ross, Danforth. *The American Short Story.* Minneapolis: University
    of Minnesota Press, 1961, pp. 34–35.
  Sanderson, pp. 29–30.
  Shaw, pp. 29–32.
  Tanselle, G. Thomas. "Hemingway's 'Indian Camp,' " *Explicator*, XX
    (February 1962), Item 53.
  Waldhorn, RG, pp. 54–55.
  Young, 1st, pp. 3–4. [Reprinted in Weeks, Robert P., ed. *Hemingway:
    A Collection of Critical Essays.* Englewood Cliffs, N.J.: Prentice-
    Hall, 1962, pp. 96–97.] Young, 2nd, pp. 31–32.

53. Indian Country and the White Army (Unpublished; "The Limited
    Objective")
    (1956/ . . . / . . . / . . .)
  Baker (Life), p. 534.

54. The Indians Moved Away (Fragment)
    (. ? . /1972/*The Nick Adams Stories*/ . . .)

55. The Judgment of Manitou (Juvenilia)
    (ca. 1915/1916/*Tabula*/EHA)
  Baker (Life), p. 23.
  Baker, S., p. 7.
  Montgomery, pp. 43–44, 46–47 [story itself appears pp. 44–45].

56. The Killers ("The Matadors")
    (1926/March 1927/*Scribner's Magazine*/MWW, CS, NA)
  Atkins, p. 7.

Baker (*Artist*), p. 123.

Baker (*Life*), pp. 169, 175, 184, 453, 509, 592; film, 458, 462, 651.

Baker, S., p. 30.

Bakker, pp. 22–23, 254.

Beards, Richard D. "Stereotyping in Modern American Fiction: Some Solitary Swedish Madmen," *Moderna Sprak*, LXIII (No. 4, 1969), 329–337.

Benson, pp. 73, 142–44, 145.

Bonazza, Blaze O., and Emil Ray. *Instructor's Manual to Accompany "The Dimensions of the Short Story,"* James E. Miller and Bernice Slote, eds. New York: Dodd, Mead, 1964, pp. 42–46.

Booth, Wayne C. *The Rhetoric of Fiction*. Chicago: University of Chicago Press, 1961, pp. 151–52.

Brooks, Cleanth and Robert Penn Warren. "The Killers," *American Prefaces*, VIII (Spring 1942), 195–209. [Reprinted, with revisions, in *Understanding Fiction*. New York: F. S. Crofts & Company, 1943, pp. 316–24; second edition, New York: Appleton-Century-Crofts, 1959, pp. 303–12; and in part in Weeks, Robert P., ed. *Hemingway: A Collection of Critical Essays*. Englewood Cliffs, N.J.: Prentice-Hall, 1962, pp. 114–17.]

Bruccoli, Matthew J. "Ole Anderson, Ole Andreson, and Carl Anderson," *Fitzgerald/Hemingway Annual 1971*, Matthew J. Bruccoli and C. E. Frazer Clark, Jr., eds. Washington, D.C.: N.C.R. Microcard Editions, 1972, p. 341.

Crane, R. S. "The Killers," in *The Idea of the Humanities and other Essays Critical and Historical*, II, 1967, pp. 303–14.

Daniel, Robert. "Hemingway and His Heroes," *Queen's Quarterly*, LIV (Winter 1947–48), 471–85. [pp. 471–78: "The Killers"]

Davies, Phillips G. and Rosemary R. Davies. " 'A Killer Who Would Shoot You for the Fun of It': A Possible Source for Hemingway's 'The Killers,' " *Iowa English Yearbook*, XV (1970), 36–38.

DeFalco, pp. 63–71.

Evans, Oliver. "The Protagonist of Hemingway's 'The Killers,' " *Modern Language Notes*, LXXIII (December 1958), 589–91.

Fenton, p. 94.

Freeland, Bayne. "Letter to the Editor of *Studies in Short Fiction*," *Studies in Short Fiction*, V (Spring 1968), iii–v.

Frey, Leonard H. "Irony and Point of View in 'That Evening Sun,' " *Faulkner Studies*, II (1953), 39–40.

Grebstein, pp. 21, 109–10.

Grebstein, Sheldon Norman. "The Tough Hemingway and His Hard-Boiled Children," in Madden, David, ed. *Tough Guy Writers of the*

56. The Killers, cont.

Thirties, Carbondale: Southern Illinois University Press, 1968, pp. 26–27.

Gurko, Leo. "The Achievement of Ernest Hemingway," *English Journal,* XLI (June 1952), 292–93; also in *College English,* XIII (April 1952), 370.

Gurko, pp. 188–91.

Hagopian, John V., and Martin Dolch. "The Killers," in Hagopian, John V. and Martin Dolch, eds. *Insight I: Analyses of American Literature.* Frankfurt: Hirschgraben, 1962, pp. 99–103.

Heiney, Donald. *Recent American Literature.* Great Neck, New York: Barron's Educational Series, Inc., 1958, pp. 162–63.

Hovey, pp. 28–29.

Jaffe, Adrian H. and Virgil Scott. *Studies in the Short Story.* New York: Holt, Rinehart & Winston, 1949, pp. 208–13.

Kempton, Kenneth Payson. *The Short Story.* Cambridge: Harvard University Press, 1947, pp. 39–41, 110–12, 126.

Lesser, Simon O. *Fiction and the Unconscious.* New York: Random House, 1957, pp. 101–02.

Livingston, Howard. "Religious Intrusion in Hemingway's 'The Killers,' " *English Record,* XXI (February 1971), 42–44.

Maloney, Michael F. "Ernest Hemingway: The Missing Third Dimension," in Gardiner, Harold C., ed. *Fifty Years of the American Novel.* New York: Scribner, 1952, p. 188.

Marcus, Fred H. *Perception and Pleasure: Stories for Analysis* (Manual), Boston: Heath, 1968, pp. 10–11. *Perception and Pleasure: Stories for Analysis,* Boston: Heath, 1968, pp. 77–78.

Moore, L. Hugh, Jr. "Mrs. Hirsh and Mrs. Bell in Hemingway's 'The Killers,' " *Modern Fiction Studies,* XI (Winter 1965–1966), 427–28.

Morris, William E. "Hemingway's 'The Killers,' " *Explicator,* XVIII (October 1959), Item 1.

Moseley, Edwin M. *Pseudonyms of Christ in the Modern Novel: Motifs and Methods.* Pittsburgh: University of Pittsburgh Press, 1962, pp. 111–12, 124–25.

Nahal, pp. 93–94.

Oliver, Clinton F. "Hemingway's 'The Killers' and Mann's 'Disorder and Early Sorrow,' " in Timko, Michael and Clinton F. Oliver, eds. *38 Short Stories: An Introductory Anthology,* New York: Alfred A. Knopf, 1968, pp. 69–78.

Owen, Charles A., Jr. "Time and the Contagion of Flight in 'The Killers,' " *Forum,* III (Fall–Winter 1960), 45–46.

Peterson, p. 95.

Sampson, Edward C. "Hemingway's 'The Killers,' " *Explicator*, XI (October 1952), Item 2.

Short, Raymond W., and Richard B. Sewell. *A Manual of Suggestions for Teachers Using "Short Stories for Study,"* revised edition. New York: Holt, 1950, pp. 24–26.

Stephens ("Appendix B: More Sources, Analogues, and Echoes"), p. 370.

Stone, Edward. "Some Questions about Hemingway's 'The Killers,' " *Studies in Short Fiction*, V (Fall 1967), 12–17.

Taube, Myron. "The Nada and Plato's Cave," *CEA Critic*, XXVI (May 1964), 5–6.

Walcutt, Charles C. *Man's Changing Masks: Modes and Methods of Characterization in Fiction.* Minneapolis: University of Minnesota Press, 1966, pp. 305–07.

Waldhorn, RG, pp. 61–62.

Walz, Lawrence A. "Hemingway's 'The Killers,' " *Explicator*, XXV (January 1967), Item 38.

Ward, J. A. " 'The Blue Hotel' and 'The Killers,' " *CEA Critic*, XXI (1959), 7–8.

Weeks, Robert P. "Hemingway's 'The Killers,' " *Explicator*, XV (May 1957), Item 53.

West, Ray B. *The Short Story in America, 1900–1950.* Chicago: Regnery, 1952, pp. 97–100; Gateway edition, 1952, pp. 94–96.

White, p. 14.

Wilson, Edmund. *The Wound and the Bow: Seven Studies in Literature.* New York: Oxford University Press, 1947, pp. 214–42. ["Hemingway: Gauge of Morale" first appeared in *Atlantic*, CLXIV (July 1939) as "Ernest Hemingway: Bourdon (sic) Gauge of Morale."] [Reprinted in McCaffery, John K. M., ed. *Ernest Hemingway: The Man and His Work.* New York: Cooper Square Publishers, Inc., 1969, pp. 236–57.]

Wimberly, Lowry Charles. "Hemingway and Horatio Alger, Jr.," *Prairie Schooner*, X (Fall 1936), 208–11.

Wright, Austin McGiffert. *The American Short Story in the Twenties.* Chicago: University of Chicago Press, 1961, pp. 33–34.

Young, 1st, pp. 20–22. [Reprinted in Weeks, Robert P., ed. *Hemingway: A Collection of Critical Essays.* Englewood Cliffs: Prentice-Hall, 1962, pp. 107–08.] Young, 2nd, pp. 48–49, 60.

57. A Lack of Passion (Unpublished)
   (1927/ . . . / . . . / . . .)
Baker (*Life*), p. 595.

58. Landscape with Figures (Unpublished; "In the Old Homestead")
[See Young and Mann, Item 61.]

59. The Last Good Country (Fragment)
(. ? . /1972/*The Nick Adams Stories*/ ...)

60. The Light of the World
(1933/October 27, 1933/*Winner Take Nothing*/CS, NA)
Atkins, pp. 204–05.
Baker (*Artist*), p. 140.
Baker (*Life*), pp. 238, 241.
Baker, S., pp. 30–31.
Bakker, pp. 23–25, 257.
Benson, pp. 57–60.
Bruccoli, Matthew J. "The Light of the World: Stan Ketchel as 'My Sweet Christ,'" *Fitzgerald-Hemingway Annual 1969*, Matthew J. Bruccoli and C. E. Frazer Clark, Jr., eds., Washington, D.C.: NCR Microcard Editions, 1969, 125–30.
Canaday, Nicholas, Jr. "Is There Any Light in Hemingway's 'The Light of the World?'" *Studies in Short Fiction*, III (Fall 1965), 75–76.
DeFalco, pp. 81–88.
Hovey, pp. 18–20.
Martine, James J. "A Little Light on Hemingway's 'The Light of the World,'" *Studies in Short Fiction*, VII (Summer 1970), 465–67.
Montgomery, pp. 27, 91–95.
O'Faolain, Sean. *The Short Story*. New York: Devin-Adair, 1951, pp. 215–16.
Schafer, William J. "Ernest Hemingway: Arbiter of Common Numerality," *The Carlton Miscellany*, III (Winter 1962), 100–04.
Thomas, Peter. "A Lost Leader: Hemingway's 'The Light of the World,'" *Humanities Association Bulletin* (Canada), XXI (Fall 1970), 14–19.
Waldhorn, RG, pp. 59–61.
Young, 1st, pp. 22–23. [Reprinted in Weeks, Robert P., ed. *Hemingway: A Collection of Critical Essays*. Englewood Cliffs, N.J.: Prentice-Hall, 1962, pp. 108–09.] Young, 2nd, p. 50.

61. A Man of the World
(1957/November 1957/*Atlantic*/ ...)
Baker (*Life*), p. 538.
DeFalco, p. 216.
[See Section I: Astro and Benson, Delbert E. Wylder, "Internal Treachery." See also Section IV: Julian Smith, "Eyeless in Wyoming."]

62. A Matter of Colour (Juvenilia)
(1916/1916/*Tabula*/EHA)
Baker (*Life*), p. 22.
Baker, S., pp. 7–8.
Montgomery, p. 47 [story itself appears pp. 47–49].

63. The Monument (Unpublished)
(1956/ . . . / . . . / . . .)
Baker (*Life*), p. 534.

64. The Mother of a Queen
(ca. 1932–33/October 27, 1933/*Winner Take Nothing*/CS)
Atkins, pp. 188–89.
Baker (*Life*), p. 606.
Bakker, p. 144.
Hovey, pp. 21–22.

65. Mr. and Mrs. Elliot ("Mr. and Mrs. Smith")
(1924/Autumn-Winter 1924–25/*Little Review*/IOT, CS)
Baker (*Life*), pp. 133, 141, 181, 585.
Benson, pp. 66, 107.
DeFalco, pp. 155–58.
Fenton, p. 154.
Grebstein, pp. 81–82, 181.
Hovey, p. 13.
Jost, p. 123.
Killinger, p. 38.
Peterson, pp. 174–75.
Shepherd, Allen. "Taking Apart 'Mr. and Mrs. Elliot,' " *Markham Review* II (September 1969), 15–16.

66. My First Sea Vouge (Juvenilia)
(1911/1969/*Ernest Hemingway: A Life Story*/ . . .)
Baker (*Life*), pp. 12, 14 [Story itself reprinted on p. 12].

67. My Old Man
(1922/Summer 1923/*Three Stories and Ten Poems*/IOT, CS)
Baker (*Life*), pp. 100, 102–03, 106, 109, 111, 118–19, 159, 470; film, 648.
Baker, S., pp. 26–27.
Bakker, p. 50.
Davis, Robert Gorham. *Instructor's Manual for Ten Modern Masters.* New York: Harcourt, Brace, 1953, pp. 25–26.
DeFalco, pp. 56–62.

67. My Old Man, cont.

Fenton, pp. 149–50.

Greet, T. Y. and John M. Munro. *The Worlds of Fiction.* Boston: Houghton Mifflin Company, 1964, pp. 78–84.

Hovey, pp. 39–41.

Joost, pp. 62–64.

Krause, Sidney J. "Hemingway's 'My Old Man,'" *Explicator*, XX (January 1962), Item 39.

Lewis, p. 13.

Peterson, pp. 70–71.

Rovit, p. 43.

Singleton, Ralph H. *Instructor's Manual for "Two and Twenty: A Collection of Short Stories."* New York: St. Martin's Press, 1962, pp. 6–7. Young, 2nd, pp. 177, 177n.

68. A Natural History of the Dead

(1932/September 23, 1932/as part of Chapter XII of *Death in the Afternoon*/WTN [revised], CS)

Atkins, pp. 10–11.

Baker (*Life*), p. 604.

Baker, S., pp. 35, 87.

Clark, John Abbott. "A Footnote to a Footnote to a Footnote," *National Review*, I (December 28, 1955), 19–21.

Fenton, p. 57.

Grebstein, p. 77.

Hovey, pp. 105–07.

Maloney, Russell. "A Footnote to a Footnote," *New Yorker*, XV (July 15, 1939), 26.

Portz, John. "Allusion and Structure in Hemingway's 'A Natural History of the Dead,'" *Tennessee Studies in Literature*, X (1965), 27–41.

Waldhorn, RG, pp. 133–34.

Weeks, Lewis E., Jr. "Mark Twain and Hemingway: 'A Catastrophe' and 'A Natural History of the Dead,'" *Mark Twain Journal*, XIV (Summer 1968), 15–17.

Yunck, John A. "The Natural History of a Dead Quarrel: Hemingway and the Humanists," *South Atlantic Quarterly*, LXII (Winter 1963), 36–43.

69. Night Before Battle

(1938/February 1939/*Esquire*/FUS)

Baker (*Life*), pp. 334, 339.

[See Section IV: Martin Light, "Of Wasteful Deaths," and Julian Smith, "Christ Times Four."]

70. **Night Before Landing** (Fragment from unfinished novel, *Along with Youth: A Novel*)
    (1925/1972/*The Nick Adams Stories*/ . . .)

71. **Nobody Ever Dies** ("Flower of the Party")
    (1938/March 1939/*Cosmopolitan*/ . . .)
    Baker (*Life*), p. 338.

72. **Now I Lay Me** ("In Another Country—Two. A Story")
    (1927/October 14, 1927/*Men Without Women*/CS, NA)
    Baker (*Life*), pp. 184, 228.
    Baker, S., pp. 33, 38.
    Bakker, pp. 25–27, 256.
    Barrows, Herbert. *Suggestions for Teaching "15 Stories."* Boston: Heath, 1950, pp. 7–9.
    Benson, pp. 7, 129–30.
    DeFalco, pp. 104–14.
    Gettmann, Royal A., and Bruce Harkness. *Teacher's Manual for "A Book of Stories."* New York: Rinehart, 1955, pp. 34–36.
    Hovey, Richard B. "Hemingway's 'Now I Lay Me': A Psychological Interpretation," *Literature & Psychology*, XV (Spring 1965), 70–78.
    Hovey, pp. 8, 47–53, 219.
    Johnston, Kenneth G. "The Great Awakening: Nick Adams and the Silkworms in 'Now I Lay Me,' " *Hemingway Notes*, I (Fall 1971), 7–9.
    Kuppuswamy, B. "Hemingway on Insomnia," *Literary Half-Yearly*, I (July 1960), 58–60.
    MacDonald, Scott. "Implications of Narrative Perspective in Hemingway's 'Now I Lay Me,' " *Studies in American Fiction*, I (Autumn 1973), 213–20.
    Montgomery, pp. 28–29.
    Peterson, pp. 34, 81.
    Rovit, p. 79.
    Stephens, ("Appendix B: More Sources, Analogues, and Echoes"), p. 371.
    Waldhorn, RG, pp. 62–63.
    Young, 1st, pp. 29–30. [Reprinted in Browne, Ray B., and Martin Light, eds. *Critical Approaches to American Literature, II.* New York: Crowell, 1965, pp. 276–77.] Young, 2nd, pp. 57–58.

73. **Old Man at the Bridge** ("The Old Man at the Bridge")
    (ca. 1938/May 19, 1938/*Ken*, as "The . . ."/CS)
    Atkins, pp. 24–25.

73. **Old Man at the Bridge,** cont.
    Baker (*Life*), pp. 332, 337.
    Bakker, pp. 152–53, 271.
    DeFalco, pp. 121–27.
    Hovey, pp. 150–51.
    Lid, Richard W. "A Student Discussion of Hemingway's 'Old Man at the Bridge,' " *The Short Story: Classic and Contemporary.* Philadelphia: J. B. Lippincott Co., 1967, pp. 517–38.
    Lid, Richard W. "Hemingway and the Need for Speech," *Modern Fiction Studies*, VIII (Winter 1962–63), 401–07.
    Rovit, p. 83.
    Waldhorn, RG, pp. 168–69.

74. **On the Quai at Smyrna** (Vignette: "Introduction by the Author")
    (1930/October 24, 1930/*In Our Time*, 2nd ed./CS)
    Baker (*Life*), p. 601.
    Bakker, p. 52.
    DeFalco, pp. 127–29.
    Fenton, pp. 186–87.
    Hovey, p. 15.
    Leiter, Louis H. "Neural Projections in Hemingway's 'On the Quai at Smyrna?' " *Studies in Short Fiction*, V (Summer 1968), 384–86.
    Peterson, pp. 68, 77.
    Woodward, R. H. "Hemingway's 'On the Quai at Smyrna,' " *Exercise Exchange*, X (March 1963), 11–12.
    Young, 2nd, p. 57.

75. **On Writing** (Fragment)
    (. ? ./1972/*The Nick Adams Stories*/ . . .)
    Nahal, pp. 193–94.

76. **One Reader Writes**
    (1932/October 27, 1933/*Winner Take Nothing*/CS)
    Baker (*Life*), p. 227.
    Bakker, pp. 144–45.
    DeFalco, pp. 159–60.
    Edelson, Mark. "A Note on 'One Reader Writes,' " *Fitzgerald/Hemingway Annual 1972*, Matthew J. Bruccoli and C. E. Frazer Clark, Jr., eds. Washington, D.C.: N.C.R. Microcard Editions, 1973, pp. 329–31.
    Hovey, p. 16.
    Waldhorn, RG, p. 22.

77. **One Trip Across**
    (ca. 1933/April 1934/*Cosmopolitan*/[became Part I of *To Have and Have Not*])

Baker (*Artist*), p. 203.
Baker (*Life*), pp. 252, 268, 279, 607.

78. **Out Of Season** ("Before the Season")
    (1923/Summer 1923/*Three Stories and Ten Poems*/IOT, CS)
    Baker (*Artist*), pp. 121–22.
    Baker (*Life*), pp. 109, 111, 170–71, 509, 581.
    Baker, S., p. 18.
    DeFalco, pp. 163–68.
    Grebstein, p. 156.
    Hovey, pp. 10–11.
    Johnston, Kenneth G. "Hemingway's 'Out of Season' and the Psychology of Errors," *Literature and Psychology*, XXI (November 1, 1971), 41–46.
    Sanderson, pp. 22–24.
    Stephens ("Appendix B: More Sources, Analogues, and Echoes"), p. 365.
    Waldhorn, RG, pp. 44–45.
    Young, 2nd, p. 178.

79. **Paris, 1922** (Sentence-length sketches)
    (1922/1969/*Ernest Hemingway: A Life Story*/ ...)
    Baker (Life), pp. 90–91, 108.

80. **The Passing of Pickles McCarty** ("Woppian Way"; unpublished)
    (1919/ ... / ... / ...)
    Baker (*Life*), pp. 60, 84, 100, 169, 574.

81. **A Pursuit Race**
    (1927/October 14, 1927/*Men Without Women*/CS)
    Baker (*Artist*), p. 123.
    Baker (*Life*), p. 184.
    Bakker, pp. 85–86.
    DeFalco, pp. 58–59.
    Fenton, p. 49.
    Grebstein, pp. 21, 186–88.
    Hovey, p. 17.
    Killinger, pp. 51–52.
    Waldhorn, RG, p. 22.
    Wilson, Edmund. "The Sportsman's Tragedy," *New Republic*, LIII (December 14, 1927), 102–03.

82. **The Revolutionist** ("Chapter XI" from *in our time*: "In 1919 he was traveling on railroads in Italy")
    (1923/Spring 1924/*in our time*/IOT, CS)
    Atkins, p. 24.

82. **The Revolutionist,** cont.

Bakker, pp. 50–51.

DeFalco, pp. 88–91.

Groseclase, Barbara S. "Hemingway's 'The Revolutionist': An Aid to Interpretation," *Modern Fiction Studies*, XVII (Winter 1971–72), 565–70.

Johnston, Kenneth G. "Hemingway and Mantegna: The Bitter Nail Holes," *Journal of Narrative Technique*, I (May 1971), 86–94.

Shepherd, Allen G. "Hemingway's 'The Revolutionist': A Proto-Story for Study," *Exercise Exchange*, XVIII (Spring 1974), 19–20.

Stephens ("Appendix B: More Sources, Analogues, and Echoes"), p. 364.

Watts, pp. 135, 137.

83. **A Room on the Garden Side** (Unpublished)

(1956/ . . . / . . . / . . .)

Baker (*Life*), p. 534.

84. **The Sea Change**

(ca. 1931/December 1931/*This Quarter*/WTN, CS)

Baker (*Artist*), p. 139.

Baker (*Life*), p. 227.

Bakker, pp. 143–44.

DeFalco, pp. 176–79.

Grebstein, pp. 110–11, 113–14.

Kobler, J. F. "Hemingway's 'The Sea Change': A Sympathetic View of Homosexuality," *Arizona Quarterly*, XXVI (Winter 1970), 318–23.

Peterson, pp. 81, 82–83, 89–90.

Wycherley, H. Alan. "Hemingway's 'The Sea Change,'" *American Notes and Queries*, VII (January 1969), 67–68.

Young, 2nd, pp. 178n, 183n, 286n.

85. **Sepi Jingan** (Juvenilia)

(1916/1916/*Tabula*/EHA)

Baker (*Life*), p. 27.

Baker, S., pp. 8–9.

Montgomery, pp. 49–50, 53–54, 169, 170 [story itself appears pp. 50–52].

86. **The Short Happy Life of Francis Macomber** ("Happy Ending")

(1936/September 1936/*Cosmopolitan*/CS)

Atkins, pp. 5–6. 16–18, 47, 86, 138–40, 143, 186, 237.

Bache, William B. "The Red Badge of Courage and 'The Short Happy

Life of Francis Macomber,' " *Western Humanities Review*, XV
(Winter 1961), 83–84.

Baker (*Artist*), pp. 189–91. [Reprinted in Weeks, Robert P., ed.
Hemingway: A Collection of Critical Essays. Englewood Cliffs,
N.J.: Prentice-Hall, 1962, pp. 118–21.]

Baker (*Life*), pp. 284, 314, 340, 453, 509, 513.

Baker, S., pp. 98–101.

Bakker, pp. 129–37, 155.

Beck, Warren. "The Shorter Happy Life of Mrs. Macomber," *Modern
Fiction Studies*, I (November 1955), 28–37. [Reprinted in Howell,
John M., ed. *Hemingway's African Stories: The Stories, Their
Sources, Their Critics*. New York: Charles Scribner's Sons, 1969,
pp. 119–28.]

Bell, H. H., Jr. " 'The Short Happy Life of Francis Macomber,' " *Explicator*, XXXII (May 1974), Item 78.

Benson, pp. 146–48.

Brooks, Cleanth. *The Hidden God*. New Haven: Yale University Press,
1963, pp. 15–16.

Bruccoli, Matthew J. "Francis Macomber and Francis Fitzgerald,"
Fitzgerald/Hemingway Annual 1970, Matthew J. Bruccoli and C. E.
Frazer Clark, Jr., eds. Washington, D.C.: N.C.R. Microcard Edi-
tions, 1970, p. 223.

Crane, R. S. "On 'The Short Happy Life of Francis Macomber,' "
English "A" Analyst (Northwestern University English Department), Number 16. [Reprinted in Howell, John M., ed. *Hemingway's African Stories: The Stories, Their Sources, Their Critics*.
New York: Charles Scribner's Sons, 1969, pp. 129–36; in *The Idea
of the Humanities and Other Essays Critical and Historical*, Chicago,
1967, Vol. II, pp. 315–26; in Locke, Louis, William Gibson, and
George Arms, eds. *Introduction to Literature*, 3rd edition, New
York: Rinehart, 1957, pp. 470–79.]

Davidson, Arnold E. "The Ambivalent End of Francis Macomber's
Short Happy Life," *Hemingway Notes*, II (Spring 1972), 14–16.

Davis, Robert Gorham. *Instructor's Manual for Ten Modern Masters*.
New York: Harcourt, Brace, 1953, pp. 27–29.

DeFalco, pp. 202–07.

Ennis, Lambert. " 'The Short Happy Life of Francis Macomber' "
English "A" Analyst (Northwestern University English Department), Number 9.

Fleissner, R. F. "The Macomber Case: A Sherlockian Analysis," *Baker
Street Journal*. XX (September 1970), 154–56, 169.

Gaillard, Theodore L., Jr. "The Critical Menagerie in 'The Short

86. The Short Happy Life of Francis Macomber, cont.

Happy Life of Francis Macomber,' " *English Journal*, LX (January 1971), 31–35.

Goldhurst, William. *F. Scott Fitzgerald and His Contemporaries*. Cleveland: World Publishing Company, 1963, pp. 194–96.

Grebstein, pp. 14–15, 84–85, 103–05.

Greco, Anne, "Margot Macomber: 'Bitch Goddess,' Exonerated," *Fitzgerald/Hemingway Annual 1972*, Matthew J. Bruccoli and C. E. Frazer Clark, Jr., eds. Washington, D.C.: N.C.R. Microcard Editions, 1973, pp. 273–80.

Gurko, pp. 196–98.

Handy, William J. *Kant and the Southern New Critics*. Austin: University of Texas Press, 1963, pp. 87–88.

Heiney, Donald. *Recent American Literature*. Great Neck, N.Y.: Barron's Educational Series, Inc., 1958, pp. 164–65.

Hill, John S. "Robert Wilson: Hemingway's Judge in Macomber," *University Review*, XXXV (Winter 1968), 129–32.

Holland, Robert B. "Macomber and the Critics," *Studies in Short Fiction*, V (Winter 1968), 171–78. [Reprinted in Howell, John M., ed. *Hemingway's African Stories: The Stories, Their Sources, Their Critics*. New York: Charles Scribner's Sons, 1969, pp. 137–41.]

Hovey, pp. 123–27.

Howell, John M. "The Macomber Case," *Studies in Short Fiction*, IV (Winter 1967), 171–72.

Howell, John M., and Charles A. Lawler. "From Abercrombie & Fitch to *The First Forty-Nine Stories*: The Text of Ernest Hemingway's 'Francis Macomber.' " *Proof (The Yearbook of American Bibliographical and Textual Studies*, ed. Joseph Katz), II (1972), 213–81.

Hutton, Virgil. "The Short Happy Life of Macomber," *University Review*, XXX (Summer 1964), 253–63.

Jackson, Thomas J. "The Macomber Typescript," *Fitzgerald/Hemingway Annual 1970*, Matthew J. Bruccoli and C. E. Frazer Clark, Jr., eds. Washington, D.C.: N.C.R. Microcard Editions, 1970.

Killinger, pp. 44–46, 76.

Kobler, J. F. "Francis Macomber as Four-Letter Man," *Fitzgerald/Hemingway Annual 1972*, Matthew J. Bruccoli and C. E. Frazer Clark, Jr., eds. Washington, D.C.: N.C.R. Microcard Editions, 1973, 295–96.

Lewis, Clifford. " 'The Short Happy Life of Francis Macomber,' " *Études Anglaises*, XXIII (July–September 1970), 256–61.

Lewis, pp. 79–93.

May, Merrill M. "Macomber as Hero," *English "A" Analyst* (Northwestern University English Department), Number 10.

McMahon, T. "Hemingway: Philosophy of Action," *Yale Literary Magazine*, CXV (December 1947), 16–20.

Mizener, Arthur. *The Sense of Life in the Modern Novel*. Boston: Houghton Mifflin, 1964, pp. 223–26.

Morris, William E. "Hemingway's 'The Short Happy Life of Francis Macomber,' " *Explicator*, XXIV (December 1965), Item 31.

Nagel, James. The Narrative Method of 'The Short Happy Life of Francis Macomber,' " *Research Studies*, XLI (March 1973), 18–27.

Nahal, pp. 95–101.

Orvis, Mary Burchard. *The Art of Writing Fiction*. New York: Prentice-Hall, 1948, pp. 26–27, 99–101, 129–32.

Peirce, J. F. "The Car as Symbol in Hemingway's 'The Short Happy Life of Francis Macomber,' " *South Central Bulletin*, XXXII (Winter 1972), 230–32.

Peterson, pp. 86–87, 155–56.

Ross, Woodburn O., and A. Dayle Wallace. *Short Stories in Context*. New York: American Books, 1953, pp. 310–14.

Rovit, pp. 72–74.

Sale, William M., Jr., James Hall, and Martin Steinmann, Jr. *Critical Discussions for Teachers Using "Short Stories: Tradition and Direction."* Norfolk: New Directions, 1949, pp. 40–44.

Sanderson, pp. 73–75.

Scott, pp. 27–29.

Shaw, pp. 82–84.

Shepherd, Allen. "The Lion in the Grass (Alas?): A Note on 'The Short Happy Life of Francis Macomber,' " *Fitzgerald/Hemingway Annual 1972*, Matthew J. Bruccoli and C. E. Frazer Clark, Jr., eds. Washington, D.C.: N.C.R. Microcard Editions, 1973, pp. 297–99.

Stein, William Bysshe. "Hemingway's 'The Short Happy Life of Francis Macomber,' " *Explicator*, XIX (April 1961), Item 47.

Stephens, pp. 268–73.

Vaidyanathan, T. G. "Did Margot Kill Francis Macober?" *Indian Journal of American Studies*, I (1970), 1–13.

Voss, Arthur. *The American Short Story*. Norman: University of Oklahoma Press, 1973, pp. 235–37.

Wagner, M. J. "A Note on the Ending of the Story," *English "A" Analyst* (Northwestern University English Department), Number 9.

Waldhorn, RG, pp. 147–51.

86. The Short Happy Life of Francis Macomber, cont.

Waterman, Arthur E. "Hemingway's 'The Short Happy Life of Francis Macomber,' " *Explicator*, XX (September 1961), Item 2.

Watts, pp. 141–42.

West, R. R. *The Short Story in America, 1900–1950*. Chicago: Regnery, 1952, pp. 99–101; Gateway edition, 1952, pp. 95–97.

West, Ray B., Jr. "Three Methods of Modern Fiction: Ernest Hemingway, Eudora Welty, Thomas Mann," *College English*, XII (January 1951), 193–203. [Explication of "The Short Happy Life of Francis Macomber," on pp. 194–96. Reprinted in Locke, Louis G., ed., et al., *Introduction to Literature*. New York: 1952, 2nd edition, pp. 479–81; in West and Stallman, *The Art of Modern Fiction*. New York: Rinehart, pp. 259–62.]

White, p. 18.

White, W. M. "The Crane-Hemingway Code: A Reevaluation," *Ball State University Forum*, X (Spring 1969), 15–20.

Young, 1st, pp. 41–46, 168–69. [Reprinted in Browne, Ray B., and Martin Light, eds. *Critical Approaches to American Literature, II*. New York: Crowell, 1965, pp. 284–88.] Young, 2nd, pp. 69–74, 197–98.

87. A Simple Enquiry

(1927/October 14, 1927/*Men Without Women*/CS)

Baker (*Artist*), p. 140.

Baker (*Life*), pp. 182, 184.

Bakker, p. 85.

DeFalco, pp. 131–32.

Hovey, pp. 20–21.

Wilson, Edmund. "The Sportsman's Tragedy," *New Republic*, LIII (December 14, 1927), 102. [Reprinted in his *The Shores of Light: A Literary Chronicle of the Twenties and Thirties*. New York: The Noonday Press, 1952, p. 341.]

88. The Snows of Kilimanjaro

(1935/August 1936/*Esquire*/CS)

Atkins, pp. 9–10, 62–63, 224–25, 237, 240.

Bache, William B. "Nostromo and 'The Snows of Kilimanjaro,' " *Modern Language Notes*, LXXII (January 1957), 32–34.

Baker (*Artist*), pp. 191–96. [Reprinted in Weeks, Robert P., ed. *Hemingway: A Collection of Critical Essays*. Englewood Cliffs, N.J.: Prentice-Hall, 1962, pp. 122–26.]

Baker (*Life*), pp. 286, 289, 292, 295, 314, 322, 355, 476, 509, 578–79, 583, 611.

Baker, Carlos. "The Slopes of Kilimanjaro: A Biographical Perspective," *Novel: A Forum on Fiction*, I (Fall 1967), 19–23. [Reprinted as "The Slopes of Kilimanjaro" in *American Heritage Magazine*, XIX (August 1968), 40, 42–43, 90–91; and in Howell, John M., ed. *Hemingway's African Stories: The Stories, Their Sources, Their Critics*. New York: Charles Scribner's Sons, 1969, pp. 55–59.]

Baker, Howard. "The Contemporary Short Story," *Southern Review*, III (Winter 1938), 585–89.

Baker, S., pp. 97–98.

Bakker, pp. 137–39, 155, 268–69.

Bassett, Charles W. "Katahdin, Wachusett, and Kilimanjaro: The Symbolic Mountains of Thoreau and Hemingway," *Thoreau Journal Quarterly*, III (1971), 1–10.

Benson, pp. 130–34.

Bevis, R. W. and M. A. J. Smith, Jr. "Leopard Tracks in 'The Snows of Kilimanjaro.'" *American Notes and Queries*, VI (April 1968), 115.

Childs, Barney. "Hemingway and the Leopard of Kilimanjaro," *American Notes and Queries*, II (September 1963), 3.

Cunningham, Donald H. "Hemingway's 'The Snows of Kilimanjaro,'" *Explicator*, XXII (February 1964), Item 41.

DeFalco, pp. 207–10.

Dussinger, Gloria R. "'The Snows of Kilimanjaro': Harry's Second Chance," *Studies in Short Fiction*, V (Fall 1967), 54–59. [Reprinted in Howell, John M., ed. *Hemingway's African Stories: The Stories, Their Sources, Their Critics*. New York: Charles Scribner's Sons, 1969, pp. 158–61.]

Dussinger, Gloria R. "Hemingway's 'The Snows of Kilimanjaro,'" *Explicator*, XXVI (April 1968), Item 67.

Dworking, Martin S. "A Dead Leopard and an Empty Grail," *The Humanist*, XIII (July–August 1953), 164–65.

Engstrom, Alfred. "Dante, Flaubert, and 'The Snows of Kilimanjaro,'" *Modern Language Notes*, LXV (March 1950), 203–05.

Evans, Oliver. "'The Snows of Kilimanjaro': A Revaluation," *PMLA*, LXXVI (December 1961), 601–07. [Reprinted in Howell, John M., ed. *Hemingway's African Stories: The Stories, Their Sources, Their Critics*. New York: Charles Scribner's Sons, 1969, pp. 150–57.]

Fenton, pp. 180–81, 186.

Fisher, Marvin. "More Snow on Kilimanjaro," *Americana Norvegica*, II (1968), 343–53.

Goldhurst, William. *F. Scott Fitzgerald and His Contemporaries*. Cleveland: World Publishing Company, 1963, pp. 203–08.

Gordon, Caroline and Allen Tate. *The House of Fiction*. New York:

88. The Snows of Kilimanjaro, cont.

Charles Scribner's Sons, 1950, pp. 419–23. [Reprinted in Howell, John M. ed. *Hemingway's African Stories: The Stories, Their Sources, Their Critics.* New York: Charles Scribner's Sons, 1969, pp. 142–44.]

Grebstein, pp. 15–16, 21–22.

Gurko, pp. 198–201.

Heiney, Donald. *Recent American Literature.* Great Neck, N.Y.: Barron's Educational Series, Inc., 1958, pp. 163–64.

Hovey, pp. 127–31.

Howell, John M. "What the Leopard was Seeking," *American Notes and Queries,* VII (January 1969), 68.

Howell, John M. "Hemingway's Riddle and Kilimanjaro's Reusch," *Studies in Short Fiction,* VIII (Summer 1971), 469–70.

Joost, p. 59.

Killinger, pp. 43–44, 60, 71.

Lewis, pp. 97–110.

Lewis, Robert W., Jr. and Max Westbrook. "The Texas Manuscript of 'The Snows of Kilimanjaro,' " *Texas Quarterly,* IX (Winter 1966), 66–101.

Lewis, Robert W., Jr. "Vivienne de Watteville, Hemingway's Companion on Kilimanjaro," *Texas Quarterly,* IX (Winter 1966), 75–88. [Reprinted in part in Howell, John M., ed. *Hemingway's African Stories: The Stories, Their Sources, Their Critics.* New York: Charles Scribner's Sons, 1969, pp. 101–09.]

Lewis, Robert W., Jr. and Max Westbrook. " 'The Snows of Kilimanjaro,' Collated and Annotated," *Texas Quarterly,* XIII (Summer 1970), 64–143.

Lynskey, Winifred. *Reading Modern Fiction.* New York: Charles Scribner's Sons, 1952, pp. 266–68; second edition, 1957, pp. 266–68; third edition, 1962, pp. 266–68.

MacDonald, Scott. "Hemingway's 'The Snows of Kilimanjaro': Three Critical Problems," *Studies in Short Fiction,* XI (Winter 1974), 67–74.

Maloney, Michael. "Ernest Hemingway: The Missing Third Dimension," in Gardiner, Harold C., ed. *Fifty Years of the American Novel.* New York: Charles Scribner's Sons, 1952, p. 186.

Maynard, Reid. "The Decay Motif in 'The Snows of Kilimanjaro,' " *Discourse,* X (Autumn 1967), 436–39.

Montgomery, Marion. "The Leopard and the Hyena: Symbol and Meaning in 'The Snows of Kilimanjaro,' " *University of Kansas City Review,* XXVII (June 1961), 277–82. [Reprinted in Howell, John M., ed. *Hemingway's African Stories: The Stories, Their Sources,*

Their Critics. New York: Charles Scribner's Sons, 1969, pp. 145–49.]

Nahal, pp. 109–118.

O'Connor, William Van. "Two Views of Kilimanjaro," *History of Ideas News Letter*, II (October 1956), 76–80. [Reprinted in *The Grotesque: An American Genre and Other Essays*. Carbondale: Southern Illinois University Press, 1962. pp. 119–24.]

Orrok, Douglas Hall. "Hemingway, Hugo, and Revelation," *Modern Language Notes*, LXVI (November 1951), 441–45.

Peterson, pp. 29–30, 49–50.

Rovit, pp. 35–39.

Sanderson, pp. 75–76.

Shaw, pp. 84–86.

Spiller, Robert E. *The Third Dimension: Studies in Literary History*. New York: Macmillan, 1965, p. 171.

Stallman, R. W. *The Houses that James Built and Other Literary Studies*. East Lansing: Michigan State University Press, 1961, pp. 193–99.

Stephens, pp. 273–82.

Stephens, Robert O. "Hemingway's Riddle of Kilimanjaro: Idea and Image," *American Literature*, XXXII (March 1960), 84–87. [Reprinted in Howell, John M., ed. *Hemingway's African Stories: The Stories, Their Sources, Their Critics*. New York: Charles Scribner's Sons, 1969, pp. 93–94.]

Tarbox, Raymond. "Blank Hallucinations in the Fiction of Poe and Hemingway," *American Imago*, XXIV (Winter 1967), 312–43.

Taylor, J. Golden. "Hemingway on the Flesh and the Spirit," *Western Humanities Review*, XV (Summer 1961), 273–75.

Tedlock, Ernest W., Jr. "Hemingway's 'The Snows of Kilimanjaro,' " *Explicator*, VIII (October 1949), Item 7.

Thomaneck, Jurgen K. A. "Hemingway's Riddle of Kilimanjaro Once More," *Studies in Short Fiction*, VII (Spring 1970), 326–27.

Voss, Arthur. *The American Short Story*. Norman: University of Oklahoma Press, 1973, pp. 237–39.

Walcutt, Charles C. "Hemingway's 'The Snows of Kilimanjaro,' " *Explicator*, VII (April 1949), Item 43.

Waldhorn, RG, pp. 143–47.

Walz, Lawrence A. " 'The Snows of Kilimanjaro,' A New Reading," *Fitzgerald/Hemingway Annual* 1971, Matthew J. Bruccoli and C. E. Frazer Clark, Jr., eds., Washington, D.C.: N.C.R. Microcard Editions, 1971, pp. 239–45.

Watts, pp. 35–37, 143, 145.

88. The Snows of Kilimanjaro, cont.

Westbrook, Max. "The Stewardship of Ernest Hemingway," *Texas Quarterly*, IX (Winter 1966), 89–101.

White, William. "Hemingway's (?) Kilimanjaro," *Literary Sketches 10* (February 1970), 11.

Young, 1st, pp. 45–50. [Reprinted in Browne, Ray B. and Martin Light, eds. *Critical Approaches to American Literature, II.* New York: Crowell, 1965, pp. 288–91.] Young, 2nd, pp. 69, 74–78, 127, 197–98.

[See in this volume: Gennaro Santangelo, "The Dark Snows of Kilimanjaro."]

89. Soldier's Home

(1924/June 1925/*Contact Collection of Contemporary Writers* [anthology]/IOT, CS)

Atkins, pp. 222, 243.

Baker (*Life*), pp. 132, 238, 585.

Baker, S., p. 27.

Bakker, pp. 48–50, 53.

DeFalco, pp. 137–44.

Fenton, pp. 71, 151.

Grebstein, pp. 81, 156.

Gurko, pp. 181–83.

Hays, Peter L. " 'Soldier's Home' and Ford Madox Ford," *Hemingway Notes*, I (Fall 1971), 21–22.

Hovey, pp. 8–9, 41–42.

Killinger, pp. 33–34, 51.

Lewis, Robert W., Jr. "Hemingway's Concept of Sport and 'Soldier's Home,' " *Rendezvous* (Special Hemingway Issue), V (Winter 1970), 19–27.

Nahal, pp. 108–09.

Peterson, pp. 47–48, 60.

Petrarca, Anthony J. "Irony of Situation in Ernest Hemingway's 'Soldier's Home,' " *English Journal*, LVIII (May 1969), 664–67.

Skaggs, Calvin and Merrill Maguire Skaggs. *Instructor's Manual for Mark Schorer's Galaxy: Literary Modes and Genres*, New York: Harcourt, Brace & World, 1967, pp. 39–42.

Stephens ("Appendix B: More Sources, Analogues, and Echoes"), p. 363.

Waldhorn, RG, pp. 67–68.

90. Summer People

(ca. 1923/1972/*The Nick Adams Stories*/ ...)

91. Ten Indians ("After the Fourth"; "A Broken Heart")
(1925/October 14, 1927/*Men Without Women*/CS, NA)
Aiken, William. "Hemingway's 'Ten Indians,' " *Explicator*, XXVIII
(December 1969), Item 31.
Atkins, pp. 220–21.
Baker (*Life*), pp. 157, 169, 184, 186, 592.
Bakker, pp. 21–22.
Benson, pp. 11–12.
DeFalco, pp. 49–52.
Friedman, Norman. "What Makes a Short Story Short?" *Modern Fiction Studies*, IV (Summer 1958), 103–17. [Reprinted in Rideout, Walter B., and James K. Robinson, eds., *A College Book of Modern Fiction*. Evanston, Illinois: Row, Peterson, 1961, pp. 552–65.]
Grebstein, pp. 107–08.
Hovey, pp. 6–7, 37–38.
Lewis, pp. 9–10.
Montgomery, pp. 61, 96–106.
Rideout, Walter B. and James K. Robinson, eds. *A College Book of Modern Fiction*. Evanston, Illinois: Row, Peterson, 1961, pp. 552–65.
St. John, Donald. "Hemingway and Prudence," *Connecticut Review*, V (April 1972), 78–84.
Thurston, Jarvis, ed. *Reading Modern Short Stories*. Chicago: Scott, Foresman and Company, 1955, pp. 15–16, 22, 171–76.
Waldhorn, RG, pp. 56–57.
Young, 2nd, pp. 48, 62.

92. The Three-Day Blow
(1924/October 5, 1925/*In Our Time*/CS, NA)
Atkins, pp. 90, 180.
Baker (*Artist*), p. 136.
Baker (*Life*), pp. 64, 132, 539, 574, 585.
Baker, S., p. 123.
Bakker, pp. 18–20.
Benson, pp. 19, 66–68.
DeFalco, pp. 44–49.
Grebstein, pp. 80–81, 158–59.
Hovey, pp. 7–8, 37.
Killinger, p. 43.
Lewis, pp. 10–11.
Mellard, James M. *Four Modes: A Rhetoric of Modern Fiction*. New York: The Macmillan Company, 1973, pp. 285–89.

92. The Three-Day Blow, cont.

Millet, Fred B. *Reading Fiction*. New York: Rinehart, 1952, pp. 65–66, 114–15, 261–62.

Montgomery, pp. 134–40.

Rovit, pp. 84–85.

Stephens ("Appendix B: More Sources, Analogues, and Echoes"), pp. 362–63.

Waldhorn, RG, pp. 37, 68.

Young, 2nd, pp. 34–35.

93. Three Shots (Fragment)

(. ? . /1972/*The Nick Adams Stories*/ . . .)

94. Today is Friday ("One More for the Nazarene"; "The Seed of the Church")

(1926/Summer 1926/*Today is Friday* [pamphlet]/MWW, CS)

Baker (*Life*), pp. 184, 321, 593.

Baker, S., pp. 59–60.

Bakker, pp. 86–87.

DeFalco, pp. 186–91.

Gordon, Caroline. *How to Read a Novel*. New York: Viking Press, 1957, pp. 100–02.

Grebstein, pp. 114–15.

Hovey, p. 26.

Killinger, p. 79.

Peterson, p. 202.

Shepered [one name only; also spelled "Sheperd"]. " 'Today is Friday': A Note," *Diliman Review*, XVIII (April 1970), 173–75.

Waldhorn, RG, pp. 88–89.

95. The Tradesman's Return

(1935/February 1936/*Esquire*/[revised to become Part II of *To Have and Have Not*])

Baker (*Life*), p. 281.

96. The Undefeated ("The Bullfighters: A Story")

(1924/Summer 1925/*Querschnitt*, as "Steirkampf" in German/ MWW, CS)

Baker (*Artist*), p. 122. [Reprinted in Litz, Walton, ed. *Modern American Literature*. New York: Oxford University Press, 1963, pp. 232–33.]

Baker (*Life*), pp. 138, 141, 143, 175, 184, 219.

Baker, S., pp. 60–61.

Bakker, pp. 81–82, 83, 263.

Christensen, Francis. "A Lesson From Hemingway," *College English*, XXV (October 1963), 12–18.

DeFalco, pp. 197–201.

Grebstein, pp. 102–03, 105–47, 159–60.

Gurko, pp. 194–96.

Hovey, pp. 26–27, 96–97.

Joost, pp. 143, 145–46.

Joost, Nicholas. "Ernest Hemingway and *The Dial*," *Neophilologus*, LII (April, July 1968), 180–90, 304–13. [pp. 305–07: "The Undefeated"].

Kronenberger, Louis. Review of the *Best Short Stories of 1926*, ed. Edward J. O'Brien. N.Y. *Herald Tribune Books* (January 16, 1927), p. 4.

Maloney, Michael F. "Ernest Hemingway: The Missing Third Dimension," in Gardiner, Harold C., ed., *Fifty Years of the American Novel*. New York: Charles Scribner's Sons, 1952, p. 186.

Nahal, p. 95.

O'Brien, Edward J. *The Short Story Case Book*. New York: Farrar and Rinehart, 1935, pp. 262–323 [story and commentary together].

Rovit, pp. 60, 83–84.

Stephens ("Appendix B: More Sources, Analogues, and Echoes"), pp. 367–69.

Stewart, Randall and Dorothy Bethurum, eds., *Modern American Narratives*. Chicago: Scott, Foresman, 1954, pp. 68–70.

Waldhorn, RG, p. 26.

Watts, pp. 116–17.

West, Ray B. *The Short Story in America, 1900–1950*. Chicago: Regnery, 1952, pp. 91–95; Gateway edition, 1952, pp. 87–90.

97. Under the Ridge
   (1939/October 1939/*Cosmopolitan*/FUS)

Baker (*Life*), p. 339.

French, Warren. *The Social Novel at the End of an Era*. Carbondale: Southern Illinois University Press, 1966, pp. 91–93.

Spender, Stephen. "Books and the War. Part IV: The Short Story Today," *Penguin New Writing*, No. V (April 1941), pp. 131–42.

[See Section IV: Martin Light, "Of Wasteful Deaths," and Julian Smith, "Christ Times Four."]

98. Untitled manuscript ("The day we drove back from Nancy to Paris after being interrogated by the inspector general")
   [See Young and Mann, Item 35.]

99. Untitled manuscript ("The galleria in Milan. . .")
   [See Young and Mann, Item 40.]

100. Untitled manuscript ("He was quite thin and blind. . .")
[See Young and Mann, Item 47.]

101. Untitled manuscript (Fragment: "In those days everyone was fond of
my father. . .")
[See Young and Mann, Item 89.]

102. Untitled manuscript (Fragment: "This is the story of the death of
Eldred Johnstone. . .")
[See Young and Mann, Item 88.]

103. Untitled manuscript ("The train moved through the hot valley. . .")
[See Young and Mann, Item 92.]

104. Untitled manuscript (Fragment: "The woman came out to the road
from the big farmhouse when we stopped the jeep")
[See Young and Mann, Item 97.]

105. Up in Michigan
(1921/Summer 1923/*Three Stories and Ten Poems*/CS [revised])
Atkins, p. 221.
Baker (*Artist*), p. 135.
Baker (*Life*), pp. 64, 87, 100, 103, 111, 118, 134, 182, 332, 574, 588,
595.
DeFalco, pp. 55.
Fenton, pp. 149, 152–54.
Grebstein, pp. 77–80, 163.
Hovey, p. 8.
Lewis, pp. 4–5.
Montgomery, pp. 119–27.
Waldhorn, RG, pp. 43–44.
Young, 2nd, pp. 179–80, 180n.

106. A Very Short Story ("Chapter X" from *in our time*: "One hot evening
in Milan")
(1923/Spring 1924/*in our time*/IOT, CS)
Baker (*Artist*), p. 98n.
Baker (*Life*), pp. 147, 574.
Bakker, p. 51.
Benson, pp. 55–56.
DeFalco, pp. 162–63.
Hovey, p. 16.
Kaplan, Harold. The Passive Voice: *An Approach to Modern Fiction.*
Athens: Ohio University Press, 1966, pp. 94–95.
Meyers, Marshall. "A Tagmemic Analysis of Hemingway's 'A Very
Short Story,' " in Hays, Daniel G., and Donald M. Lance, eds., *From*

Soundstream to Discourse: Papers from the 1971 Mid-American Linguistics Conference. Columbia: University of Missouri, 1972, pp. 158–66.
Montgomery, p. 115.
Peterson, pp. 71–72.
Shaw, pp. 19–20.
Young, 2nd, p. 89.

107. A Way You'll Never Be
(1932/October 27, 1933/*Winner Take Nothing*/CS, NA)
Baker (*Life*), pp. 228, 468.
Baker, S., pp. 34–36.
Bakker, pp. 29–30, 32–33.
Benson, p. 73.
DeFalco, pp. 114–21.
Grebstein, pp. 18–19, 118–19.
Hovey, pp. 29–32.
Miller, Patrick. "Hemingway's 'A Way You'll Never Be,' " *Explicator*, XXIII (October 1964), Item 18.
Rovit, pp. 79–80.
Sanderson, p. 37.
Stephens ("Appendix B: More Sources, Analogues, and Echoes"), pp. 371–72.
Waldhorn, RG, pp. 63–65.
Watts, pp. 154–55, 156, 156n.
Yokelson, Joseph B. "A Dante-Parallel in Hemingway's 'A Way You'll Never Be,' " *American Literature*, XLI (May 1969), 279–80.
Young, 1st, pp. 23–26. [Reprinted in Weeks, Robert P., ed. *Hemingway: A Collection of Critical Essays.* Englewood Cliffs, N.J.: Prentice-Hall, 1962, pp. 109–10.] Young, 2nd, pp. 50–54.

108. Wine of Wyoming
(ca. 1929–1930/August 1930/*Scribner's Magazine*/WTN, CS)
Baker (*Artist*), pp. 141, 141n.
Baker (*Life*), pp. 210, 227, 246, 597.
Bakker, pp. 145–46.
DeFalco, pp. 52–53.
Grebstein, pp. 60, 63–67.

109. Wolves and Doughnuts (Unpublished)
(1919/ . . . / . . . / . . .)
Baker (*Life*), pp. 65, 84.